T0305492

Driving Identities

Driving Identities examines long-standing connections between popular music and the automotive industry and how this relationship has helped to construct and reflect various socio-cultural identities. It also challenges common assumptions regarding the divergences between industry and art, and reveals how music and sound are used to suture the putative divide between human and non-human.

This book is a ground-breaking inquiry into the relationship between popular music and automobiles, and into the mutual aesthetic and stylistic influences that have historically left their mark on both industries. Shaped by new historicism and cultural criticism, and by methodologies adapted from gender, LGBTQ+, and African-American studies, it makes an important contribution to understanding the complex and interconnected nature of identity and cultural formation. In its interdisciplinary approach, melding aspects of ethnomusicology, sociology, sound studies, and business studies, it pushes musicological scholarship into a new consideration and awareness of the complexity of identity construction and of influences that inform our musical culture.

The volume also provides analyses of the confluences and coactions of popular music and automotive products to highlight the mutual influences on their respective aesthetic and technical evolutions.

Driving Identities is aimed at both academics and enthusiasts of automotive culture, popular music, and cultural studies in general. It is accompanied by an extensive online database appendix of car-themed pop recordings and sheet music, searchable by year, artist, and title.

Ken McLeod is an Associate Professor of Music History at the University of Toronto. He has published widely on identity politics in popular music, and the intersections between technology, science fiction, and rock music. His first book, *We Are The Champions: The Politics of Sports and Popular Music* (Ashgate, 2011), examines the interconnection of sport and popular music in constructing racial, gender, socio-economic, and national identities.

Ashgate Popular and Folk Music Series

Series Editors: Stan Hawkins, Professor of Popular Musicology, University of Oslo and Lori Burns, Professor, University of Ottawa, Canada

Popular musicology embraces the field of musicological study that engages with popular forms of music, especially music associated with commerce, entertainment and leisure activities. The Ashgate Popular and Folk Music Series aims to present the best research in this field. Authors are concerned with criticism and analysis of the music itself, as well as locating musical practices, values and meanings in cultural context. The focus of the series is on popular music of the twentieth and twenty-first centuries, with a remit to encompass the entirety of the world's popular music.

Critical and analytical tools employed in the study of popular music are being continually developed and refined in the twenty-first century. Perspectives on the transcultural and intercultural uses of popular music have enriched understanding of social context, reception and subject position. Popular genres as distinct as reggae, township, bhangra, and flamenco are features of a shrinking, transnational world. The series recognizes and addresses the emergence of mixed genres and new global fusions, and utilizes a wide range of theoretical models drawn from anthropology, sociology, psychoanalysis, media studies, semiotics, postcolonial studies, feminism, gender studies and queer studies.

Women in the Studio: Creation, Control and Gender in Popular Music Sound Production
Paula Wolfe

The Art of Record Production: Creative Practice in the Studio, Volume 2
Edited by Simon Zagorski-Thomas, Katia Isakoff, Lacasse Serge, and Sophie Stévance

Beggars Banquet And The Rolling Stones' Rock And Roll Revolution: 'They Call My Name Disturbance'
Edited by Russell Reising

The Tragic Odes Of Jerry Garcia And The Grateful Dead Mystery Dances in the Magic Theater
Brent Wood

For more information about this series, please visit: www.routledge.com/music/series/APFM

Driving Identities
At the Intersection of Popular Music and
Automotive Culture

Ken McLeod

Routledge
Taylor & Francis Group

LONDON AND NEW YORK

First published 2020
by Routledge
2 Park Square, Milton Park, Abingdon, Oxon OX14 4RN

and by Routledge
605 Third Avenue, New York, NY 10017

First issued in paperback 2021

Routledge is an imprint of the Taylor & Francis Group, an informa business

© 2020 Ken McLeod

Publisher's Note
The publisher has gone to great lengths to ensure the quality of this reprint but points out that some imperfections in the original copies may be apparent.

British Library Cataloguing-in-Publication Data
A catalogue record for this book is available from the British Library

Library of Congress Cataloging-in-Publication Data
A catalog record has been requested for this book

ISBN 13: 978-1-03-223616-2 (pbk)
ISBN 13: 978-1-138-31705-5 (hbk)

DOI: 10.4324/9780429455346

Typeset in Times New Roman
by Taylor & Francis Books

The audio examples can be accessed via the online Routledge Music Research Portal: www.routledgemusicresearch.co.uk.

Please enter the activation word RRMusic and your email address when prompted. You will immediately be sent an automated email containing an access token and instructions, which will allow you to log in to the site.

To my wife, Julie Pedneault-Deslauriers, and my son, Nolan Alexander McLeod

Contents

Figures

Acknowledgements

This book arose out of a realization that despite the fact that we commonly connect cars and popular music in our cultural imaginations, there had been very little work devoted to the intersection of the two industries and their important nexus in the construction and reflection of identity.

This project would not have come to fruition without the continuing support of my family, friends, and colleagues. I also wish to express my appreciation to moderators, panels, and audiences at the American Musicological Society (AMS), the Association for the Study of Popular Music (IASPM), and the Society for Ethnomusicology (SEM) meetings where various aspects of this work were initially presented. I would also like to acknowledge my graduate seminar students at the University of Toronto, all of whom, in various ways and at various times, provided invaluable feedback and insight into various aspects of this project. I would be particularly remiss not to express my sincere gratitude for and appreciation of the work done by my research assistants, Jeremy Strachan, Jack Harrison, Nicole Pasqualini, and Laura McLaren, without whose help and hard work many aspects of this book would not have been realized. I am also in debt to Neil Soiseth for his sage insights and suggestions.

I would also like to express my sincerest gratitude to my parents, Don and Louise, my grandparents, and my sister Ann for their love and support throughout my life. Above all else, however, I would like to thank my wife Julie Pedneault-Deslauriers for all her truly invaluable help with this project. Whether reading drafts of chapters, looking after our son Nolan, or talking through various issues, this book simply would not have been possible without her.

I would also like to gratefully acknowledge the Social Sciences and Humanities Research Council of Canada for supporting and funding this research through an Insight grant.

Introduction: revving up

This book explores the intersection of popular music and automobile culture in North America and Europe, from the advent of internal combustion engine vehicles in 1885 to the present. More particularly, it examines the historical connections between popular music and automobiles and how the two have combined to construct, contest, reinforce, and re-envision gender, racial, sexual, and locational identities in both abstract aesthetic and explicit political contexts.

The central thesis of this study is that popular music and automobiles are connected not only through the myriad of songs that incorporate automotive themes but also in their function as synergistic agents in the construction of identity and community. Although they are too often considered in isolation from one another, the connections between popular music and automobile culture occur in a wide variety of ways. These include the significant use of automotive sounds in popular music; the nexus of automobiles and popular music in constructing gender, class, and racial identities (e.g., Hispanic lowrider culture and the important place of automobiles in African-American blues, jazz, and hip hop); the influential role of cars and popular music in defining various locations (e.g., Detroit as Motown); and the entwined emphasis on techno-culture, futurism, and speed. Moreover, significant industry-related initiatives further contribute to bind automotive and music cultures in mutually productive and commercial relationships, such as the evolution of audio systems and the related immersive experience of listening to music in cars, the use of popular music in car advertising and artist sponsorships, and issues relating to sound studies and the urban-industrial environment. Through a comprehensive examination of sound recordings, music videos, lyrics, scores, advertising media, and a selection of automotive literature from the late nineteenth century to the present, *Driving Identities* analyzes the multifaceted nature and breadth of the music–automobile relationship and gauges its significance in shaping critical discourses around issues of identity and fashioning the modern self.

Since its inception, the car has had a significant effect on Western popular culture. Automobiles were incorporated into almost all popular media, from magazines, books, and newsprint to early radio, television, and movies. The themes of such works typically centred on the liberation that the automobile afforded. For examples, books and movies frequently depicted young men freeing themselves from middle-class restraints to travel and seek adventure. Throughout the twentieth century, car ownership for men, as well as for women and racial minorities, came to be associated with independence, freedom, and improved social status. Nowhere, however, was the liberating power of the car expressed and celebrated more strongly than in the world of popular music.

Much scholarly inquiry into artistic reactions to modernity has focused on visual media (e.g., painting and photography) and literature that mediated the onset of industrial society. However, the machine age is, perhaps, best characterized by its aural impact, and so a study of machine aesthetics forms an underlying part of this project. In the words of Alan Burdick (2001), we must "listen—to the cable cars … Jupiter Rockets, surgical banter, steam locomotives, punch clocks: the work songs of the whole carbon-based enterprise" (p. 70 and qtd. in Dinerstein, 2003, p. 7). The automobile's connection to the world of sound and music was forcefully established early in the twentieth century when Italian Futurists envisioned the years ahead sonically, as a powerful "roaring car" speeding away from traditional European artistic and social conventions. On February 20, 1909, *Le Figaro* published Filippo Tommaso Marinetti's "The Founding and Manifesto of Futurism," which famously proclaimed:

> We affirm that the world's magnificence has been enriched by a new beauty: the beauty of speed. A racing car whose hood is adorned with great pipes, like serpents of explosive breath—a roaring car that seems to ride on grapeshot is more beautiful than the [Greek sculpture] *Victory of Samothrace.* We want to hymn the man at the wheel, who hurls the lance of his spirit across the Earth, along the circle of its orbit (Marinetti, 2009, p. 51).

The manifesto focused not just on the car and the beauty of speed, but on its sonic element—the explosive "roaring" engine, creating a "hymn" to the driver. It overtly asserted the aesthetic value of the machine. The machines the Futurists particularly valued were those dedicated to speed: the car, the train, the aeroplane, machines that made it possible to literally and figuratively mobilize bodies. Marinetti (2009), for example, dedicated his 1908 poem "To My Pegasus" to the racing car:

> Vehement god of a steel race,
> Automobile thirsting for space
> shuffling and trembling in anguish,
> pulling at the bit with strident teeth!
> O formidable Japanese monster,
> with a forge's eyes,
> fed by flames and mineral oils,
> hungry for horizons and sidereal preys …

I will set free your heart with its diabolical beat
and its gigantic pneumatic tires,
for the dance that you will lead
on the white roads of the world! (p. 425)

The car here is envisioned as a living, breathing, even racialized god-like entity that will lead the rest of mankind on a "dance." Fellow Futurist Luigi Russolo, more than simply celebrating the sound of machinery and cars in prose and poetry, provided what is likely the first instance of incorporating the sound of an internal combustion engine into a musical work in his concerto, *The Meeting of Automobile and Airplane* (1913).

In development contemporaneously to Marinetti's manifesto, only four years later, in 1913, Henry Ford introduced his first complete automotive assembly line in Detroit. These events can be considered the inauguration of a century that placed trust in the ability of technology to ensure the future. The assembly line and its merging of human beings and machinery define the age of industrial mobilization of social energies directed to speeding up productivity. Acceleration, speed, and the cult of the machine were the values emphasized by both the aesthetic ideology of the Futurist Manifesto and the practice of Ford's assembly line.

The machine age changed our sonic environment and, in turn, impacted in manifold ways the construction and reflection of various identities. In 1936, the eminent architect Le Corbusier, influenced by the Italian Futurists in his essay "The Spirit of the Machine, and Negros in the USA," remarked on "the grinding of the street cars … the pounding of machines in factories," and argued that "from this new uproar they [African Americans] make music" (Dinerstein, 2003, p. 2). Despite his sometimes essentializing tone, Le Corbusier recognized that African Americans had successfully integrated modern technology and the chaotic rhythms of the urban soundscape into their musical practice. This is but one example of the sound of the machine informing music and identity construction. The intersection of car culture and music in the construction and reflection of not only African-American identities but of various gender, sexual, and locational identities forms a central objective of this study.

In addition to analysing the relationships between cars and music in the shaping and expressions of these identities, a significant portion of this book is aimed at understanding the sonic influence of automotive culture on popular music (and, to some extent, the reverse). To a large degree, popular music often projects the surrounding sonorities of its environment. For instance, in discussing the impact of The Velvet Underground, music critic Ellen Willis (2011) explains how rock and roll sounds like the city: "rock-and-roll's oldest metaphor for modern city life [is] anarchic energy contained by a tight repetitive structure" (p. 55). Her formulation entails two components. First, rock n' roll functions as a musical metaphor, a sonic suggestion or musical simulation of the experience of urban life rather than a mere lyrical or vocal narration of stories or emotions. Second, this metaphor operates through a tension of opposites: chaos and order, uncontainable noise and inescapable rhythm. Such a position resonates with Adam Krims' (2007) concept of an "urban ethos," a framework for analysing musical representations of social life:

> [T]here is a range of possible, and more or less likely, representations of the city in the corpus of ... commercial popular music, and ... certain representations call for framing at certain times. ... It is the scope of that range of urban representations and their possible modalities, in any given time span, that I call the urban ethos. The urban ethos is thus not a particular representation but rather a distribution of possibilities, always having discernable [*sic*] limits as well as common practices. It is not a picture of how life is in any particular city. Instead, it distills publicly disseminated notions of how cities are generally, even though it may be disproportionately shaped by the fate of particular cities (p. 7).

Much along the same lines of thought as Willis and Krims, British sociologist Chris Rojek (2011) argues for the concept of an "urban-industrial backbeat" against which modern pop music emerged in the twentieth century. This refers to the concrete contexts and settings that give meaning and motivation to our uses and activities surrounding popular music, and that provide a "window" into a specific "structure of feeling" that acts as a summation of a discernible geography, history, and culture (p. 80). In this manner, popular music has been imbued with the sound of the car, the rocking of the engine pistons, and the rolling freedom of wheels in motion that combine to invigorate and move the human body.

Another important thread running through this book is an exploration of how, in our intimate haptic connections with it (whether as drivers or passengers), the car has long been a contested symbol of the merging of humans and machines. Gasoline- and electric-powered machines surpass the limitations of mere muscles, blurring the distinction between living organism and machine, and imparting a related rise in the value of machine aesthetics. Behind the wheel, the driver is stronger, faster, and more powerful than his/her non-motorized and less-mobile brethren. The connection between cars and their drivers is so strong that much automobility literature refers not to discrete entities of driver and car, but rather to a human–machine hybrid, compound, or "assemblage." The car both functions to heighten our notion of self-identity—variously reflecting our personality, lifestyle, and status—yet simultaneously blurs our corporeal identity as we amalgamate in an assemblage with a mass-produced machine. Jack Katz (1999), for example, suggests that "Driving requires and occasions a metaphysical merger, an intertwining of the identities of driver and car that generates a distinctive ontology in the form of a person-thing, a humanized car or alternatively, an automobilized person"; it is a "process in which one ... becomes sensually intertwined with mechanical tool and perceptual field" (pp. 33, 41). Mimi Sheller (2007) similarly describes driving as "a practice that intertwines and mixes the human and the inhuman, the person and the thing, the material and the informational" (p. 177). Some theorists have even recently adopted the term "autoself" or "automobile self" to refer to the fused identity of the car–driver entity. Richard Randell (2017), for instance, proposes the following:

> The autoself is not a disembodied self but is composed of the dual bodies of person and automobile. The latter, the "metallic and glass shell" that is the body that is routinely encountered on the road, allows for only limited communication: through the flashing of headlights, tailgating, sounding of horn, and so forth. The autoself (unlike the cyberself) is incapable of engaging in anything beyond rudimentary discourse; ironically, it is unable even to reflect discursively upon its own existence (p. 673).

While one might argue that enhanced, hands-free telephone and Internet devices allow for more than rudimentary communication, the concept of an "autoself" is likely the most extreme example of our identities being influenced by and even subsumed into the automobile. The act of driving, however, often involves precisely such a form of mental disengagement from our discrete selves, one that mirrors and is amplified by the distraction that listening to music often induces. As drivers gain experience with their vehicles the embodied skills and actions of driving typically appear to be performed in relatively unconscious "automatic" and un-reflexive ways such that the experience of driving sinks into our "technological unconscious" (Thrift, 2004, p. 41). Driving can, at least in non-stressful conditions, involve a certain detachment from the world, a process of daydreaming or, for Baudrillard (1988), "a spectacular form of amnesia"—a loss of reflective self-identity and merging into the act of driving the car that an accompanying musical soundtrack would seem to heighten (p. 9).

Echoing the ecstatic, spiritual tones of Marinetti's Futurist ideology, for many observers the car has become an entity of almost religious self-identification, a material object of beauty and reverence that promises the perfection and transformation of man. Writing in 1957, Roland Barthes (1991) felt that cars were:

> almost the exact equivalent of the great Gothic cathedrals: I mean the supreme creation of an era, conceived with passion by unknown artists, and consumed in image if not in usage by a whole population which appropriates them as a purely magical object (p. 88).

Describing the new Citroën DS (a play on the French word *Déesse*, for goddess), he lauded it as:

> the best messenger of a world above that of nature: one can easily see in an object at once a perfection and an absence of origin, a closure and a

brilliance, a transformation of life into matter (matter is much more magical than life) (p. 88).

For Barthes, no longer did the automobile express mere brute speed; instead, it infused speed with beauty and grace. More than inanimate machines, cars represented major cultural creations replete with their own spiritual mythology.

Not everyone, however, was as susceptible to the automobile's allure. In contrast to Barthes' deification of the car, Theodor Adorno (2005) yearned for "the good old days" in his essay "More Haste, Less Speed." There once was a time, he claimed, when walking implied the relaxed rhythms and tempos associated with human dignity, a dignity that, with the advent of machine-driven and automotive transportation, had become a mere memory:

> Traffic regulations no longer need allow for wild animals, but they have not yet pacified running. It estranges us from bourgeois walking. The truth becomes visible that something is amiss with security, that the unleashed powers of life, be they mere vehicles, have to be escaped. The body's habituation to walking as normal stems from the good old days. It was the bourgeois form of locomotion: physical demythologization, free of the spell of hieratic pacing, roofless wandering, breathless flight. Human dignity insisted on the right to walk, a rhythm not extorted from the body by command or terror. The walk, the stroll, were private ways of passing time, the heritage of the feudal promenade in the nineteenth century. With the liberal era walking too is dying out, even where people do not go by car. The Youth Movement, sensing these tendencies with infallible masochism, challenged the parental Sunday excursions and replaced them by voluntary forced marches, naming them, in medieval fashion, *Fahrt* [journey, drive] when the Ford model was about to become available for such purposes. Perhaps the cult of technical speed as of sport conceals an impulse to master the terror of running by deflecting it from one's own body and at the same time effortlessly surpassing it. The triumph of mounting mileage ritually appeases the fear of the fugitive. But if someone is shouted at to "run" … the archaic power makes itself heard that otherwise inaudibly guides our every step (p. 162).

For Adorno, the normative pace and rhythm of walking faded away in the era of mass production, displaced by the faster tempo and repetitively mechanistic rhythms engendered by the dominance of car culture. Adorno's distaste for the increasing pace of society was directly attributable to and identified with the "Youth Movement" and, as addressed in his 1941 essay "On Popular Music," its equally objectionable fascination with popular music. Albeit indirectly, Adorno's philosophy was an early instance of the supposed deleterious effects of the convergence of automotive culture, popular music, and identity. For many others, however, the automobile represented a form of mobile sonic expressiveness to be celebrated through songs, advertising, and various cultures of engine and sound system modification.

The effects of automobiles on everyday life have often been the subject of controversy. While the introduction of the mass-produced automobile represented a revolution in mobility and convenience, the modern consequences of heavy automotive use contributed to the reliance on non-renewable fuels, a dramatic increase in the rate of accidental death, social isolation and the disconnection of community, rise in obesity, generation of air and noise pollution, and the facilitation of urban sprawl and decay. This book should in no way be regarded as an apology for the automotive industry, but rather an attempt to understand the significant impact it has exerted on popular music—and vice versa. Nor does this book aim to offer a full history of the relationship between music and motor vehicles. It does, however, offer an examination of key historical connections in order to better contextualize the period under consideration. While recent scholarship has addressed the discrete, individual roles of automotive culture and music in shaping locational and social identities, there exists at present no scholarly study of the convergences and mutual reinforcement of these elements in constructing such identities. Similarly, neither the important connections between popular music and automobiles in film and television nor the related uses of popular music in automotive industry advertising and sound branding in the construction of identity have received in-depth critical attention. This work attempts to rectify these lacunae and offer new understanding of the scope and socio-cultural function of the historical synergy between automotive culture and popular music.

This study is inherently interdisciplinary in nature and draws on aspects of musicology, sociology, gender studies, African-American studies, marketing and advertising, art and industrial design, and philosophy (particularly involving ideas surrounding identity construction, accelerationism, post-humanism, and material culture). As such, it echoes recent shifts in humanities research. Intersections, synergistic connections, and exchanges between seemingly distantly related methodologies and disciplines, such as between bodies and machines, have become central questions not only in music history but in the humanities and social sciences more generally. In offering a greater understanding of the cultural web in which I inscribe the music/automobile relationship, this volume seeks to contribute to the increasing focus on connected histories, networks, liminal borders, and topics shared by multiple disciplines.

To this end, this book pursues three interrelated objectives: 1) to analyze the historical interrelationship of popular music and automobiles in order to better understand the complexities of their mutually influential aesthetics; 2) to provide a previously unexplored analysis of the synergistic role of cars and popular music in constructing identity; and 3) to challenge stereotypical concepts surrounding the division of art and industry, particularly to understand the entwined nature of music and the automobile industry manifested in advertising, audio systems design, safety, and environmental issues. It therefore illuminates and challenges common assumptions regarding the divergences between industry and art, underscoring how the automotive and commercial music industries have mutually evolved and benefited from both aesthetic and technological commonalities.

Additionally, in an era of post-human critiques of the materialist nature of humanity, it interrogates our personal, social, and cultural relationships with automotive technology, and reveals how music and sound are used to suture the putative divide between human and non-human and to complicate traditional limits of subjectivity. It thereby provides a unique understanding of the ability and use of popular music and designed sounds to bridge the divide between the body and the machine, the human and the non-human.

Despite the intense degree of integration of automotive culture with popular music, there has been little dedicated scholarly study of the phenomenon or the context of its production. A number of books have analysed the general impact of car culture on American cultural life, the most salient of which are Berger (1979, 2001), Dunn (1998), Flink (1970, 1975, 1990), Foster (2003), Lhamon (1990), Miller (2001), Parkin (2017), Passon (2011), Rae (1959, 1965, 1971), and Volti (2004). Most of these works, however, are several decades old, and almost entirely eschew questions related to popular music and identity construction.

A recent scholarly thread has focused on the psychological and cognitive ramifications of driving while listening to music. In addition to articles by Brodsky (2002), Bull (2001), Dibben and Williamson (2007), Furnham and Allas (1999), Stutts et al. (2003), and Wiesenthal, Hennessy, and Totten (2000), Warren Brodsky's recent *Driving with Music* (2015) explores the cognitive aspects of music listening while driving a car in order to understand how music-related behaviour in a car can either enhance or imperil driver safety. Coming largely from the perspective of sound studies, Bijsterveld, Cleophas, Krebs, and Mom's *Sound and Safe* (2013) is perhaps the most comprehensive look at the connection of sound culture and driving. It offers a significant analysis of the rise of "quiet culture" in car advertising and engineering, and of the role of sound and music in fears around safety. This study differs from these others in that the focus is not principally on the driving experience or on the cognitive science behind it, but rather on the socio-cultural implications of music and sound in contributing to and creating felt experiences and identities while driving, and in enhancing an often anthropomorphized relationship with our cars. It also provides a distinct historical overview of how music consumption has influenced car design and how cars have, in turn, influenced musical content and its consumption.

The car's relationship to race, gender, and locational identity has been the subject of inquiry in Jeremy Packer's *Mobility without Mayhem* (2008). However, Packer does not consider these identities in relationship to music. Notions of race and car audio modification culture have also been explored in relation to Chicano lowrider culture (Chappell, 2012; LaBelle, 2008; Tatum, 2011). Again, however, relatively little attention is given to understanding the actual music of that culture. Suzanne E. Smith's *Dancing in the Street* (1999) represents one of the only studies that discuss the influence of the car industry on music, specifically the rise of the Motown sound in Detroit. Similarly, Joel Dinerstein's *Swinging the Machine* (2003) has provided an insightful perspective on the influence of machine culture more generally on African-American swing and jazz between the First and Second World Wars. In linking the aesthetics of art and industry, these latter two works provide particularly valuable insights for the current study, although this study significantly extends the scope (in terms of time period, musical and sonic examples, location, and identities at stake) of these inquiries.

The relatively few studies that have touched upon popular music and automobile culture are limited to articles and chapters in larger works, including a notable essay by E. L. Widmer (2002) entitled "Crossroads: The Automobile, Rock and Roll, and Democracy." John L. Wright's "Croonin' about Cruisin'" (1978) demonstrates how, since its inception, the automobile has been a "vehicle of musical inspiration" for popular songs. More recently, Paul Gilroy (2001) and George Lipsitz (2006) insightfully examine aspects of the complicated relationship between African-American musicians and car culture. Likewise, Timothy Taylor (2007, 2012) analyzes the use of techno music in car advertising. Mark Laver (2015) provides insightful analyses regarding the use of jazz in various automotive marketing campaigns. Justin Williams (2010, 2013, 2014) also contributes well-considered and illuminating articles and chapters on the relationship between automobile sound systems and hip hop production practices.

This study attempts to offer a unique analysis of how car advertising influences popular music; investigates how listening to music and designed sounds in cars enhances an anthropomorphic relationship to and with the car; and probes the critically under-studied relationship between musical culture and industry. It provides the first comprehensive and long-overdue analysis of the historical evolution of car songs in popular music and their role in both constructing identity and normalizing and incorporating the sounds of the urban/suburban industrial age. This book seeks to create a far more detailed understanding of how deeply intertwined our musical values, practices of consumption, and industrialization really are. It provides understanding of the ability and use of popular music and designed sounds to bridge the divide between body and machine, human and non-human, and consumer and product, and argues that we are increasingly hybridized, interpenetrated constructions of corporate and machine influences, thus challenging conventional notions of human identity and subjectivity.

The seven chapters of this book each deal with different aspects of identity and identity construction in the car–popular music nexus. Chapter 1 provides a historical overview of car songs in popular music, from sheet music incarnations of Tin Pan Alley through to today—including examples from blues, early rock n' roll, singer-songwriters, techno, and rap, among others. It focuses on specific works that illuminate the evolving relationship of popular music to cars, and discusses how early sheet-music songs and car-manufacturer sponsorship of radio advertising, in contrast to journalism that associated the car with moral decay (Blanke, 2007), served to normalize and humanize the automobile in North American society while also creating and naturalizing many (now) stereotypical conceptions of the automobile. Following from Tin Pan Alley, the evolution of car songs is traced through blues and r & b works that often treated the car as a symbol of social status and liberation, but also used it as a sexual metaphor and a personification of women. The 1950s and 1960s expressed a fascination with futuristic technology, and I show how the speed and utopian liberation it represented characterized much of the design and content of both the automotive and rock and roll industries. Singer-songwriters of the 1970s related to the car less as an icon of youthful rock n' roll rebellion than as a more utilitarian, if somewhat mythologized, vehicle with which to move through everyday life, whereas punk and new wave songs in the 1980s particularly focused on the dystopic effects of the automobile. Finally, the 1990s and 2000s, while witnessing a decline in car songs in mainstream popular music, saw them prominently featured in hip hop, often as a manifestation of status similar to that previously occurring in blues and r & b. The chapter also highlights the aesthetic and sonic influences of the car on popular songs, including the incorporation of engine and horn sounds, and sounds gleaned from the automobile manufacturing process (topics also discussed in Chapters 4 and 5).

Chapter 2 focuses on the intersection of popular music and cars in the construction of African-American identities. A central feature of this chapter is the advent and evolution of the Motown sound, perhaps the most overt and influential articulation of the bonds between black identity, music, and the automotive industry. This chapter also discusses how car ownership in the early twentieth century represented black upward mobility, but also signified the mobile "threat" of blackness crossing into white space. Of particular focus are the songs of Chuck Berry, who briefly worked in two automobile manufacturing plants and was especially fascinated with the symbolic social status afforded by automobiles. Additional issues explored in this chapter include the role of music and analogous notions of improvisation and car modification as means of signifying in both Hispanic lowrider and African-American hip hop culture, and the place of the automobile as an icon of social and physical liberation in African-American blues and jazz.

Chapter 3 analyzes the nexus of automobiles and popular music in constructing images of femininity and masculinity, and LGBTQ+ identities. It begins with the premise that cars, as objects of desire and devotion, have often been linked through song with women or anthropomorphized as female personae. The years following the Second World War saw car songs come into prominence at a time when men were in the driver's seat of both the automotive and the recording industries. Consequently, most early rock n' roll car songs reflected male experiences and ambitions. Following an analysis of the rise of hypermasculine identities in hard rock and hip hop car songs, the chapter turns to female challenges to these voices (e.g., Joni Mitchell, Aretha Franklin, and Shania Twain, among others) and elaborates on new literatures of gendered "feeling" for cars (Sheller & Urry, 2006; Kent, 2015). As women entered the rock n' roll and automotive arenas in increasing numbers, they altered the meaning of the automobile in popular music to reflect their own perspectives. This chapter thus provides an additional location from which to consider how the automobile has impacted women's lives, as well as how women's experiences and ambitions have influenced rock n' roll and American car culture. Finally, the chapter explores the intersection of automobile culture and music in relation to LGBTQ+ identities, which are typically overlooked in discussions of masculine, hetero-normative automotive culture. Even so, several car companies have overtly targeted gay and lesbian consumers, and a number of artists have focused on unfamiliar and non-heteronormative narratives and feelings for cars in lyrics and videos in order to further queer discourses. Through the combined lens of popular music songs and car advertising campaigns and their soundtracks, the chapter illuminates and highlights recent challenges to and contestations of the stereotypical image of the car as a heteronormative machine.

Chapter 4 discusses the ways in which the automotive industry approaches concepts of sound branding in order to delineate both product and consumer identities. It elucidates how sonic aspects of the car–driver experiences—such as distinctive engine sounds or the variety of interior warning indicators and chimes—are carefully designed to appeal to various target markets. Additionally, this chapter discusses the role of music in television and radio advertising for automobiles, the increasing ubiquity of utilizing popular musicians to help brand various models, and the growing influence that such product endorsement deals exercise over popular music content. The central feature of this chapter is an analysis of how manufacturers employ sound and popular music in order to create anthropomorphic, haptic connections between cars and consumers.

Chapter 5 looks at the various uses of musical concepts, language, and aesthetic practices as applied in the automotive industry, and identifies various sonic and musical components of automotive manufacturing and engineering culture drawn from stereo- and headphone-listening technologies (including the penchant for using musical car names, the musical terms and technologies that are used to tune, codify, and identify engine sounds, and the seemingly endless quest for a quiet driving experience and pristine listening environment) that mark much automotive design. The chapter concludes with a discussion of how the automotive industry attempts, often by relying on musical or sonic means, to imbue cars with sentient emotional "agency" that would encourage consumers to understand cars as empathetic, emotional actors that merge in forms of a human–machine hybridity.

Chapter 6 examines the car as a vehicle for both the consumption and production of music and expressive sound. Whether through the medium of car radios, cassette tapes, CD players, or MP3 player ports, cars have facilitated our listening habits and reflected the latest in listening and playback technology. Indeed, the popularity of radios in cars has even influenced radio programming. Following the discussion of the musical concepts and metaphors used in manufacturing and "tuning" cars, this chapter outlines the history of automotive sound systems and related devices (e.g., car horns and sirens) in terms of their influence on popular music and as expressive devices in their own right. A prime feature of this chapter addresses the car as an instrument for projecting musical identities through various car stereo modification cultures (hip hop booming and Jeep beats, Houston SLAB, and Chicano lowrider, for instance). A part of car modification culture known as "tuning"—the enhancement or even building of stereo systems—contests the mass-produced, homogenous identities and listening experiences offered by automotive manufacturers, and allows the sonic projection of individual and community identities that redefine the embodied listening experience in unique ways. I apply Deleuze and Guattari's (1987) notions of "assemblage" and Lefebvre's (1991) ideas surrounding the construction of social space to formulate a new understanding of these modified car–driver constructions and show how they allow the performance of resistive, hybrid assemblages of various ethnic, racial, class, and locational identities.

Chapter 7 weaves together several disparate strands linking popular music and automobile culture and identity. Beginning with movie and television soundtracks, the chapter discusses the role of popular music in depicting a variety of car-related activities such as chase scenes or travel and racing montages, and how it subsequently provides a major narrative of identity in these films. Similarly, cars often play a major role in music-based television shows such as *The Monkees* (with its Monkeemobile) or *The Partridge Family* (with the Partridge Family Bus), in these cases delineating a common identification with the road and touring musicians in the 1970s. The role of anthropomorphic talking cars (such as KITT from *Knight Rider*) is also explored in relation to the auto industry's increasing penchant for actual "interactive" or "intelligent" cars. From these increasingly humanized and sentient cars, the chapter transitions to the quasi-spiritual connections that sometimes link drivers to their cars and how popular music has often reinforced them. From the intimate moments of listening to music while driving to songs directly evoking spirituality, the experience of car travel and music often combine to enhance both physical and emotional journeys. The chapter further addresses key places and locations whose identity is largely defined by the relationship between cars and popular music: for example, how Detroit's legendary music scene—from the manufactured Motown sound to proto-punk garage rockers like The MC5 (short for Motor City Five)—is directly related to its automotive industry; or how particular roads in America (such as Los Angeles' "Sunset Strip" and the iconic "Route 66") have also come to be delineated by the merging of popular music and automotive culture. This chapter also argues that roads and streets themselves are spaces that have a complex sonic and rhythmic component made up of multiple elements such as footsteps, construction, or the regulated noise of traffic, and that this contributes to an often-overlooked aspect of locational identity. The chapter concludes with a discussion of car companies' attempts to integrate themselves into various locational communities through their patronage of cultural and artistic events and venues.

In sum, this book attempts to understand the multifariousness and importance of the mutual influences between popular music and automotive culture, and how they have combined to construct human identities. Feelings about driving are often similar to feelings about music, and are one way that emotions are embodied in relationships not only with other humans but also with material things, including kinaesthetic aspects of how human bodies interact with the material world.

1 "Come away with me, Lucille"

A brief history of popular song and automobiles

As several studies have recognized, the centrality of automobility has exerted itself across the globe (Brodsky, 2015; Gartman, 2004; Sheller, 2004; Wollen, 2002a). It is estimated that in 2014 the number of cars in use throughout the world exceeded 1.2 billion, a 20 per cent increase since 2010 (Voelcker, 2014). In 2013, the United States alone had over 254 million registered vehicles (Bureau of Transportation Statistics, 2013). Furthermore, some scholars predict that expanding markets in developing countries will result in as many as two billion cars in operation by 2030 (Lutz & Fernandez, 2010).

Until the 1920s, the expense of automobile ownership meant it was mostly reserved for the wealthy. It was a vehicle for conspicuous consumption that projected and identified one's social class and financial means. The advent of mass-production techniques developed by Henry Ford allowed his eponymous car company, along with competitors Chrysler and General Motors (GM), to produce roughly 72 per cent of the world's automobiles by the mid-1920s (Gartman, 2004). This signalled an incursion of the car into the daily lives of less affluent consumers such that it now holds a central identifying status across all social classes (Inglis, 2004).

Since its inception, the car has made a particularly significant impact on Western popular culture. Automobiles have been incorporated into almost all mediums of entertainment—magazines, books, newsprint, radio, television, and movies. Typically, the themes of such works have centred on the freedom the automobile affords. Books and movies have focused on individuals, typically young men, who succeed in liberating themselves from a restrictive middle-class life in order to travel and seek adventure in the exotic. The common idea of the car as liberating has always rested on an odd contradiction—a desire to escape from those conditions that allow one to possess a car in the first place. Nonetheless, car ownership came to be associated with independence, freedom, and increased social status. Nowhere, however, has the liberating effect of the car been more celebrated than in the world of popular music. Indeed, the two industries have been mutually interconnected almost from the moment of their respective formations. For well over one hundred years, the subject of automobiles and automotive culture has been employed in almost every genre of popular music. A complete study of lyrical and sonic references is beyond the scope of this chapter. Instead, the aim will be to provide a topical, and roughly chronologic, overview of the evolution of popular music relating to cars, from Tin Pan Alley parlour songs through to contemporary popular music. In so doing, it will outline the historical prevalence and current extent of the interconnections between popular music and automobiles, and illuminate a new understanding of their mutually influential aesthetic. Particular attention will be paid to the sonic influence of automobile culture on popular music—how the sounds of engines, horns, and car customization have impacted popular music aurally—and how the relationship between cars and popular music has evolved in constructing and reflecting various identities.

Early automotive songs

In 1885, Gottlieb Daimler invented in Germany what is often recognized as the prototype of the modern internal combustion gas engine. North America's first gasoline-powered commercial car manufacturers were Charles and Frank Duryea, whose Duryea Motor Wagon Company produced 13 different models by 1896 (Bellis, 2016). And within a decade of the appearance of automobiles on America's roads, Tin Pan Alley was creating car-related hits with a speed and regularity that compared favourably to the auto industry's mass-production pace. Between 1905 and 1907, more than 120 songs were written with the automobile as subject (Widmer, 1990, p. 82). The automotive themes of these songs reflected the general culture of the automobile industry: sexual adventure, upward mobility, liberation from social control, and masculine power. Such themes reflected not only the ideals overtly promoted by the auto industry but also, in part, those generated by songwriters as they interpreted the car's significance.

At the time, sheet music sales dominated the commercial music industry. Much of the early music about the automobile, such as "Motor Car" (1903) and Hamilton J. Hawley's "The Auto Race" (1904), consisted of instrumental works for piano or band that were designed to imitate the unique mechanical sounds of the new and exciting invention. Many of these sheet music works translated well into the relatively new medium of recording, partly because of their onomatopoeic content. For example, "The Auto Race," as performed by the Edison Concert Band and recorded in 1905, features an early recording of a car backfiring as it starts up, followed by several hoots from a hand-pump car horn that are imitated by the winds and interjected at various moments. Such imitative musical features are suggestive that the car was not simply a machine understood only in functional terms, but that it was also a work of art in itself that inspired other artists. As a spoken word preamble on the recording explains, the idea of the "race" pits different instruments against each other in a rollicking *perpetuum mobile* of racing sixteenth notes as different instruments take up the main melody and thus "overtake" others.

Indeed, composers of many instrumental genres, including dance music, ragtime, and marches, wrote music celebrating, and often imitating, the frequently erratic motorized sounds of the new automobile. Typically evoking a seemingly unnatural mechanical intrusion on the sonic lives of listeners, the tempos alternated between fast and slow, with repetitive drone-like melodies and noise effects evoking the various spluttering and monotonous sounds of an engine. March music relating to the car was particularly prevalent in works such as George Rosy's "The Motor March" (1906), Joseph Howard's "The Peerless March" (dedicated to the Peerless Motor Company, 1917), Harry Zickel's "The Ford March" (1908), Harry Sawyer's "The Taxi Cab March" (1910), J. W. Ladd's "The Automobile March" (1900), George W. Moraine's "The Auto King March" (1911), and Richard Goosman's "Auto Patrol March" (1908). Dances, mostly two-steps, included Grace Walls Linn's "The Automobile Spin" (1899), Frank P. Banta's "Kareless Koon" (1899), E. H. Pendleton's "The Ebony Flyer" (1903), and E. Hardy's "The Auto Glide" (1915).

Advertising

As cars became increasingly common in American life, so too did music written about them. In 1904, some 29 songs were published about automobiles, 40 in 1905, and 53 in 1908 (Heitmann, 2009). Henry Ford, inventor of the popular Model T, alone was mentioned in over 60 songs composed between 1908 and 1940. Much as with record company Motown's symbiotic association with the automotive industry later in the century, songs that employed car brand names served to increase the marketing and sales of both products. Car companies were quick to realize and seize the advertising potential of sheet music. Many began to give out sheet music to the public, hoping to bring in potential customers (although those who already owned a particular make of car celebrated in song may also have been interested). A song proclaiming the virtues of a product might have been practised and played multiple times in people's homes, perhaps even hundreds of thousands of times over across the country if the tune were memorable or popular enough. Of course, the composer of the song also enjoyed spin-off benefits of this success, although it is hard to gauge the overall commercial influence of such practices, be it their influence on car sales or on the careers and incomes of sheet music composers.[1]

The commercial associations between the music and auto industries began as early as 1899, with the publication of L. Marda's heavily syncopated "The Studebaker Grand March." Aside from the lyrical promotion of the product in the song, the artwork that frequently appeared on the sheet music covers was a prime means of bringing advertising messages into the potential consumer's home. The front cover of "The Studebaker Grand March," for example, celebrated 50 years of the Studebaker Bros. Manufacturing Company, with artwork depicting its factory as it originally looked in 1849 and again in 1899. The back cover extolled the capacity of the factory, proclaiming it the "Largest in the World, covering 98 acres," with "Vehicles of Every Description" and an "Annual capacity [of] 75,000 Vehicles." While the melody and lyrics of advertising sheet music songs provided a sonic and aural testimony to the quality and features of the car, the imagery, as manifest in the "Studebaker March" and actual representations of Henry Ford (as discussed below), offered a less ephemeral reminder of the manufacturer.

Figure 1.1 Front Cover of L. Marda, "The Studebaker Grand March" (1899). Image Supplied by Lester S. Levy Collection of Sheet Music, Sheridan Libraries, Johns Hopkins University

Figure 1.2 Back Cover of L. Marda, "The Studebaker Grand March" (1899). Image
supplied by Lester S. Levy Collection of Sheet Music, Sheridan Libraries,
Johns Hopkins University

C. R. Foster and Byron Gay's "The Little Ford Rambled Right Along"
(1914) exemplifies the type of advertisement that a car song could provide.
The song is a comedic ode to the reliability of a Ford Model T (depicted on
the cover of the sheet music) and testifies to the amount of driving abuse it
could withstand yet still "ramble along":

You can smash the top and smash up the seat,
You can twist it out of shape till both ends meet;
Smash the body and rip out a gear,
Smash up the front and smash up the rear,
Smash up the fender and rip off the tires,
Smash up the lamps and cut out the wires,
Throw in the clutch and then forget the juice,
And the little old Ford will go to beat the deuce.

The song thus portrays the merits of the Ford, its reliability and practicality, in comparison to a "big limousine": as "the gas burned out in the big machine / The little old Ford don't need gasoline." As such, it is an ode to class identity, contrasting the down-home reliability of the middle or working class, who would have been the market for the Model T, to the relative unreliability of the upper classes in their limousines. The chorus of "And the little old Ford it rambled right-along" is set to an undulating sixteenth-note melody underlain by a syncopated left-hand piano part that evokes both the rumbling sound of the engine and the notion of rambling movement. In Billy Murray's hit version of the song, recorded in 1915, the rumble and syncopations are supplemented by actual car-horn honking.

Ford commissioned many other songs as advertising odes to the Model T and later Model A. Jack Frost's witty wordplay in "You Can't Afford to Marry If You Can't Afford a Ford" (1915) emphasized the low price of the Model T. Playing off the common practice of anthropomorphizing cars in song, Larry Shay's "When Lizzie Changed Her Name to Baby Lincoln" (1927) was commissioned by Ford to advertise the name change of the Model T, whose popular nickname was Lizzie. The same anthro-pomorphizing occurred in Walter O'Keefe's "Henry's Made a Lady Out of Lizzie" (1928), which announced the new Model A: "She once had rattles in her wheel, But now she's full of 'sex appeal' / She's like all the other vamps, Pretty shape and lovely lamps." Several other songs were simply paeans to Henry Ford himself that also boasted the Model T's reliability. Examples of these include "My Henry Ford" by Joe Austin and Ralph Loveland (1915), "Mr. Ford You've Got the Right Idea" by Ray Sherwood and J. Fred Coots (1916), and "That Wonderful Ford" by Geneva Cranston (1915). Many of these songs—again, commissioned by the company—featured a picture of a young Henry Ford on the front cover, connecting the songs and the cars to the cult of personality he embodied.

However, not all songs relating to Henry Ford were positive. In 1922, for example, Billy Rose and Ballard MacDonald penned the cynical "Since Henry Ford Apologized to Me," a satirical response to Ford's public apology to the Jewish people. Ford had extended the apology to ward off a lawsuit following a series of overtly anti-Semitic remarks he had published in his newspaper, *The Dearborn Independent* (Lewis, 1976, pp. 144–145). The song casts a doubtful eye over the sincerity of Ford's admission of guilt:

I was sad and I was blue but now I'm just as good as you
Since Henry Ford apologized to me
That's why you threw away your little Chevrolet
And bought yourself a Ford cou-pay.
I told the superintendent that the Dearborn Independent doesn't have to
hang up where it used to be
You're happy now because he settled half the case
I'm sorry I cut off my nose to spite mayn [*sic*] race
Are you glad he changed his point of view?
Yes, I like even Edsel too
Since Henry Ford apologized to me.

Meant to be sung as a duet in a thick Yiddish accent, it became a minor hit, mostly after it was performed and recorded by the Happiness Boys in 1927.[2] The song remains a rare instance of public criticism of Ford's anti-Semitic views.

Cars and brokenness!

As demonstrated in the lyrics to "The Little Ford Rambled Along" and other Ford-related songs that emphasized the Model T's reliability, the automotive experience at the turn of the century was not an unalloyed love affair. Indeed, the automobile had many detractors and was derided in song as often as it was celebrated. For example, Dave Reed Jr's "Git a Horse" (1902) comically outlines the low regard in which many people held the increasing incursion of the automobile:

Automobile coming down the street,
Git a horse, git a horse;
You will hear this all along the beat,
Git a horse, git a horse.
When you're just about to turn a corner
A rock or something hits you in the ear,
You say your pray'rs and think you are a goner
But soon the saying falls upon your ear,
Git a horse, git a horse …

It's enough to make your angel brother cross.
All the young ones in the land
In your path are sure to stand,
Then they dodge away and yell with awful force,
"Git a horse, git a horse."
You're mad enough to kill the kids of course.
But a hint to you I'll drop,
If you want to make them stop,
Git a horse, git a horse.

The song overtly, and somewhat humorously, alludes to opposition to the new presence of a mechanized mode of transportation and the seeming lack of human control over the technology compared to the traditional, more responsive, and natural horse. All references to the automobile, for example, are set with consistent repeated quarter notes that proceed to "break down" into more erratically syncopated beats. The expression "horseless carriage," of course, was a well-known term for early automobiles and, like today's cord-less vacuum cleaners or driverless cars, was an instance of new technology labelled by what was missing in comparison to older forms.[3]

Songs about the unreliability of the new automotive technology, often cast in negative comparison to the comparative reliability of horses, were also common. Kerry Mills and Ren Shields' "Take Me Out For a Joy Ride" (1909), the song that coined the term still in use today (and that also carries subtle sexual connotations), ironically outlines how a bad automotive experience could distract from, rather than aid, an automotive courtship. The lyrics relate how "sweet Gwendolin" is forced to walk "a Marathon" after her suitor's car breaks down:

> Fly little, sly little Rudolph O'Neil,
> Took her out once in his automobile,
> Ten miles from town motor broke down, of course,
> Farmers all gathered and yelled, "Get a horse."
> Nothing to carry her home could be found,
> A Marathon she had to do back to town,
> And now she's laid up with both feet in a sling,
> So never again will sweet Gwendolin sing

That same year, the Edison motion picture company released the short comedy *The Interrupted Joy Ride*, in which a litany of near misses befalls a hapless, inexperienced driver. A certain mistrust of and hostility to the car and car owners was evident in such songs, and spoke to the propensity of early autos to breakdown. One of the most famous examples of the break-down song is Maurice Abrahams' "He'd Have to Get Under—Get Out and Get Under (To Fix Up His Automobile)" (1913). Here, the car's breakdown is characterized by a slowing tempo and a descending melodic line to the lyric, "Then something happened to the old machinery." Although it was sung by other stars of the day, the song became a huge hit for Al Jolson in 1913, selling over 2 million records and over 800,000 copies of the sheet music (Hillstrom & Hillstrom, 2006, p. 240). Other songs, such as Irving Berlin's "Keep Away From the Fellow Who Owns An Automobile" (1909), Billy Murray's "I Think I Oughtn't Auto Anymore" (1907), and Reed's "Git a Horse," testify to the mixed feelings that many songwriters and their audiences had for the relatively new invention.[4]

Some sheet music songs not only promoted the reliability of various brands of automobiles, but, by the 1930s, also began to promote driving and road safety. In a precursor to the "mental hygiene" films of the 1950s and 1960s that provided instruction to teens about safe driving, in 1937, Irving Caesar, composer of "Tea for Two" (1925), published the first collection of car songs for children. Called *Sing a Song of Safety*, the album included 21 songs intended for use in classrooms across the country to teach children about the potential dangers of traffic. Caesar claimed that the idea came to him as he gazed out of his office window and watched children walking along the streets, blithely disregarding traffic and the warning shouts of their mothers (Caesar, 1937).

The number and variety of musical works devoted to the car not only reflected, in part, the general obsession with and infatuation over the automobile at the time, but also how the motor car was changing the soundscape of both urban and rural North America and Europe. As the city and countryside began to be inundated by the seemingly alien and man-made mechanical sounds of pistons, crankshafts, car horns, backfiring, and others associated with the internal combustion engine, so too were the sound and landscape of contemporary popular music directly influenced by the automobile. In turn, the onomatopoeic musical works both drew attention to the new sounds and noises associated with the automobile and served to familiarize and normalize these sounds in the public mind. From this perspective, popular music incorporated and thus humanized the alienating sounds of the unnatural automotive machine.

Early car songs and race

An ugly offshoot of automobile songs of this period was the presence of overtly racist "coon songs," such as "The Ebony Flyer" and "Kareless Koon." Coon songs were based on the syncopated rhythms of ragtime, although the two genres are distinctly different from one another in tone and form. The coon song craze of the late 1800s and early 1900s was perpetuated largely by white composers, although some black composers, such as Ernest Hogan and Bob Cole, also participated. Coon songs were racist contrivances that, under the guise of humour, exploited every conceivable imagined negative, black characteristic and stereotype for comic possibilities. African-American aspirations for social advancement and their imagined criminality, food preferences, and inclinations toward gambling were all exploited. Black people were characterized as ignorant and indolent, devoid of honesty or honour, and given to drunkenness and lasciviousness. They were portrayed as making money through gambling, theft, and hustling, rather than honest toil. The elevation of white people as the progenitors and masters of science and technology (and the attendant faith in science and technology) contributed to an ideology of white supremacy, of which owning and operating an automobile played a part. Songs such as R. Mellville Baker and Josephine Sherwood's "Jes' Come Around' Wid an Automobile (I Don't Ride In No Hitch Like Dat)" (1902), aside from using the "N" word, also parodies black patois.

Harry Zaun and Halsey K. Mhor's "I Got a White Man Running My Automobile" (1906) is likewise riddled with racist sentiments, and accuses the protagonist of accident fraud as the only means by which he can afford a car:

Abe Jackson was a lucky coon
and he always had the dough
He broke his leg on a trolley car
and got five thousand or so,
He said I think I've enough spare change
for to buy an automobile,
With a poor white man to run it for me
how happy I would feel

I got a white man running my Automo automo,
running my automobile,
You never can know, till you get the dough
how happy it makes you feel,
I eats the best of chicken stew,
If my money gives out I'll steal,
Just to keep that white man running my automo,
running my automobile

This yaller coon's coin soon gave out
and he tried that game a game
He said if I break off both legs this time
perhaps they'll give me ten,
He got on a car but he jumped too far
and was hit by an auto passing by,
On a grave stone near in words carved clear
they put there when he died.

Typically, these songs reflected white notions of African Americans' inability to understand or deserve the new and relatively sophisticated technology associated with the automobile, and to underline the notion that technological achievement and mastery were hallmarks of white superiority. In the latter song, the "yaller" (meaning a light-skinned) black person, having fraudulently gained the means to acquire an automobile through an accident, is unable to even pronounce the word correctly until taking several runs at it.

The relationship between African Americans and cars is long and complex. Coon songs about cars were thankfully short-lived. Following World War II, the availability of affordable, fast, technologically advanced cars allowed some African Americans, many of whom had migrated north to work in the automotive plants of Detroit, to buy cars. Engaging in a poetics of diasporic transit stretching from the underground railroad to freedom rides, driving became a kind of "liberation from their apartheid" for African Americans. Car ownership, a symbolic representation of their socio-economic progress and status, is often still celebrated in African-American popular music (Gilroy, 2001, p. 94). Car ownership in the early twentieth century, then, represented a sign of black upward mobility. It figuratively and literally signified the mobile opportunity (or threat, depending on the perspective) of blackness crossing into white space. Chuck Berry, for example, briefly worked in two automobile manufacturing plants and was particularly fascinated with the symbolic social status afforded by automobiles. Berry's "No Money Down" (1955), to give but one instance, extols the acquisition of social status achieved through ordering on credit various accessories for his Cadillac. As discussed later in this chapter, and explored in more detail in Chapter 2, the equation of cars and car customization with socio-economic success is still evident in contemporary forms of African-American music.

Women, cars, and courtship

From the beginning of the automobile age, cars have been intimately connected with romance and courtship. At the very least, they allowed couples to range further afield from restrictive parents and overly inquisitive friends and neighbours. The ability to meet up with people and potential love interests was also greatly expanded beyond limitations previously imposed by the horse and buggy. Automotively empowered couples also had a much wider choice of activities in which to engage. They could now travel much further for picnics, dances, concerts, and other forms of entertainment, while being less constrained by weather or season.

Of course, the influence of the automobile on courtship extended past the freedom it afforded as a mode of transportation. The automobile also provided a convenient private setting for sexual relations. Previously, the horse and buggy, with its carriage open to odours, flies, and various other horse-related irritations, was hardly the epitome of a romantic environment. Early cars, modelled on the buggy, were typically open, with riders sitting on narrow elevated seats. As such, they were exposed to both the elements and onlookers. Gradually, however, improvements were made to make the automotive experience more pleasant. Although the infamous open-air "rumble seat" (adapted from horse carriages) was still included on many makes of cars into the late 1930s, by the 1920s cabins became enclosed, heaters were added, and seats, sometimes detachable, were made wider and more comfortable. To judge the effect on love and courtship practices that these improvements yielded, one need only look to the proliferation of "Lovers' Lanes" that soon became a feature of almost every community in North America. The car provided an intimate and potentially exciting setting that most young people, who normally lived with their parents, could not find at home.[5]

In the early part of the twentieth century, the link between automobiles and courtship was propagated and celebrated in popular culture through endless valentines, advertising, and cartoons. Nowhere, however, was the connection more evident than in the songs of Tin Pan Alley. A plethora of songs celebrated romance and automobiles, often conflating the two such that the heartfelt feelings a young man might have for his sweetheart were transferred to, or emblematic of, the love for his car. As early as 1899, in Alfred R. Dixon's song "Love in an Automobile," the car was portrayed as a means to seduce women. A once-rejected lover sees his luck change when he suggests, "Say, wouldn't you go for a honeymoon in a cozy automobile? / When she heard my bright suggestion, why, she fairly jumped with joy / Her reply was just a question 'Oh say, when do we start, dear boy?'" The music is set to a seductively lilting waltz tempo and characteristic oom-pah-pah accompaniment, with an extended, suggestive pause on the word "tight" in the repeated phrase "gripping the lever tight." The trope of women instantly seduced by automotive technology and the men who operated it (or dominated it) soon became commonplace. A few of these songs linking the automobile to thinly veiled references to sex include: Kerry Mills and Ren Shields' "Take Me Out For a Joy Ride" (1909); Lawrence and William Dillon's "On the Old Back Seat of the Henry Ford" (1916); Joseph Carey's "In Our Little Love Mobile" (1917); Joseph Blake's "Riding in Love's Limousine"(1920); Archie Fletcher et al.'s "I'm Going to Park Myself in Your Arms" (1926); Fred Cootes and Charles Newman's "Tumble in a Rumble Seat" (1933); and David Mack et al.'s "Fifteen Kisses on a Gallon of Gas" (1939).

Other early songs and instrumental marches conflated automobiles and women as similar objects of desire. This overt type of objectification is found in works whose titles squarely map the woman onto the machine, such as R. J. Morris' "My Automobile Girl" (1900), Sidney Chapman's "The Automobile Girl" (1906), Charles Campbell and Julian Edward's "The Motor Girl" (1909), Leon De Lora's "Motor Maid" (1912), and Richard Rodgers' first published tune, "Auto Show Girl" (1917). Something of this conflation is found in Collins Davis' "My Automobile Girl From New Orleans" (1900), in which the male protagonist is attracted to his car as much as to his female companion—and then only because she has the means to provide him with a car. "We ride each night in this horseless machine; There's no reins so I hold my queen / My automobile girl from New Orleans I love to count her money in my dreams."[6] Both the woman and the car are seen as vehicles for his upward social mobility.

The romantic personification of the car was taken to new heights with songs such as Harry Carrol's "The Love Story of the Packard and the Ford" (1915), in which "Mr. Packard and Miss Fliverette" (Fliver being another nickname of the Model T) are depicted in a romance between two cars that eventually marry and produce a "little Buick." Another incarnation of this type of car/woman conflation is found in Earl C. Jones and Richard Whiting's "The Big Red Motor and the Little Blue Limousine" (1913). The song epitomizes much of the motor-courtship experience, depicting "Daisy" and "Billy" stealing away in their cars to "spoon and make tender eyes," or showing their cars communicating with each other in a none-too-subtle sexual way: "With my 'clutch,' I'll show you how to 'spark'."

Daisy White drove a nice blue Limousine,
Billy Bright had a great, big, red machine
And they rode each day down a country way,
(just to be alone).
There they'd spoon and make such tender eyes,
That their love once caused a great surprise,
For Bill's red machine
Told Daisy's Limousine.

[chorus]
Come and be my true blue Limousine, (Glide along, glide along, glide along)
I am full of love and gasoline (Ride along, ride along, ride along)
Lovers stroll where it is dark,
Let us roll right thro' the park,
With my "clutch," I'll show you how to "spark," "spark," "spark" (Little Limousine.)
Show your "speed" my wheels will never "tire," (Rubber tire, never tire, never tire.)
My poor heart for you is all afire, fire, with desire,
I'll be true so never doubt when I run a "Run-a-bout,"
Said the Big Red Motor to the Little Limousine.

Most of the Tin Pan Alley automotive love songs were light-hearted, with simple lyrics that typically revolved around some episode of slightly suggestive courtship facilitated by the car. Puns based on the various aspects of the car and human passion were common. As in the example above, the term "spark" or "sparking" was often used to refer to both the process of courtship (as in sparking up a romance) and to refer to the analogous means by which engines were ignited. Of course such metaphors equated love and courtship to something mechanical, evoking, albeit unintentionally, the culture industry's erosion of the human as feared by Adorno and others.

By far the most successful and certainly most enduring of these early automotive love songs was the 1905 hit "In My Merry Oldsmobile," with lyrics by Vincent Bryan and music by Gus Edwards, which sold between 600,000 and 1 million copies of sheet music (Heitmann, 2009, p. 92). The lyrics reflect the common connections that people made between romance and the automobile. The song recounts the story of Johnnie Steel, his Oldsmobile, and his "dear little girl" Lucille. In a gently lilting 3/4 waltz time, the song is full of sexual innuendo and includes the following lines:

They love to spark in the dark old park / As they go flying along, she says she knows why the motor goes; the sparker is awfully strong / Each day they spoon to the engine's tune, their honeymoon will happen soon.

The chorus includes the somewhat suggestive line, "You can go as far as you like with me in my merry Oldsmobile." Notably, the car here becomes a musical accompaniment to the couple's lovemaking as they "spoon to the engine's tune."

Underlining the often symbiotic connection between automobile companies and popular music production, General Motors used the song (but did not originally sponsor it) as an advertising jingle for their Oldsmobile brand for several decades, ensuring the song's instant recognizability. The lyrics, however, were altered slightly to avoid some of the more overt sexual connotations. Oldsmobile sponsored several television shows starring Patti Page in the 1950s, including *The Patti Page Show* (1955–1956), *The Big Record* (1957–1958), and *The Oldsmobile Show Starring Patti Page* (1958–1959). "In My Merry Oldsmobile" was used as the theme song on every telecast, and Page often sang some form of it with new lyrics:

> Young Johnny Steele has an Oldsmobile
> He loves a dear little girl
> She is the queen of his gas machine
> She has his heart in a whirl
> Now, when they go for a spin, you know,
> She tries to learn the auto, so
> He lets her steer, while he gets her ear
> And whispers soft and low;
>
> [Chorus]
> Come away with me, Lucille
> In my merry Oldsmobile
> Down the road of life we'll fly
> Automobubbling, you and I
> To the church we'll swiftly steal
> Then our wedding bells will peal,
> You can go as far as you like with me
> In my merry Oldsmobile.
>
> They love to "spark" in the dark old park
> As they go flying along
> She says she knows why the motor goes
> The "sparker" is awfully strong
> Each day they "spoon" to the engine's tune
> Their honeymoon will happen soon
> He'll win Lucille with his Oldsmobile
> And then he'll fondly croon.

In 1932, Fleischer Studios (responsible for the characters Popeye and Betty Boop) produced a highly suggestive animated spot, entitled *In My Merry Oldsmobile*, in which a peeping tom invades Lucille's bedroom while she is undressing. While the short contains overtly suggestive phallic images, sexual tension, and voyeurism, Lucille fights back and ultimately drives off her unwanted suitor. The succeeding filmed advertisement of a couple in an Oldsmobile, presented in a "follow the bouncing ball" sing-along style, also promoted the independence that driving could afford women.

In My Merry Oldsmobile was produced during the women's liberation movement of the 1930s, and so this short can actually be read as an early instance of a car manufacturer advocating women's autonomy, similar to some later public relation stunts to advertise cigarettes to women.[7] Beyond the other more lurid aspects of this film, the cartoon connected driving with a woman's independence. Indeed, when one looks at the catalogue of motorcar songs from the turn of the century, despite the litany of car-as-woman metaphors and innuendos of the car as a machine of sexual seduction, and perhaps contrary to common assumptions, many appear to empower women. The car afforded women an opportunity to take control of their own transportation, independent of men. As the lyrics in "My Merry Oldsmobile" assert, Lucille "tries to learn the auto, so He lets her steer, while he gets her ear." One can imagine the day when Lucille will drive on her own, without someone "getting her ear." As such, women are portrayed as actively engaged in automotive culture as a means of figurative if not, as in this case, literal escape. Thus the car is again portrayed as an agent of liberation.

As automobile scholar James Flink (1990) writes,

> Despite the traditional association of the automobile as a mechanical object with men and masculinity in American culture, automobility probably had a greater impact on women's role than on men's, and the women have been enamoured with the motor car from the onset of its diffusion (p. 162).

Operating an automobile mostly required technical skill rather than physical strength, and so women could operate a car much more easily than a team of horses. They were at first primarily users of electric cars, which were silent, cleaner, and did not require hand-cranking to start the engine.[8] The introduction of Charles Kettering's automatic self-starter in 1912, often referred to as the "ladies' aid," and of the closed cabin after 1919, which did away with the need to wear special clothes while motoring, encouraged larger numbers of middle-class women drivers of conventional gasoline automobiles to take to the roads (Flink, 1990, p. 162).[9] For women, much as for men, the automobile facilitated new possibilities for romance, recreation, and work outside the home. Through their ability to operate, sometimes repair, and own their own automobiles, women were able to create a new identity for themselves that included the ability to master machines.

Women were among the earliest drivers when steam- and electric-powered automobiles were introduced in the 1890s, although the exact numbers are difficult to prove because automobile licensing did not begin in America until

1900 (1903 in England) and many women drove automobiles registered in their husband's name (Wosk, 2001, p. 115). In 1904, the Ladies Automobile Club was founded in Britain and comprised over 300 members by the end of the year. Despite this state of affairs, and also despite well-publicized accounts of women's driving achievements, such as Vera Hedges Butler's 1500-mile tour from Paris to Nice in 1901, the sight of women driving was still something of a novelty. In 1907, however, the *New York Times* proclaimed that many women were now switching from electric to "high-powered gasoline cars" and were able "to operate an auto as well as many of the best men pilots" (Women autoists skillful drivers, 1907; Wosk, 2001, p. 117).

The Tin Pan Alley songs of the period, to some extent, recognized and celebrated the presence of women on the road. Songs such as Frederick Leeds' "The Belle of 1900" (1899), Alfred Calzin's "The Automobile Girl" (1901), Sidney Chapman's "The Automobile Girl" (1906), Arthur Hauk's "The Lady Chauffeur" (1907), and Charles Campbell and Julian Edwards' "The Motor Girl" (1909)—for whom "life's a merry whirl / For the daring, scaring, flashing, dashing Motor girl"—all testify to the respect accorded female drivers. Susan Lewis and Joe Nathan's "The Girl on the Automobile" (1905) sums up many of the empowering sentiments driving afforded for women:

> The maiden of yore would feel rather sore,
> If she could see the girl of today ...
>
> No more sweet perfume, it has met its doom!
> Why it's really a thing of the past;
> For, instead of rose-dream,
> It's mild gasoline!
> Its perfume forever will last.
> The maid on the bus, who would make a big fuss
> If the horse would run, shy, or would fall,
> Runs into a fence, and the scene is immense!
> She gets up, and don't mind at all.

The song is set as a rather forthright march in C major that reinforces the sense of control imparted by the lyrics. Rather than suggest female drivers were radical thrill seekers who could not be trusted on the road, songs such as these (and often the visual imagery of the sheet music covers that accompanied them) helped legitimate women's abilities while still evoking an aura of dignity and calm, as well of an emergent strength of constitution needed to cope with the exigencies of automobile operation. These songs did not create or reflect the sexist clichés of hapless and helpless women drivers, but rather were forceful emblems of women's capacity for control.[10] In 1909, Dorothy Levitt, perhaps the most famous female motorist of her day, noted in her handbook, *The Woman and the Car*, that 20 or 30 years earlier "some acquaintance with mechanics and the ability to understand local topography ... were supposed to be beyond the capacity of a woman's brain." "Where as now," she continued, "indeed the average woman is probably quicker than the average man in gathering from a map the information it has to offer" (Levitt, 1909, pp. 87–88; also see Wosk, 2001, p. 123).[11] The ability to repair and even tinker with their cars by adding lights, luggage racks, heaters, and other features became an increasingly important skill set for early women drivers, challenging common representations of them as passive consumers. Tin Pan Alley songwriters, to their credit, recognized the parallel market for celebrating the mechanical accomplishments of women. Indeed, one might assume that it was, at least in part, through the distribution of and exposure to empowering female motor songs that increasing numbers of women sought out the excitement of automotive experiences.[12]

Automobility liberated increasing numbers of women from the narrow confines of the home, allowing them to experience new freedom, power, and pleasure behind the wheel, while simultaneously helping to change them from producers of food and clothing into consumers of national-brand canned goods, prepared foods, and ready-made clothes. Despite the images of the joyriding, liberated woman propagated in sheet music songs and some advertising, Laura Behling (1997) has pointed out that the majority of car advertising in the 1920s reinforced traditional representations of male dominance. The automotive advertising from this period directed towards women typically concentrated on "safety, dependability, security, and comfort, beauty or fashion" (p. 13). It would take several generations before such stereotypes in advertising began, however gradually, to dissipate. Notwithstanding this interpretation, the liberating images and songs about the abilities of women drivers at the beginning of the century provided a source of empowerment for women; but they also, of course, helped build and reinforce a substantial pool of consumers for the automobile companies who benefited from expanding their market to women. That advertising from this period often promoted positive and empowering images of women driving in a controlled and dignified manner is unsurprising if car companies hoped to make their products attractive to 50 per cent of the population.[13]

The sexually expressive nature of cars, in sum, has been part of the automotive musical culture from its inception. Tin Pan Alley songwriters—indeed, songwriters of almost all eras and genres—have thus capitalized on the car as an anthropomorphized, typically female object of male desire and as the lyrical location of sexual encounters. As outlined in this section, however, Tin Pan Alley songwriters and automotive companies also often attempted to appeal to women as empowered, increasingly liberated drivers and consumers.

Flying cars and roving jeeps

Although significantly predating the era of space exploration and its eventual conflation with cars and popular music—as evidenced by Jackie

Brenston's hot rod ode to an Oldsmobile, "Rocket 88" (1951), discussed below—several Tin Pan Alley songs celebrated the technological achievement of the car and its seemingly limitless potential to transport people, figuratively and literally, to new and unfamiliar places. Perhaps the best example of this was Carl Carlton and C. D. Paxton's "From Earth to Mars in a Jackson Car" (1908),[14] which makes the case that "Jackson cars" are the choice of angels for space travel:

> Last night as I lay sleeping
> an angel appeared unto me,
> With great white wings a-sweeping
> and thus spoke unto me,
> Away up yonder in the great milky way
> among the comets and the stars,
> They're using automobiles today
> and the best are Jackson cars.

A significant number of songs about airplanes, such as George Evans and Ren Shields' "Come Take a Trip in my Airship" (1904) or Fred Fisher and Alfred Bryan's "Come Josephine in My Flying Machine" (1910), also expressed, albeit with some ironic caution, the technological optimism of the era: "Whoa, dear! Don't hit the moon! / No, dear ... Not yet, but soon!"

As the novelty of the car began to wane in the 1920s, so too did the number of popular songs written about them. Although a few popular car songs emerged—such as "Clarence Gaskill's "I'm Wild About Horns on Automobiles That Go Ta-Ta-Ta-Ta" (1928) or Vincent Lopez's "The Chauffeur and the Debutant" (1938)—sheet music sales went into relative decline as audiences increasingly turned their attention towards movie musicals and dance halls. During the Depression, folksinger Woody Guthrie wrote several songs lamenting life on the road, such as "Talking Dust Bowl Blues" (1940), in which he "swapped my farm for a Ford machine / And I poured it full of this gasoline / And I started, rockin' an' a-rollin' / Over the mountains, out towards the old Peach Bowl." Yet again Guthrie represents the automobile as a means of liberation from the economic depression of the Oklahoma Dust Bowl.[15]

Following the heyday of Tin Pan Alley, automobile songs enjoyed a brief revival during World War II. During this period, North America witnessed increased exposure to military mechanization, and songs about military vehicles subsequently captured the public's imagination. The jeep in particular became a beloved symbol of rugged American determination. Examples of this type of song include Marsh Crosley's "Why Don't They Put a Saddle on This Doggone Jeep?" (1944), Hoagy Carmichael's "I'm a Cranky Old Yank in a Clanky Old Tank" (sung by Bing Crosby in 1942), and Irving Berlin's "What Are We Going To Do With All the Jeeps?" (1944). Despite these somewhat scattered examples, automotive songs were relatively rare (perhaps due to rationing of tires and gasoline and the paucity of new car production, or the unseemliness of crooning about domestic luxury in a time of national sacrifice, cars did not carry the same romantic allure), and it was not until the late 1940s and 1950s that they reappeared in significant numbers.

Immediately preceding the war, Cliff Bruner had a huge hit in 1939 with Ted Daffin's "Truck Driver's Blues," one of the biggest-selling songs of that year. The increasing popularity of honky-tonk and Western music in the postwar period, however, saw new songs about the loneliness of the road, yet also the freedom to roam across the country. Hank Williams, in particular, had hits with Leon Payne's "Lost Highway" (1952) and the suggestive "Hey Good Lookin'" (1951), which featured the line, "I got a hot rod Ford, and a two-dollar bill / And I know a spot right over the hill." In the 1950s, Terry Fells' honky-tonk "Truck Drivin' Man" (1954) reinvigorated the genre of truck-driving songs, opening the door in the 1960s for songs like Frankie Miller's "Truck Driving Buddy" (1965). Meanwhile, the Willis Brothers scored a top-ten country music hit in the US with "Give Me Forty Acres (to Turn This Rig Around)" (1964). The songwriting duo of Charlie Moore and Bill Napier also wrote several Western-swing trucking songs, including "Lonesome Truck Driver" (1964) and "Truck Driver's Queen" (1963). Indeed, country singer Dave Dudley built a career out of truck-driving anthems. His recording of "Six Days on the Road" became a million-selling hit in 1963 and was later covered by numerous artists, such as Steve Earle and George Thorogood and the Destroyers. Dudley later recorded an entire album of truck-driving songs called *Truck Drivin' Son-of-a-Gun* (1965). Then, in the mid-1960s, broadcaster Charlie Douglas pioneered an all-night truckers' radio program in Louisiana, after which new songs about long-haul drivers and their lives appeared with regularity. In the 1970s, the genre grew in popularity as rock and roll bands covered the occasional trucking song. It reached the height of its popularity in 1976, when C. W. McCall's "Convoy" topped both the country and pop music charts.[16]

The rich variety of truck-driving songs deserves much more attention and reflects something of the perilous culture surrounding the transport industry. Songs typically touched on the pressures that life on the road places on relationships, the monotony or freedom of life on the road, and industry-related hazards like falling asleep at the wheel, crashes, drug and alcohol addiction, and police harassment. Truck-driving songs obviously appealed to truckers themselves, but, as the above examples illustrate, had significant success in crossing over to the general public. To some extent, the popularity of trucking songs can be viewed in relationship to a heightened concern for the fate of the individual. The lone long-haul truck driver as a distinctly working-class figure dealing with life on the road became a romantic icon not dissimilar to the cowboy in a period that normalized an increasingly homogenized middle-class existence. To some extent such trucking songs can be regarded as both a defiant proclamation of masculinity and a lament.

Automotive blues

Following on the heels of its high profile in Tin Pan Alley songs, the automobile became the subject of many blues recordings. Bluesmen, much like numerous country and popular musicians, became accustomed to the grinding nature of long-distance road trips. In the 1930s and 1940s, however, African-American car owners were rare, and so most experienced automobiles vicariously or by hitchhiking. As such, rather than romanticizing the automobile, many blues tunes, such as Robert Johnson's "Crossroad Blues" (1936), reflect emotions of fear, unfamiliarity, and feeling lost: "Standin' at the Crossroads I tried to flag a ride / Didn't nobody seem to know me, babe, everybody pass me by."

Transportation is nonetheless one of the most common themes in the blues. Frequent subjects included walking or trains, but by the 1920s, when blues recordings became more commonplace, the car fully dominated American culture. Blues musicians sang about all kinds of makes and models, but, as with Tin Pan Alley, the most common brand immortalized in early blues was the Ford Model T. Mass production of the Model T transformed Ford's vision into the car of the people. Black consumers often identified with it, perceiving it as analogous to their own lives—hardworking, durable, and just as ignored for their virtues— even though it was a commodity that symbolized a lifestyle often out of reach. Moreover, as will be further explored in Chapter 2, with the rise of Motown, the Model T was built by a significant black workforce. A lot of bluesmen may have desired the prestige of a Cadillac, but they were driving a Ford.

In "DB Blues" (1928), Blind Lemon Jefferson sings about his love of several different kinds of car after he shows up in his new Ford:

> Gonna get out of my four-cylinder Dodge, I'm gonna get me a Super Six
> Get out of my four-cylinder Dodge, get me a Super Six
> I'm always around the ladies, and I like to have my business fixed
>
> I'm crazy about a Packard, but my baby only rates a Ford
> I'm crazy about a Packard, but my baby only rates a Ford
> A Packard is too expensive, Ford will take you where you want to go

Jefferson here recounts his preference for driving Dodges, Packards, and the Super Six, a model produced by the Hudson Motor Car Company. However, in the end it is only the "Ford [that] will take you where you want to go."[17] The song also reinforces sexualized female conflations with cars, as it is clearly a Ford that his girlfriend drives and takes him "where you want to go."

Sleepy John Estes also reinforced the notion that the Model T was the choice of common folks when he recorded "Poor Man's Friend (T Model)" in 1937. The Model T was out of production by 1927, so this song was probably composed several years before being recorded, or reflective of the fact that to a poor man the only car available is long outdated. The Model T was still clearly an iconic automobile:

Well, well, when you see it in the winter, please throw your winder over in
the bin
Well, well, when you see it in the winter, I want you to throw your winder
over in the bin
Well, well, probably next spring, I want to rig up my T-Model again

Well, well, a T-Model Ford, I say, is a poor man's friend
Well, well, a T-Model Ford, I say, is a poor man's friend
Well, well, it will help you out, even when your money's thin

Elsewhere, the song refers to somebody who "done stole my winder out on
the road," referring to the hand-crank used to start the car.

In yet another ode to a Ford, Roosevelt Sykes recorded a song named for
the founder of the Ford Motor Company, "Henry Ford Blues," in 1929:

Now, lady, won't you let me drive your Ford
Now, miss lady won't you let me drive your Ford
Now I ain't your chauffeur, but I can't hold it anymore

Now there was a woman, now she owned a Chevrolet
Now there was a woman, now she owned a Chevrolet
Now she been driving fourteen years, hasn't had an accident yet

Among other issues, the song, as discussed previously, testifies to the prevalence, and skill, of female drivers.

Other blues tunes unabashedly used the car and its engine as metaphors for
sexual intercourse. E. L. Widmer (1990) comments on this situation:

In 1926, Virginia Liston lamented that her "Rolls Royce Papa" had a bent
piston rod; a year later, Bertha Chippie Hill, in "Sports Model Mama,"
claimed to receive punctures every day; and in 1929, Cleo Gibson ...
belted out "I've Got Ford Engine Movements in My Hips" (p. 84).

Robert Johnson's "Terraplane Blues" (1936) was one of the earliest blues
songs to anthropomorphize a car as a woman. In a song that sold nearly 5000
copies, Johnson used the high-powered yet inexpensive Hudson model called
the Terraplane as a metaphor for sex. In the song's narrative, the car refuses
to start and Johnson suspects that his girlfriend let another man drive it while
he was gone. In describing the various mechanical problems with his Terraplane, Johnson spins thinly veiled sexual innuendo. It contains the overtly
sexualized lines, "I'm gonna hoist your hood, mama, I'm bound to check
your oil ... And when I mash down on your little starter, then your spark
gonna give me fire."[18]

The car/sex metaphor was not limited to male artists. Many female blues
singers unashamedly connected the automobile to sex and the body, from
Virginia Liston's "Rolls Royce Papa" (1926) and Bertha Hill's "Sports Model

Mamma" (1927) to Memphis Minnie's proclamation, "he drives me so easy, I can't turn him down" in "Me and My Chauffeur" (1941).

Notwithstanding some of the early blues songs by women that connected the car to sex, the link between popular music and automobiles (particularly rock music styles of the 1950s and later) is typically rooted in hypermasculine notions of phallocentric power, freedom, and technology. Jean Baudrillard (1996) argues that it is not only men who experience the car as a female objectification:

> The motorcar ... may be a projectile or a dwelling place. But basically, like all functional mechanical objects, it is experienced—and by everyone, men, women, and children—as a phallus, as an object of manipulation, care and fascination. The car is a projection both phallic and narcissistic, a force transfixed by its own image (p. 69).

Indeed, the vast majority of car songs were written and performed by men. The often masochistic tone of such imagery—controlling a woman as one controls technology—was also connected to the common personification of women as a guitar, as demonstrated in B. B. King's "Lucille" or Jimi Hendrix's famous simulated sex with a guitar.

After World War II, the availability of affordable, fast, and technologically advanced cars allowed increasing numbers of African Americans to buy an automobile, many of whom having migrated north to work in the automotive plants of Detroit. As Paul Gilroy (2001) notes, "Automobility ... helps to show up the deepening lines of class division inside racialized communities" (p. 85). As previously mentioned, car ownership and participation in automotive culture was a means of challenging the hierarchical racism of white control of science and technology; but it was also a means of representing or "signifyin(g)," to use Henry Louis Gates' (1988) well-known term, both racial socio-economic progress and individual status. As will be discussed more thoroughly in Chapter 2, but also later in this chapter, such attributes continue to be celebrated in African-American popular music today, particularly as manifest in the ongoing fetishization of cars in hip hop.

"Rocket 88" and the advent of rock n' roll

In the 1950s, car culture took hold of the popular imagination of both black and white consumers, and the enervating speed and rollicking beats of rock n' roll made it the perfect musical vehicle to celebrate their combined potential for economic and physical liberation. In the culture of early rock n' roll, cars were venerated beyond their mere function as a means of transport, serving as symbols of economic success and socio-sexual freedom. The combination of cars and popular music even took on political overtones, as during the postwar period they became associated with the superiority of capitalism. The car and the highway offered a freedom that communism simply could not offer.

In an attempt to kick-start a sputtering economy and quell fears of Russian technological advances in the wake of Sputnik, Karal Ann Marling (1996) explains that, in 1958, President Dwight D. Eisenhower's advertising men "tried to persuade consumers to step on the gas: 'You Auto Buy!' was the official slogan of the government's psychological offensive against unpatriotic, stay-at-home thrift" (p. 133). The timely combination of both affordable mass-produced cars and rock n' roll records represented the autonomy of a generation of young people. The new experience of sexual and economic freedom manifest in rock n' roll found a sympathetic resonance in car culture, and together they proclaimed the emancipation of young people from all walks of life.

With the migration of so much of the North American white middle class to the suburbs in the 1950s, car culture and its associated infrastructure of highways, gas stations, roadside attractions, motels, diners, and drive-in movies rapidly expanded. Postwar car culture often reflected futuristic notions of travel and exploration. One of the leading candidates for the first ever rock n' roll song is, indeed, Jackie Brenston and Ike Turner's hot rod ode "Rocket 88" (1951), which honoured the new Oldsmobile model of the same name, itself an allusion to the developing military and transportation technology. Rock n' roll developed roughly contemporaneously with the era of space exploration. The confluence of the futuristic rocket and upbeat, energetic r & b music immediately wedded the car and the song to the liberating techno-future of space travel and 1950s' youth rebellion.

The lyrics for "Rocket 88" allude to the sound of the car. In both Brenston's and Bill Haley's slightly later versions (also recorded in 1951), the rhythm section plays a perpetual-motion sixteenth-note syncopated groove punctuated by horn sounds. The rollicking rhythm and horn-honking imitation thus create the onomatopoeic quality of an actual jalopy. In Bill Haley's version, a real-life aggressive car horn and screeching tires are mixed into the song and it concludes with a fade-out of a revving engine. The song, for example, immediately references the sound of jalopies and hearing "the noise they make."[19] In addition to recalling the sound of the car as exemplified in earlier Tin Pan Alley and blues, "Rocket 88" also plays on familiar themes of the car as a vehicle for sex and displaying one's socio-economic status. The lyrics, for example, are an invitation for women to go "ridin'... for joy" and evoke phallic "rocket" imagery. They also list the car's outstanding features, including a V-8 engine, convertible top, and modern design. In so doing, they link the car to the increased economic power of youth and to the general rise in consumer culture that followed in the wake of World War II.

The success of "Rocket 88" inspired numerous imitations, including Billy Love's "Drop Top" (1951), Howlin' Wolf's "Cadillac Daddy" (1952), and Johnny London's "Drivin' Slow" (1952), in addition to Brenston's own follow-up, "Real Gone Rocket" (1951). (The latter's opening piano riff later served as inspiration for Little Richard's "Good Golly Miss Molly" [1956]).

Figure 1.3 Print Ad for Oldsmobile "Rocket 88" (1951). Courtesy General Motors LLC

The Playmates' "Little Nash Rambler" (1958) and Charlie Ryan's "Hot Rod Lincoln" (1955) were also early rock n' roll hits based on particular cars. In these and other songs, the tight relationship between rock n' roll music and the automobile was cemented.[20]

As demonstrated in "Rocket 88" and in the onomatopoeic rhythms of many earlier Tin Pan Alley car songs, the incorporation of the sound-machine technology into popular music had precedents in other genres. Joel Dinerstein observes that the exposure of many African Americans to the industrialization of northern cities signified that the machine was another type of rhythm to integrate into their sonic world perspective. This is particularly evident in the popular fascination for railroad songs, such as Duke Ellington's "Take the 'A' Train" (1941) or Count Basie's "Super Chief" (1939). Many of these songs rely on a feature that Albert Murray describes as "locomotive onomatopoeia," consisting of a rhythmic acceleration and sonic layering that mimic the sound of a steam train leaving the station and building momentum (Dinerstein, 2003, p. 72). Thus, rock n' roll continued the sonic incorporation of machines that began in the early part of the century.

The growing influence of car culture epitomized in songs from the 1950s reflected perceptions of widespread prosperity in postwar North America. The rise of suburbs, with their disparate supermarkets and shopping centres, made car ownership an indispensable part of North American life. Youth and marginalized classes were able to act as independent consumers—many for the first time—and create their own leisure styles, even if, in many cases, only vicariously through the songs of the rock n' roll stars of the day.

Following Elvis Presley and Chuck Berry, a host of rock n' rollers adopted car references, from Little Richard's claim that "Long Tall Sally" (1956) is "built for speed" to Buddy Holly's "Not Fade Away" (1957), in which he proclaims his love to be "bigger than a Cadillac." Many groups even took inspiration for their names from car brands, such as the Imperials, the Eldorados, the Continentals, the Cadillacs, and the Edsels. The deaths of James Dean and Eddie Cochran in car crashes also romanticized the tragic aspect of car culture, as celebrated in songs such as Ray Peterson's "Tell Laura I Love Her" (1960), Jan and Dean's "Dead Man's Curve" (1964), and the Shangri-Las' "Leader of the Pack" (1964). Indeed, the topical fascination with automobiles in rock music in general can at least in part be explained in the performative experience common to both activities. The risks and rewards of driving a fast car and performing rock music are often similar. Echoing the experience of drag racers (and perhaps even gunslingers from the Old West), rock musicians, through their electric guitars and amplifiers, were similarly fused with technology and expected to go for broke, hold nothing back, and risked their reputations if they could not reinvent themselves and win over fans with every performance. Early rock n' roll and automobile culture were thus linked in their mutual significations of simultaneous pleasure and danger.

Hot rodding

Hot rod culture originated in the dry-lake racing culture of Southern California and became prevalent following World War II, when, thanks to the popularity of periodicals such as *Hot Rod Magazine* and fiction such as

Henry Gregor Felsen's novel *Hot Rod* (1950), it spread to other parts of the US. Hot rodding was favoured by young men with limited budgets tinkering with and modifying their cars to make them run faster and look better. As such, it was a culture of expressing personal identity through the individualized modification of cookie-cutter, factory-produced cars.

In addition to popular literature and movies incorporating hot rodding—such as the original *The Fast and the Furious* (1954), *Hot Rod Girl* (1956), and *Drag Strip Riot* (1958)—the 1950s saw the advent of a significant number of songs dedicated to the practice. Arkie Shibley and his Mountain Dew Boys performed George Wilson's "Hot Rod Race" in 1950, and the song instantly became a classic hot rod hit. The song recounts a race between a Ford and a Mercury, and includes references to several core themes in hot rodding—including slang surrounding car modification such as "twin pipes and a Columbia butt," risky behaviour, and youth challenging the police who were unable to keep up with them and forced to "run and hide."[21] Later, both the Ford and the Mercury are left in the dust by another hot rod, "a kid in a hopped-up Model A." Shibley's recording consists of a Western swing style with a perpetual-motion downbeat rhythmic pulse mimicking the engine, and a particularly striking horn honking accent performed on the lead electric guitar. In three later versions of the song that were all released in 1951, the original racially charged lyrics "rippin' along like white folks" were changed, variously, to "plain folks" (Ramblin' Jimmie Dolan), "rich folks" (Tiny Hill), and "poor folks" (Red Foley). These changes reflected something of the importance of the car song in defining identity, be it by race or class. "Hot Rod Race" proved to be immensely popular and served as the model for numerous hot rodding songs that followed in its wake, most notably Charlie Ryan's "Hot Rod Lincoln" (1955). This latter song was an explicit answer to "Hot Rod Race." It begins with a direct reference to Shibley's earlier ballad, stating:

> You heard the story of the hot rod race that fatal day / When the Ford and the Mercury went out to play / Well, this is the inside story and I'm here to say / I'm the kid that was a-drivin' that Model A.[22]

Hot rodding songs later featured prominently in the California sound of the early 1960s, as celebrated in the music of Jan and Dean and the Beach Boys. Jan and Dean reached their commercial peak in 1963 and 1964 after they met songwriter/producer Brian Wilson of the Beach Boys. The duo scored 16 Top 40 hits on the *Billboard* and *Cash Box* magazine charts, with a total of 26 chart hits over an nine-year period (1958–1966). Jan Berry and Brian Wilson collaborated on roughly a dozen hits and album cuts for Jan and Dean, including the number-one hit "Surf City" (1963), written by Wilson. Subsequent top-ten hits featured hot rodding themes such as "Drag City" (1964, #10), the eerily portentous "Dead Man's Curve" (1964, #8),[23] and "The Little Old Lady from Pasadena" (1964, #3) who, as the lyrics describe, "Has a pretty little flower bed of white Gardenias / But parked in a rickety old garage / Is a brand new shiny red super stocked Dodge."[24]

"The Little Old Lady from Pasadena" provides an interesting case study of the influence of automotive manufacturing on music and of the integration of the automobile into North American culture in general, and Californian culture in particular. The origin of the song stems from a popular television advertising campaign that Southern Californian Dodge dealers debuted in early 1964. Starring 72-year-old actress Kathryn Minner, the commercials depicted a white-haired, elderly lady speeding down the street (and sometimes a drag strip) at the wheel of a modified Dodge. She would stop, look out of the window, and holler, "Put a Dodge in your garage, honey!"

"The Little Old Lady from Pasadena" played on a folk archetype in Southern California. At the turn of the twentieth century, many Americans moved from the Midwest to the region in order to take in the healthful coastal climate and mitigate the effects of one of the period's great epidemic illnesses, tuberculosis. This migration continued through to World War II. Since men tended to die earlier than women, California, and Pasadena in particular, became known for its high percentage of elderly widows. Part of this lore was that many an elderly man who died in Pasadena supposedly left his widow with a powerful car that she rarely, if ever, drove, such as a "Superstock Dodge." Used-car salesmen in California, so the story went, would tell prospective buyers that the previous owner of a vehicle was "a little old lady from Pasadena who only drove it to church on Sundays," meaning that the car had little wear. From this premise came the comic song about a "little old lady from Pasadena" who had a hot "Superstock Dodge" in her "rickety old garage." These vehicles had low-production number "Max Wedge" engines (Maximum Performance Wedge Engine)—lightweight race specials built in 1964 for drag racing that are highly collectible today. The song's twist was that, unlike the subject of the usual joke, this little old lady not only drove the hot car, but was also a fearsome and accomplished street racer—the "terror of Colorado Boulevard." Jan and Dean even enlisted Minner to appear on "The Little Old Lady from Pasadena" record sleeve.

Achieving even greater commercial success than Jan and Dean, the Beach Boys (brothers Brian, Dennis, and Carl Wilson, their cousin Mike Love, and the Wilsons' friend Al Jardine, in their original incarnation) were noted for their intricate vocal harmonies, arrangements laden with catchy hooks, and songs that celebrated and reinforced an idealized Southern California youth culture (white, suburban, and middle class) of surfing, romance, and cars. The Beach Boys had their first significant commercial success with "Surfin' Safari" in 1963. On the B-side of the record was "409," a song describing a Chevrolet with a 409-cubic inch V-8 engine. Somewhat ironically, Brian Wilson knew very little about surfing or cars, but his songwriting partner, Gary Usher, did, and he was able to help Wilson tap into these staples of Californian culture. As John Heitmann (2009) relates, the Chevy 409 was "a family car that when equipped with a four-speed transmission, two four-barrel carburetors, and a posi-traction rear end could go 0–60 in less than 5 seconds" (p. 117). The "giddy-up giddy-up 409" backing vocals are a humorous reference to the horsepower involved in the race. The song is also yet another instance of the car/woman conflation, beginning with the protagonist declaring "She's real fine, my 4–0-9," and later that "nothing could catch her." It also features the sound of a muscle car rhythmically revving its engine at the beginning of the song. Brian Wilson recorded the engine, likely not a 409 but a rather a 1958 Chevy 358, on his reel-to-reel Wollensack tape recorder. Thus, in the manner of early Tin Pan Alley songs and "Rocket 88," "409" is yet another example of the sound of automobiles actively influencing and infiltrating the sound of popular music.

Following the initial success of "409," the Beach Boys released a string of hit hot rod and car songs. Leaving aside covers, such as their version of Jan and Dean's "Little Old Lady from Pasadena," a list of the Beach Boys' better-known car songs includes: "I Get Around" (1964); "Little Deuce Coupe" (1963); "Shut Down" (1963); "Fun, Fun, Fun ('til Her Daddy Takes Her T-bird Away)" (1964); "This Car of Mine" (1964); "Drive In" (1964); "Little Honda" (1964); "Custom Machine" (1964); and "Spirit of America" (1975), the latter inspired by race-car driver Craig Breedlove's land speed record, set in 1963. Indeed, "I Get Around" and "Little Deuce Coupe" were two of the band's biggest-selling singles.

One of the most iconic of the Beach Boys' hot rod/street-racing songs is "Shut Down" (1963), written by Wilson and car enthusiast Roger Christian. The song tells the story about a drag race between a "four-thirteen" Superstock Dodge Dart and the narrator's "fuel-injected Stingray," using language that borrows the hot rod slang of the kids who participated in such events. As a result, "Shut Down" is full of the colourful vernacular typical of street-racing culture—the racers are described as "two cool shorts standing side by side," while the lyrics detail racer tactics such as "to get the traction I'm riding my clutch" and "power shift here we go." The musical content of "Shut Down" accentuates the excitement of the race by interspersing the narrative verses with short choruses that build tension in the manner of shifting through gears. The Beach Boys' recording of "Shut Down" enhances the song's frenetic quality by having the rhythm tracks speeding along at double-time in comparison to the melody of the lyrics. The song starts with a mildly threatening, if anthemic, "tach it up, tach it up, buddy gonna shut you down," with the melody rising on "tach it up" and rapidly descending on the word "down." It then cruises along on a combination of quickly down-strummed surf guitar and cymbal-heavy drum work. The instrumentation is simple, but Wilson artfully uses the group's renowned close vocal harmonies to colour the tune, including gliding, harmonized vocables ("oooh pump it up now") during the verses and a multi-part delivery on the chorus. The result is a fast-paced classic that, almost in the real time of a drag race, tells its story in under two minutes. "Shut Down" became an early hit for the Beach Boys and, along with "409" and "Little Deuce Coupe," established the group as just as skilled at hot rod and drag-racing songs as they were at surf rock. "Shut Down" later became a staple cover for hot rod rockers like the Rip Chords and the Road Runners.

Though there are many, one other Beach Boys car song is particularly worthy of comment. "Custom Machine" (1963) provides a litany of customized parts and alterations made to a Corvette. Among the most prized customization, however, is to the stereo system, which is replete with "vibrasonic sound." Vibrasonic sound systems were after-market accessories that created a slight delay between the front and rear speakers—creating a modest reverb effect, it was an attempt to enhance the in-car stereo listening experience. In a form of self-reflexive construction, the song cleverly alludes to the fact that many would have heard this Beach Boys song through precisely such a system. In addition, the Beach Boys supplied a vocally harmonized imitation of the sound of the engine: "When I step on the gas she goes wa aa aa."[25] This is notable in that it is a rare example of the human voice evoking the sound of a car engine rather than being imitated by instruments. Once again, the car is anthropomorphized as "she," a fact that is reinforced by the high vocal falsetto representing the engine's highly tuned state.[26]

In one of the stranger instances of popular music and automotive convergence, the Beach Boys also briefly had a more direct relationship with cars in marketing their records. In 1966, Capitol Records commissioned the "King of Kustom Kars," George Barris—designer of the Batmobile, among other famous movie and television cars—to build a series of customized Austin Mini Mokes, which were to be called Mini Surfers. Five of these cars were built and given to each of the Beach Boys. A further series of 20 cars were then constructed as promotional vehicles to be raffled off to fans at exclusive radio station promotional events. The Mini Surfers featured red-and-white, candy-striped paint (inside and out!), a matching striped and fringed rag-top roof, 8-track sound systems with removable speakers, chrome bumpers, and fake air intakes on the bonnet. Moreover, the hubcaps were designed to look like gold records, and a Weber surfboard was attached to each roof (Barris & Featherstone, 1996, p. 119). A record company commissioning cars to market a group is almost unheard of today. However, as will be discussed in more detail in Chapter 4, the use of popular musicians to market cars became more prominent throughout the 1960s and 1970s, and still continues.

Rock n' roll n' automotive technology

Much like the automotive celebration that took place in sheet music at the turn of the century, the 1950s saw the automobile again take centre stage in the North American popular imagination. No form of artistic popular culture celebrated the automobile more than the newly emergent musical form of rock n' roll. In its appeal to youth and teenage culture, early rock n' roll praised the car as an icon of speed and liberation. The term "roll" of rock n' roll immediately linked the genre to mechanized movement, and the energy and power of the car was matched by a similar energy in the sound, rhythms, and lyrical content of the music. The customization of cars found in hot rod culture spilled over to rock n' roll with lyrics that could be individually interpreted. As proof of the intimate link between rock n' roll and the automobile, one need look no further than the visual culture of that genre and, beginning in the 1950s, the extraordinary number of record jackets that featured photographs of cars.[27]

The rise of car songs and the merging of automotive culture in rock n' roll were, to a large degree, predicated on the fact that both industries marketed affordable, mass-produced commodities. Young people from all walks of life were empowered to move around more freely and listen to more music where and how they pleased. Both industries enabled and appealed to the idea of autonomy for a generation of young people.

Indeed, the introduction of new technology played an important role in the cross-pollination of rock n' roll and automobiles in the 1950s. New pushbutton radios, first introduced in the 1930s but only made popular in the 1950s, enabled listeners to switch between stations while sitting at traffic lights. The car radio was the first truly mobile personal sound system, presaging the Walkman and today's digital players and smartphones by decades. Cars were effectively jukeboxes on wheels. Similarly, the transistor radio was introduced as a portable car radio in the mid-1950s and became an option available in all cars by 1955. Radio and television were already important mediums for bypassing regional controls (especially regarding racial matters). Transistor radios further compromised parental control, and cars with radios represented yet one more degree of seeming teenage anarchy. With their modest weight, reliability, and easier volume control, car sound systems took on a new importance. A number of other factors contributed to this increase in automotive music consumption. The US Federal Communications Commission (FCC) increased the number of AM radio licences after 1947 to roughly twice their previous levels (Heitmann, 2009, p. 156). This allowed for a diversity of station formats over the previous model of national network broadcasters (e.g., CBS, NBC) and their affiliates' domination of radio content. New, independent stations were free to choose whatever format and content they felt would sell in their respective markets. The wartime migration of African Americans to the North also formed a notable part of postwar radio diversification, exposing young white ears to blues and r & b, and intruding on the turf of Tin Pan Alley and New York. Various popular music formats began to appear in the late 1940s, and by the early 1950s the "Top Forty" format had arrived.[28]

Innovations in radio programming were, to a large degree, mirrored by the technological innovation in popular music itself. In 1949, Leo Fender introduced the prototype of his Telecaster, the first commercially available, solid-body electric guitar that allowed guitarists to play as loudly as they liked without the annoyance of feedback. In 1954, he added the double cutaway Stratocaster that, along with Gibson's Les Paul (first produced in 1952), became the most copied and played guitar in modern popular music. The names Telecaster and Stratocaster evoked the technological innovations of the space age, associating the instruments with the speed and utopian futurism that jet and rocket travel promised. Automobile design was similarly influenced, as swept-back tail fins, aerodynamic bullet-like fuselages, and tail-lights mimicking jet and rocket engines became commonplace. Manufacturers also adopted futuristic space-age names to market their vehicles, such as Buick Electra (1959), Ford Galaxie (1959), Hudson Jet (1953), and Pontiac Star Chief (1954). As previously mentioned, the Oldsmobile "Rocket" 88 (1951) was also tied to this trend.

The fascination with futuristic technology and the speed and utopian liberation it represented characterized much of the design and content of both the automotive and rock n' roll industries throughout the 1950s and 1960s. To some extent, both industries represented a fetishization of the energy of youth, specifically the pent-up, postwar sexual vitality of the Baby Boom.

Since the 1970s

The evolution of car songs throughout the decades represents both the evolution of the automotive technology and the wider change of generational values. In the wake of 1950s' and 1960s' hot rod and muscle car culture, the 1970s saw somewhat more sedate and mundane musical odes to the car. Reflecting the fact that many Baby Boomers were no longer teenagers and were losing a lot of the romanticism of youth, many songs of this period relate to the automobile less as an icon of youthful rock n' roll rebellion than as a more utilitarian, if somewhat mythologized, vehicle with which to move through everyday life.

One of the most iconic car songs of all time, and an exception to the more sedate expression of car culture in the 1970s as discussed below, is Janis Joplin's searing rendition of "Mercedes Benz" (1970), a song that underscores something of the generational change in attitude towards the car. The *a cappella* track, which graced Joplin's posthumous album *Pearl* (1971), is a blatant hippie-era rejection of consumerism in which Joplin ironically asks the Lord to buy her a Mercedes Benz (her friends "all drive Porsches"), a colour television, and "a night on the town." Rather than celebrating the speed, power, or features of the car, as would have been more common in 1950s' rock n' roll or 1960s' hot rod songs, Joplin views the possession of a Mercedes as an almost mythical goal, one that can only be met through an absurd request to God. It remains among the most revered songs about a luxury car, yet also one of the most raw, recorded in just one take. That Joplin died three days after recording the song or the ironic anti-consumerist sentiments it expresses has never stopped Mercedes-Benz from using it in a number of the automaker's advertisements.

Beyond songs written about cars, many have involved other aspects of car culture, including the experience of travel on roads and highways, as already discussed in relationship to truck-driving music in the 1950s and 1960s. Indeed, the roads and highways themselves were often frequent subjects in popular music. Such songs have included Robert Johnson's "Crossroads"

(1936), Bobby Troup and Nat King Cole's "Route Sixty Six" (1946), Jan and Dean's "Dead Man's Curve" (1964), and Bob Dylan's album *Highway 61 Revisited* (1965).

The 1970s saw a plethora of road-and-travel songs that were powerful emblems of change and renewal following the social turbulence of the 1960s. Road songs such as Vanity Fair's "Hitchin' a Ride" (1970), John Denver's "Take Me Home, Country Roads" (1972), America's "Ventura Highway" (1972), Don McLean's "American Pie" (1972), Gordon Lightfoot's "Carefree Highway" (1974), Gerry Rafferty's "Baker Street" (1978), AC/DC's "Highway to Hell" (1979), and Willie Nelson's throwback to the early country rambling man, "On the Road Again" (1980), captured the imaginations of FM audiences. Perhaps under the influence of Johnson's "Crossroads" (purportedly located at the confluence of Highways 61 and 49 near Clarksdale, Mississippi, where Johnson supposedly sold his soul to the Devil in exchange for his legendary guitar skills), many of these songs portray the road as a quasi-religious or spiritual metaphor for the path to either heaven or hell. Likewise, African-American dance music, such as Eddie Kendricks' "Keep on Truckin'" (1973) and Rose Royce's iconic disco anthem "Car Wash" (1977), celebrated automotive culture as an almost fantastical part of American life.

While the car has been the subject of countless songs, its sonic influence on those songs has received little consideration. Yet, as I have discussed throughout this chapter, cars have consistently influenced the sound of popular music—whether in the incorporation of repetitive sixteenth-note rhythms accompanying many automotive Tin Pan Alley songs, the rollicking *perpetuum mobile* and horn-honking techniques of early rock n' roll songs such as "Rocket 88," or the incorporation of increasing tempos to mimic gear changes in the Beach Boys' "Shut Down." This trend continued well into the 1970s. In its mechanistic approach, perhaps no other song epitomized the melding of automobiles, music, and place more than Kraftwerk's 22-minute ode to the German highway, "Autobahn" (1974). Kraftwerk co-founder Ralf Hütter commented that after listening to the work, the bulk of which was comprised of onomatopoeic ambient electronic sounds of car engines and highway traffic noises, "you will discover that your car is a musical instrument" (Bracewell, 2002, p. 288). The concept of the car as a musical instrument directly recalls the "mechanical symphonies" of Italian and German Futurists. Rather than celebrating the future through fetishizing technology, however, Kraftwerk embraced a nostalgic, even romanticized evocation of technology. Replete in their retro suits and haircuts, and evincing a cynical critique of stereotypical German efficiency, Kraftwerk invited their audience to explore a romanticized landscape of industrial capitalism, the latter represented by a mythologized sonic terrain of the Autobahn that plays with ideas of monotony, repetition, and a seemingly subhuman robotic lack of emotion. It is a machine-dominated landscape, the efficiency of which is, ironically, disturbed only by the presence of humans.[29]

As intimated in "Autobahn," roads and streets themselves are spaces that have a complex sonic component that is made up of, among other sounds, footsteps, conversations, and the noise of traffic passing. There is often a subtle rhythm to these sonorities delineated by traffic lights, stop signs, speed limits, flow restrictions, and the like that create loose patterns of tension and release. In this manner, the car–music relationship contributes to the overall transitory complexity and rhythms of the soundscape of the street. At the level of the individual, as Michael Bull (2001, 2004a) has recognized, the use of self-selected musical accompaniment, whether on foot through personal listening devices or via a car sound system, allows us to exert a personalized structure to the otherwise uncontrollable rhythms and sounds imposed by existing architectures and configurations of the street and other social spaces. For some, such as Theodor Adorno (1941), listening to music in the midst of other surrounding "noise" serves merely to distract listeners from larger concerns. In such cases, music is used as a distraction/disengagement from the listener's true alienation from others and him/herself. In this sense, listening to music while driving merely "decorates" or masks the sound of industrial capitalism as manifest in the sound of the car, the sound of the road, and other associated and uncontrollable noise. The issues surrounding the consumption of music while driving or riding in a car are complex and, among other concerns, call into question the role of music in facilitating human relationships with the machine. These issues will be explored more thoroughly in Chapter 4.

Although it is perhaps a particularly pronounced theme of much early rock n' roll, the relationship between rock music and car culture is one that spans almost every rock/pop genre and style. Cars have served as lyrical subjects for songs as diverse as the glam rock of Queen's "I'm in Love With my Car" (1975), Bruce Springsteen's working-class anthem to American teenage angst, "Born to Run" (1975), Gary Numan's new wave ode to a future lived entirely in "Cars" (1979), or the Clash's punk-inflected "Brand New Cadillac" (1979; a cover of Vince Taylor's 1958 rockabilly tune) and Rush's "Red Barchetta" (1981). Even the Beatles had recorded the iconic vocal horn honking in "Drive My Car" (1965). This list does not include the plethora of songs about motorcycles and trucks, such as Steppenwolf's iconic "Born to Be Wild" (1968) and C. W. McCall's "Convoy" (1975). Reflecting its working-class imaginary, cars and trucks also form a consistent thematic element in country music including Hank William's "hot rod Ford" in "Hey Good Lookin'" (1951), Jerry Reed's "East Bound and Down" (1977), Alabama's "Roll On (18 Wheeler)" (1984), Toby Keith's "Big Ol' Truck" (1994), Brad Paisley's "All I Wanted Was A Car" (2007), and Tim McGraw's "Truck Yeah" (2013), to name but a few.

In general terms, this brief list reflects something of the high point of the Baby Boom fascination with and fetishization of cars that coincides with the heyday of the American automobile industry of the 1960s and 1970s. Drawing on the influence of early electronic music innovators such as Kraftwerk, the advent of synth-pop and alternative music in the 1980s saw some of the most powerful statements of the dystopian effects of the automobile, and, more generally, of technology on Western culture. The American new wave group The Cars, for example, in their minimalist guitar-synth style, embodied a terse nihilistic alienation. Their most successful single, "Drive," from the album *Heartbeat City* (1984), is marked by a haunting synthesizer sounds-cape and the enigmatic line "Who's gonna drive you home tonight?" that summed up something of the sense of anguish about the future that many young people experienced in the 1980s.

By far the most famous of example of this techno-futuristic angst was Gary Numan's hit single "Cars." Numan was well known for his fascination with futuristic themes. In "Listen to the Sirens" (1978), he demonstrates inspira-tion in the science fiction works of Philip K. Dick and in technological dys-topia more generally. "Cars" features a stripped-down, brooding synth-pop instrumental that lasts for well over a minute before Numan's expressionless, robotic vocals begin to intone a vision of the future where life is led exclu-sively in cars:

> Here in my car
> I feel safest of all
> I can lock all my doors
> It's the only way to live[30]

As Numan describes it, the song was inspired by a road rage incident:

> I was in traffic in London once and had a problem with some people in front. They tried to beat me up and get me out of the car. I locked the doors and eventually drove up on the pavement and got away from them. It's kind of to do with that. It explains how you can feel safe inside a car in the modern world. ... When you're in it, your whole mentality is dif-ferent. ... It's like your own little personal empire with four wheels on it (Anderson, 2001).

Canadian progressive rock band Rush also dabbled in the dystopian future and its connection to cars. "Red Barchetta," from the album *Moving Pictures* (1981), narrates the tale of driving an Italian race car in a futuristic world of overbearing traffic laws. The late Neil Peart, Rush's drummer and main lyri-cist, was an automotive fan (and the author of several books on motorcycle touring), and the song commemorates his favourite car, the Ferrari Barchetta (Bowman, 2015, p. 58). It is inspired by the short story "A Nice Morning Drive" by Richard Foster, published in the November 1973 issue of *Road and Track* magazine. In the 1940s and 1950s, the Barchetta ("little boat" in Ita-lian) referred to an open, two-seater sports car made for racing. The song is marked by ethereal harmonic guitar work and a synthesizer wash that coa-lesces into a hard-driving pulsating rock groove driven by snare drum cracks that mimic the sound of the car's pistons when the protagonist fires up the old engine. The car responds "with a roar" and "tires spitting gravel," and he drives "with the wind in my hair" while listening to the "mechanical music" and feeling the "adrenaline surge."[31] The propulsive rhythmic flow of the song matches the visceral feeling of "wind in my hair" and the "adrenaline surge" of the joyride. The reference to "mechanical music" here is also redolent of the shift in sound that Rush was undergoing in *Moving Pictures* as they began to incorporate more synthesizers, electronic effects, and aspects of a new wave influence into their previously more progressive, rock-guitar dominated works. The video for the song also borrows from popular analogue car-racing video games of the early 1980s, adding another level of near-futuristic engagement.

A somewhat different form of dystopic alienation is found in Tracy Chapman's hit single "Fast Car" (1988). Instead of outlining the trepidation of a technologized, overly rule-driven future, the song describes a hoped-for escape to a better, more economically successful life:

> I know things will get better
> You'll find work and I'll get promoted
> We'll move out of the shelter
> Buy a bigger house and live in the suburbs[32]

"Fast Car" upends the trope of freedom celebrated in most male-dominated car songs. By the end of the song, Chapman, who has now found "a job that pays all our bills," tells her alcoholic boyfriend to take his "fast car and keep on driving." Thus Chapman's ode speaks to women who have suffered abusive and/or dead-end relationships at the hands of men. As Sheila Whiteley (2000) observes, "Fast Car" is a personal documentary, "a song which tells of the need to escape and the hopelessness of knowing that it is simply a dream" (p. 176). Furthermore, "Fast Car" is sung in an intimate style with a simple acoustic guitar accompaniment. Gone are any sonic or musical references to the motoristic sounds of engines and machines that are often associated with male-centred car songs of the 1950s or 1960s and suggesting a female alienation from the car as a romantic ideal. While evincing an antithesis of technology in its production, the song still echoes the desire for liberation that the car afforded early disadvantaged blues and African-American rock n' rollers such as Chuck Berry, albeit in starker and much more sombrely realistic terms. As such, the song evokes the car not in the festive or sexually cathectic terms that might have characterized classic 1950s' rock n' roll, but as an almost mundane utilitarian object. Ostensibly, the unalloyed romance with the car was now, with occasional exceptions, essentially over.

While darker visions of a dystopian future characterized several iconic car songs of the era, the 1980s saw a variety of other popular musical comments on automotive culture. In a throwback to earlier pop music fascination with sex and cars, Prince's "Little Red Corvette" (1983) narrates a one-night stand with a promiscuous woman (the "Little Red Corvette") whom he urges to "slow down" and "find a love that's gonna last." In addition to the title, Prince uses several other automobile metaphors, such as comparing their lovemaking to a ride in a limousine. For sheer rock exuberance in a car-themed song, Van Halen's "Panama" (1984) has few equals. Released on the hit album *1984* from the same year, it features singer David Lee Roth (who owned a car he called Panama) describing his attraction to a woman in automotive terms, thus making the same woman-as-car conflation as earlier bluesmen and rock n' rollers. There "ain't nothing like ... her shiny machine," Roth intones. The scene then shifts to "an on-ramp coming through my bedroom" and a rather explicit description of sex behind the wheel: "Got the feeling, power steering / Pistons popping, ain't no stopping now."[33] Also in 1984, future Van Halen singer Sammy Hagar gained fame with the hard rock classic "I Can't Drive 55," a song that describes the experience of getting a speeding ticket. It quickly became a rallying call for all those disgruntled with the 55-mile-per-hour national maximum speed law in the United States.[34]

In recent years, some have argued that there has been a noticeable decline in the number of car songs. Du Lac (2008), for example, makes the claim that "a curious thing happened in rock: the car-song trend sputtered and lurched and finally went kaput." Indeed, it is possible that a more mature popular music culture chose to leave car songs in the past. English group Prefab Sprout's "Cars and Girls" (1988), for example, critiqued Bruce Springsteen's seemly limited and outdated lyrical themes—"Brucie dreams / Life's a highway / Too many roads bypass my way"—and suggests "Some things hurt more, much more than cars and girls."[35] Of course, a variety of other authors have also claimed that rock itself has essentially sputtered and died, and indeed the question of why we keep questioning its currency is explored in Kevin Dettmar's *Is Rock Dead?* (2006). Du Lac (2008) rests his argument on a belief that cars have become far more utilitarian in their design, and hence are necessarily less interesting and inspiring to songwriters than cars in the postwar period:

> Back before cars became utilitarian things—Point A-to-Point B conveyances with computerized everything's powered by $4-a-gallon gas— they were objects of lust, symbols of liberation and power, the center of the youth movement's sexual universe in post-World War II America. (What happens in the back seat stays in the back seat!)

In response to du Lac, Chris Lezotte (2013) posits that car songs have, in fact, remained popular themes in popular music, and that it is not the cars but rather the voices that have changed as female singer-songwriters have taken up the form:

> Contrary to du Lac's assertion, the passing of the classic car song is not due to changes in the automobile that inspired it, but rather, in the voices

and experiences of those who sing about it. The female singer-songwriter who came late to both automobility and rock 'n' roll has infused the automobile and popular music with multiple new meanings. Women from a variety of musical genres—rock 'n' roll, R&B, country, and pop—have called upon the automobile as a vehicle of freedom, escape, recollection, and rebellion, performed through the voice of women's experience. In the process, they have reconfigured the car song from a recounting of the white teenage male's rite of passage into a metaphor for the multiplicity of women's lives (p. 162).

Tracy Chapman's "Fast Car," as discussed above, is one such case. As Lezotte argues, the popularity of car songs in classic rock n' roll results to a large degree from the intersection of two male-dominated realms, automotive culture and rock n' roll. It is not surprising that car songs, even today, are largely considered through a lens of heterosexual masculinity.

While dystopian and sexual metaphors of car songs predominated in the 1980s (though likely part of a larger dystopic alienation in music culture at large), the 1990s and 2000s saw much more variegated references to automotive culture. Notably, songs about automobiles or car culture in general came to be dominated by two genres, alternative music and hip hop. Relatively recent alternative artists who have employed the automobile as a common motif include, for example, Wilco's "Passenger Side" (1995), Elastica's "Car Song" (1995), Metallica's "Fuel" (1997), The Bottle Rockets' "1000 Dollar Car" (2004), Snow Patrol's "Chasing Cars" (2006), Kings of Leon's "Camaro" (2007), Modest Mouse's "Dashboard" (2007), Arcade Fire's "Keep the Car Running (2007), Justice's "Horsepower (2011), Macklemore and Ryan Lewis' "White Walls" (2012), Lolawolf's "Drive (Los Angeles)" (2013), Deadmau5's "Mercedes" (2014), Mike Snow's "Back of the Car" (2016), and Frank Ocean's "White Ferrari" (2016). This brief list testifies to the ongoing fascination with automobile themes, particularly in the independent, college, and alternative rock scenes.[36] By far, however, the largest number of contemporary automotive references is found in hip hop.

The presence of car culture in hip hop may be understood as a continuation of a phenomenon of 1950s' African-American culture. In 1950s' black America, the car was symbolic of a successful lifestyle, an indicator of social status, and so songs such as Chuck Berry's blues-styled "No Money Down" (1955) revelled in the acquisition of various accessories for his Cadillac: "Mister, I want a yellow convertible, 4-door De Ville, with a Continental spare and wire chrome wheels."[37] The equation of cars with socio-economic success is mirrored in several recent hip hop songs that treat high-end cars as a symbol of status. Consider 50 Cent's "Get in My Car" (2005), in which he proclaims: "So much chrome on my Benz, you see ya face in my rims."[38] The popularity of MTV's *Pimp My Ride* (2004–2007), hosted by rapper Xzibit, underscores the connection between hip hop, cars, and the challenge of restricted socio-economic ascendency afforded to many African Americans.

The hip hop songs mentioning or centred on cars are too numerous to list in detail, but suffice it to say that they have spanned all eras of the genre, although they undoubtedly peaked during the gangsta rap era of the 1990s. Works centred on cars from this era include Sir Mix-A-Lot's "My Hooptie" (1989), LL Cool J's "Illegal Search" (1990), "The Boomin' System" (1990), and "Back Seat (of my Jeep)" (1993), Dr. Dre and Snoop Dogg's "Let Me Ride" (1993), and Outkast's "Two Dope Boyz (in a Cadillac)" (1996). The legacy of car songs remains prominent in hip hop. Automobiles are particularly noteworthy in works by The Game, such as "My Low Rider" (2005), "Let's Ride" (2006), "In My 64" (2011), "Ferrari Lifestyle" (2011), and "Standing on Ferraris" (2015). Indeed, one hip hop website claims that some 269 tracks cut by The Game, an astounding 64 per cent of his entire output, reference cars in some way, shape, or form (MC Big Data, 2015).

Many hip hop lyrics allude to the practice of cruising. Listening to music while driving or sitting in a car allows for an intensified personal audio experience that simultaneously extends into the realm of public display. As such, the car and its accompanying musical experience can often become a form of identity performance. When fitted with the latest in customized sound amplification systems, the car becomes a resonating chamber in and of itself—in essence, the entire automobile turns into a sound reproduction device. For many drivers, projecting music from their cars represents a public marker of identity, one that can even signify a form of aural invasion of territory. Mexican-American lowriders and African Americans involved in hip hop culture often radically customize their stereos and modify their cars with non-factory rims, interiors, and shock absorbers, among other changes. Such customized sound systems continue the tradition of appropriating and co-opting technology that has its basis in the white corporate power structure for the purposes of cultural identification and distinction. Much as in the hip hop practice of transforming a turntable intended as a means of sound reproduction into a means of sound production, so, too, such modifications turn the car from merely a means of transportation into a means of sound projection. The car becomes a sonic, visual, and mobile means of announcing and projecting cultural identity, as well as a means of resisting white corporate control. A more detailed exploration of the nexus between hip hop, automotive culture, and African-American identities will be developed in Chapter 2.

Conclusion

The automotive industry around the globe is currently undergoing a major economic disruption. North American car companies in particular have been forced to borrow billions of dollars in order to keep operating, and well-known brands such as Pontiac, Saturn, and Saab have been discontinued, while others are threatened. Despite these apparent setbacks, the future of automobile culture promises advanced concepts such as driverless cars and automated or intelligent highways, as well as extensions of current integrated communications systems such as General Motors' OnStar and other GPS-based systems. Paradoxically, technology is being used to both facilitate free-dom of mobility and access to information, with iPods, smartphones, and intelligent cars; yet, simultaneously, it is being used to inhibit or at the least closely track freedom of movement in the form of identity chips in credit cards, luggage and body scanners, closed-circuit cameras (CCTV), and GPS-locating technologies. If these technologies are brought to their ultimate frui-tion, human control in automotive experiences in these scenarios may well be limited to programming their destination and preferred playlist.

Although the next stage of the auto industry remains to be determined, given the increasing concerns with fuel consumption and environmental sus-tainability, it will doubtless look quite different from the one at the time of this book's publication. With this redefinition of car culture, the popular music that typically accompanies and reinforces it will necessarily be different. Excepting nostalgic cover tunes, one can surmise that there will likely be less musical valorization of the gas-guzzling hot rod than was common in the 1950s and 1960s. Indeed, given the growing environmental stance against cars in favour of bicycles and various alternative forms of public transportation, it seems that popular music involving cars may yet become an increasingly rare commodity. The ethic of liberating individualism found in earlier songs may well be displaced by a more communal, socially motivated ethic of environ-mental emphasis. Indeed, the utopian aesthetic of speed, power, and libera-tion represented by automobile culture and associated popular songs is progressively being displaced by the speed, power, and virtual mobility affor-ded by digital technology and Internet navigation. It remains to be seen, however, whether future discourse will look at the twentieth century's love affair with automobiles as a lost golden age or a horrible misstep that con-tributed to an environmental catastrophe.

Nonetheless, it is clear that the car will not immediately disappear and that we will thus continue to use it for the foreseeable future as a key venue for consuming music, and that music will continue to serve as a major marketing tool in car advertising. Consider Bono's (2010) New Year's resolution in the *New York Times*, which was led off by a call not for world peace or an end to hunger, but rather an impassioned plea for a "return of the automobile as a sexual object." He asked:

> How is it that the country that made us fall in love with the automobile has failed, with only a few exceptions, to produce a single family sedan with the style, humor, and grace of cars produced in the '40s, '50s and '60s?

Testifying to a similar loss of musical romance, a 2002 Chevrolet ad cam-paign, seeking to evoke past glories, put up billboard signs that read, "They Don't Write Songs About Volvos." Mark LaNeve, who heads GM's North American marketing, has stated that the company's influence on popular culture is "part of the automobile being woven into the fabric of American culture." He also points out: "there aren't too many songs about your first Toyota. That's a big advantage for us" (Kushma, 2008). In a manner similar to the use of Tin Pan Alley songs to advertise cars, automotive companies today thus seem to be acutely aware of the power and value of musical nostalgia, even as nostalgia necessarily accepts the death of a past ideal, as a trigger for revitalizing their image and sales.

Much as we will continue to rely on internal combustion engine cars for the immediate future, our fascination with creating musical soundtracks to enhance our driving experiences will likewise continue. As this chapter has sought to illuminate, the nexus of popular music and cars has often directly influenced both the sound and content of both industries, and this evolving interrelationship is a central feature of identity formation. As will be explored in more detail in subsequent chapters, the intersection of popular music and automobiles often proclaims aspects of race, gender, sexuality, and location too often ignored in the construction of identity. The prevalence of music in the driving experience ultimately mediates notions of intimate private space and public space as drivers navigate through various landscapes and make public spaces private and private spaces public.

Notes

1 Advertising in general was undoubtedly central to the success of automobile sales. During the 1920s, the automobile industry was one of the heaviest users of magazine and newspaper space, along with other types of media such as sheet music. Expenditures for automobile advertising in magazines alone climbed from $3.5 million in 1921 to $6.2 million in 1923, and then to $9.269 million in 1927 (Flink, 1990, p. 191).

2 The use of the over-the-top Yiddish accent could also cast doubt on who was being satirized here. That is, by drawing attention to a Jewish stereotype, it could provide anti-Semitic fuel of supposed Jewish foreignness, especially in the highly xenophobic 1920s.

3 Before recently being phased out, Volkswagen's top-end luxury vehicle, the Phaeton, took its name from the Phaeton carriage, a light, sporty, open carriage drawn by two horses that was popular in the late eighteenth and early nineteenth centuries. The name Phaeton derives from Phaëton, the son of Helios in Greek mythology, who nearly set the world on fire when he lost control of the sun chariot. The term was subsequently adapted to describe early, open-top touring cars before being used by Volkswagen's model from 2002 to 2016 (Ramey, 2015).

4 Nicknamed "The Denver Nightingale," and one of the most popular performers of the vaudeville era, tenor Billy Murray recorded both "He'd Have to Get Under" and "I Think I Oughtn't Auto Anymore." The latter is a narrated account of a car that is frequently in need of repair, and of the reckless driver who crashes it. Murray recorded a number of other songs about cars throughout his career, including "In My Merry Oldsmobile" (1905) and "The Little Ford Rambled Right Along" (1915).

5 Later in the century, the intimacy of the car was further reinforced through the medium of the drive-in theatre, which became known by both enthusiasts and detractors as "passion pits."

6 "My Automobile Girl from New Orleans" is also notable for its overtly racist content, including the line, "I drive down in the old French part of a town / Where

the girls ain't coons although they are brown." However, such lyrics also suggest the allure of this type of transgression that the car facilitated.

7 For example, women marching in the 1929 Easter Day parade in New York were given cigarettes by the American Tobacco Company. The cigarettes were labelled "torches of freedom" in an effort to connect women's independence to this product, thereby commodifying women's social progress and desire for sexual equality (Jones, 2000, p. 254).

8 Battery-powered cars were not uncommon at the turn of the century. While somewhat slower than their steam- or gasoline-driven counterparts and hampered by longer cold-weather start-ups, they accounted for 38 per cent of car sales in America at the turn of the century (The history of the electric car, 2014).

9 The term "ladies aid" of course may have been employed as much to denote the emasculation of men as much as the empowerment of women.

10 Indeed, evidence suggests that women were actually better drivers than men at the time. As early as 1925, the American Automobile Association announced that tests had conclusively proved that women drivers were not only as competent as men, but more stable and predictable in their responses to driving situations (Flink, 1990, p. 163).

11 Known as "the fastest girl on Earth," Dorothy Levitt was an English sporting "motoriste." She set the women's land speed record at nearly 91 miles per hour in 1905. A pioneer of women's independence, her book advocated holding up a small hand mirror "from time to time in order to see behind while driving in traffic"—thereby inventing the first rearview mirror before it was introduced by manufacturers in 1914—and that for women drivers travelling alone, "it might be advisable to carry a small revolver" (Levitt, 1909, pp. 28, 30).

12 It is possible that songwriters were also playing to the role of middle-class women in this period as guardians of the domestic sphere. Sheet music and domestic performance were likely going to be under the direction of women, so appealing to her would make commercial sense. If so, it is a curious example of women using their confined status to access cultural texts that challenge it.

13 The automakers in the first half of the century not only marketed their cars as sex objects, they also consciously or subconsciously began to incorporate sex into their designs in increasingly overt ways. Cars became longer, lower, and more inspired by the male phallus, while the headlamps, bumper guards, and radiator grilles were simultaneously "perceived as female sexual symbols" (Lewis, 1983, p. 127). On the other hand, Henry Ford purportedly sought to inhibit lovemaking in his Model T by reducing the size of the back seat. Likely the most well-known advocacy of the car as sexually cathected object came from Dr. Joyce Brothers' famous psychoanalytic reading of the car and masculinity. In the 1970s, Brothers maintained that, for many men, their car "was an extension of themselves and a powerful symbol of masculinity and virility. The more immature the male, the more his sexuality is apt to be linked to ... cars." She also posited, "In their minds [males] ... may equate driving with sexual function which leads to the assumption that the bigger the car the better" (ibid.).

14 This song was written for the Jackson Automobile Company, which produced cars in Jackson, Michigan, from 1903 to 1923.

15 Interestingly, the song employs the term "rockin' an' a-rollin'" to refer to the unsteady motion of travelling in an unsteady and overloaded car. Perhaps Guthrie's most famous automotive song, however, is the children's song "Riding in My Car" (1954) in which he imitates various engine sounds with his voice.

16 Roger Miller's crossover hit "King of the Road" (1964) is sometimes mistaken for a trucking song, but is, in fact, about a life jumping trains: "Third boxcar, midnight train, destination, Bangor, Maine."

17 The "DB" in the title is an abbreviation of Dodge Brothers.

18 For a more complete list of car-inspired blues songs, see Widmer (1990 p. 90, n10).
19 Words and music by Jackie Brenston. Copyright Warner Chappell Music Inc.
20 The arrival of Elvis Presley and his infatuation with Cadillacs, the symbolic epi-tome of socio-economic success in the 1950s, only reinforced the love affair. Elvis' purchases of Cadillacs for gifts were legendary. One incident in 1974 had him buying 14 such cars and distributing them in the course of one evening.
21 Lyrics by George Wilson.
22 Lyrics and music by Charles Ryan, W. Stevenson, and W. S. Stevenson. Copyright Sony/ATV Music Publishing LLC.
23 In 1966, Jan Berry, driving the same Corvette Stingray featured in the song, suf-fered a near-fatal accident, close to the location described in the song. Berry was in a coma for nearly two months, suffering brain damage and partial paralysis.
24 Lyrics by Gary L. Usher and Roger Christian. Copyright Sony/ATV Music Pub-lishing LLC.
25 Lyrics by Michael Love and Brian Wilson. Copyright Sony/ATV Music Publishing LLC.
26 The female personification in "Custom Machine" is put into further relief by the fact that it is performed by the five Beach "Boys" who were marketed as the middle-class, young white male ideal.
27 Grushkin (2006) provides little analysis, but traces the history of the connection between automotive and rock 'n roll cultures through visual culture (e.g., record jackets, advertising).
28 Stemming from the number of records a jukebox could hold and be played in rotation, local radio stations would play countdowns of the 40 most popular records, and later used commercial jingles to aggressively promote their Top Forty format.
29 In a novel extension of the representation of highways sounds in Kraftwerk's "Autobahn," in several locations around the globe, including Japan, Denmark, and the US, engineers have built musical roads that emit audible melodies when they are driven over. The concept works by using grooves cut at specific intervals in the road surface. Just as travelling over small speed bumps or road markings can emit a rumbling tone throughout a vehicle, the "melody road" uses the spaces between to create different notes. The moving car literally plays the melody, with the pitch and tone varying according to the car's speed. For a demonstration and discussion of the practice, see Your car as a musical instrument (2008).
30 Lyrics and music by Gary Anthony James Webb. Copyright Universal Music Publishing Group.
31 Lyrics by Neil Peart. Copyright Core Music Publishing.
32 Lyrics by Tracy Chapman. Copyright Purple Rabbit Music.
33 Lyrics and music by Alex Van Halen, Edward Van Halen, and David Lee Roth. Copyright Warner Chappell Music, Inc.
34 The National Maximum Speed Limit was a provision of the US federal 1974 Emergency Highway Energy Conservation Act that prohibited speeds higher than 55 miles per hour (90 km/h). It was enacted in response to disruptions in the supply of oil, along with its related escalating price, during the 1973 oil crisis.
35 Lyrics and music by Paddy McAloon. Copyright Sony/ATV Music Publishing LLC.
36 Although the focus of this chapter is popular music written about cars, the auto-mobile has even occasionally found its way into classical music. Erik Satie's absurdist cabaret song "L'omnibus automobile" (1906), for example, describes an empty bus carrying sacks of plaster and driving through crowds of people on Bastille Day. Robert Moran, wrote the avant-garde work "39 Minutes for 39 Autos" (1969), which employs the use of 39 car horns along with the cars them-selves. Similarly, John Adams' minimalist orchestral work "A Short Ride in a Fast

Machine" (1986), with its direct onomatopoeic reproduction of a car changing gears and increasing in speed, pays homage to the automobile. Other notable classical works include Virgil Thompson's one-act ballet *Filling Station* (1937), John Williams' "Scherzo for Motorcycle" (1989), and Yuval Sharon and Invisible Cities' novel production of *Hopscotch* (2015), a mobile opera that takes place in 24 different cars.

37 Lyrics and music by Chuck Berry. Copyright Ole Media Management.
38 Lyrics and music by Curtis James Jackson and Tony L. Cottrell. Copyright Kobalt Music Publishing Ltd.

2 "No particular place to go"

Cars, music, and African-American identity

What is often referred to as the Great Migration was one of the most trans-formative events in twentieth-century American history. Between the 1910s and 1970s, millions of African Americans from the rural South made their way to the cities of the North and West in search of higher-paying jobs and freedom from Jim Crow laws. The experiences in their new communities, however, were a mixed bag. Homesickness and the temptations of urban life, not to mention the racism of white neighbours, often gave them, for lack of a better term, the blues. The music they carried with them and that was influenced by this migration captured the reality of their existence, from their aspirations to the hard realities of urban life, representing a sonic re-humanizing salve for the too often de-humanizing and alienating experiences of factory work and an industrially centred society still marked by racial prejudices.

Whether travelling by rail, bus, or car, mechanized transportation was a particularly central experience in the Great Migration. The automobile industry was one of the main sources of employment for the migrants, particularly in areas around Detroit. The presence of black labour in the history of the automotive industry has been given a fair amount of attention. Despite Henry Ford's personal beliefs that black people were racially inferior and should be segregated, his factories provided work opportunities and came to be regarded as institutions of racial uplift. By 1926, Ford employed approximately 10,000 African Americans, representing 10 per cent of his workforce (Heitmann, 2009, p. 40). However, they were frequently given the most physically demanding jobs, "the most dangerous, dirty, and disagreeable jobs—chiefly in paint spraying and foundry work" (Flink, 1990, p. 127). The twentieth-century transformation of black America—the rise and fall of Jim Crow, the Great Migration, the dramatic growth in the black industrial labour force, and the rise of a black-oriented consumer culture—coincided with and was shaped by the rise of the automobile.

This chapter begins by outlining the nexus of music and transportation technologies in delineating the African-American experience, including railroad songs and notions of Afrofuturistic travel as exemplified in the music of Cybotron. I then move to a discussion of the car's role within the African-

American community as a status symbol, as variously expressed in the "motovatin'" songs of Chuck Berry, the notable valorization of the Cadillac in song and within the music industry in general, and the musical analogues of car modification culture in hip hop. I also pay specific attention to Motown Studios, likely the most iconic reflection of the intersection of black identity, music, and the automotive industry. In particular, I focus on the often conflicted nature of the relationship in which the influence of auto-motive manufacturing techniques and promotional associations with many car companies greatly contributed to the success and visibility of black artists even as the industry often exploited its black workforce. Finally, drawing on cultural theorist Paul Virilio's (1986) notions of "dromology," this chapter looks at the desire for speed and acceleration in defining transformations in the social status of African Americans and analogous musical manifestations, perhaps most acutely realized in Chuck Berry's "Promised Land" (1964).

African-American music and transportation technologies

Following America's manufacturing boom in the wake of World War II, the availability of affordable, fast, and technologically advanced automobiles allowed more African Americans, many of whom had migrated north to work in the automotive plants of Detroit, to buy cars. As Paul Gilroy (2001) notes, "Automobility … helps to show up the deepening lines of class division inside racialized communities" (p. 85). Engaging in a poetics of diasporic transit stretching from the underground railroad to freedom rides, driving for Afri-can Americans became "liberation from their apartheid" and car ownership a symbolic representation of their socio-economic progress and status, one often still celebrated in African-American popular music today (ibid., p. 94).

As discussed in Chapter 1, following on the heels of its prevalence in Tin Pan Alley songs, the automobile became the subject of many blues recordings. In the 1930s and 1940s, however, African-American car owners were relatively rare, most having experienced the car only vicariously or via hitchhiking. Consequently, rather than romanticizing the automobile, many blues tunes, such as Robert Johnson's "Crossroads" (1936), reflect fear, unfamiliarity, and feeling, figuratively if not literally, lost.

The incorporation of machine technology into African-American popular music has arguably predated such songs and is found in other genres. As outlined by Joel Dinerstein (2003), the exposure of many African Americans to urbanization and industrialization in northern cities has meant that the mechanistically repetitive sounds associated with manufacturing and assembly lines became another type of rhythm to integrate into their sonic world per-spective. The speed, drive, power, and repetition of the machine are all hall-marks of West African dance and drumming, and all have subsequently become trademarks of American vernacular music. This is particularly evi-dent in the fascination with railroad songs, such as Duke Ellington's "Take the 'A' Train" (1941) or "East St. Louis Toodle-Oo" (1927), or Count Basie's

"Super Chief" (1939). Many of these songs rely on a feature that Albert Murray describes as "locomotive onomatopoeia," consisting of a gradual rhythmic acceleration and sonic layering that mimics the sound of a steam train leaving the station and building momentum (Dinerstein, 2003, p. 72). From Curtis Mayfield's "People Get Ready (There's a Train a Comin')" (1965) to Gladys Knight and the Pips' "Midnight Train to Georgia" (1973), for many African Americans the railroad represented the promise of industrial liberation and the literal and figurative move to a better life. The railroad, however, was a somewhat conflicted icon of black liberation. While it was a means of escape and potential liberation from the oppression of Jim Crow laws, expressed most prominently in the enduring history of the "underground railroad," the railroad's very existence in the South was largely the result of direct and indirect slave labour.

As with the railroad, the relationship of many African Americans to Western European-developed technology, transportation technology in particular, is often conflicted. As a result of the slave trade and segregation, the African-American relationship with technology was largely synonymous with being controlled by it. Slave ships, the cotton gin, voting machines, and segregated buses were all machinery purposefully designed and manufactured to silence and oppress African Americans. More recently, preoccupation with technology by African Americans has represented an active form of resistance and control. Perhaps the most powerful manifestation of this has occurred in hip hop's appropriation and fetishization of sound technologies such as turntables, digital samplers, and auto-tune machines. These technologies have been intentionally repurposed from their original (largely white-conceived) function—a sound reproduction device turned into a sound production device in the case of the turntable, a device originally intended to interpret seismic data in the case of auto-tune. In gangsta or hardcore rap styles, even the microphone becomes an active technology of resistance. As Robin Kelley (2004) argues, in hardcore rap "the mic becomes a Tech-9 or AK-47, [and] imagined drive-bys occur from the stage" (p. 189). In such real or imagined cases, African Americans co-opt and control technology associated with both weapons and automobiles.

African-American popular music has long been characterized by a fascination with and incorporation of technology, particularly in relation to facilitating literal and figurative empowerment and social mobility. Cultural critic Mark Dery (1993) has coined the termed "Afrofuturism" to refer to African-American signification that appropriates images and uses of advanced technology and alien and/or prosthetic-enhanced (cyborg) futures. Afrofuturism is found in a variety of artistic genres, including the science fiction writings of authors such as Steve Barnes, Octavia Butler, Samuel R. Delany, and Charles Saunders, and in films such as John Sayles' *The Brother from Another Planet* (1984). Afrofuturistic art and music is typically concerned with black nationalism and empowerment, and the creation of mythologies based on connections between historical prophetic imagination, such as Egyptian theories of the afterlife, and modern, alienated black existence (McLeod, 2003). Afrofuturist artists include the experimental cosmological jazz of Sun Ra and his Intergalactic Jet-Set Arkestra, pioneers of the use of synthesizers and African percussion, and George Clinton's alter ego of an alien named Star Child who was sent down from the mothership to bring funk to earthlings. Similarly Herbie Hancock's jazz-cyber funk album *Future Shock* (1983) or Bernie Worrell's *Blacktronic Science* (1993) sonically project futuristic images of black exploration and experimentation. As Mark Dery (1993) observes, "African Americans are, in a very real sense, the descendants of alien abductees" (p. 736). In this manner, black diasporic consciousness attempts to return to an inaccessible homeland, an imaginary utopian homeland in which the previously marginalized aliens have reclaimed control. In terms of popular music, this dynamic has often been metaphorically expressed through black artists co-opting previously white-dominated technologies of sound production and recording, as discussed above, in service of creating powerful sonic images of the potential for black wealth and power. Similarly, the incorporation of mechanized transportation, whether by rail or motor vehicle, into African-American social life, including musical expression, reinforced this narrative of liberating motion and migration.

Proponents of Afrofuturism often rely, in an expression of strategic irony, on older technology and sounds (such as turntable scratching in hip hop) that represent a conscious misuse and/or a contestation of typically mainstream/white-controlled technology. As Tricia Rose (1994) states,

> Many of [hip hop's] musical practitioners were trained to repair and maintain new technologies for the privileged, but have instead used these technologies as primary tools for alternative cultural expression. This technology has not been straightforwardly adopted; it has been significantly revised in ways that are in keeping with longstanding black cultural practices (p. 63).

In this sense, there exists a continuum of black "misuses" and reclamations of technology: from the broken bottleneck applied to the blues guitar or the oil drum bashed and buffed to create Trinidad steel sound, to the Roland 808 drum machine (picked up second-hand by black producers in Chicago who turned its "unmusical" sounds into the basis of house music) and the more recent ubiquity of Auto-Tune, a device originally designed to interpret seismic data before its initial commercial vocal application in Cher's "Believe" (1998). The exploration of original sounds that arise from this intentional misuse of technology is intimately connected to what Kodwo Eshun (1998) calls "Afro-Diasporic futurism," a digital diaspora of "computerhythms, machine mythology and conceptechnics which routes and reroutes and criss-crosses the Black Atlantic" (p. –006).

The relationship between African Americans and musical expressions of utopian travel can be understood as reaching as far back as nineteenth-century Negro spirituals. The very titles of many spirituals express a desire to reject the Earth and its hardship and suffering. "Swing Low, Sweet Chariot," "All God's Chillun Got Wings," and "This World Is Not My Home" all have the unifying theme of rejecting the material world and travelling to a better place. Equating these spiritual journeys with terrestrial travel is not difficult. Indeed, many African-American artists bring the idea of spiritual travel to the street. In an irreverent spoof of "Swing Low, Sweet Chariot," jazz musician Dizzy Gillespie sang "Swing Low, Sweet Cadillac" (1967)—a telling comment on the place of the car in black popular culture. In a similar trope of the same spiritual, George Clinton and Parliament Funkadelic's classic "Mothership Connection" (1975) equates space travel and the car through lyrics such as "swing low sweet chariot / stop and let me ride."[1]

Afrofuturistic travel connected to the car is also a particularly cogent aspect of more recent rave and techno music. One of the seminal moments in the development of techno was the formation of Cybotron in 1981. Comprised of black turntable wizards Juan Atkins and Rick Davis (aka 3070), this group launched the Detroit techno scene on their Deep Space label. Influenced by a local DJ called Electrifyin' Mojo, who specialized in playing European synth-pop acts like Gary Numan, Ultravox, Human League, and Kraftwerk, their music was a minimalist wash of analogue Roland, Arp, and Korg MS 20 synthesizers that, according to Davis, "extrapolated the necessity of interfacing the spirituality of human beings into the cybernetic matrix: between the brain, the soul and the mechanisms of cyberspace" (Savage, 1993). One of Cybotron's most influential songs, "Cosmic Cars" (1982), is a stark, vocoded vocal and bass-heavy analogue synth piece that draws from Numan's equally dystopian song "Cars" (1979), and, like the spirituals that preceded it, dreams of an automotive virtual or physical escape from the realities of earth. The protagonist describes being alone and far from home in his "cosmic car" with the music "playing loud" and wishing he could "escape this crazy place" before accelerating and only seeing "stars" around him.[2] The music is relatively up-tempo, with a strong bass synth groove and a Roland DR-55 drum machine backbeat that mechanistically repeats throughout the entire track, emulating the repetitive percussion of an internal combustion car engine. Rhythmic synthesized horn honks also punctuate phrases and bring the more mundane sound of contemporary cars into the mix. While essentially designed as dance music, the darkly mechanistic style of Cybotron also spoke to Detroit's economic collapse in the late 1970s, following the city's heyday as the centre of the American automobile industry. (The stripped-down aesthetic was also, of course, a function of the limited analogue technology available to such early innovators.) "Cosmic Cars" references a form of futuristic street cruising with the "music playing loud." It emphasizes speed, "accelerating fast," and a desire for change through technological means.

Detroit techno as illustrated by Cybotron aimed to erase the sonic memory of the Fordist sounds associated with Motown (discussed below) and to mimic the robotic production lines that had replaced the variable capital of black physical labour with the constant capital of machines. In advance of actual machine-based automation, the African-American workforce at manufacturing plants were treated as living robots, performing mind-numbing and physically repetitive work and subjected to the systematic speeding up of the line to meet production quotas. Management credited higher production with the shift to automation; protesting black workers referred to it more tellingly and pejoratively as "niggermation" (Georgakas & Surkin, 1998, p. 85).

Audiomobility and identity

Listening to music while in a car allows for an intensified personal audio experience while simultaneously extending the listening experience into the realm of public display. As such, the car and accompanying music experience can often become a form of identity performance. Moreover, when fitted with the latest in customized sound amplification systems, the car becomes a resonating chamber in and of itself—that is, the entire car becomes a sound reproduction device. For many drivers, projecting music from their cars represents a public marker of identity, and even a form of aural projection of territory and place. Mexican-American lowriders (discussed in more detail in Chapter 6) and African Americans involved in hip hop culture often radically customize their stereos and modify their cars with non-factory rims, interiors, and shock absorbers, among other changes. Such customized sound systems continue the tradition of appropriating and co-opting technology that has its basis in the white corporate power structure for the purpose of cultural identification. Much as in the hip hop practice of transforming a turntable into a means of sound production, such modifications turn the car from a means of transportation into a means of sound projection. Like the use of ghetto blasters or boom boxes by African-American and Hispanic youth in the 1980s, the car becomes a sonic, visual, and mobile means of announcing and projecting cultural identity. It also becomes a means of claiming sonic territory.

Such cultural appropriations of car technology can be regarded as an expansion of what Joel Dinerstein (2003) calls "survival technology." Dinerstein uses the term to explain how "the presence (or 'voice') of machinery became integral to the cultural production of African American storytellers, dancers, blues singers, and jazz musicians" (p. 126). According to Dinerstein, the machine aesthetic was particularly powerful in the 1930s when African-American artists integrated the monumentality, drive, precision, and rhythmic flow of factory work and modern cities into Big Band swing. By incorporating such an aesthetic, African-American musicians and dancers successfully transferred the de-humanizing experience of the machine into something pleasurable, sonically re-humanizing the landscape in which they lived. Lowriders and hip hop enthusiasts extend this practice, inverting a process to incorporate their dance and music practices directly into their machines. By modifying white-marketed, mass-produced technology, the car and its sound system become re-colonized extensions of both Hispanic and black cultural identities, and part of an overall culture of resistance to hegemonic white conformity. These modifications, however, are also often linked to issues of safety, criminality, and gangsterism. Such practices reinforce the duality of the automobile as a site for free mobility and expression while simultaneously rendering minority participants as visibly marginalized members of a white-dominated society.

Following the economic recovery of World War II, the availability of affordable, fast, and technologically advanced cars allowed increasing numbers of African Americans to buy automobiles. *Ebony* magazine estimated that 20 per cent of black households intended to buy new cars in the 1958 model year alone. Throughout the postwar years, car companies began to target black consumers, placing advertisements in black newspapers and especially in new magazines like *Ebony* and *Jet* that catered to the small but growing black middle class. Gilroy (2001) observes that "African Americans ... spend some 45 billion dollars on cars and related products and services and ... they are 30% of the automotive buying public although they are only 12% of the US population" (p. 90). For many African Americans, the automobile offered a material antidote to the severely restricted mobility they had endured through generations of slavery, indentured servitude, and segregation.

For African Americans, and for Americans more generally, cars were, and often remain, symbols of status. As anthropologist Grant McCracken (2005) observes, "When Americans talked about 'getting ahead,' 'going somewhere,' 'traveling in the fast lane,' and 'heading straight for the top,' these were not cavalier remarks or empty metaphors. They were reflections of an important aspiration and reality in American life" (p. 70). Hence, not only did the automobile provide a new way of signifying social prestige during the early twentieth century; it also helped fundamentally change the way we think and talk about social status. Furthermore, McCracken claims that, because of the blurred division between the automobile and its operator, "drivers [are often] inclined to take credit for properties that belonged to the car. They [become] large, gleaming, and formidable" (p. 77). This explains much of the connection between cars, music, and social status discussed here.

Car ownership in the early twentieth century thus represented a sign of black upward mobility; for many whites, it also literally and figuratively signified the mobile threat of blackness crossing into white space. As outlined by George Lipsitz (2006), "automobile ownership symbolized a degree of status and success inappropriate for blacks" and often engendered death threats and violent reactions from whites (p. 164). Take, for example, Ralph Ellison's 1973 short story "Cadillac Flambé," in which a jazz musician riding in his new Cadillac hears a racist senator on the radio refer to the Cadillac as a "coon cage" (Packer, 2008, p. 190).

Indeed, the role of the Cadillac and its celebration in song, in particular, should not be underestimated in its influence on the formation of African-American identity.[3] According to cultural theorist Dick Hebdige (1988), throughout the 1950s and 1960s the Cadillac represented the aspirations of the "disadvantaged [black] American" (p. 66). In America, the Cadillac was the motorized chrome embodiment of the American Dream. It represented the epitome of aspirational car ownership for both black and white. After all, as Elvis Presley declared, "A Cadillac puts the world on notice that I have arrived" (Widner, 2002, p. 70; also qtd in Laver, 2015, p. 84). In emulation of Presley's sentiments, the Cadillac was particularly desired by and prevalent in the African-American community. This was despite the fact that, according to company policy, Cadillac dealers were forbidden to sell to African Americans until well into the 1940s; before then, African Americans were typically limited to buying used Cadillacs (Laver, 2015, p. 105).

Notwithstanding, or perhaps even on account of, such racist marginalization from this aspect of American car culture, and from mainstream American society in general, African Americans cultivated a deep desire for the Cadillac. The 2008 musical biopic *Cadillac Records* was titled for the fact that Leonard Chess, owner of Chess Records, bought a new Cadillac each time one of its roster of black stars—such as Muddy Waters, Little Walter, Chuck Berry, or Etta James—achieved a number-one record.[4] R & B legend Ray Charles was another who favoured the Cadillac, as both a symbol of wealth and as a high-powered version of manhood. As expressed in the opening of Charles' 1953 classic "It Should've Been Me," women are unable to resist a man who has the wherewithal to own and drive a Cadillac. The song's protagonist loses out on connecting with an attractive woman "when a Cadillac cruised up and 'swish' she was gone."[5] Charles laments that it should have been him driving the "real fine car." There is more than simple greed and lust at work in these lyrics. In the racial context of 1950s America, there were also the matter of aspiration and pride, of overcoming the white majority's limited view of black value. The phenomenon is still seemingly relatively commonplace as many black youth attempt to establish their status through purchasing the most expensive sneakers and aspiring to the hyper-consumerism and conspicuous consumption associated with successful black musicians, entertainers, and sports personalities.

In 1949, *Ebony* attempted to explain to its readers "Why Negroes Drive Cadillacs," arguing that a Cadillac was a tool to further black equality—at least in terms of image. The article proclaims:

> The fact is that basically a Cadillac is an instrument of aggression, a solid and substantial symbol for many a Negro that he is as good as any white man. To be able to buy the most expensive car made in America is as graphic a demonstration of that equality as can be found (Johnson, 1949, p. 34).

In essays such as this, *Ebony* promoted the notion that consumption and economic power were synonymous and key to social mobility. Critics, however, decried the article for reproducing an un-nuanced, white, middle-class inspirational vision for African Americans that both obscured socio-cultural realities for many blacks and simply treated them as dark-skinned whites (Chambers, 2016, p. 66). It is also important to note that *Ebony*, even with its base of African-American readership and staff, was completely ignored by car advertisers until 1953, eight years after its first issue, and it was not until 1966 that the magazine first featured a car ad using African-American models (Laver, 2015, p. 105).

Chuck Berry, whose songs typically described the idiosyncrasies of teenage life, was particularly fascinated with cars and the related acquisition of social status. Berry briefly worked in two automobile manufacturing plants, and automobiles played a central role in both his life and art, as dramatically demonstrated by his arrest for driving a car as part of an interracial couple in 1959. Berry's fascination with cars and what he called his "motorvatin'" songs began with his first hit single, "Maybellene" (1955). One of the seminal works of rock n' roll, the song was an adaptation of "Ida Red," a hillbilly song by Bob Wills & the Texas Playboys from the early 1950s. Lyrically, the song tells the story of a woman who keeps cheating on her man. Berry sings about "motorvatin' over the hill" and chasing Maybellene in his V8 Ford while she drag races him in a Cadillac Coupe de Ville. Musically, much like "Rocket 88," the song is built on a loose but mechanically insistent driving rhythm with an up-tempo accented backbeat that resembles the sound of an engine. The repetitive and relatively dynamically static four-to-the-floor vocal delivery and repetitive verse–chorus structure of the song also add both to the inherent tension and thrilling speed of the rolling chase. Berry's dissonant guitar solo, momentarily breaking the narrative, provides an almost onomatopoeic sound of horn honking, and possibly the engine backfiring and overheating. The song conflates Maybellene with the car she is driving, an object of envy and desire for Berry. He similarly has to have his Ford V8 engine cooled down by a passing rainstorm (the sexual metaphors here are clear and not particularly subtle).[6] Sean Cubitt (2000) claims that the "greatest novelty" of this song:

> is in the eroticization of the motor car, a process that was already well under way in the marketing of consumer durables at the end of the period of post-war austerity, but compounded with a representation of black sexuality to introduce an element of threat … "Maybellene" concentrates on a representation of power in sexuality that reproduces the subject in a patriarchal ideology of masculinity (p. 155).

At the end of the song, Berry has seemingly "caught Maybellene at the top of the hill," but the early use of a fade-out seems to imply that the "chase"—for love/sex, material goods, and social status—will continue indefinitely.[7] Berry's "No Particular Place to Go" (1964) makes another familiar car/woman conflation, and underlines the 1950s' youth philosophy that destinations have become superfluous in the face of the pleasures, often sexual, of automobile life.

In the 1950s, the car was also symbolic of a successful lifestyle, an indicator of social status, and songs such as Berry's blues-styled "No Money Down" (1955) celebrates the acquisition of various accessories for his Cadillac. While he is "motorvatin' back in town," he bargains with a Cadillac dealer for an extensive list of what he wants in a new car in return for trading in his "broken-down, raggedy Ford."[8] The list includes a yellow convertible (four-door de Ville) with power steering and brakes, air conditioning, "automatic heat," short wave radio, a TV, a phone, and a "full Murphy bed in my back seat." Before acquiring the car, he also adds four carburettors, two straight exhausts, railroad air horns, a military spark, a five-year guarantee, and an insurance policy. The song illustrates an early example of the resistive black modification of white techno-culture. The litany of demands, ultimately obtained for no money down, is also symbolic of the liberation of consumer buying power that was embodied in the purchase of a new car. In these scenarios, the black consumer, if only as imagined through Berry's song, has the power to make such demands. The promise of buying a car, then, held the liberating qualities that extended beyond those associated with transportation and movement, and reached into the ability to exercise economic purchasing power typically only associated with white consumers.

The equation of car with African-American socio-economic success is also mirrored in blaxploitation films of the 1970s. The heroes of films such as *Sweet Sweetback's Baadasssss Song* (1971), *Shaft* (1971), and *Superfly* (1972) all drove modified, lowriding hot rods conspicuously adorned with chrome and gold trim. Particularly as manifest in Isaac Hayes' iconic "Theme from Shaft" (1971), with lavish studio production, classical orchestral arrangements, and extended melodic phrasing building to dynamic climactic crescendos, the soundtracks to these films projected both notions of black masculine hypersexuality—"Who's the black private dick / That's a sex machine to all the chicks? (Shaft) Ya damn right!"[9]—and the sound of black wealth and economic power. In the 1980s and 1990s, high-end cars also figured prominently in rap. Public Enemy, one of the most popular rap groups of the late 1980s and early 1990s, dedicated a song to the virtues of the Ninety-Eight, the largest, most powerful, and most luxurious of the Oldsmobile sedans. The lyrics to "You're Gonna Get Yours (My Oldsmobile 98)" (1987) delight in the Oldsmobile's speed and power—"It's the reason I'm ahead of the pack"—and the fact that its tinted windows looked like the superhero's car that "the Green Hornet had."[10] Similarly, Kool G. Rap and DJ Polo include "dope" car attributes such as Pirelli tyres, leather seats, and gold rims in their song "Cars" from the album *The Road to the Riches* (1989).

As touched upon in Chapter 1, contemporary rap continues to celebrate high-end cars as status symbols. Consider Drake's "Poundcake/Paris Morton Music 2" (2013), which boasts "I had Benzes 'fore you had braces / The all black Maybach but I'm not a racist."[11] The song "MotorSport" (2017) by hip hop trio Migos (Quavo, Takeoff, and Offset), featuring Nicki Minaj and Cardi B, while infamously the initial manifestation of a personal feud that erupted between the two singers, ties into several themes in this book. The lyrics and accompanying video are heavily invested in sexualized automotive culture. The video, for example, sees both Minaj and Cardi B suggestively posing in front of luxury high-performance sports cars (a red Ferrari Testarossa, and a white Lamborghini Countach respectively), essentially embodying the cars and portraying sex as a motorsport. The song is also rife with references to upward mobility and economic success. Minaj at one point raps "Pull up in the space coupe, I done linked with Marty [Marty McFly's DeLorean from *Back to the Future* (1985)] / I can actually afford to get a pink Bugatti."[12] The video also features futuristic flying cars (Uber Lyfts) and brings in *Blade Runner*-esque skyscraper imagery with neon Japanese characters and dragons. The song uses stark production with robotic, heavily Auto-Tuned vocals. The effect, in combination with the video featuring high-performance cars that resemble space-ships, or a "space coupe," the metallic alien-like costumes worn by Minaj and Cardi B, and glowing neon lighting, imparts a distinct Afrofuturistic aura to both the song and the video.[13]

The popularity of MTV's *Pimp My Ride* (2004–2007), hosted by rapper Xzibit, cemented the connection between hip hop, cars, and the insubordination of previously restricted socio-economic access for most African Americans. The show was set in Los Angeles and involved participants convincing the host that their typically worn-out car needed to be "pimped" or customized. The car was then taken to a customization shop and given a complete customized makeover, including state-of-the-art sound and entertainment systems, which typically reflected the personality of the car owner. In a somewhat odd update, in 2016 the NFL Network aired a revamped version of the show entitled *Tackle My Ride*, produced by Michael Strahan and hosted by National Football League (NFL) player LaMarr Woodley and car customizer James Torrez. The premise is the same as *Pimp My Ride*, but the car customizations are now turned into "fan cars" in support of participants' favourite NFL teams.

African-American projection of identity through their cars, and related notions of status and conspicuous consumption, is by no means universal. William DeVaughn's classic song "Be Thankful For What You Got" (1974) stands in marked contrast to the aspirational materialism associated with many songs about automobiles (Gilroy, 2010, p. 41). DeVaughn's song, originally titled "A Cadillac Don't Come Easy," sold over two million copies and was number one on the r & b charts. Delivered in DeVaughn's laidback soulful style and accompanied by a relaxed bongo beat and organ, the song reinforces the notion that one could still be "Diggin' the scene / With a gangsta lean" without buying into the consumerist trappings of a luxury car—"you may not have a car at all … but you can still stand tall."[14]

As expressed in Berry's "No Money Down" and *Pimp My Ride*, a central feature of many African Americans' relationship with the car lies in its modification. Jeremy Packer (2008, p. 233) asserts that automotive customizing—such as window tinting, the addition of non-factory stereo systems, pneumatic shock absorbers, custom rims, and interiors—is typically associated with minority car cultures. The conspicuous nature of many of these features has led to racial profiling by police and government agencies, with the inordinate attention to black motorists commonly referred to as the mock-crime "driving while black."

One of the most evocative, if not fetishistic, manifestations of black car modification culture is found in Houston's SLAB scene. Although the cars are often somewhat similar in look to lowriders found in many American cities, Houston's SLAB scene has developed in particularly unique ways that define both local space and identity. According to Pat Jasper, Houston Arts Alliance Director of Folklife and Traditional Arts, "SLABs are a uniquely Houston expression developed in the Sunnyside neighborhood in the '80s and '90s" (Smith, 2013). Coined in the 1980s, SLAB originally referred to the lowriding stance of the cars and their closeness to the concrete or curb "slab." Later, SLAB came to be more popularly understood as an acronym for "Slow, Low, Loud and Bangin'" (Mehta, 2014). Much like the use of old and/or outdated musical technologies in much Afrofuturist music, SLAB cars are typically highly modified versions of outdated, old-school luxury cars such as the ubiquitous Cadillac, but also Buicks, Oldsmobiles, and Lincolns. In addition to lowering the suspension, typical SLAB modifications reflect the individual tastes of the owner and include everything from stylized candy paint jobs to trunk-popping devices, re-upholstered interiors, after-market LED lights, flat-panel TVs, oversized brand logos, and, of course, powerfully enhanced stereo systems. The most original features of SLAB cars, however, and what most overtly sets them apart visually from other lowrider cars, are their massively protruding wire-rimmed hubcaps (called "pokes" or "elbows") that often extend 18 inches or more from the wheels.

Echoing its SLAB car modification culture, Houston is also known for its unique brand of hip hop known as "chopped and screwed." In the early 1990s, Houston's DJ Screw was pioneering the chopped and screwed technique, which rearticulated how the forefathers of hip hop had (mis)used turntables some 15 years earlier in the South Bronx. DJ Screw took the newest popular rap songs, sampled various sections, and, "screwing" the pitch controller on his turntable, drastically slowed down the tempos such that the voices of the original rappers were stretched out to a dreamy, leisurely flow. Although DJs typically adjust the pitch control to match the pace of one record to others to create a seamless transition from one recording to another, DJ Screw used the pitch controller to drastically reduce the tempo of songs to around 70 beats per minute. In so doing, he took a 45 rpm record and played it at 33 rpm, then committed that remix to a cassette tape. The "chopped" aspect of the technique refers to the "cuts, scratches, pauses, and rewinds that accompany the slowed-down mix" (Sarig, 2007, p. 320).

Chopped and screwed is also connected to the ingestion of "Purple Drank," a concoction that, like both SLAB and chopped and screwed, originated in Houston and represents a modification of a pre-existing product, in this case cough syrup (often Robitussin). The drink is a homemade mixture of codeine/promethazine cough syrup, light-coloured soda (such as 7-Up or Mountain Dew), and often Jolly Rancher candies for added sweetness. Purple Drank (also variously known as sizzurp, lean, barre, Texas tea, sip-sip, and purp) produces euphoric effects, and often induces the feeling that everything is being experienced in slow motion—effects similar to the slow beat rate of the music itself. DJ Screw's mixtapes were overtly linked to the drug and frequently employed titles like *Sippin Codeine, Leanin' on a Switch*, and *Show Up and Pour Up*. DJ Screw included "instructions for listening" in the liner notes to his album *3 'N the Morning*: "Get with your click and go to the other level by sippin' syrup, gin, etc., smoke chronic indo, cess, bud, or whatever gets you to that other level" (Hall, 2001, p. 6).

There are many analogies to be made between the modification culture of SLAB cars and the chopped and screwed style. In addition to the modifications made to older cars or recordings, the slow tempo of chopped and screwed, for example, melds with and reflects the slow-cruising, to-be-seen aspect of SLAB car gatherings. Indeed, many music artists have sung about SLAB culture or reference the cars in their songs. Houston rapper Lil' Troy's "Wanna Be a Baller" (1999), for example, features a sample of Prince's "Little Red Corvette" and the recurring lyrics "Twenty-inch blades—on the Impala."[15] Rapper Fat Pat's "Tops Drop" (1997) is another ode to Houston's SLAB culture, featuring lyrics such as "Welcome to the land, where ... Trunks keep popping [and] Tops keep dropping down in Houston."[16] The song both samples and chops and screws Yarbrough and Peoples' earlier jam, "Don't Stop the Music" (1980). In this manner, Houston rappers employ the chopped and screwed style in combination with references to SLAB car modification culture to creatively signify their locational identity.[17] The slow, low, and loud ethos of the style also notably involves a different bodily relationship to the car and driving than the typical suburban quest for a quiet, fast, and unobtrusive commute. SLAB style, like many other forms of car modification culture, creatively inverts and/or resists many of the standardized values associated with upper- or middle-class white car consumers, many of whom would likely question the need for and the practicality of protruding 18-inch spokes or the ability to pop one's trunk for display purposes while driving.[18]

While the car has always been an important symbol of both wealth and mobility in African-American culture, it has been particularly celebrated in hip hop as a means of signification, a way of announcing one's power and prestige through the attention-drawing visibility of a modified luxury car or intimidating SUV. Ironically, cars are also celebrated in rap music for the anonymity they can provide. For many rappers, aside from a visible manifestation of their wealth or prestige, the fetishization of their cars is related to the privacy vehicles afford. Despite the attention-getting bling and booming stereo systems, inside the often dark space of the car, occupants are not easily observable. As Erik Nielson (2010) observes,

It is hardly a coincidence, then, that the often preferred driving position is in a laid back almost reclining position, deemphasizing individual presence, and that vehicles in rap music videos almost always have tinted windows, further augmenting their inherent capacity to frustrate surveillance (p. 1266).

Many rap songs, as Nielson points out, actively refer to the anonymity their cars provide.[19] Consider the following lyric from "Can't C Me," from Tupac Shakur's *All Eyez on Me* (1996): "When I'm rollin' by / Niggas can't see me." In similar fashion, the Wu Tang Clan song "Redbull" (2000) includes Inspectah Deck's claim, "Behind the tinted windows I lie low."[20] In 2006, Chamillionaire rapped about evading surveillance from the police in his car in his Grammy-winning song "Ridin'," an ode to the perils of driving while black. The lyrics allude to the fact that the police are trying to catch him "ridin' dirty" with drugs (possibly with Purple Drank or "lean," as in the lyric "Police think they can see me lean"), but are unable to see into his car because of the tinted windows.[21] Thus, while the police and public are able to observe the luxurious trappings of wealth in "the shine on the deck and the TV screen," his car simultaneously provides privacy from outside surveillance. A combination of modifications, tinted windows, and/or a reclined driving position thus enables a form of black resistance to the control and authority of the state, and allows for various forms of individual authorization.

Motown and black identity

The Motown sound is perhaps the most overt and influential articulation of the bonds between black identity, music, and the automotive industry. Through iconic songs such as Martha and the Vandellas' "Dancing in the Streets" (1967), Smokey Robinson's "Cruisin'" (1979), Marvin Gaye's "What's Going On?" (1971), and the Temptations' "Ball of Confusion (That's What the World is Today)" (1970), the music that emanated from Berry Gordy's Motown Studios represented how the sound of Detroit's streets could articulate and depict the state of black Americans.

Motown Studios was founded by songwriter and businessman Berry Gordy, Jr. in 1958, and was initially located in a small house on West Grand Boulevard in Detroit. The staff of the company soon began referring to their operation as "Hitsville USA," and started attracting and recruiting the best African-American talent in the region. The record label engineered its first hit in 1960 with Barrett Strong's recording of "Money (That's What I Want)," written by Gordy and Janie Bradford. In the following year, Motown released The Miracles' "Shop Around," featuring Smokey Robinson, who co-wrote the song with Gordy. The song became Motown's first record to sell a million copies and launched a string of commercial hits for the label. In the wake of this initial success, Motown lived up to its nickname by producing and releasing music by an amazing array of artists, including The Four Tops,

Gladys Knight and the Pips, Stevie Wonder, Mary Wells, The Marvelettes, Diana Ross and the Supremes, Edwin Starr, The Jackson Five, The Commodores, Lionel Ritchie, Michael Jackson, and Boyz II Men. In a ten-year period from 1960 to 1969, this relatively small company claimed an incredible 79 records in the Billboard Hot 100.

While there is no denying the influence and success of Motown artists and the Motown sound in the history of popular music, the actual influences and impact of the automotive industry on the sound and production practices of the label have, with the possible exception of Suzanne E. Smith's book *Dancing in the Street* (1999), been little studied. Music was an influential factor in the history of Detroit long before the formation of Motown, and was often overtly linked to the automotive industry. African-American workers initially migrated to the city in large numbers in order to capitalize on Henry Ford's promise of a minimum wage of five dollars a day in 1914. As Smith outlines, blues artists were often influential in publicizing Ford's offer to African Americans with songs such as Blind Blake's "Detroit Bound Blues" (1928), which proclaimed "I'm goin' to Detroit, get myself a good job … I'm goin' to get me a job, up there in Mr. Ford's place / Stop these eatless days from starin' me in the face" (p. 12). Among other issues, we see clearly here an early instance of the synchronicity of industry and music in forming and influencing African-American musical identity.

A number of influential blues artists were part of the Great Migration to Detroit and actively incorporated their experience with the automotive industry into their art. John Lee Hooker, for example, was born in Coahoma County, Mississippi, but made his way to Detroit in 1948 to work for the Ford Motor Company, as well as to launch one of the most storied careers in postwar blues music. His recordings of the now-iconic "Boogie Chillen" (1948) detail the excitement that new arrivals to Detroit could find in the city's bars and clubs. In one version of the song, Hooker sings about coming to town for the first time and asking a stranger where he was, with the reply: "This is Detroit, boy, it really jumps here."[22]

Similar sentiments are found in many blues songs of the 1930s and 1940s, particularly performers' fondness for Hastings Street, the centre of black culture and entertainment in Detroit during that era. Songs evoking a love of the street include Blind Blake and Charlie Spand's classic piano and guitar boogie woogie recording of "Hastings Street" (1929), Big Maceo's "Detroit Jump" (1945), and Detroit Count's "Hastings Street Opera" (1948), which is highlighted by a slow-walking blues, spoken-word description of all the bars, businesses, and experiences to be had on the street. Montana Taylor's "Detroit Rocks" (1929) is also notable for its motoristic, 12-bar, blues boogie/barrelhouse style. It is also important for being one of the earliest recordings to feature the term "rocks," and as such is one of the earliest precursors of the term "rock n' roll." Hastings Street was part of Detroit's "Black Bottom" neighbourhood (named by early French settlers for the dark topsoil in the area) and its proximity to an area known as Paradise Valley that was famous for its plethora of nightclubs where artists such as Billie Holiday, Ella Fitzgerald, Duke Ellington, Pearl Bailey, and Count Basie, among others, regularly performed (Woodford, 2001, pp. 171–172).

Aside from the simple referencing of Detroit, many musicians were actively influenced by their employment in various automotive manufacturing plants. Urban bluesman and autoworker Bobo Jenkins, for example, often commented on the inspiration that his long hours on the automotive assembly line at Chrysler had on his music: "That whirlin' machinery gives me the beat. It's like hearin' a band playing all day long. Every song I ever wrote that's any good has come from me standin' on that line" (Smith, 1999, p. 12). Of course, the sheer monotony and often de-humanizing pace of the automobile assembly line was also on the mind of many bluesmen. In his well-known "Please Mr. Foreman" (1959), Joe L. Carter outlines how beaten down he feels, pleading, "Please Mr. Foreman, slow down your assembly line / No, I don't mind workin', but I do mind dyin'."[23]

As manifest in "Please Mr. Foreman," prosperity and a better life were not always found in the automotive factories in Detroit. Many musicians lamented their move north after negative experiences in the big city, and promised to return home to the South. As Arthur Alexander sings in the classic "Detroit City" (1968), "Home folks think I'm big in Detroit City / From the letters I write they think I'm fine / But by day I make the cars, by night I make the bars / If they could only read between the lines."[24] He vows to hop the next freight train south to return to his family. Tampa Red's "Detroit Blues" (1945) relates a similar experience as the men of Detroit steal his woman and he vows to return to Tennessee. Abner Jay's song "Depression" (released in 2009) also captures the restlessness and despair experienced by many migrants. The song's protagonist sings of leaving his home in Georgia, where his parents were sharecroppers who had nothing to eat but "grasshoppers." Setting out for a better life, he fails to find success, singing, "I hitchhiked to New York City, Chicago, Cleveland, and Detroit ... everywhere I went along everything I do is wrong / Oh Lord, shoulda never left home."[25] Such feelings of emptiness, loneliness, resignation, failure, and a desire to return to southern rural homes were common themes.

Many of the songs that capture the experience of the Great Migration still ring true today, particularly in the wake of Detroit's economic crises and declaration of bankruptcy in 2013. Indeed, one wonders whether the city's "glory days" that exist in the collective nostalgia of many Detroit natives ever truly existed. Detroit's industrial economy was devastated by the Great Depression, and many migrants decided to return to the South. Victoria Spivey's lyrics to "Detroit Moan" (1936) are relevant to many descendants of the Great Migration living in Detroit today. Spivey describes Detroit as "a cold, hard place" that she has to leave "if I have to flag number ninety-four," and "I ain't never comin' to Detroit no more."[26] In catching the #94 train out of the now famously abandoned and dilapidated Michigan Central Station, the despair Spivey feels is almost palpable.[27] In 1963, country singer

Bobby Bare repeated the sentiments in his song "Detroit City," in which he "ride[s] the freight train north to Detroit City," only to spend years in unrealized dreams before putting his pride "on the southbound freight" and returning to "the ones he left behind."[28] These songs epitomize and chronicle the feelings of loneliness and disillusionment felt by thousands of both black and white rural southerners who left home hoping to find a better life in industrial Detroit.

The automotive industry in Detroit, then, influenced African-American music in both a positive and negative manner. On the one hand, it could provide a form of sonic and socio-economic inspiration as well as the financial security needed to be able to create music. On the other hand, it was at the root of unrealized dreams and demoralizing and soul-destroying fatigue and frustration. In 1968, however, the relationship between music and the automotive industry took on a new twist. On May 2 of that year, a racially integrated group of about 4000 autoworkers staged a wildcat strike at the Dodge [Chrysler] Main Plant in Detroit. The immediate reason for the strike was a recent speeding up of the assembly line, but other underlying concerns and grievances motivated the action. What began as an integrated action soon divided along racial lines when a disproportionate number of black workers were fired by Chrysler, including one of the strike leaders, General G. Baker. As a result of these actions, the black leaders of the strike made the decision to form their own advocacy group to specifically represent the needs of their black union brotherhood. This new group called themselves the Dodge Revolutionary Union Movement (DRUM) and took on the larger cause of organizing black workers on a national scale such that "the black working class would be the vanguard of the revolutionary struggle in this country" (qtd in Smith, 1999, p. 234).

DRUM grew rapidly throughout 1968, using the militant *Inner City Voice* newspaper to reach a circulation of nearly 10,000 readers. The *Inner City Voice* published a variety of poems, cartoons, and photographs to enhance its political messages. It was instrumental for inspiring several other like-minded labour organizations to form in Detroit, eventually organizing under the umbrella group, the League of Revolutionary Black Workers. In addition to the *Inner City Voice*, DRUM relied on various means of independent cultural expression to publicize and promote its cause. At one wildcat protest outside a Chrysler plant on July 12, 1968, activists, many garbed in African robes, brought bongo drums as a symbol of the new militant organization. They began beating the bongos while other DRUM members danced to African rhythms. A documentary produced by the League of Revolutionary Black Workers, *Finally Got the News*, featured politicized songs such as Carter's "Detroit I Do Mind Dying." Notably, as outlined by Smith (1999, pp. 223–224), the *Inner City Voice* was openly critical of Gordy's Motown Records, claiming it was more concerned about its own profit margins than improving the working conditions and economic opportunities of the black community that put it on the map.

Despite criticism from some black activists in Detroit, at times Motown did take an active role in the politics of promoting race relations. Among other activities, for example, on August 28, 1963, the label released a recording of Martin Luther King's Detroit speech entitled "The Great March to Freedom." Influenced by this recording, Langston Hughes signed a contract with Motown to release later in the same year an album of his poetry, *Poets of the Revolution*, in collaboration with local Detroit poet Margaret Danner.[29] Motown additionally arose and functioned in a city dominated by the auto industry, an industry that, while profiting from black labour, routinely excluded African Americans from controlling the means of production. A black-owned record label producing and recording black music and operating in the heart of white corporate America was a political act almost by default.

While Motown operated as an independent and almost subversive political operation within the heart of the automotive industry, it nonetheless simultaneously co-opted many of the production techniques, emerging technologies, and marketing practices associated with the industry—practices that allowed it to reach some of the largest audiences in the history of black-owned cultural production. Indeed, Motown often overtly aligned itself with the auto industry in its songs and marketing when it was expedient to do so. The assembly line process of music and star creation is well known; but Motown routinely aligned its star performers with the auto industry, such as Martha and the Vandellas' televised performance of "Nowhere to Run" (1967), filmed on location at Ford's River Rouge plant assembly line (discussed below).

Berry Gordy took sonic and rhythmic inspiration from the assembly line. Before founding Motown, he worked at the Fort Wayne Assembly plant in Indiana, and would often hum tunes and compose songs in his mind to mitigate the boredom of the assembly line (Smith, 1999, p. 14). While the assembly line might tangentially have influenced Gordy's songwriting, it overtly influenced Motown's production methods, which were directly influenced by the efficiency of Ford's automotive production line. In his autobiography, Gordy (1994) writes,

> At the plant cars started out as a just a frame, pulled along on conveyor belts until they emerged at the end of the line—brand spanking new cars rolling off the line. I wanted the same concept for my company, only with artists and songs and records. I wanted a place where a kid off the street could walk in one door an unknown and come out another a recording artist—a star (p. 140; also see Smith, 1999, p. 14).

Gordy's overall strategy for launching songs and artists at Motown involved a three-stage process that he labelled "create, make, sell." Each of the three phases of this assembly line involved a distinct division of labour. In the "creative" phase, songwriters, producers, and performers were only responsible for their immediate area of expertise. Songs were typically broken down into similarly discrete units such that, as in the auto industry, a part could be easily exchanged, replaced, or assembled at a later date. In the studio, in-house band The Funk Brothers, for example, typically compartmentalized the recording of voice, bass, treble, and melody parts, recording rhythm tracks for songs that did not even have melodies written for them and/or repurposing background vocals originally recorded for one song into another. The guitarists (of which there usually were three) even divided the different ranges of a song, with one playing the high parts, one the middle, and one the low register, so that one or more could be eliminated or swapped out.

Following the creative stage of the process, a song moved down the assembly line to the "making" or production phase. The producers decided on the final components to be used in a song, and then brought it to the legendary quality control department headed by Billie Jean Brown. Brown collected and collated all the available recordings for appraisal at weekly Friday morning meetings over which Gordy presided. Gordy relied on her instincts more than he did any other person at Motown, and for some 19 years it was up to Brown, a former journalism student, to decide whether a recording was up to the record label's standards and worthy of being released. Her decisions were based solely on whether she believed a particular recording would sell sufficiently. As Gordy tells it,

> Billie Jean was feared by almost every producer in the room because they knew "she had my ear." She had as keen a sense of what was a hit as anyone I knew. And she knew it. That's why she sat there like a diva in the last act waiting for her solo. She was expressionless, nothing moving except her squinting eyes, which darted back and forth from one hopeful producer to another as if to say "Yes, I hold your fate in my hands" (Betts, 2014, n.p.).

While he was the ultimate decision maker and evokes sexist stereotypes of "diva" behaviour in this description, Gordy nonetheless testifies to the relative power that women wielded at various stages in the Motown manufacturing operations. It is also noteworthy that Brown's power points to a contradiction in a process that applied scientific management to musical production: from this determined and merciless process of efficiency to one person's ears ultimately deciding whether the results were acceptable. The Motown process took individual power out of the hands of the artists in favour of management, and then reintroduced that individual power at the final stage. Brown all but became the artist in the process.

The next stage in the process, "sell" or marketing, owed as much to the practices of the automobile industry as did the modular creative phase. The label's artist development department was typically the next stage of the assembly line. Also known as "charm school," the artists were taught the basics of etiquette, deportment, choreography, make-up, and stage presence, thus ensuring a unified and polished presentation among all Motown artists. Just as with other aspects of the production process, each area of charm school was taught by an individual solely responsible for that area. Charles "Cholly" Atkins, for example, was responsible for choreography and creating dance routines, while Maxine Powell taught etiquette and stage presence. Motown's concern for the general presentation and public decorum of their artists was a holdover from previous beliefs regarding the need to avoid racist stereotypes about uncivilized or uneducated African-American behaviour. It should be remembered that the charm school model was not unique to the Motown system, but was used by Hollywood studios and business executives in various corporations. While Gordy rarely (if ever) signed anyone who needed to be "re-made," Motown strove to present its artists and songs in a manner that would reflect well on black people as a whole and free them from mainstream white accusations of uncouth deportment. Of course, this entailed more mercenary outcomes in seeking to make Motown artists more acceptable and palatable to the larger market of mainstream white America. At its heart, Motown mined black culture in Detroit, then refined and reassembled it into a profitable commodity.

Occasionally the auto industry provided more than just a production model for Gordy and his artists. The Funk Brothers (Motown's celebrated house band that played on most of the label's hit recordings) were well known for their sonic innovations and improvisations in the studio, such as the use of snow-tyre chains to create an industrially stark percussive backbeat on songs like Martha and the Vandellas' hit, "Nowhere to Run."[30]

By the 1960s, the automation of the assembly lines that had initially attracted and provided stable employment opportunities for thousands of black workers in the first half of the century began to work against job opportunities. Instead, improvements in automation on the lines had significantly reduced the need for many skilled and semi-skilled workers. James Boggs, a Chrysler autoworker and activist organizer of the Freedom Now Party, wrote about the deleterious effects of automation for black workers in his book *The American Revolution: Pages from a Negro Worker's Notebook* (1963):

> Automation replaces men. This of course is nothing new. What *is* new is that now, unlike most earlier periods, the displaced men have nowhere to go. The farmers displaced by mechanization of the farms in the 20's could go to the cities and man the assembly lines. As for the work animals like the mule, they could just stop growing them. But automation displaces people, and you don't just stop growing people even when they have been made expendable by the system. Under Stalin the kulaks and all those who didn't go along with the collectivization of agriculture were just killed off. Even then, if they had been ready to go along, Stalin could have used them. But in the United States, with automation coming in when industry has already reached the point that it can supply consumer demand, the question of what to do with the surplus people who are the expendables of automation becomes more and more critical every day (Boggs, 1963/2009, p. 33).

Adding to the problem of automation and the technological displacement of workers was the fact that the big three auto makers, Ford, General Motors, and Chrysler, began relocating their manufacturing plants to suburban locations outside the Detroit city limits, thereby limiting access of black workers who largely resided in the inner city.

Automotive technology and automation, then, had become a double-edged sword for Motown. On the one hand, it contributed to the loss of income and employment opportunities for its black audiences. On the other, assembly line procedures and other technological advances of the auto industry provided models for its production practices. Developments such as the car radio also directly influenced the sound and production of the Motown style and facilitated a wider distribution of its music than would have otherwise occurred. It has often been recognized that the car radio influenced both the form and sound of early Motown hits. In addition to radio generally influencing the length of songs (i.e., shorter songs resulted in greater frequency of radio play), commentators also noted, for example, that "Motown's light, unfussy, evenly stressed beats, its continuous loop melodies, were the ideal accompaniment to driving" (Morse, 1971, p. 23; also in Smith 1999, p. 123). Moreover, Motown record producers and studio engineers were among the first to set up car speakers in the recording studios in order to replicate how a song would sound when heard from a car radio—an idea that would later become common studio practice.[31]

At times, the music industry and Detroit's auto industry intentionally aligned themselves with each other, such as when Ford began marketing its new Mustang, one of the first cars to be specifically marketed to America's youth, reflecting their increased purchasing power. Ford was thus attempting to appeal to the same demographic that listened to Motown, and rock n' roll music in general. As part of its campaign to capture the youth market, Ford began to sponsor "hootenanny" folk concerts on various college campuses.[32] The hootenannies were eventually released as an album "[s]pecially produced by your local Ford dealer by RCA Victor," entitled *Ford Hootenanny* (1964) and featuring artists such as Harry Belafonte, the Sons of the Pioneers, The Limeliters, and Miriam Makeba among others. Cashing in on the folk music craze for hootenannies, Ford also advertised various "BIG HOOTE-NANNY" sales at their dealerships around the country in newspapers.[33] The ads featured a cartoon banjo-playing car dealer with the catchphrase "COME BUY 'EM FOR A SONG, FOLKS!"

Motown, for its part, often borrowed from the cachet of the automobile industry when marketing its artists. Much like today's celebrity associations with automobiles (see the use of celebrity musicians and branding in Chapter 4), Motown often marketed its stars with publicity shots that included a high-end car, typically a Cadillac, in order to evoke a transference of value in the minds of potential customers of a similar aesthetic and economic quality. In this reciprocal arrangement, the car underlined and reinforced the success of the artist via its elite distinctiveness and celebrity cachet. Potential consumers of both music and automobiles were thus presented with the apparent combined epitome of musical and automobile aesthetics and engineering. As with much of the rest of America, as witnessed by Elvis' infatuation for the brand, the Cadillac was viewed as the car of choice within Motown. Singer Mary Wilson (2000) described the role the car played in providing incentives within the company, describing "a fleet of brand-new Cadillacs parked all over West Grand Boulevard. As soon as a writer, producer or performer got his first check it was as good as endorsed over to the local Cadillac dealership" (p. 149). According to Wilson, Motown executives, wishing to preserve their distinctiveness, even bickered over the colour of the car they might purchase. "One day Mickey Stevenson drove up in a Caddy the same color and style as Berry's new one, a light color, like grey. *Someone* would have to exchange his car, a few days later Mickey was tooling around in a black Cadillac" (ibid., emphasis in original).

While Motown stars and employees conspicuously showed off their success by associating themselves with Cadillacs or other high-end automobiles, the company was also conscious of not alienating its working-class fan base and so inserted itself into the industrial landscape of the city. Several Motown promotions saw artists photographed within the auto assembly plants themselves. On June 28, 1965, CBS broadcast the show *It's What's Happening, Baby*, hosted by popular DJ Murray "the K" Kaufman and featuring artists such as the Dave Clark Five, Herman's Hermits, Marvin Gaye, the Supremes, Tom Jones, and Ray Charles, among other top hit makers of the day. The show began with Martha and the Vandellas' performance of "Nowhere to Run," staged on the Mustang assembly line of the Ford River Rouge plant in Detroit. The group playfully ran around actual assembly line workers and machinery in the plant, metaphorically enacting the lyrics of the song that describe an obsessive love—"free of you I'll never be … nowhere to run to … nowhere to hide"—from which the protagonist cannot free herself.[34] The lyrics and the enacted a mock chase through the factory floor can thus be read as a metaphor for the obsessively recurring repetition of the assembly line and of factory working conditions. It was a situation from which workers had almost nowhere to hide or many, if any, options to run towards, and so could never be free from the bonds of the car manufacturing companies. The performance concluded with Murray the K driving a fully assembled Ford Mustang out of the plant as Martha and the Vandellas waved goodbye. The segment, while potentially showing its manufacturing plant in a negative light, offered free publicity for Ford's new Mustang by underlining its association with youth and the star power of Hitsville USA, and simultaneously aligned Martha and the Vandellas (and Motown) with the gritty blue-collar realities of the factory workers.

Motown also reciprocally engaged with Ford, albeit indirectly, when promoting its artists on CBS's top-rated *Ed Sullivan Show*. Ford sponsored the program, and Sullivan himself became an "ambassador" for the Lincoln-Mercury brand in 1955.[35] As Smith (1999, p. 134) notes, Sullivan was well known to be sympathetic to African-American entertainers on his show, which at times put him in conflict with southern Ford dealers who sponsored his show and resented his affection for black guests. Sullivan, however, refused to bow to these objections. In the wake of The Supremes' acclaimed national debut on his show in December 1964, Motown began to employ Sullivan's show as the last station on its production line. Sullivan subsequently booked appearances by other Motown artists releasing new songs, including the Temptations, the Four Tops, and the Miracles, in addition to return appearances by the Supremes. While certain elements of Ford sought to limit the visibility of black artists on television (largely out of fear of a negative impact on sales among white viewers of programs they sponsored), Sullivan's show brought increased visibility for black entertainers, specifically those affiliated with Motown. This, in turn, helped reinforce and support the black labour that built both the Motown sound and the cars the show promoted.

In a more recent update of the relationship between Motown and the auto industry, in late 2012 Chrysler launched the "Motown Edition" of its popular 300 series sedan. The Fiat Chrysler Automobiles (FCA) press release about the new model claimed: "If cars are the heart of the Motor City, music is its soul." Chrysler particularly used the life and legend of Berry Gordy to enhance and cement what it refers to as its "brand partnership" and "collaboration" with Motown:

> "Berry Gordy is a true inspiration and has paved the way to signify the sound and the drive that reflects the spirit of Detroit and the people who live in it," said Olivier François, Chief Marketing Officer, Chrysler Group LLC. "It is a privilege to have such a legendary icon partner with the Chrysler brand and the 300 Motown Edition."
>
> "The Chrysler brand's imagination moved the world, while our rhythms forever changed music adding a sound and uplifting spirit that could only be from the Motor City. And our new Chrysler 300 Motown is a tribute to both," said Saad Chehab, President and CEO–Chrysler Brand, Chrysler Group LLC. "More than just a *brand partnership, our collaboration* with Motown Records elevates our passion to express our Detroit roots further and inspire a new limited-edition 300 sedan that embodies the soul and originality of our city" (FCA, 2012, emphasis added).

The promotion was focused on a 60-second commercial titled "Who We Are," which features Gordy riding in the back of the Motown Edition 300 from Detroit to New York City to see the opening of *Motown: The Musical* on Broadway. As described in the press release:

> The spot opens with Berry Gordy sitting in the backseat of the Chrysler 300 Motown Edition parked outside the Motown Museum in Detroit, the building where Motown Records was created. As the car pulls away the voiceover begins to tell the story of sound and drive of the city of Detroit,

a sound that still moves people and a drive that allows it to overcome any challenge that comes its way.

As he drives through the streets, images of a young Stevie Wonder, Smokey Robinson and the Miracles, the Supremes and the Temptations flash across the screen and viewers are taken through iconic visuals of the streets of Detroit and eventually transported to the streets of New York where Berry Gordy's destination is revealed in front of the "Motown: The Musical" marquee at the Lunt Fontanne Theatre in New York City. The spot ends with Berry Gordy stepping out of the vehicle and saying, "We are Motown and this is what we do," and announcing the musical coming to Broadway in March 2013.

In keeping with its musical branding, the 300 Edition prominently featured an upgraded audio system. It employed Beats Audio technology with a 12-channel amp to push 10 speakers with the proprietary Beats Audio equalization algorithm. The Uconnect® infotainment system also featured what Chrysler billed as "the segment's largest touchscreen" at 8.4 inches, which allowed seamless connectivity with other devices, infotainment, and multimedia features. Notably, the Uconnect's audio system featured an SD card reader pre-loaded with a card containing 100 songs by original Motown artists. Albeit in a different format from the assembly line production techniques and sounds that originally inspired Gordy and the Motown sound, the merging of automobile technology with the record label was again apparent, in this instance a technological merging of brands and products.

The Motown Edition 300 was one of a series of Chrysler's efforts to market itself by showcasing its close association with Detroit. These included the company's decision in 2011 to use the tagline "Imported from Detroit" in its advertising. No doubt Chrysler hoped that memories of legendary music produced by Motown Records, not to mention Gordy's image, would strike an emotional chord with car buyers. The spot, nonetheless, cemented the historically reciprocal relationship between Motown and the auto industry. It should be noted, however, that Motown, perhaps ironically, appears to have no particular brand loyalty itself, given its artists' and executives' preference for Cadillacs, a General Motors product, back in the 1960s. For marketing purposes, and in order to align itself with the younger audience who might buy their records, Motown advertised its artists in relationship with the Ford Mustang, à la Martha and the Vandellas' performance on *It's What's Happening, Baby*. In the new millennium, it appeared that Gordy's new car of choice is no longer a Cadillac (perhaps now viewed as too old school and ostentatious), but rather the Chrysler 300 series.

Motown's complex and often conflicted relationship with African-American culture and identity has been discussed at length elsewhere (Smith, 1999; Early, 2004; Werner, 2006). As a black-owned business promoting and marketing black music and performers, Motown was continually forced to negotiate turbulent waters where issues of race and civil rights were concerned. Throughout the 1960s, its ability to promote and sell African-American talent that appealed to both black and white consumers advanced notions of racial integration and provided many in the black community with a source of pride. In the wake of the assassination of Malcolm X, the Watts uprising, and the Selma Voting Rights Campaign, black nationalists called some of Motown's achievements into question. Motown's music was slickly packaged and tightly controlled so as to avoid controversy, and thus appeal to as wide (read: white) an audience as possible. Some black supporters conceived of Motown's ability to appeal to a white audience as a positive sign that interracial understanding was possible. More militant black critics felt that Motown should be more concerned with advancing racial pride alone, and less about bridging divides and appeasing white consumers. To quote Suzanne Smith (1999), "Many of Motown's performers began to feel 'twice tried'—wanting to be accepted as entertainers, but also remembering that 'they are Negroes'" (p. 140). Motown's complicated relationship with the automotive industry mirrored to some degree its position in the black community itself. As already discussed, it borrowed technology and production methods from the auto industry, and often appropriated the cachet obtained by associating and marketing its stars with the products of the automobile manufacturers. At the same time, Motown was conscious of the fact that the auto industry was increasingly alienating the African-American community through its labour practices. In many ways, Motown's relationship with racial issues and the automobile industry is a case study for W. E. B. Du Bois' (1897) belief that black Americans operate within a condition of double-consciousness that involves

> this sense of always looking at one's self through the eyes of others, of measuring one's soul by the tape of a world that looks on in amused contempt and pity. One ever feels his two-ness—an American, a Negro; two souls, two thoughts, two unreconciled strivings; two warring ideals in one dark body, whose dogged strength alone keeps it from being torn asunder (p. 194).

On the one hand, Motown needed to succeed simply as an "American" company on its own terms like any other, appealing to the broadest commercial market possible; yet, on the other hand, it felt compelled to view itself from a racialized "Negro" perspective and the related objectives of promoting consciousness-raising that could be perceived as being in direct "warring" conflict with the former objectives. This, of course, assumes that we allow that the Motown corporation (it was officially incorporated as Motown Record Corporation on April 14, 1960) can be viewed as analogous to a corporeal body, as indeed the term legally implies. To a large extent, this is the universal history of black Americans and black-owned and -controlled businesses—a history that does not discriminate by social or economic class, but rather a history of the longing to attain self-conscious personhood.

The automobile thus often represents another type of "striving" within African-American culture, that of conspicuous consumption and the triumph of consumerism.[36] Paul Gilroy (2001) nevertheless notes the dangers of reductively linking black identity to car culture:

> It is not only that the resulting forms of attention can release violent envy and compound the petty hatreds of a violently segregated world. The historian David Nye has pinpointed some of the tragic consequences that can follow when this intimate, transient bond is carried over into the world of automotivity: "to the extent that the buyer invested personal meaning in a car, its obsolescence underlined how unstable the sense of identity can be when underwritten by consumption" (p. 87).

While it is a given that issues of racial identity are far more complex than a particular identification with or proclivity for certain products or brands, it is also still true that the nexus of automotive culture and popular music has played a large role in shaping a variety of African-American identities in various places and locations. From Detroit's Motown to Houston's SLAB and chopped and screwed cultures of modification, popular music and cars have synchronously and mutually influential factors in constructing individual and regional identities. Indeed, the modification culture of lowriders and SLAB (and of hip hop in general) acts as a metaphor of identity construction itself. In keeping with Deleuze and Guattari's (1987) notions of assemblage, both cars and musical productions are mechanical constructions comprised of a constellation of traits:

> We will call an assemblage every constellation of singularities and traits deducted from the flow—selected, organized, stratified—in such a way as to converge (consistency) artificially and naturally; an assemblage, in this sense, is a veritable invention. Assemblages may group themselves into extremely vast constellations constituting "cultures" (p. 406).

By extension, as far as identity construction is concerned, we might all be understood as assemblages of various constellations of the external projections of community or cultural identification from the cars we drive, the music we listen to, the clothing we wear, and even our shared, though individualized, histories of race, ethnicity, gender and sexual identity, and class and religion. Just as music and cars are assembled from a constellation of different parts, albeit in service of economic corporate goals, so too do we often choose the parts of our lives and products with which we identify in order to assemble our idealistic projections of the self. African-American processes of car and music modification, however, add a layer of disruption to what might be perceived as the normative material assembly of a car, musical track, or even a drug such as Purple Drank. The disruptive, unexpected juxtapositions of materials and sensorial qualities result in particularly creative and defiant cultural productions that continually resist subsumption into dominant forms of cultural production.

Race and the need for speed

Regardless of racial identity, to a large degree the often symbiotic relationship between popular music and the automotive industry lies in a common human fascination with and desire for speed. Speed is found in information exchange, in the electronic media realm of television and film, in travel, in every instance where humans hook up with and are saturated by technologies. Speed is also at the heart of the manipulation of wealth. Cultural theorist Paul Virilio coined the term "dromology," rooted in the Greek term *dromos*, meaning "road," to refer to the science of speed in relationship to the development of societies. Virilio believes that speed precedes wealth, and that power always grows out of the possession of the means of velocity. He outlines his ideas to Sylvère Lotringer in *Pure War* (first published in 1983):

> Speed is the unknown side of politics, and has been since the beginning: this is nothing new. The wealth aspect in politics was spotlighted a long time ago. ... [I]t was a mistake ... to forget that wealth is an aspect of speed. ... People forget the dromological dimension of power: its ability to inveigle, whether by taxes, conquest, etc. Every society is founded on a relation to speed. Every society is dromocratic. ... We have two sides of the regulation of speed and wealth. Up until the nineteenth century, society was founded on the brake. Means of furthering speed were very scant. You had ships, but sailing ships evolved very little between Antiquity and Napoleon's time; the horse even less; and of course there were carrier pigeons. The only machine to use speed with any sophistication was the optical telegraph, then the electric telegraph. In general, up until the nineteenth century, there was no production of speed. They could produce brakes by means of ramparts, the law, rules, interdictions, etc. They could brake using all kinds of obstacles (Virilio & Lotringer, 2008, p. 58).

The dromocratic revolution is Virilio's name for the Industrial Revolution, for the key to the steam engine and the combustion engine was the fabrication of speed. He continues:

> And so they can pass from the age of brakes to the age of the accelerator. In other words, power will be invested in acceleration itself. We know that the army has always been the place where pure speed is used, whether it be in the cavalry—the best horses, of course, were army horses—the artillery, etc. Still today, the army uses the most pertinent speeds—whether it be in missiles or planes. ... There is no political power that can regulate the multinationals or the armed forces, which have greater and greater autonomy. There is no power superior to theirs. Therefore, either we wait for the coming of a hypothetical universal State, with I don't know what Primate at its head, or else we finally understand that what is

at the center is no longer a monarch by divine right, an absolute monarch, but an absolute weapon. The center is no longer occupied by a political power, but by a capacity or absolute destruction (pp. 59–60).

For Virilio, everything about our modern society revolves around an acceleration derived from our interaction with machines. Acceleration, for example, is the key driver of capitalism—to develop ways to produce more in a finite period. Whether it is the hyper-fast tempos of speed metal, hardcore punk, and some rap, or the flow of and access to information over the Internet or communication by satellite technology and cell phones, all function by accelerating flows and creating multiple interfaces between bodies and hyperactive machines.

Sound is closely linked to the vector of speed. To go faster than the speed of sound, to break the sound barrier, has been the iconic measure of technological achievement throughout the twentieth and into the twenty-first century. Popular music has particularly been driven by the components of acceleration and speed. Music videos, for example, de-territorialize perception by a seemingly overwhelming rush of images and noise, but then re-territorialize it as a commodity. In a similar fashion, the Internet has facilitated the cultivation and acceleration of innumerable music styles and subgenres. Genres such as mallsoft, vaporwave, or hypnogogic pop, to name but a few, arise in a heartbeat and die out before many people, certainly mainstream music listeners, are likely even aware of them. For Virilio, "Overaccelerated speed renders us unconscious" (Potter, 1987, p. 14). Like sex, speed sells; but it also can take us over a threshold of human perception whereby our senses cannot, for all practical purposes, keep up. Some have even speculated that we are entering a final stage in the cult of sensation, in which our bodies are unable to enjoy the extreme pleasures that have been prepared for them with frenetic excess (Potter, 1987).

While Virilio's perspective applies to the excesses and accelerations of stylistic change in many aspects of Western culture—and popular music particularly would seem to have particular resonance concerning questions of marginalization and issues of race—if one accepts Virilio's proposition that power stems from the possession of the means of velocity, then, much as in the Afrofuturist agendas already discussed, speed and the control of the machinery capable of producing it are central to the drive for African-American social equality and the quest for accelerated political change. To a large extent, this "accelerationism" and, in some instances, challenges to it are evident in the myriad of creative African-American musical styles and approaches that characterize and shape contemporary popular music

In 1954, Chief Justice Earl Warren delivered the US Supreme Court's landmark decision in *Brown v. Board of Education of Topeka, Kansas*, urging the rapid desegregation of the nation's public schools. The actual phrase Warren used to underscore the urgency of this directive was the seemingly contradictory "with all deliberate speed." In his book *Deliberate Speed*, W. T.

Lhamon, Jr considers this a key phrase for the times, going beyond the urgency for social change to describe the tempo of 1950s' popular culture as a whole. Life was moving forward at breakneck speed on a number of fronts. The United States was in the throes of transformation, shedding the skin of an industrial society and entering the post-industrial age. From Jack Kerouac's *On the Road* (1957) to the music of Miles Davis, Little Richard, and Chuck Berry, Lhamon sees an aesthetics of speed as brought about by the rise of youth culture and the associated "wanton squandering of energy" that accompanied it. For Lhamon (1990), the multiple significations of the racialized Sambo figure "was the conceit enabling the popularity of rock n' roll" (pp. 8, 76). In particular, Lhamon looks at the speed with which manifestations of this slippery representation would appear in different mediums and cultural works, and in the case of his reading of Chuck Berry's character in the car chase song "Maybellene," simply referring to him as "Mobileman." This concept of the mobility of identity again resonates with Dubois' notion, discussed above, that black Americans operate within a condition of double-consciousness. In many ways, African Americans all take on the position of the Mobileman/Mobilewoman as they must instantaneously react to and shift between the "warring ideals" of black and white America and a more profound double-consciousness that recognizes, paradoxically, the insufficiency of consciousness itself and concomitant need for radical social transformation.

The theme of traveling and mobility, whether of racial consciousness or of physical space, is central to Chuck Berry's "Promised Land" (1964), which he wrote while in prison and was the first single he recorded and issued upon his release. Underscoring the theme of mobility and transportation, the song appeared on the album *St. Louis to Liverpool* (1964). Wishing to capitalize on his popularity during the British invasion, Berry and Chess Records put together this album to appeal to younger consumers. *St. Louis to Liverpool* includes four of the five charting singles he enjoyed in 1964, including "No Particular Place to Go," "You Never Can Tell," "Promised Land," and "Little Marie," which was a sequel to "Memphis, Tennessee" (1959).

"Promised Land," written to the melody of the well-known train song "Wabash Cannonball," is nominally about travelling across the country from Norfolk, Virginia, to the so-called "promised land" of Los Angeles. Like "The Wabash Cannonball," it lists a number of locations and destinations that the narrator encounters along the way. Substituting a bus for a train, the "poor boy" narrator boards a Greyhound coach in Norfolk, Virginia. He passes through Raleigh and stops in Charlotte, North Carolina, but bypasses Rock Hill, South Carolina. As Lhamon points out, the bypassing of Rock Hill is related to Freedom Riders and a racially motivated beating that took place at the bus station there in 1961. (Elvis Presley's cover of "Promised Land," released in 1975, conveniently omitted this verse.) The bus then rolls out of Atlanta but soon breaks down, leaving him stranded in downtown Birmingham, Alabama. The song's protagonist, ostensibly Berry himself, then takes a train "across Mississippi clean" to New Orleans. From there, he goes to Houston, where people "who care a little 'bout me" buy him a silk suit, luggage and a plane ticket to Los Angeles. Upon landing in Los Angeles, he calls back to Norfolk ("Tidewater four, ten-oh-nine") to tell the folks back home he has made it to the promised land.[37]

Musically, the song is a blues-based rocker that moves along at a breakneck pace. Its most definitive musical feature is Berry's characteristically enervated down-strummed rhythmic guitar that adds a sense of physical tension and added energy of the song. When Berry wakes up "high over Albuquerque" on a jet to the promised land, his interjected guitar solo doubles in pace in a frenetic bout of flutter-picked chords that mimic the increased speed associated with jet travel. The flutter-picked solo chords return as a concluding fade-out to the song when Berry phones home from the so-called promised land. The pace of the music never diminishes, however, and the fade-out of hyperactive flutter chording suggests that the quest for the promised land continues and will, perhaps, never be obtainable.

Berry also refers to the spiritual "Swing Low, Sweet Chariot," a reference that is juxtaposed with the modern jet he has taken to Los Angeles and an even faster form of communication, the telephone: "Swing low sweet chariot … cut your engines, cool your wings, and let me make it to the telephone." In making this conflation, Berry is brought into alignment with Afrofuturist notions, the idea of liberation based on return to a past/future of African domination of space and technology. His lyrics convey a sense of time travel, of a man out of place and time, as the plane is likened to a Pegasus-like horse-drawn chariot that needs to cool its wings after its accelerated journey. Indeed, earlier in the song Berry does not just passively get on a bus, but rather actively rides it: "I straddled that Greyhound and rode him into Raleigh and on across Caroline." There is an underlying juxtaposition of references to natural manifestations of speed as embodied in horses, greyhounds, and wings on the one hand, and against man-made mechanical manifestations represented by buses, cars, and jet planes on the other. It is clear that Berry is reliant on transportation technology, which is often flawed and breaks down, to reach his mythic goal. But it is only by co-opting the unnatural and by negotiating a maze of white-dominated transportation and communication technologies that he is able to reach his objective. Throughout the song, he variously walks and takes a bus, a taxi, a train, and a jet plane, before finally, in a final act of technological mobility, he uses a telephone to instantaneously project his voice back home.

The role of transportation in African-American life, much of it automotive, is central to the underlying meaning of the song. As mentioned above, Berry wrote this work while in prison. On December 23, 1959, Berry was arrested in St. Louis on charges relating to his transportation of a 14-year-old girl across state lines for "immoral purposes." The Mann Act was the common name for a piece of federal legislation properly called the United States White-Slave Traffic Act of 1910. Although intended as a tool for cracking down on organized prostitution, the vague language of the Mann Act regarding the transportation of women for "immoral purposes" rendered its provisions broadly unenforceable. It was selectively applied in various high-profile cases over time, however—most famously in Berry's and in that of the heavyweight boxing great Jack Johnson. The automobile, then, was instrumental to Berry's loss of freedom.

Furthermore, Norfolk, Virginia, whence the narrator feels compelled to leave and begin his quest, was well known for its resistance to the integration imposed in *Brown vs. Board of Education*. During the period Berry wrote the song, the advent of new suburban developments saw many white middle-class residents moving out of the city along new highway routes, leaving black people to live in the increasingly impoverished downtown core.

Understood in this context, then, the song is essentially an ode to the historical and present journeys and struggles of African Americans for the mythical "promised land" of racial equality. However, the song fades out and is open-ended, as Lhamon (1990) recognizes:

> No such place has yet materialized for blacks in White America, not even California. The term [promised land] signifies a place necessary but impossible to believe in on earth. Hence the plane has become the chariot swinging low as it lands, the airport has become the terminal gate, both as real and unreal as the signifying term can pump up (p. 82).

In some sense, the song is a metaphor of the double-edged nature of the African-American experience as mapped through the doubled-edged nature of automobility and mechanized transportation in general. All facets of the song are imbued with transportation, largely automotive. The song's inception stems from Berry's imprisonment for transporting (driving) a minor across state lines. It is melodically and rhythmically modelled on the "Wabash Cannonball" train, though it features a much faster up-tempo driving beat in keeping with the seemingly urgent desperation of reaching the promised land. It is lyrically centred on a Greyhound bus trip across the country that alludes to incidents involving the Freedom Riders and that bears comparison to the trials and tribulations of journeys not dissimilar to those made on the underground railroad. Thus the song manifests notions of both the promised liberation afforded by automobile, train, and plane travel and of their related dangers—breakdowns, for example, plague the bus ride and the narrator hopes the plane will "come down easy."

Berry's "Promised Land" is a wonderful evocation of the mobility, both physical and psychological, that motivated many African Americans in the 1950s and 1960s. Its rapid tempo, at times almost frantic in Berry's lead electric guitar strumming, intimates a repulsion from the past and, perhaps, a desperation to move forward to a new and better place. It embodies the aspects of the black experience of the historic underground railroad, the present Freedom Riders, and the imagined future of a promised land in

California. It also encapsulates a conflicted relationship with transportation technology and African-American identity. Written during his prison sentence, the song is a marked change in tone from Berry's previous relationship with automobiles. From the relaxed sexual innuendos of "No Particular Place to Go" or "Maybellene," "Promised Land" imparts a less optimistic and less romanticized account of black mobility.

Berry's "Promised Land" is a musical manifestation of speed and, ultimately, represents a desire for accelerated social change. Nevertheless, many styles of music associated with African Americans and other racial minorities actively resist normative conventions of speed and/or fast tempos. Speed and acceleration are often viewed as the natural outcomes of modern industrial capitalism. The commonly heard equation that "time equals money" drives a resulting and concomitant need to speed up production and innovation as well as that of the circulation and consumption of goods and information. However, as seen in the chopped and screwed style linked with SLAB, radically slower tempos are the norm. In much the same manner, Hispanic lowriders prefer "low and slow" beats corresponding to their car cruising style. In these cases, a literal and figurative deceleration of musical tempos and of car cruising speeds serve to invert the normative expectations of conformity and power. Here deceleration represents a political rearticulation of physical embodiment, a creative and resistive slowing down of one's body in relationship to car travel, one that simultaneously signifies an attachment to a particular community.

A relationship to speed and the technology that enables it, or in some cases allows for its deceleration, underscores much African-American music. The speed implied in the Afrofuturist space travel of Sun Ra or George Clinton, the acceleration of automobile assembly lines and the associated feelings of robotic "niggermation" that resulted in Motown and Detroit techno, or Chuck Berry's almost frantic electric guitar chording in "Promised Land" are all examples of the nexus of black music and technology used to promote and advance social change, racial uplift, and empowerment with all due speed.

Conclusion

This chapter has outlined some aspects of the often conflicted African-American relationship with transportation technologies as they have been expressed in popular music. As manifest in artists and musical styles ranging from Chuck Berry's motorvatin' rock n' roll songs to Cybotron's Afrofuturistic techno odes to car travel, African-American artists have incorporated the car to express various aspects of their social life and to reinforce a narrative of liberating motion and migration. Often incorporating insistent, mechanically propulsive rhythms, black artists have celebrated the sound of the car and its associated liberating power, speed, and advanced technology in numerous songs such that it has become inculcated into their identity. Perhaps above all else, cars, particularly luxury cars such as Cadillacs, have been and still are, particularly in hip hop, commonly celebrated in song as aspirational symbols and manifestations of upward social mobility and status. As demonstrated by Houston's SLAB scene, African-American car modification culture also overlaps and becomes entwined with the musical modification culture of hip hop. Both function as synchronous demonstrations of resistance to, variously, mainstream white corporate culture and police authority, and as literal and figurative vehicles to express self and community identity. Motown Studios is doubtless the most famous and overt articulation of the influence of and crosspollination with the automotive industry in African-American music. To some extent Motown was a microcosm of the conflicted relationship between the black community and the automobile. Motown famously and successfully borrowed production techniques adopted from automotive assembly lines, yet continued to align itself with auto manufacturers in the face the industry's increasing automation and concomitant alienation of the African-American community through its labour practices. The chapter concluded with a theoretical exploration of the need for speed in understanding the valorization of mechanized transportation in the African-American community. As manifest in Chuck Berry's "Promised Land," speed, and the faster the better, is paramount in redressing issues surrounding racial inequality and injustice.

Notes

1 Lyrics and music by George Clinton, William Collins, and George Worrell. Copyright Bridgeport Music Publishing.
2 Lyrics and music by Juan Atkins and Richard Davis. Copyright Sony/ATV Music Publishing LLC.
3 According to one study, Cadillacs are likely "the most referenced brand in U.S. popular culture." The same holds true for popular music, where "in 2004 alone the Cadillac was mentioned some 70 times in song lyrics, up from some 46 the year before" (Myers & Dean, 2007, p. 160).
4 In *One-Dimensional Man*, Herbert Marcuse (1964) cites the example of "the negro who owns a Cadillac" to demonstrate the extent to which subordinate groups have been assimilated and won over by "passive consumerism" in order to "serve the preservation of the Establishment" (p. 8). Of course the "negro" to whom Marcuse refers is alienated from the predominantly racist, white-dominated mainstream society. In his quest to fit in, to affirm his humanity, he has little choice but to participate in the empty, de-humanizing materialism of capitalist life. He attempts to find and affirm his sense of bodily humanness in a material object, his car.
5 Lyrics by Eddie Memphis Curtis. Copyright Warner Chappell Music, Inc.
6 W. T. Lhamon (1990) insightfully assesses the Chuck Berry of "Maybellene" as "[a] man who has overcome his victimization [as an African American] by chasing down the fanciest Cadillac on a rainy road ... intuitively drawn on the language and riffs of his folk ways, intertwined them with the twang and rhythm of his neighbor's [white country music] counter tradition, and snuck his anthem of pride past all natural and cultural roadblocks" (p. 79).
7 Lyrics and music by Chuck Berry. Copyright Ole Media Management.
8 Lyrics and music by Chuck Berry. Copyright Ole Media Management.
9 Lyrics and music by Isaac Hayes. Copyright Universal Music Publishing Group.

10 Lyrics and music by Carlton Ridenhour and James Henry Boxley III. Copyright Universal Music Publishing Group.
11 Lyrics and music by James Eliot, Matthew Samuels, Aubrey Graham, Isaac Hayes, David Porter, Corey Woods, Dennis Coles, Gary Grice, Clifford Smith, Jason Hunter, Lamont Hawkins, and Shawn C. Carter. Copyright Kobalt Music Publishing Ltd.
12 Lyrics and music by Belcalis Almanzar, Francisco Saldana, Kevin Gomringer, Kiari Cephus, Kirsnick Khari Ball, Onika Maraj, Quavious Marshall, Ramon Ayala, Shane Lindstrom, Tim Gomringer, and Victor Cabrera. Copyright Warner Chappell Music, Inc.
13 Lil Nas X's "Old Town Road (I Got the Horses in the Back)" (2018) is a notable addition to the nexus of hip hop and car culture. Aided by its association with the Western-themed video game *Red Dead Redemption 2*, it famously reached number 1 on the *Billboard* Hot 100 and number 19 on the Hot Country charts before the magazine re-evaluated the song's genre and deemed that it did not qualify for the country chart. Blending timbral and lyrical aspects of country and rap, it is typically described as being in a country rap, or country trap style as popularized by rapper Young Thug. Of more interest for the current study however is that the song, in something of a "back to the future" scenario, conflates horses and cars as featured in lyrics such as "Ridin' on a tractor / Lean all in my bladder" and "Ridin' on a horse, ha / You can whip your Porsche." The song thus draws parallels between the real or imagined risk-taking hypermobile life of outlaws in the Old West and that of modern hip hop artists. Lyrics and music by Atticus Ross, Billy Ray Cyrus, Jocelyn Donald, Kiowa Roukema, Montero Lamar Hill, and Trent Reznor. Copyright Kobalt Music Publishing Ltd.
14 Lyrics and music by William DeVaughn. Copyright Sony/ATV Music Publishing LLC.
15 Lyrics and music by Bruce Isaac Rhodes, Jarvis Lemon, John Edward Hawkins, Patrick L. Hawkins, Terence Glen Prejean, and Troy Birklett. Copyright Universal Music Publishing Group.
16 Lyrics and music by Bernard Edwards and Nile Rodgers. Copyright Sony/ATV Songs LLC.
17 Likely the most high-profile mention of SLAB culture is found in Beyoncé's song "No Angel" from her eponymously titled album in 2013. She does a shout-out to her hometown, Houston, when she references SLABs and a "ride around with that H-town." In fact, the video accompanying "No Angel" was shot at Houston's first ever "Slab Parade and Family Festival" in October 2013. Lyrics and music by Beyoncé Knowles, Caroline Elizabeth Polachek, and James Fauntleroy. Copyright Kobalt Music Publishing Ltd.
18 For more on the politics of car customization, see Chapter 5.
19 There are exceptions to rappers desiring anonymity in their cars. Drake's "Pound Cake/Paris Morton Music 2," for example, exclaims, "Fuck it, I don't even tint it, they should know who's in it." Lyrics and music by James Eliot, Matthew Samuels, Aubrey Graham, Isaac Hayes, David Porter, Corey Woods, Dennis Coles, Gary Grice, Clifford Smith, Jason Hunter, Lamont Hawkins, and Shawn C. Carter. Copyright Kobalt Music Publishing Ltd.
20 Music and Lyrics by Clifford Smith, Hugh Brodie, Jason Hunter, Reggie Noble, and Robert F. Diggs. Copyright Universal Music Publishing Group.
21 Lyrics and music by Juan Salinas, Oscar Salinas, Anthony Henderson, and Hakeem Seriki. Copyright Sony/ATV Music Publishing LLC.
22 Lyrics and music by John Lee Hooker. Copyright Sony/ATV Music Publishing LLC.
23 Lyrics and music by Joe Lee Carter. Copyright Hi Records under Exclusive Licence to Fat Possum Records.

24 Lyrics and music by Danny Dill and Mel Tillis. Copyright Universal Music Publishing Group.
25 Lyrics and music by Abner Jay. Released version copyright Mississippi Records.
26 Lyrics by Victoria Spivey. Copyright Document Records.
27 Once the tallest railway station in the world and, with its Beaux-Arts classical style, one of the grandest in the country, Michigan Central Station has since been made famous as the subject of countless "modern ruins" photographs.
28 Lyrics and music by Danny Dill and Mel Tillis. Copyright Universal Music Publishing Group.
29 For a detailed and informative description of the circumstances surrounding the inception and recording of this album, see Smith (1999, pp. 107–111).
30 The Funk Brothers, anonymous on Motown recordings, consisted of a changing line-up of predominantly African-American musicians. Although the name is sometimes applied to any of the backing musicians who played on a Motown recording session, it is generally accepted that there were 13 main members, as recognized in their Grammy Lifetime Achievement Award (2004) and on their star on the Hollywood Walk of Fame.
31 It would not have gone unnoticed by Motown executives that, by 1964, 80 per cent of all new Mustang buyers requested a car radio option. See The Mustang–A new breed out of Detroit (1964).
32 Such advertising to the folk music community evinced something of a contradiction. Though most folkies were white, middle-class college students with buying power, they also claimed to reject the crass materialism of their parents, so an album sponsored by Ford should have been regarded with some suspicion.
33 See, for example, Big Hootenanny (1964), from the Lexington, NC, *Dispatch*.
34 Lyrics and music by Edward Holland Jr, Lamont Dozier, and Brian Holland. Copyright Sony/ATV Music Publishing LLC.
35 Sullivan was seemingly responsible for significantly influencing Ford's sales. One Ford spokesperson claimed, "Mercurys have come up fast in sales, thanks to Sullivan. Monday is now our busiest day, following his Sunday show" (Smith, 1999, p. 133).
36 According to one study, an "African-American family with the same income, family size, and other demographics as a white family will spend about 25 percent more of its income on jewelry, cars, personal care, and apparel. For the average black family, making about $40,000 a year, that amounts to $1,900 more a year than for a comparable white family" (Postrel, 2008).
37 Lyrics and music by Chuck Berry. Copyright Arc Music Corp.

3 "Gotta feel for my automobile"
Cars, music, gender, and sexuality

This chapter will analyze the nexus of automobiles and popular music in constructing representations of femininity, masculinity, and various LGBTQ identities. It begins with the premise that cars—as objects of desire, devotion, and obsession—have often been linked with women through song (as in "Maybellene" [1955] or "Mustang Sally" [1965]) or given female personas (e.g., the Beach Boys' proclamation in "409" [1962] that "She's real fine, my 409"). The years following the Second World War saw car songs come into prominence at a time when men were in the driver's seat of both the automotive and recording industries. The car song was produced and marketed by men principally for consumption by young white male drivers, and so most early rock n' roll car songs reflected a male experience (Lezotte, 2013).

Following an analysis of the rise of masculine identities in car culture and of the tendency to anthropomorphize cars as women, both in advertising and in song, the chapter will turn to female challenges to these norms (Joni Mitchell, Shania Twain, and Tracy Chapman, among others). As women entered the rock n' roll and automotive arenas in greater numbers, both as singer-songwriters and drivers, they altered the meaning of the automobile in popular music to reflect their own experiences. This chapter thus provides an additional location from which to consider how the automobile impacts women's lives, as well as how women's experiences have influenced rock n' roll and American car culture.

Finally, this chapter will explore the intersection of automobile culture and music in relation to LGBTQ identities, which are typically overlooked in discussions of stereotypically masculine, heteronormative automotive culture. Yet, several car companies have specifically targeted gay and lesbian consumers (such as Subaru's active cultivation of gay and lesbian customers in the mid-1990s), and some artists, such as Frank Ocean and Queen, have employed unfamiliar and non-heteronormative narratives and feelings for cars in lyrics and videos to further queer discourses. Through the combined lens of popular music songs and car advertising campaigns and soundtracks, this chapter illuminates and highlights recent challenges to the stereotypical image of the car as a heteronormative, masculine machine.

Hypermasculinity and car culture

While there is not a great deal of scholarship devoted to the car song in general, what exists typically focuses on music produced and performed by men, and in which the automobile is constructed as a vehicle of male identity, rebellion, and power. The myriad of meanings the automobile holds for women, as voiced through popular car songs, is generally absent in analyses of the relationship between the automobile and music (Lezotte, 2013, p. 163).

As discussed in Chapter 1, Jackie Brenston and Ike Turner's "Rocket 88," a song inspired by the Oldsmobile Model 88, is not only the prototype of early rock n' roll, but also of the association of the car song with male power. The song extols both the virtues of the automobile and those of the man who drives it. The protagonist's main intent is to attract girls who "will ride in style" as well as, suggestively, "goin' on the corner and havin' some fun / takin' my Rocket on a long, hot run."[1] As Paul Grushkin (2006) writes, "Turner had cooked up a mellow, cruising boogie with a steady-as-she-goes back beat that, married to Brenston's enthusiastic, sexually suggestive vocals, spoke of opportunity, discovery and conquest" (p. 26).

Also discussed in the first chapter of this book, many male drivers and songwriters alike have imbued the car with a female persona. Although some early Tin Pan Alley songs valorized the exploits of female drivers, the car as female was depicted as an often temperamental machine that must be controlled, manipulated, and mastered by men in order to achieve their desires.

To a large degree, the predilection to anthropomorphize and, indeed, animate cars lies behind the proclivity of such conflations. Anthropologist Stewart Guthrie claims that we typically "animate and anthropomorphize [automobiles] at the same time," thus imbuing the car with an added level of vitality (Parkin, 2017, p. 146). People have thus often treated their cars as possessing at least some aspect of humanity, giving them names, talking to them, or interpreting human facial characteristics in their grilles. Of the numerous ways in which we understand or imagine our cars to be human, the gendering of automobiles is perhaps the most significant. As Kathrine Parkin (2017) points out, "it was the car's ability to perform gender that allowed individuals to affirm their own gender roles and engage in a largely unexamined intimate relationship" (p. 146).

"Tin Lizzie," the nickname of Ford's 1908 Model T, was the first of many female names for cars, affirming a female association that still persists. A consumer study conducted in 2014 found that the top five nicknames names employed for cars were all feminine or typically associated with female characteristics: Baby, Betsy, Bessie, Black Beauty, and Betty (DMEautomotive, 2014). The same survey found that contemporary women and younger millennial car owners are the most likely to personify their cars and associate a gender with their vehicle. Doug Van Sach, DMEautomotive's vice president, strategy and analytics, claims:

> The accepted cliché is that men have a more passionate, personal relationship with their beloved cars, while women view them as utilitarian machines that get you from Point A to B. But this research provides a different insight: women are significantly more likely to christen their vehicles, and also associate a female gender with them, while more men perceive their vehicles as male. And while we've seen numerous headlines on the fact that millennials are the least car-passionate generation in history, they're far more likely to personify and name their vehicles. This indicates an emotional and personal vehicle attachment in these demographics, one that auto marketers might want to explore and leverage (DMEautomotive, 2014).

The emotional attachment to and tendency to personify cars as feminine is not solely a Western phenomenon. Anthropomorphism plays a particularly important role in Japanese car culture, where cars are not so much signifiers of status as objects of endearment. Toyota, for example, actively anthropomorphizes the look of its cars. Referring to the latest edition of its popular Prius model, Toyota chief engineer Shoichi Kaneko claims, "The first three generations had what we call a 'happy face'. … With the fourth generation, we tried to appeal to younger customers as well, so we changed the face to be more defiant" (Bell, 2017). Toyota's new zero-emission hydrogen fuel cell car (which first became publicly available in 2018) is called Mirai, a female Japanese name meaning "future" (ibid.).

The proclivity to conflate women with cars, and perhaps with technology more generally, is underscored by the preponderance of disembodied female voices used to give voice to everything from automated answering machines to transit system announcements and GPS navigation devices. Female voices were used when automakers began to use automated voice prompts in cars, reminding us, among other things, that "your door is ajar." Since 2013, General Motors' OnStar in-car communication system in North America has been voiced by Diane Williamson. She reads from prepared scripts in a voice that the company, somewhat eerily, refers to as "Danielle" (Adams, 2013). The vast majority of GPS navigation systems also use a default female voice. One notable exception, however, occurred in Germany in the late 1990s, when BMW was forced to recall a female-voiced navigation system on its 5 Series cars after being inundated with calls from German men refusing to take directions from a woman (Griggs, 2011).

The feminization of car technology has recently extended into the world of virtual assistants that is also almost exclusively populated by female voices. Microsoft's Cortana, Amazon's Alexa, Google's Assistant, and Apple's Siri (voiced by Susan Bennett) are all programmed to use female voices as the default option. Rather than seeing this as perpetuating sexist stereotypes, Amazon conceives of Alexa as an empowered female:

> [W]e believe Alexa exudes characteristics you'd see in a strong female colleague, family member or friend—she is highly intelligent, funny, well-

read, empowering, supportive and kind. This is intentional. Alexa is a self-identified feminist (ask her!) and a proponent of human rights in general—and that is incredibly core to her personality and the way she interacts with our broad customer base (Liberatore, 2017).

Regardless of the above rationale, studies have shown that both men and women find a female voice "warmer and more understanding" than a male one (Liberatore, 2017). One might also consider the influence of science fiction movies to account for this phenomenon. Whether it is the homicidal HAL 9000 computer from *2001: A Space Odyssey* (1968), the rogue computer program in *WarGames* (1983), or Auto, the spaceship's autopilot function in *WALL-E* (2008), automated voices of authority or menace tend to be male. More subservient talking machines, such as the onboard computer from the *Star Trek: The Next Generation* television series or "Holly" from the British science fiction comedy series *Red Dwarf*, are more often female (Griggs, 2011). Amazon's characterization of Alexa as an empowered feminist aside, the use of automated female voices reinforces a common gender stereotype that connects women with notions of subservience and compliance and has the additional effect of making the technology appear more "natural" and benign than a male voice.

As manifest in the Mirai, female gender personification of the car still persists and is commonly reinforced in movies and popular culture. Electric cars such as the Toyota Prius have particularly been subject to female conflation. For example, in the 2011 comedy *No Strings Attached*, when a male character sees a Prius, he proclaims, "it's kind of girly." In a similar fashion, though evoking a potentially new reductive stereotype, *The Dilemma* (2011) sees the lead character asserting, "Ladies and gentleman, the electric car … is totally gay" (Parkin, 2017, p. 153).

Although cars have typically been associated with the feminine, whether in song, marketing, design, or simply in personal relation, it should not be ignored that cars have also been linked with aspects of male identity. Stick-shifts, emergency brakes, and pistons have all been commonly seen as having phallic symbolism. Muscle cars and trucks, in particular, have also been given masculine personas, often explicitly (and even aggressively) heteronormative and masculine. In an ad campaign for the 1997 Camaro, Chevrolet targeted straight white men with the bombastic, if not homophobic and racist, claims: "If everyone owned one, maybe we could have prevented disco," and that disco "was a pimple on the face of music history." The Camaro was unambiguously a car for "real men" (Parkin, 2017, p. 158).

The automobile is an expressive object that in part reflects the dominance of masculine machine culture. Cars are coded either as masculine—"figured as rocket, bullet, or gun, that is as a sexual extension of the male"—or conflated into a female being, "as flashy possession, mistress or wife" (Wernick, 1991, p. 74). Through such attitudes, "Prevailing patriarchal constructions of masculinity as dominance (where the car simply becomes an extension of the man) and femininity as submission (she handles really well) are reinforced" (Paterson, 2007, p. 47). The car/woman conflation, evident in the term "Tin Lizzie" to refer to an old Ford Model T (or, more generally, a run-down vintage automobile of any make), is rife in popular song.[2] Indeed, the male Irish rock band Thin Lizzy, best known for their hit "The Boys are Back in Town" (1976), was named for the Irish dialect pronunciation of "Tin."

In the early twentieth century in particular, the romance of the road seduced men into a belief that masculinity did not just promise freedom and mobility; it was defined by them. Conceived, designed, produced, and operated almost entirely by men, the automobile became a tangible sign of patriarchal power and authority that only relatively recently has become subject to appropriation by those who are not white, heteronormative males. As reinforced in popular literature and movies, the fast, powerful car represents the strong, virile male, regardless of physical size or sexual prowess. The skilful manipulation of a powerful car can be likened to the virtuosic control of a musical instrument such as an electric guitar. Both become instruments of masculine power and control and are assertive signifiers of male aggression, transforming into cathected objects that reveal male egos. More generally, cars, like music, are sources of both emotional intensity and physical or bodily stimulation.

To a large degree, the presence of cars in music videos, movies, and other media is a signifier of the masculine qualities of their drivers. They are, essentially, meant to be viewed as extensions of male identity. The cars are typically large, powerful, and often threatening in appearance. To own such a car is confirmation that one belongs to the culture of North American masculinity. Heteronormative males of almost any ethnicity or race are concerned with the maintenance of power. The phallus is the essential sign of power, and is typically metaphorically aligned with the automobile. Firearms can also be seen as representing a similar reinforcement of masculinity. In movies and music videos, the larger, more powerful the gun and the faster, more expensive the car, the more potent the masculinity of the man.

Car songs and gender conflations

As outlined in Chapter 1, popular songs portraying automobiles as women are not uncommon. The car/woman conflation, for example, is perhaps never more evident than in Prince's "Little Red Corvette" video from 1983. The woman's identity is completely tied to her identification with the car. Moreover, she is nameless and never speaks. The song's protagonist directly compares her to the Corvette, proclaiming, "Baby, you're much too fast," but that her "ride is so smooth, you must be a limousine."[3] The red colour of the car and the French diminutive feminine "ette" of the Corvette brand name also associate her with heat and sexuality. The woman is reduced to an inanimate sexualized object; she is a machine to be driven or manipulated according the sexual desires of the male protagonist.

Despite the ongoing tendency to conflate and objectify women with and as cars, several women have composed songs that demonstrate an empowered relationship with the car. Tracy Chapman's "Fast Car" (1988) and Melissa Etheridge's "You Can Sleep While I Drive" (1995), for example, both use the metaphor of driving to escape relationships with men. Chapman's song revisits and transforms the traditional association of masculine power with a "fast car" by reframing it as symbol of male oppression. These songs stand in marked distinction to such iconic Bruce Springsteen songs as "Born to Run" or "Thunder Road" (both from 1975) in which women are relegated to being passive passengers of active male drivers. Springsteen also makes overt car/ woman conflations. In his 1984 song "Pink Cadillac," he declares: "They say Eve tempted Adam with an apple … but … I know it was her pink Cadillac."[4]

Following the lead of their male counterparts who personify women as cars, and doubtless influenced by the litany of female/car conflations in car advertising (Parkin, 2017), some female singers have reversed the traditional narrative by comparing themselves to cars. In the year following Springsteen's "Pink Cadillac," Aretha Franklin personified herself as a "Pink Cadillac" in her Grammy-winning version of "Freeway of Love" (1985), encouraging her male protagonist to "jump in, it ain't no sin / Take a ride in my machine."[5] As a black woman from Detroit, there is a particular symbolism to Franklin's choice of a Cadillac. As Chris Lezotte (2013) observes:

> The vehicle not only reflects Franklin's significant status and success, but her position as driver rather than passenger marks her as an individual with a great amount of power and control. Through her appropriation of the car song, Aretha Franklin emboldens women to take control of the car, relationships, and their lives (p. 173).

In Lezotte's reading, Franklin is simply the driver of the car, not its embodiment. However, Franklin's suggestive invitation to "take a ride in my machine" shows her metaphorically conflating herself with the car. To be sure, she is in control; but her body is also the machine in which her love interest will metaphorically ride.

Evincing a similar form of automotive empowerment in her 2007 song "Shut Up and Drive," Rihanna also compares herself to a car, proclaiming: "I'm a fine tuned supersonic speed machine … My engine's ready to explode so start me up and watch me go, go, go."[6] The final line above even recalls a similar lyric from Franklin's "Freeway of Love": "drop the pedal and go, go, go." The song plays with and appropriates masculine car tropes, sonically forefronting heavy guitar power chords throughout. In the accompanying video, Rihanna provocatively drapes her body over the body of a car in the manner of a pin-up girl. The video, however, undermines such stereotypes by depicting a garage full of women mechanics all working on their cars, underscoring non-traditional female automotive empowerment, as does the admonition for men to simply "shut up and drive." Like Franklin before her, Rihanna is the one firmly in control.

Automobiles have also played a significant role in the work of Canadian country singer Shania Twain. In her hit 2002 single "In My Car (I'll Be the Driver)," Twain claims the car as a place of female agency and empowerment in her relationship. The protagonist describes how she does not mind if her boyfriend thinks he is the strong one in the relationship, "but in my car, I'll be the driver ... I come alive and ... I'm in control."[7] Twain highlights the need for negotiation with male relationships, but also the importance for women of having a space in which they are completely in control—a place, in a car or otherwise, in which they can "come alive" and escape the demands and expectations of others.

Taking a somewhat different approach from either Franklin or Rihanna, Twain overtly rejects the car/woman conflation. In "That Don't Impress Me Much" (1997), she rebuffs men who treat their cars as potential mates and objects of obsession comparable to women. The protagonist of the song complains about her partner's infatuation with his car, proclaiming: "I can't believe you kiss your car goodnight ... you must be jokin' right!"[8] Though something of a parody rather than an active call for women's empowerment, the song expresses a familiar female frustration over some men's automotive obsessions. The sentiment is taken up by Lady Gaga in her song "Glitter and Grease" (2010), in which she describes the love a past beau felt for his car, a watermelon-green Chevrolet El Camino. She complains that "Even though I'm real sexy he loves his car ... he's always with his car."[9] In response she is forced to compete by putting on more make-up or "glitter and grease."

The female disdain of men's female personification of and love for their cars has even extended into songs in which betrayed women take out their anger on their boyfriend's car. Carrie Underwood's "Before He Cheats" (2006), for example, makes a car/woman conflation between "a bleached-blonde tramp" and "his pretty little souped-up four-wheel drive," and takes out her vengeance on both the car (by carving her name into the leather seats, smashing the headlights, and slashing the tires) and, by analogy, the woman with whom her former lover was cheating.[10] Beyoncé's film version of her 2016 album *Lemonade*, in which she expresses her rage and frustration over her husband Jay Z's infidelity, also features her smashing parked cars with a baseball bat and crushing a row of cars behind the wheel of a monster truck. To some extent, we might interpret a reversal of the car-as-female conflation here. While the crushed cars may represent his many female relationships, they could also simply represent Jay Z himself. More clearly, however, Beyoncé seems to embody the image of the empowered monstrous truck.

In late 2018, Cadillac used the song "Bang Bang" (2014), recorded by Jesse J, Ariana Grande, and Nicki Minaj, to advertise its 2019 Cadillac XT4. The up-tempo song prominently features the line, sung by Jesse J, that makes a by now familiar car/woman conflation: "She got a booty like a Cadillac / But I can send you into overdrive."[11] Again, even in a trio of powerful women, the familiar car/woman conflation is forefronted. In an interview about the song, however, Jesse J saw it as empowering young women:

I looked at Nicki and myself and Ariana, all three of us look so different, and we're all equally confident. I was pointing at Nicki in the video, I was like, "she's got a booty like a Cadillac, but *I* can send you into overdrive!" I'm not going to rival what she has, but I've got what I've got. That's what I feel like young women, especially, need to hear. You have to love yourself, before anyone else can even come in. So for me, as a slim, tall-legs-no-boobs-no-bum kind of girl, I've got to represent (Garber-Paul, 2014, emphasis in original).

Underscoring the liberating message, at least as Jesse J sees it, the Cadillac commercial depicts a group of confident women driving the crossover SUV through a city while others skateboard down the sidewalk. The tag line voice-over proclaims: "Once again, driving is joyful." If nothing else, the song and advertisement speak to the somewhat disappointing normalization of the car/woman conflation in popular music and automotive culture and the extent to which women have come to identify with, and even personify themselves as, automobiles.

Car songs and female empowerment

As discussed in Chapter 1, in the hands of female singer-songwriters, such as in Tracy Chapman's "Fast Car," the automobile can be treated as a somewhat ironic tool for female liberation from male oppression. This trope was notably highlighted in the acclaimed road trip movie *Thelma and Louise* (1991). The two protagonists, played by Geena Davis and Susan Sarandon, respectively, find fleeting moments of joy and liberation while on the run in their 1966 Ford Thunderbird convertible. The car is also the tool by which they agree to commit suicide. In the iconic final scene, pursued by the police and expecting a lifetime in prison, the two embrace before gunning the accelerator pedal and driving off the side of the Grand Canyon.[12] As seen in *Thelma and Louise*, "Fast Car," and other female car songs such as Lucinda Williams' "Car Wheels on a Gravel Road" (1998), the car becomes a double-edged vehicle of female identity. On the one hand, it represents the potential for female liberation and escape from the mundane in a vein similar to what was previously typically available to men. On the other hand, it is also a potent symbol of the very culture of patriarchal dominance and control from which many women want and need to escape.

Joni Mitchell is among the most frequent and prominent female singer-songwriters to engage with the car as symbol. Songs such as "Big Yellow Taxi" (1970), "Car on a Hill" (1974), and "Refuge of the Roads" (1976) depict a complex, if not sometimes conflicted, relationship with the automobile. One of her most iconic songs, "Big Yellow Taxi," for example—aside from being an ode to environmental issues ("they paved paradise and put up a parking lot")—only mentions the titular taxi in the final verse, when late at night a "big yellow taxi took away my old man."[13] As such, the yellow taxi (which some have interpreted as a Metro Toronto Police car, which were painted yellow until 1986) facilitates her boyfriend/lover either walking out on her in an actual taxi or being taken away by the police. In either instance, the car is an obvious intruder on the environment, and represents a dystopic lost relationship, whether of our connection to nature or of a personal human love.

Mitchell's critically acclaimed, jazz-inflected album *Hejira* (1976) takes its title from the Arabic word for journey, specifically that of the prophet Muhammad from Mecca to Medina in 622. For Mitchell, the journey refers to a solo car trip she made from Maine to Los Angeles in 1975. The album's final track, "Refuge of the Roads," presents a somewhat different relationship with the car to that of "Big Yellow Taxi." Commenting on a picture of the Earth taken from space in a highway service station restroom, similar to the paving of paradise in "Big Yellow Taxi," Mitchell juxtaposes idyllic images of nature with the man-made construction of the highway: "you couldn't see a city ... or a highway ... or this baggage overload / Westbound and rolling taking refuge in the roads."[14] The highway and its attendant connection to the car, however, are seen here as a means of taking refuge, of escape. Later Mitchell claimed that the song was inspired by Chögyam Trungpa, a Buddhist teacher with whom she stayed for three days as she drove through Colorado on her way to Los Angeles. Trungpa, she claimed, took her to a place of "enlightenment where you have no ego and no drive ... It is bliss and it is nothing" (Fischer, 2006). Coming at the end of a record about the highway, this song interprets the car and highway driving as places of meditative spiritual liberation. Mitchell's "Car on a Hill," from her *Court and Spark* album (1974), provides yet another, perhaps more stereotypical female relationship with the car. The song narrates the experience of a woman waiting for her lover to return to her, listening in vain for the sound of his car driving up a hill: "I've been listening to the sirens and the radio ... I've been waiting for his car on the hill ... waiting for a car."[15] The car here is clearly a sonic representation of her lover who is out socializing without her. She waits for the sound of the car as she waits for him; and, thus, rather than view the car as an intruder on a relationship as in "Big Yellow Taxi" or as a metaphoric means of spiritual enlightenment and escape as in "Refuge of the Roads," in this instance she seems to reduce it to stereotypical masculine identity.

Thus Mitchell proves to have a multifaceted and sometimes conflicted relationship with the car. This is underscored by Chris Lezotte (2013), who, in discussing Mitchell's early song "(Born to) Take the Highway" (1966), observes:

[S]he does not use the automobile to describe feelings of power, status, or control, nor does she call upon the genre to reflect upon her conquests and success, sexual or otherwise. Rather, Mitchell's songs most often concern themselves with the small things that constitute women's lives. She speaks of the conflicts between independence and belonging, work and home, and love and pain (p. 167).

Challenging typical gender expectations, Mitchell reimagines the automobile as a metaphor for female experiences, positive and negative. She claims the car as a space of female self-determination, of refuge and deliberate escape, but also as an object of heartbreak and loss.

Car culture and women

While the most prevalent voices in the history of cars songs have been male, women have been as acutely affected by cars and car culture. Lezotte (2013) remarks:

> Men and women experience cars differently. Gendered expectations of driving behavior and automobile use influence how men and women think about cars. While women have, in the twenty-first century, become "as, if not more, wedded to the car than their male counterparts" [Walsh, 2008, p. 395], the reasons they value cars often differ considerably from those of male drivers (p. 164).

Despite the fact that women (not to mention homosexual, bisexual, and transgender individuals) "experience" the car as much as men, they are largely absent from histories of car culture. Influential automotive cultural studies such as by James Flink (1975) or Cynthia Dettelbach (1976), for example, mostly omit women's voices altogether. The general alienation and exclusion of women from technology has many roots. The historical development of capitalism in the West, relocating manufacturing from domestic, private dwellings to factories, is often seen as creating a gendered division of labour that "laid the foundations for male dominance of technology" (Wajcman, 1991, p. 21). Such inequities, of course, still inform much of today's popular music industry, which sees technologically centred occupations such as producer or studio engineer as overwhelmingly male realms.[16]

To a large degree, the hypermasculinization of car songs stems from the prevalent mythology about the inability of women to cope with technology and machines in general. To a large degree technology has been viewed as part of the productive sphere, which has been stereotypically characterized as masculine, whereas consumption has been imagined as feminine. In 1902, *Car Illustrated* published an article titled "Beauty at the Helm" in which a wealthy socialite, Mrs Harold Harmsworth, always drives with her mechanic because she "modestly professes to understand nothing of the mechanism of her motor" (Beauty at the helm, 1902). Nearly 50 years later, in 1949, *Vogue* magazine published a similar article, "Women and Their Cars," portraying several well-heeled female drivers, including Mrs Henry Ford and Bette Davis, as knowing "less about the insides of their cars than Peter Rabbit" and being "mechanically half-witted" (Women and their cars, 1949). Such mythologies ignored more than one instance of feminine mechanical proficiency, not the least of which was the active role that women played as automotive mechanics in wartime. In Britain during the First World War, for example, the Women's Army Auxiliary Corps (WAAC) actively recruited female driver-mechanics to service army automobiles. In the US, the Women's Motor Corps (founded in 1917) mandated that recruits possess both a state chauffeur's and mechanic's licence (Wosk, 2001, p. 141). The situation was little different in the Second World War, when women again worked as military mechanics thanks to American Congresswoman Edith Nourse Rogers, who introduced a bill to establish the Women's Army Corps (WAC). In England, Princess Elizabeth trained as a driver and mechanic as part of the Auxiliary Territorial Service (ATS). On the domestic home front, women were enlisted into various roles that ranged from playing baseball to repairing the older cars needed to get essential workers to their jobs. A slogan on the famous "Rosie the Riveter" posters proclaimed, "Do the job *HE* left behind."

The iconic "Rosie the Riveter" character arose first in popular music, not in visual art. A song of that title was written by Redd Evans and John Jacob Loeb in 1942 and issued by Paramount Music Corporation of New York. Released in early 1943, it was played on the radio and broadcast nationally. It was also performed by various artists in conjunction with popular big band leaders of the day. The lyrics feature Rosie "protecting" her boyfriend Charlie, who is a Marine, by "working overtime on the riveting machine." The song became quite popular, particularly in a version recorded by the Four Vagabonds, an African-American group, and rose up the hit parade. It seems likely that Norman Rockwell heard this song and was possibly influenced by it, given that he wrote the name "Rosie" on the lunch box in his cover for a 1943 issue of *The Saturday Evening Post* that forever popularized the image in the minds of the American public.

The Second World War undoubtedly challenged the image of women as mechanically inept, but unfortunately it was mostly only superficial and temporary. In reality, many women returned to being homemakers during the prosperity of the 1950s. Indeed, as suggested in Chapter 1 and to be further discussed in Chapter 5, men coming back home from the war were exposed to the latest in military communications and transportation technology, and brought the tinkering skills they acquired during the war to bear on the home front in the forms of hot rod and amateur audiophile culture.

From the inception of the automotive industry, women were often merely seen as adjuncts. Stephen Bayley's book *Sex, Drink and Fast Cars* (1986) typifies "man's relationship" with his car as being about power as articulated by designers, stylists, the advertising creative team, and marketers. For Bayley, a woman in a powerful car is "at once titillating and de-masculating" and represents an "overt sexual statement" (p. 32). The book underscores the by now familiar car/woman conflation. Indeed, to this day women are used to market cars in various media and at car shows as human representations of the car. As marketers are fond of saying, sex sells, and women have been commonly used to eroticize cars as objects of desire since automobiles came into existence. As early as 1903, Oldsmobile, for example, began using women in their advertisements (Wosk, 2001, p. 120). Although the iconography of women driving cars was also, in part, a cultural emblem of women's modernity, independence, and mobility (Hollywood studios, for example, commonly photographed stars such as Greta Garbo and Marlene Dietrich seated in automobiles to connect them with elegance, glamour, and success), more often than not the automotive industry simply fused women and cars as homologous entities of eroticized aspirational longing.

To this day, the use of attractive female models at car shows as silent adjuncts to this year's "model" of car is perhaps the most commonly recurring car-as-female conflation in the automotive industry. Women drape their bodies over cars as common objects of desire and control. In music, this state of affairs was expressed in The Cars' album *Candy-O* (1979), which is instantly recognizable for its cover art painting by *Playboy* and *Esquire* artist Alberto Vargas, a full-colour pin-up girl sprawled across a line drawing of a Ferrari. The Cars later reprised this look in their cover for *Heartbeat City* (1984), which featured an image of a pop art pin-up next to a 1971 Plymouth Duster 340 muscle car. This type of erotic car album art is, of course, not limited to The Cars and has been found in almost every type of popular music. Just a few examples include the covers of The Rip Chords' *Three Window Coup* (1964), which featured a hot rod 1934 Ford; Cannonball Adderley's *Sophisticated Swing* (1957), a Mercedes 300s; Ben Folds' *Super D* (2004), a Buick Super; or ZZ Top's iconic *Eliminator* (1983), a customized 1933 Ford Coupe that appeared in many of the band's subsequent videos.

Where women have not been simply used to sexualize the car, they have been cast by producers of car culture as figures who influence the purchases of men. In the interwar period, concern about women's corrupting influence on design pointed to an increasing emphasis on comfort and aesthetics. For example, 1920s' car manufacturer Edward "Ned" Jordan was acutely aware of the influence of women on car purchases, and so began incorporating and emphasizing ideals of comfort, beauty, and style in his car designs and advertising copy. His advertisement "Somewhere West of Laramie" (1923) is considered a seminal use of the power of emotion to sell a product. The copy made no mention of price or quality of the car, or of any of its features, but used instead an abstract drawing of a young woman on a horse racing against a Jordan Playboy Roadster:

> Somewhere west of Laramie there's a broncho-busting, steer-roping girl who knows what I'm talking about. She can tell what a sassy pony, that's a cross between greased lightning and the place where it hits, can do with eleven hundred pounds of steel and action when he's going high, wide and handsome. The truth is—the Playboy was built for her. Built for the lass whose face is brown with the sun when the day is done of revel and romp and race. She loves the cross of the wild and the tame.
>
> There's a savor of links about that car—of laughter and lilt and light— a hint of old loves—and saddle and quirt. It's a brawny thing—yet a

graceful thing for the sweep o' of the Avenue. Step into the Playboy when the hour grows dull with things dead and stale. Then start for the land of real living with the spirit of the lass who rides, lean and rangy, into the red horizon of a Wyoming twilight (Watkins, 2012, p. 50).

A stirring eulogy to women drivers in its equation of the freedom of cowboy (or cowgirl) life with the act of driving a car, the ad still underscores the masculine "Playboy" quality of the automotive industry as a whole. Much later, country artist Dave Stamey used the "Somewhere West of Laramie" ad as inspiration for his 2003 driving song of the same name.

In a rare early attempt to capture female buyers, for two model years, 1955–1956, Dodge produced the La Femme, a car specifically designed for women. The name alone, French for "the woman," overtly reinforces the female personification of cars discussed throughout this chapter. Advertising it as "The first and only car designed for Your Majesty, the Modern American Woman," the car came in white and pink ("Heather Rose") exterior while the interior featured "cashmere-soft Jacquard fabrics ... and special compartments to hold your rain apparel [and] shoulder bag." Notably the car came with matching pink rain boots and umbrella, as well as a "stunning fitted shoulder bag in soft rose, leather." The purse was also outfitted with coordinated accessories, including a make-up compact, comb, lipstick case, and cigarette case and lighter. Though Dodge discontinued the model after two years, it clearly evinced a stereotypical view of female drivers who could seemingly only be attracted to a car's sense of glamour, style, and fashion.

Lydia Simmons (1983) points out in her essay "Not from the Back Seat," for a man, a car

> is an extension of the self. For a woman it is generally a means to an end, a method of most expeditiously getting from one place to another. It is, rather than an extension of the self, a means of adornment, like a designer's dress. It is one of the primary means of setting female off from male (p. 153).

These words, though written nearly 40 years ago, continue to resonate in the current car advertising culture that still often markets cars to women by emphasizing facilitation of practical domestic chores. Car manufacturers still regularly tout features that appeal to childrearing and shopping, such as reliability, entertainment systems, cup holders, and storage.

Sexual and gendered identification has thus pervaded the car throughout its existence. It attests to the power of advertising and branding to both reflect and shape our sense of self-identity by gender and sexual orientation, in addition to age, race, and class. Personifying a car, lusting after it, or singing love songs to it, as has been common in both advertising and popular music, has served to solidify its place in the fabric of culture and as an anthropomorphic actor in our lives. The general objectification and conflation of women with cars continues to be a veritable roadblock to greater gender equality. Men's obsession with an inanimate object that they can control and modify to suit their desires clearly underscores and perpetuates the imbalance in power relations between men and women, if only by continuing to socialize others to its ideology. With regard to the influence that cars and car culture has had on shaping gender roles in society, Katherine Parkin (2017) concludes:

> An understanding of men's social and cultural control of cars does not deny the agency and power that women had in commanding their own cars, knowing how to repair them, or how to shop for them. Instead it challenges the expectation that women have had the same experience as men, and emphasizes that after more than one hundred years, women are still understood to be *poseurs* when they are at the wheel (p. 180).

As discussed above and in Chapter 1, popular music and musicians, acting almost as co-conspirators with automotive industry advertising, took an active and influential role in constructing and shaping this imaginary. Despite moments of resistance to stereotyped, highly sexualized, and objectified female conflations with cars—such as in previously discussed songs by Tracy Chapman, Joni Mitchell, or Shania Twain—both male and female singers sonically and corporeally celebrated the car/woman objectification and reinforced the automotive industry's calculated objective to sell cars to men as cathected objects of desire.

When car advertising did turn its sights on women drivers, it was careful to emphasize that the ideal consumers were unquestionably feminine and heterosexual. Just as male machismo has often been idealized by the type of car men drove, so too could a woman's sexuality be defined by the type of car she chose to drive. Lezotte (2013), for example, describes the typical characteristics of what is sometimes referred to as a "women's car":

> Sturdy, spacious, and utilitarian, the "women's car" was recognized as the perfect vehicle for carrying kids and cargo. Thus the ubiquitous station wagon of the 1950s and 1960s, the 1970 hatchback sedan, the popular minivan introduced in the late 1980s, and today's downsized SUV and crossover may be considered certifiable "women's cars." Despite changes in form, style, and cargo space over the past 60 years, the function of the woman's car has remained the same. And that is to firmly reinforce women's gendered roles as wife and mother (p. 516).

In this scenario, men drive for speed and excitement, and to experience the thrill of mechanically enabled independence. Women, however, are reduced to driving to fulfil mundane domestic tasks, thereby reinscribing heteronormatively gendered roles and expectations. An extension of the stereotypes involved in "women's cars" has been the recent introduction of an even more derisive and infantilizing term: "chick car." The term is typically used to describe a subcategory of smaller, inexpensive, fashionable, yet fun-to-drive cars. According to Lezotte (2012),

> the "chick car" category includes the Mazda Miata, Mitsubishi Eclipse, BMW MINI Cooper, VW New Beetle, Toyota RAV4, and for the more affluent, the Audi TT. The chick car category includes certain models that, in the words of journalist Ted Laturnus of the Globe and Mail, "hit women where they live." All of the cars, with the exception of the Audi, fall into the $19,000–$25,000 range, which is a lot of fun for the money. Most come in convertible versions, and many are available in a variety of colors other than silver or black. They are small, quick, and easy to maneuver; most chick cars are, in fact, two seaters. However, the most common attribute awarded to the chick car is "fun to drive" (p. 524).

Although some women may wish to drive cars with smaller and more elegant profiles that evince similar stereotypical female characteristics, others achieve a measure of what Judith Halberstam (1998) calls "female masculinity" by associating themselves with larger, more powerful, and thus stereotypically masculine cars such as trucks or SUVs.

While there is a tendency in our society to label certain makes of cars as either masculine or feminine, at least one popular brand, the Corvette, confounds this simplistic binary. Acknowledging the Corvette's feminized "ette" name, cultural theorist Jerry Passon (2011) claims the identity of the Corvette is transitive, depending on context:

> The Corvette takes on a transgressive gender role depending on how it is presented. At times the car appears to be a masculine signifier, enhancing the attractiveness and potency of its male driver. Yet the car sometimes seems to be female or takes the place of one: the Corvette itself becomes a love interest, a potential partner who replaces or rivals a human woman (p. 146).

The Corvette, in Passon's eyes, is essentially transgendered. By projecting both male and female characteristics onto the car, it remains anthropomorphized as a gendered construction—a construction that, when combined with the gendered associations of the music heard emanating within and without the car, typically enhances that identity.

While we commonly identify gender attributes with our cars, with a few exceptions gender is rarely considered in the experience of driving and using a car (Husband, Alam, Huettermann, & Fomina, 2014; Waitt, Harada, & Duffy, 2017). Mimi Sheller (2004) broaches the idea of "automotive emotions," the embodied dispositions of car users and the visceral and other feelings associated with car use (p. 223). Music, of course, is a prime actor in influencing our emotions. Gender is, in part, contingent on the affective and emotional forces triggered by how the material and expressive forces of sound and music cut across different sensory registers of bodies, and it is always situated within uneven power dynamics that differentiate bodies and spaces along the lines of gender. An Australian study on driving ethnography, for example, describes a female participant who habitually uses music as a force to make and remake sense of herself while driving. She explains how her affective and emotional capacities to drive are reduced without the presence of music and in the presence of her husband. She comments:

> I am very nervous when my husband is a passenger. … I was thinking that the other day … he makes me nervous. He got in the car. Turned my music off. Turned the heater off. "Why did you go around that truck?" "Why don't you get in this lane?" "You'd be better if you went this way." … I am much more confident when he is not in the car (Waitt et al., 2017, p. 334).

Without her familiar music and in the presence of her husband, the possibilities of who this woman can become and how she drives her car are altered. Michael Bull (2004a) claims that through their choice of music in their car, people "actively construct the meaning of their space" and change how spaces, the related journeys, and the self are configured and understood (p. 245). Consider the performance of a parent driving with or without their children. In the former instance, the music chosen might be a recording of familiar children's songs in an effort to entertain, distract, or soothe the kids during the ride. The same parent driving by themselves might be more inclined, at least momentarily, to use music as a form of therapeutic escape from their parental identity, potentially choosing music from their past that reaffirms their own sense of self and of past experiences tied to their biography associated with the music. The car provides an intimate and secure space that can facilitate a variety of self-regulating or therapeutic practices (e.g., singing or simply actively listening to recorded music) that help construct and reinforce gendered subjectivities.

Despite the continuing presence of sexist car-as-phallus or car/woman conflations and the historical male dominance of the automotive industry, recent statistics have shown a striking increase in the number of female car buyers and drivers. A survey from June 2014 by Frost and Sullivan (2015), for example, found that for the first time the number of licensed female drivers in the US outnumbered all male drivers over the age of 25. The statistics were roughly similar in Canada, Germany, and the UK. As further evidence of the increase in female influence on the industry, in 2014 Ford identified "the Female Frontier" as a top-ten micro-trend, recognizing the growing purchasing power of women. Among millennial consumers, Ford found that females were actually overtaking male buyers, making up 53 per cent of the market for that demographic. The annual Detroit auto show, once a bastion of male attention and attendance, now attracts an audience that is roughly 50 per cent women (Kwong, 2016). Further evidence of this new "frontier," so to speak, is that dealers now offer healthier snacks, spa treatments, manicures, and yoga sessions. Such attractions, perhaps unintentionally but certainly ironically, still play to gendered stereotypes relating to the objectification of women and a concomitant emphasis on regulating their bodies; but they also nonetheless mark something of a change of emphasis.[17]

With the proliferation of the car among the middle class, the 1950s witnessed some of the earliest attempts to capture female consumers. During this period, manufacturers began to persuade consumers of the benefits of owning a second car, typically to facilitate women's lives in managing their domestic responsibilities, such as shopping and picking up children from school, while simultaneously offering them a greater sense of independence. One of the most high profile of these early attempts to market to women came in the form of Chevrolet's connection to the singer Dinah Shore. In 1951, Chevrolet sponsored *The Dinah Shore Show* (1951–1960) and *Dinah Shore's Chevy Show* (1956–1963), which featured Shore singing the patriotically themed "See the U.S.A. in Your Chevrolet" (1949) at the beginning and end of every episode.[18] The short song—with the lines "See the USA in your Chevrolet ... America's the greatest land of all"—became something of an anthem for the era, approaching patriotic status.[19] As discussed by Mark Laver (2015), Shore "was presented as physically attractive without being overtly sexually provocative—an image that Chrysler marketers believed was key to appealing to the increasingly important demographic of Euro-American, suburban mothers" (p. 97). Blonde, elegantly attired, and singing non-threatening pop songs and show tunes, Shore became

> the constructed embodiment of the physical and social norms of the American mainstream [that] was critical to her credibility as Chevrolet's pitchwoman. ... To her viewers (and through Chevrolet's marketing), Shore represented the archetypal American woman—selfless, a pillar of virtue, and a metonym for the American home (Laver, 2015, p. 101).

Although it is unclear how successful the relationship was in terms of selling cars to women, Shore's patriotic ode indubitably helped make Chevrolet the most popular automobile brand in America. In the 1950s, Chevy's sales in the US averaged one million or more cars and trucks every year. A GM spokesman told *Time* magazine in December 1957 that the company considered its relationship with Dinah Shore to be "one of the most enduring love affairs in TV" (Is there anyone finah?, 1957).

Recently, car manufacturers have been more actively responding to the power of female consumers. Auto industry analyst Jessica Caldwell observes that it only makes sense to go after household decision-makers: "Women are a little more pragmatic. So they're looking at things like safety, price, fuel economy—things that make a good purchasing decision" (Kwong, 2016). This typically translates into more female interest in hybrid cars, as well as cars with attributes such as increased "ride height," which imparts the feeling of being more in control. While market research shows that men continue to be interested in technology, performance, and luxury, the same research shows that women are more likely to prioritize value, practicality, and security (Kwong, 2016). Many manufacturers have responded to this data by introducing more family-friendly features. The 2016 Chrysler Pacifica minivan, for example, offers an optional in-car vacuum cleaner, allows for moving seats forward even with a forward-facing baby seat installed, and is easier for children to step into. Such features, however, seem to limit the driving needs and desires of women to reductively and stereotypically female issues surrounding the nurturing of family safety and convenience.[20] It should also be noted, however, that despite the marked increase in the number of women buying cars and their overall influence on the market, in 2016 fewer than 18 per cent of auto industry employees were women (Kwong, 2016).

Female brand ambassadors are also becoming more influential in the realm of car marketing. In the past, women appeared in car advertising as objects displayed alongside or draped over the car, ostensibly to create some sort of anthropomorphic identification with beauty and the sexual attractiveness of the car. More recently, female celebrities are increasingly seen as important means of influencing buying behaviour. One automotive blog aimed at women asks the question:

> But realistically, how influential are female brand ambassadors? Does seeing another woman driving a car, whether she's famous or not, make us want to drive that car? I'm inclined to think yes. We are more influenced by other women in our consumer choices than we care to admit. Have you ever walked into a shop, watched the person in front of you lift something off a rail and then grab one for yourself just because she looks like she has good taste? (Wheelsforwomen, 2013)

However, as this opinion implies, celebrity female car endorsements seem limited to being primarily aimed at other female buyers, rather than at a general public. Indeed, at least one study in the UK has shown that 30 per cent of 854 respondents purchased an item because of a celebrity endorsement, and that 66 per cent of celebrity-endorsed product buyers were women (Kirkova, 2014).

Despite the perhaps condescending domestic features of the 2016 Pacifica described above, Chrysler is notable for being one of the first car brands to have employed a female celebrity as part of a national automotive advertising campaign. In 2002, Celine Dion signed a $14-million, three-year deal with Chrysler to be its celebrity spokesperson. She was subsequently featured in a series of lavish black-and-white television commercials for three models: the 2004 Chrysler Pacifica sport wagon, the Crossfire coupe, and the Town and Country Mini minivan. The Pacifica ads were underscored by her then-current hit single, a cover of Cyndi Lauper's "I Drove All Night," married to the tag line "A New Concept of Style and Confidence." The unveiling of the car was designed to coincide with the premiere of her Las Vegas show at Caesar's Palace, "A New Day ... Presented by Chrysler" (PR Newswire, 2003).

The ads feature Dion singing and driving in the various models. The Pacifica ad, for example, begins with Dion singing an *a cappella* version of "I Drove All Night" while sitting in the back seat of the stationary car. The soundtrack then transitions to the full-blown recording of the song as the car begins to move. The sleek black-and-white imagery is upscale and sophisticated, in keeping with Chrysler's strategy to attract younger, more affluent consumers. The Town and Country Mini commercial casts Dion in a stereotypical housewife role. Set to her power ballad "Have You Ever Been in Love?" it shows Dion lovingly interacting with her infant son, who is in a car seat in the minivan. Once again, the image is one of domesticity, emphasizing the sense of safety and security she provides for her son by buying the Chrysler minivan. However, focus groups told Chrysler that Dion appealed to consumers with an average age of 52. The three-year contract was ended after little more than a year. Bob Coppola, Chrysler's account marketing group director, remarked, "None of the Celine ads did especially well at breaking through the clutter. ... It was just about average" (qtd in Stein, 2003).

Male musicians who have endorsed car brands are numerous and range from Sting (Jaguar) to Bob Dylan and Berry Gordy (Cadillac), Bob Seeger (Chevrolet Trucks), Eminem (Chrysler), and Toby Keith (Ford), among many others. Car companies that have chosen to associate themselves with female musicians, however, are much rarer. In addition to the failed Celine Dion–Chrysler campaign, notable exceptions include Shirley Temple for Dodge and Jennifer Lopez for the Fiat 500.[21]

In 1936, child actress and singer Shirley Temple became the promotional spokesperson for Dodge and generated memorable tag lines in print advertising, such as "My Goodness! ... what a Grand Car!" Besides being a spokesperson for Dodge, various merchandise capitalized on Temple's wholesome image, generating a range of product endorsements, including Shirley dolls, dishes, and clothing. More recently, in 2011, Jennifer Lopez appeared in several commercials for the Fiat 500. Set to her single "Until It Beats No More," the ads depict Lopez driving through her old neighbourhood in the Bronx in the inexpensive subcompact car. However, few found the scenario plausible, and both fans and the automotive press roundly criticized it. *Adweek*, for example, sneered: "Jennifer Lopez still trying to convince you she drives a Fiat" (Stanley, 2011). Much like the failed Celine Dion campaign, the credibility gap between the celebrity musician who was judged to have very little actual relationship to or knowledge of the car in question proved toxic. While not every male celebrity endorsement has been an unqualified success, such a credibility gap is noticeably absent in most car endorsements by men.

One of the more unusual endorsements of a car by a female musician occurred in 2011 when Toyota employed the virtual Japanese vocaloid pop star Hatsune Miku to endorse its new Corolla.[22] The online ads announced

"Hatsune Miku + Corolla, driven by the sound of success"; "Corolla, the official car of Hatsune Miku"; and "The new 2011 Toyota Corolla and Hatsune Miku have two very important things in common: Big dreams in a compact package" (Toyota, 2011). The advertising also offered special giveaways to fans and featured various video advertisements showing the anime Miku driving the new Corolla.

Several other international female singers have endorsed car brands. Canadian jazz singer Diana Krall, for example, was featured in Chrysler Canada's "This is my car" campaign for the 2002 Sebring. Set to Krall's song "The Look of Love" (2001), the campaign played off Krall's elegant and sophisticated image to once again anthropomorphically sexualize the car (Laver, 2015). Spanish car manufacturer SEAT sponsored Colombian singer Shakira's European tour in 2010. As part of the deal, Shakira became a brand ambassador for its cars. SEAT launched in her honour two special editions of its Ibiza and Leon models, the so-called "Good Stuff" editions (the name taken from a song on her 2009 album *She Wolf*). A SEAT spokesperson declared, "This agreement will link the young, sporty image of the SEAT brand to the musical talent of Shakira, currently enjoying great success with her latest album, *She Wolf*" (D. Williams, 2010). Similarly, in 2011, Australian pop superstar Kylie Minogue teamed up with Lexus UK to endorse its new CT 200h. The CT 200h was launched that year as the world's first full hybrid executive compact car. The "Quiet Revolutions" advertising campaign (so called because the car can be driven in near silence relative to conventional automobiles) featured Minogue whispering "shush" to silence a cacophonous crescendo of celebrity drummers before driving off in the seemingly silent environment of the car.[23] While male pop and country singers still enjoy the vast majority of automotive endorsement deals (see Chapter 4), these examples testify, particularly in the international marketplace, to an increased willingness of car manufacturers to align themselves with female pop stars and their influence on the car-buying public.

In addition to recruiting female celebrity singers to endorse various automotive brands, a recent trend has been to link new brands of cars with unknown or independent female musicians. In a confluence of several advertising trends, Chevrolet Canada created a spot called "Canadian Dream" for its 2018 Chevrolet Cruze that features aspiring independent r & b singer-songwriter Carol Ellyn. The commercial features Ellyn driving through Toronto while singing one of her songs on the way to a recording session. Her voiceover states that she is a "full-time office project manager"; her Cruze is "my recording studio, my home office"; and her dream is "to make and share music that makes people feel great." Chevrolet's YouTube site also promotes the car as

> a safe space where she can focus, sing, and get inspired. With features like Apple CarPlay and 4G LTE Wi-Fi, Carol is able to connect with her work, with her studio, and very soon, her fans. We're inspired by people

like Carol who chase after their bigger dreams everyday (Chevrolet Canada, 2018).

The commercial and related YouTube site smartly taps into the appeal of the car to an empowered working woman and her aspirational goals, emphasizing the car's connectivity features that facilitate that empowerment and those aspirations, as well as the non-corporate artistic values associated with an independent musician.

Nissan Canada employed a similar though somewhat more dramatic scenario in its "Move to Your Own Beat" ad in support of its 2018 Nissan Kicks model. The ad depicts a young woman driving at night in a vaguely threatening dockyard area. An ominous voiceover states, "[T]he call came in [depicted on a subtitled 7 inch touchscreen display] … the meet up was on, but these aren't the kind of places that have signs, but then out of nowhere they found me." After being cut off by another car and forced to use the car's "Intelligent Emergency Braking," we realize that the Kicks' driver is a DJ arriving and being met by promoters at an after-hours, likely unlicensed, gig. The ad ends with the protagonist setting up her turntables and intoning, "And finally it was my time!" It ends with her in control of a raucous crowd of dancing admirers (Nissan Canada, 2018). Again, an aspirational female musician is shown succeeding because of the features of the car she drives. Similar to Carol Ellyn's Cruze ad, the car provides the musician with a safe environment, while her role as an accomplished yet independent DJ aligns the brand with the aesthetic and ideological values associated with an independent artist. The alliance of car companies with the values and aesthetic ideology of independent and alternative musicians is more fully explored in Chapter 4, but for now these examples suggest that car companies are increasingly realizing the value of advertising to younger working women, often co-opting the values attached with independence not only as women but also as musical individuals.

LGBTQ identities and cars

For gay North American males, the stakes surrounding automobile use and ownership can be much different than for heterosexual males. Heteronormative society still often pressures gay men to hide their sexual orientation; hence, for many, the relationship with powerful cars is a relatively limited aspect of their identity, though to be sure there is no shortage of gay car clubs. The Lambda Car Club International, for example, is the largest organization run by and for gay and lesbian automobile collectors, with 2000 members in two dozen chapters across the United States, as well as one in Toronto.[24] It is growing at a rate of 4 or 5 per cent annually (Caldwell, 2005). In a world where various kinds of car club proliferate, Lambda holds a special place, culturally and aesthetically. Though the club has some obvious social differences in terms of its gay-friendly environment, there are also differences in what is considered to be valuable in a car. As one member suggests,

> The straight men tend more to like the muscle cars, and when they start the engine at a show, they'll all run over to it. [However,] we'll race over to a car that's a beautiful pink or amethyst, and we'll all say, "Look at that brocade" (Caldwell, 2005).

Perhaps in sympathy with their own often marginalized identities, members also tend to collect "orphan" cars that are no longer manufactured, such as Ramblers and Packards. Heavily accessorized classic luxury cars, such as Lincolns and Chrysler Imperials (nicknamed PPAs, for Power-Princess Approved), are also favoured by many members, and are often painted in customized colours and adorned with added accessories, such as mink stoles and jewellery. Such overt expressions of gay-friendly car culture are, however, relatively rare.

Car culture discourses also extend into queer musical narratives and representations. Critically acclaimed, openly gay rapper and r & b artist Frank Ocean, for example, has heavily featured cars throughout his work. Unlike the stereotypical use of automobiles in hip hop as symbols of wealth, power, and masculinity, Ocean uses them as visual and lyrical symbols to narrate important moments in his life. Cars are not only lyrically foregrounded, but also placed in the background to further the storytelling and setting of the music rather than simply serve as materialistic objects. The cover of his debut mix tape, *nostalgia, ULTRA* (2001), features an image of a sunset-orange 1980s' BMW E30 M3—the singer's self-described "dream car" (Westbrook, 2017)—parked oddly at night within a park-like grassy forest. Caught in the glare of the camera's flash, it perhaps embodies the uncomfortable experience of many gay men, and perhaps even the rapper himself as a flamboyant performer, exposed and awkwardly placed in a world of stereotypically hypermasculine rap. Indeed, Ocean has actively used cars in his work to shape his emotional vulnerability and intimacy. He therefore employs vehicles for a variety of purposes, though seldom, as is stereotypically found throughout the history of rap, as a boast or marker of affluence. Most obviously, they appear in song titles such as "White Ferrari," from the 2016 album *Blond* (sometimes also titled *Blonde*), or "Mitsubishi Sony," from the visual album *Endless* (also 2016). Moreover, Ocean also uses vehicles to mark time, to situate his listeners in a setting. On the *Blond* song "Nights," he croons: "In 1998 my family had that Acura, oh, The Legend, kept at least six discs in the changer."[25]

Ocean's fixation with cars appears to be (at least in part) a complicated expression of his masculinity and sexual identity. In a 2016 essay from his magazine *Boys Don't Cry*, he speculates that his fascination with cars stems from "a deep subconscious straight boy fantasy." He continues: "Consciously though, I don't want straight—a little bent is good" (Kozack, 2016). The essay also describes a fantasy of being both confined by and liberated by the car:

The claustrophobia hits as the seatbelt tightens, preventing me from even leaning forward in my seat. The pressing on internal organs. I lean back and forward to release it. Then backwards and forward again. There it is— I got free. How much of my life has happened inside of a car? I wonder if the odds are that I'll die in one. Knock on wood-grain. Shouldn't speak like that. We live in cars in some cities, commuting across space either for our livelihood, or devouring fossil fuels for joy. It's close to as much time as we spend in our beds, more for some (Kozack, 2016).

Among other issues, and including the ubiquity and ethereal nature of interacting with cars in an urban environment, Ocean appears in this confession to internalize the car as an expression of his (at times) conflicted sexuality. Straightness is likened to a claustrophobic car with a seat belt that confines and presses against his internal organs. He has to contort his body (and perhaps his mind) to liberate himself from it.

Perhaps nowhere is Ocean's identification with the car more in evidence than in his hauntingly beautiful "White Ferrari," from *Blond*. The song narrates a relationship Ocean had when he was 16, and lyrically plays with the image of a ride in a white Ferrari as a metaphor for a fast and pure homosexual relationship: "I didn't care to state the plain, kept my mouth closed / We're both so familiar … White Ferrari"[26] The song features several samples of the Beatles' "Here, There and Everywhere" (1966) and is sung with an intimate, close mic'd vocal foregrounded in the mix. It is accompanied at times by a simple strummed acoustic guitar marked by the audible sound of fingers squeaking on the strings that lends an extra air of personal, heartfelt authenticity. Ocean performs the vocal in an emotionally wrenching half-spoken, half-sung manner. While the arrangement and lyrics clearly highlight the human pain of a past broken relationship, Ocean's voice is notably augmented by double-tracking and autotuning throughout. To some extent, we may see in this a form of duality that characterizes Ocean's aesthetic. The mixing of the human and the machine, as manifest in the autotuning and electronic manipulation of his voice (as well as the microphones and other technology with which he engages during the recording process), is another extension of his merging of human identity with the car. Reinforcing this latter point is the fact that towards the end of "White Ferrari" we hear background samples of the high-pitched whine of a revving high-performance car engine (presumably a Ferrari) into which Ocean's voice plaintively morphs and imitates. His voice, one of the prime markers of his identity, becomes that of the car. But it is not a representative imitation of the rough, throaty growl of a prototypically aggressive, macho car engine that one might expect from a stereotypically heteronormative singer. Instead, it is a delicate, almost excruciating wistful wail of a finely tuned, high-performance machine. In many ways, Ocean actively wrestles with a particularly complex form of W. E. B. Dubois' notion that black Americans operate within a condition of double-consciousness that sees them shifting between the conflicting ideals of white

America and black reality (see Chapter 2). For Ocean, however, this duality is compounded by the added double-consciousness of his non-normative sexual identity within the traditionally normatively heterosexual worlds of hip hop and r & b.

Indeed, the conflicted relationship that Ocean evokes in "White Ferrari" is made more explicit in his "Open Letter," posted on Tumblr in 2012:

> Imagine being thrown from a plane. I wasn't in a plane though. I was in a Nissan Maxima, the same car I packed up with bags and drove to Los Angeles in. I sat there and told my friend how I felt. I wept as the words left my mouth. I grieved for them, knowing I could never take them back for myself. He patted my back. He said kind things. He did his best, but he wouldn't admit the same. He had to go back inside soon, it was late and his girlfriend was waiting for him upstairs. He wouldn't tell the truth about his feelings for me for another 3 years. I felt like I'd only imagined reciprocity for years. Now imagine being thrown from a cliff. No, I wasn't on a cliff. I was still in my car telling myself it was gonna be fine and to take deep breaths (Ocean, 2012).

Again, the car is a central character in Ocean's account. Contravening stereotypical masculine identification with the car as a heteronormative object of power and control, the car in both Ocean's music and life becomes both a place of secretive confinement and claustrophobia and a place of safety and intimacy. In some sense, it is a form of closet on wheels, though one that also offers the paradoxical possibility of liberation and truthfulness. To be sure, Frank Ocean's public disclosure of same-sex desires is representative of an alternative masculinity that is articulated throughout his work. Indeed, alternative masculinities seem to be increasingly foregrounded in a music culture variously labelled by the music industry and music press as "Alt R&B," "PBR&B" (Pabst Blue Ribbon R&B), or "hipster R&B" (Dhaenens & De Ridder, 2015; Fennessey, 2011; Soderberg, 2012). Through his unconventional self-identification with high-performance cars, Frank Ocean overtly challenges the hegemonic construction of heteronormative black masculinity.

The rock group Queen provides another, earlier instance of artists engaging in an unconventional sexual identification with cars. Their song "I'm in Love with My Car (gotta feel for my automobile)" (1975) seems to overtly reinforce the common trope of personifying the car as a woman in overtly sexualized terms: "With the pistons a-pumpin'" and "With my hand on your grease gun … it's such a thrill when your radials squeal."[27] Released as the B-side to the smash hit "Bohemian Rhapsody," the song was written by the band's drummer, Roger Taylor, and features the sound of the revving engines of Taylor's car, an Alfa Romeo, at its conclusion. While at first glance it may seem a continuation of the standard hypermasculine car/woman conflation evident in a myriad of pop songs, the lyrics and Taylor's vocal delivery exhibit an almost campy, over-the-top macho tone in keeping with the band's, and particularly lead singer Freddy Mercury's, flamboyant glam rock style. Fluid sexual identities are a common theme throughout Queen's work, as evident in songs and accompanying videos to "Bohemian Rhapsody" and "I Want to Break Free" (1984), in which the band perform in drag, or the unsubtle allusions to bisexuality in "Bicycle Race" (1978), which features the lyrics "I want to ride my bicycle / I want to ride it where I like" (see McLeod, 2011).[28] "I'm in Love with My Car" seems to go beyond the standard metaphor of the woman-as-car. In this instance, the girl is actively rejected in favour of the pleasures of a physical relationship with an actual car ("Told my girl I'll have to forget her"). Here, given the rejection of a female relationship, one might suggest that the car represents something of a homoerotic relationship. The lyrics "the pistons a-pumping" and "with my hand on your grease gun" would seem to reinforce this reading.

Other LGBTQ artists have, in much the same manner as many heterosexual songwriters, actively connected cars and sex. Acclaimed queer songwriter and educator Melissa Ferrick's "Drive" (2000), for example, makes an overtly sexual connection between sex and the act of driving. "I'll hold you up and drive you all night / I'll hold you up and drive you baby 'till you feel the daylight."[29] A pulsating rhythmic accompaniment and seductively intimate vocal delivery underline the sexual metaphors at play.

Queer trip hop duo Rituals of Mine (Terra Lopez and Dani Fernandez, formerly known as Sister Crayon) portray yet another form of queer relationship with the car in their ethereal song and video, "Ride or Die" (2016). The song, much like Ferrick's "Drive," describes the sensuality of same-sex female sexual attraction and, rather simply pretending to be friends, the desire for a "ride or die." The title references hip hop/street slang, where a "ride or die chick" will stay true to her man and ride out any and all (often illicit) problems with him or die trying. Here, instead of referring to the stereotypically patriarchal act of finding a woman who will do anything for her man, the term is used in the context of same-sex female desire. The song is sung in a fragile, breathy style underpinned by a slowly pulsating bass-heavy synth accompaniment and an almost church-like chordal accompaniment, evoking a style somewhat reminiscent of trip hop artists Portishead or Massive Attack. The black-and-white video is entirely in slow motion, adding to its sensuality. Shot around the Oakland, California, neighbourhood of 34th Street and San Pablo, it is largely filmed from the perspective of someone cruising the neighbourhood in a car, viewing both people on the street and other aspects of car culture, including police cars, lowriders, and street bikes. While maintaining a gritty street culture perspective common in hardcore hip hop videos, it is notably populated by LGBT folks and other marginalized community members. As Terra Lopez explains:

> [We wanted] to film our actual friends, our girlfriends, real people who live in the hoods where we lived. … There aren't any actors in this video—it's all people in their elements, with their loved ones, their friends, their

passions in Oakland. … The spirit, the hustle, the grit, the intensity and urgency of Oakland. We also felt it was vital to showcase the under-represented (our folks in the LGBT community, POC, women). That was more important to us than anything (Rituals of Mine's video, 2016).

In a sense, the song and video act as a re-territorialization of stereotypically heterosexual male car culture. In "Ride or Die," Rituals of Mine co-opt the heterosexual male gaze and the hypermasculinity typically tied with male car culture in favour of a queer experience of the street.

The LGBTQ community is not typically the focus of car marketers who prefer, as outlined above, to target the larger market demographic of hetero-sexual men or women. However, in one of the more unusual marketing cam-paigns in the early 1990s, Subaru of America, in the face of declining sales, began to actively market their cars specifically to lesbian consumers. Subaru's unique selling point was, and still is, the fact that all-wheel drive is a standard feature on all of its models. In conducting research to reach a wider customer base, the company identified five key groups who were responsible for half of its American sales: teachers and educators, healthcare professionals, IT pro-fessionals, individuals interested in the outdoors, and lesbians. Regarding the latter category, Tim Bennett, Subaru's director of advertising at the time, explained: "When we did the research, we found pockets of the country like Northampton, Massachusetts, and Portland, Oregon, where the head of the household would be a single person—and often a woman" (Mayyasi, 2016). Further research showed that most of these women were lesbian. Subaru's marketers found that lesbian Subaru owners appreciated that the cars were dependable and good for hauling large amounts of gear without being as big as a truck or an SUV. They felt the car "fit them and wasn't too flashy" (ibid.). Many even liked the name itself—Subaru is the Japanese name for the Pleiades star cluster M45, also known as "the Seven Sisters." At the time, lesbians were shown to be four times more likely than the average consumer to buy a Subaru.

Subaru's strategy called for targeting the five core groups and creating print and billboard ads based on its appeal to each. For healthcare professionals, the ads emphasized that a Subaru with all-wheel drive could get them to the hospital in any weather conditions; for rugged individualists, a Subaru could handle dirt roads and haul gear. For lesbians, it fit their active, low-key life-style. It was a risky move for a major automobile manufacturer, taken at a time when popular culture had yet to integrate the LGBTQ cause. Main-stream movies and television shows with gay characters were still some time in the future. When Ellen DeGeneres' character in the sitcom *Ellen* came out as gay in 1997, many advertisers pulled their ads. Similar boycotts were mounted earlier in 1994 when an IKEA ad featured a gay couple. Subaru America, despite facing some internal corporate opposition and public back-lash, nonetheless went ahead with its campaign.

The first Subaru print ads that portrayed openly lesbian couples appealed to women, but did not resonate with lesbian audiences as expected (Mayyasi, 2016). Instead, a more successful strategy/approach developed ads with more covert and playful inside references to lesbian culture. One campaign, for example, showed Subaru cars that had licence plates that said "Xena LVR" (a reference to *Xena: Warrior Princess*, a television show whose female protagonists appeared to be lovers) or "P-TOWN" (a moniker for Provincetown, Massachusetts, a popular LGBTQ vacation spot). Many ads had tag lines with not so subtle double meanings. "Get out. And stay out" could refer both to exploring the outdoors in a Subaru or to coming out as gay. Other tag lines such as "It's not a choice. It's the way we're built" or "Entirely comfortable with its orientation" could refer to the fact that all Subarus came with all-wheel drive or to LGBTQ identity. Some ads featured more risqué double entendres such as "Open bed!" "Takes all your toys!" "Tie-down hooks!" "Non-stop action!" "Firm grip!" and "Wanna take a ride?"

Subaru was unabashed in its support of gay and lesbian customers. The company sponsored events like Gay Pride parades; partnered with the Rainbow Card (a credit card that offered donations to gay and lesbian causes); became a sponsor of the Showtime series *The "L" Word*; and, perhaps most notably, hired Martina Navratilova, a former tennis pro and a lesbian, to appear in its ads. The hiring of Navratilova as the face of a major car manufacturer was a particularly important moment in the world of corporate advertising as she had lamented the fact that gay athletes typically had "to hide in the closet to sell [themselves] to Madison Avenue" (Mayyasi, 2016).

At the time of its initial print campaign, Subaru executives were unsure about the potential "intrigue" created by the perception of the ad campaign's use of gay-friendly double entendres (Mayyasi, 2016). The 1990s also saw the rise of the so-called "gay-vague" ads in which a constructed scenario could be read as gay while maintaining heterosexual plausibility. Mike Wilke, founder of AdRespect, an online archive of LGBT-themed ads, coined the term "gay vague" to describe the way companies can reach queer audiences while mitigating risk of a conservative backlash (Klara, 2013). It was also in the 1990s that the gay suggestiveness of certain print advertising began to migrate to television. Consider Volkswagen's spot "Sunny Afternoon" from 1997. To the notably foregrounded accompaniment of German pop group Trio's hit song "Da Da Da" (1982), two young men rescue a piece of furniture discarded on the street using their VW Golf. The ad debuted during the famous coming-out episode of the ABC sitcom *Ellen*. Wilke explains that the show "was a media and cultural moment—and then this commercial comes on. But the two men were not overtly defined. They could be friends, roommates, or boyfriends. It allowed for multiple interpretations." These ads and the soundtracks that accompanied them were to some extent coded messages to the gay community that paved the way for more open marketing to LGBTQ consumers.

In 2006, Subaru created three custom-designed TV spots for Viacom's 24-hour gay channel, LOGO, making it one of the first advertisers to do so. After generations of invisibility, these commercials featuring kisses and affectionate displays enjoyed by same-sex couples (both gay and lesbian), and even transgender persons have been warmly received. Gay Pride is also celebrated, and some commercials seem to sell the idea of being gay more than the actual product. The soundtrack for all three commercials feature understated electro pop with aerial, breathy female vocals provided by the group Last Looks.

Subaru's gay- and mostly lesbian-focused marketing campaign was successful, and the company's efforts continue today. In focus groups and online polls, gay and lesbian consumers consistently choose Subaru vehicles as their favourite cars and/or Subaru as the most gay-friendly brand (Mayyasi, 2016). While the popularity of Subaru among LGBTQ customers did not single-handedly account for the resurrection of the company, it certainly did not hurt its reputation or sales. By the 2010s, the only car company that grew faster than Subaru was the electric car manufacturer Tesla (Mayyasi, 2016). It is somewhat heartening that the origins of the stereotypical lesbian affinity for Subarus are not the result of a cynical marketing campaign, but a progressive one. In a sense, all Subaru did was notice a group of under-represented customers and create ads for them. But it was nonetheless a significant moment in advertising in acknowledging a group that was often treated as unwelcome and invisible.

Conclusion

This chapter has outlined the various ways in which cars and music have combined to construct and/or reflect gender and sexual identities. While the vast majority of songs and sound culture surrounding cars are undoubtedly the product of and cater to heterosexual men, there is nevertheless a significant body of work that challenges this stereotype. Whether it is female singer-songwriters such as Joni Mitchell, Tracy Chapman, or Shania Twain, who wrote about the car from a variety of female perspectives, or Frank Ocean's employment of high-performance cars as metaphors for his homosexual identity, popular musicians have questioned and defied in numerous ways the apparent ubiquity of the stereotypical masculine domain of car songs. The car, as evident in these perspectives, serves as an active vehicle for creative expression of all genders and sexual identities.

Car companies often cater their products and commercial advertising to specifically appeal to male or female buyers. As part of an overall automotive culture that mostly either ignored or excluded the experiences of women and sexual minorities, cars were typically marketed as objects of masculine desire, promising men freedom and mastery of technology. As evinced in many of the songs discussed above, women were often reduced to domestic stereotypes and/or conflated with the car itself. In the latter instance, this allowed men to imagine themselves as possessing and controlling a woman as they might possess and control a car. Car companies, however, have begun to recognize the power of female customers, and have at times specifically catered to women buyers through various features and targeted marketing campaigns. There also appears to be something of an increased willingness by these companies to align themselves with female artists as spokespersons. Nevertheless, they still often resort to stereotypes of female domesticity rather than to issues of creativity, performance, or style. While sexual minorities continue to be typically overlooked and/or marginalized in terms of their automotive needs and experiences, in the case of at least one company, Subaru, lesbian and gay consumers have become an active part of its marketing strategy. Similarly, the interrelationship of LGBTQ identities and automobiles in song and popular culture is no less a defining feature of their construction and representation of identity than for heterosexuals. As I hope this chapter has at least begun to outline, the car/music nexus, therefore, goes far beyond reinforcing perceptions of stereotypical heterosexual masculine identity.

Notes

1 Lyrics and music by Jackie Brenston. Copyright Warner Chappell Music, Inc.
2 The Model T's female nickname "Tin Lizzie" was first applied in 1922 as the result of a championship race held in Pikes Peak, Colorado. Entered as one of the contestants was Noel Bullock and his Model T, named "Old Liz." Since Old Liz looked the worse for wear as it was unpainted and lacked a hood (bonnet), many spectators compared Old Liz to a tin can. By the start of the race, the car had the new nickname of "Tin Lizzie." After the unlikely car won the race, the feat was reported in newspapers across the country, leading to the use of the nickname "Tin Lizzie" for all Model T cars (Rosenberg, 2018).
3 Lyrics and music by Prince Rogers Nelson. Copyright Universal Music Publishing Group.
4 Lyrics and music by Bruce Springsteen. Copyright Sony/ATV Music Publishing LLC.
5 Lyrics and music by Jeffrey Cohen and Narada Walden. Copyright Warner Chappell Music, Inc.
6 Lyrics and music by Stephen Paul David Morris, Peter Hook, Bernard Sumner, Gillian Lesley Gilbert, Evan Rogers, and Carl Sturken. Copyright Universal Music Publishing Group.
7 Lyrics and music by Robert John Lange and Shania Twain. Copyright Universal Music Publishing Group.
8 Lyrics and music by Robert John Lange and Shania Twain. Copyright Universal Music Publishing Group.
9 Lyrics and music by Lady Gaga and Rob Fusari. Copyright Sony/ATV Songs LLC.
10 Lyrics and music by Chris Tompkins and Josh Kear. Copyright Sony/ATV Music Publishing LLC.
11 Lyrics and music by Max Martin, Onika Tanya Maraj, Rickard Göransson, and Savan Kotecha. Copyright Kobalt Music Publishing Ltd.
12 The characters were forced to run from the police after Thelma is subjected to an attempted rape and Louise shoots the attacker. The pair think the police would not believe their claim of attempted rape. In a 1999 *20/20* interview, Tori Amos said the film directly inspired her to write her song "Me and a Gun," which recounts

the story of her own rape some six years earlier (Tori Amos on being a rape survivor, 2016).

13 Lyrics and music by Joni Mitchell. Copyright Crazy Crow Music/Siquomb Music Publishing.

14 Lyrics and music by Joni Mitchell. Copyright Crazy Crow Music/Siquomb Music Publishing.

15 Lyrics and music by Joni Mitchell. Copyright Crazy Crow Music/Siquomb Music Publishing.

16 Notable exceptions to this include Sylvia Robinson, the influential hip hop producer and co-founder of Sugar Hill Records—producer of "Rappers Delight" (1979) and Grand Master Flash's "The Message" (1982)—and multiple Grammy-winning engineer Leslie Ann Jones. Moreover, many women engineers and producers are increasingly bypassing the mainstream pop music industry and turning to completely online, do-it-yourself, independent, and participatory spaces (e.g., Bandcamp, SoundCloud) to showcase and develop their production skills. One of the most influential and popular current female producers, for example, is Ramona Xavier, whose work, composed under numerous aliases (such as Vektroid or Macintosh Plus), is typically only available online.

17 It should be noted that although the vast majority of car designers are men, some women are breaking into the field. Women in the car design industry are typically confined to stereotypical female designer roles concerning interior decoration—choosing seat fabrics, colours, and trims—while male designers shape the exterior shape and look of the vehicle. However, the exterior of Acura's 2017 NSX, a seemingly macho high-performance sports car, was designed by Michelle Christensen. Similarly, the 2016 Nissan Titan, a heavy-duty pick-up truck typically used to haul everything from boats to horse trailers, was designed by San Diego-based, mother-of-two Diane Allen. Despite such successes, there is nevertheless a dearth of women in automotive design schools. Christensen, a self-described "car geek" who has been interested in motors since an early age, says, "I know that car design is an obscure career choice but I was lucky my dad exposed me to the idea. Before he suggested it, I was waffling about becoming a fashion designer or working on a pit crew." Notably, Allen, who was also involved in designing the Nissan Rogue and Infiniti M5, claims, "I realized long ago that there's no designing for a man or a woman. You just design so it looks good to everyone." Underscoring the link between car manufacturing and artistic production, Irina Zavatski, design manager at Fiat-Chrysler Automobiles and who recently worked on the 2017 Chrysler Pacifica, opines, "The best feeling is when you see people driving your car. If you are a painter or a sculptor, people have to go to a gallery to see your work. But if you're a car designer, they see your work every day all over the place" (Weingarten, 2016).

18 The song got a new lease on life in 2011 during Super Bowl XLV, when the cast of *Glee*, sang a rendition in an elaborate two-part Chevy Cruze commercial that was made to appear like an actual episode of *Glee* (with the usual *Glee* recap used at the beginning of every episode).

19 Lyrics and music by Leo Corday and Leon Carr. Copyright Chevrolet Media Management Group.

20 Of course such features reflect the evolution of the van from something that moves inanimate cargo to something that moves human cargo. The van, while marketed to appeal to women, has also become a child-centred vehicle.

21 The licensing or use of music by female artists, such as Janelle Monáe's "Tightrope" in the 2011 Canadian Chevy Cruz campaign, is different, of course, from artists who actually appear in car advertisements and marketing, and who get paid for actively endorsing the product. However, such licensing also appears to happen less frequently. While not technically a car commercial, also worthy of note is the fact that in 2008 Madonna starred in a short promotional film for the BMW M5, directed by her then-

husband Guy Ritchie and also featuring Clive Owen. The comedic short, titled *Star*, sees Madonna parody herself as a shallow and spoilt celebrity being driven to her concert by a reckless driver (Owen). The film is underscored by Blur's "Song 2" (1997) and Wagner's "Ride of the Valkyries." The short was part of a series of eight comedic branded-content films that BMW produced for the Internet from 2001 to 2016. Another short film of note is *Beat the Devil* (2002), directed by Tony Scott. It features legendary singer James Brown drag racing in a BMW Z4, trying to beat the Devil in order to regain his youth by renegotiating a deal he made as a young man when he traded his soul for fame and fortune. The film also includes Gary Oldman as the Devil and a cameo by Marilyn Manson.

22 Vocaloids are characters derived from a computer program that allows users to add synthesized human-esque vocals to their own music by inputting lyrics and a melody. Hatsune Miku is a chart-topping virtual pop idol in Japan, with songs created entirely by the input of fans and who performs "live" as a holographic 3D projection.

23 The soundtrack features famous drummers, including Pauli Stanley-McKenzie from Gorillaz, ex-Smiths drummer Mike Joyce, Joji Hirota and the Taiko Drummers, and big band aficionado Vince Dunn.

24 Other large gay and lesbian car clubs include Great Autos of Yesteryear (www.greatautos.org), based in Los Angeles and numbering about 1,200 members, and the Freewheelers Car Club (www.thefreewheelers.net), based in San Francisco.

25 Lyrics and music by Christopher Edwin Breaux. Copyright Kobalt Music Publishing Ltd.

26 Lyrics and music by Christopher Edwin Breaux. Copyright Universal Music Publishing Group.

27 Lyrics and music by Roger Meddows Taylor. Copyright Sony/ATV Music Publishing LLC.

28 Lyrics and music by Freddy Mercury. Copyright Sony/ATV Music Publishing LLC.

29 Lyrics and music by Melissa Ferrick. Copyright Wixen Music Publishing.

4 If this brand were a band

Sound and music in automotive branding[1]

Whether by animating the body through dance or transport, both popular music and cars developed as symbiotic commodities that were designed to literally and figuratively "move" us. The sounds inherently produced by automobiles—crankshafts, engine noises, and warning horns—resulted in distinct mechanistic sounds being projected onto the urban landscape. As described in Chapter 1, these sounds often influenced the sound of popular music itself.

In our daily lives the continuous flow of sound, whether encountered consciously or subconsciously, constantly informs and transforms our experience and perceptions of the world around us and, by extension, our identity. Fundamentally, noise only exists in relation to what it is not—typically something sonically meaningful—and thus transcends and deconstructs the binary oppositions between natural and unnatural, human and non-human, intentional and non-intentional. As such, noise is, in and of itself, an expressive medium of identity. Noise, and more generally sound, thus has the power to actively shape who and what we are.

The sonic experience of riding in a car is varied and complex, ranging from chaotic, uncontrollable noise to intentionally controlled music. The presence of sound systems in automobiles, regularly found beginning in the 1930s (and as discussed further in Chapter 6), allows for the personalization of one's sonic experience, replicating and expanding the freedom afforded by automobile travel itself. For many, the sound of the engine—its mechanical noises, rattles, and external road noises—provides a chaotic and somewhat annoying or even alienating sonic experience. Although designed and created by humans, engines still produce, in the minds of some, a lifeless, artificial, and disquieting industrial noise (albeit one understood by car enthusiasts to be a beautifully "tuned" sound, often described in musical terms). Potential mechanical problems, ambient wind, and traffic and noise are also often distracting to drivers and passengers. Drivers often turn to the car radio or sound system in order to quell or mitigate these disquieting or unwanted sounds and noises. Playing music or other audible entertainment while driving allows us to exert at least a degree of control over what is otherwise an often sonically uncontrolled experience. Furthermore, the designed musical sounds and tones that emanate from newer cars are meant to provide, at least in part, a recognizably "human" communicative tone that can attenuate the sense of alienation from the lifeless machinery to which we are entrusting our lives. It is important to recognize, however, that in employing both designed sounds emanating from the vehicle and in-car sound systems, we are merely using the sounds of one technology to mitigate or subdue the sounds of another. Such uses of music and sound serve to re-establish a sense of personal subjectivity and empowerment over the "noise" of the machine.

The contemporary automobile has witnessed a marked evolution in regard to the refinement, conditioning, and, in some cases, even the artificial enhancement of the noises and sounds it produces. In the past, the noises a car made were simply an unavoidable side effect of its mechanical function, the inherent consequence of the sounds of hundreds of parts working together. That era, however, is rapidly disappearing. Long familiar mechanical sounds, such as the *tick tick* sound of the turn-signal indicator, have typically been replaced by specifically designed synthesized sounds (yet often, as in the case of the indicator, these sounds mimic the familiar, and hence reassuring, mechanical sounds of the past). The aural experience of a contemporary car has been entirely and carefully crafted and tweaked by armies of sound engineers and designers. Such attention to the sonic experience can both allay fears that the machine may not be operating properly (the car needs to sound like it is "healthy") and enhance the overall sensory pleasure of driving.

In discussing the sonic components of the driving experience it is important to distinguish between sounds that are unavoidably (or seemingly unavoidably) generated by the operation of the car (the noises produced by the parts working together) and sounds that are intentionally added (e.g., various chimes and warning indicators). In the field of product sound design, the former category is typically termed "consequential sounds" and the latter "intentional sounds" (Langeveld, van Egmond, Jansen, & Özcan, 2013). While every car has its unique sonic characteristics, most automotive brands attempt to provide an experiential aural consistency that consumers can associate with particular models. The sound associated with a high-end Ferrari, for instance, should not be like that of an entry-level Ford. The refinement of sound by manufacturers is thus part of an increasing emphasis on a sensory user experience, and an extremely important part of the user interface. In these ways, sound not only plays an important role in defining particular brands and identities of automobiles but also helps define and construct our own individual aesthetic preferences and identities as consumers. To some degree our identities in this scenario are constructed from both the subjective consumption of available sounds and music and the consciously imposed influence of sound designers and marketers.

Despite its impact, the influence of sound design in automotive branding has received little scholarly attention. Significant critical attention, however, has been paid to the relationships and growing points of convergence between popular music, commerce, and advertising (Klein, 2009; Taylor, 2012; Taylor 2016). Scholars have also focused on branding and product promotion as forms of social, cultural, political, and economic exchange (Lury, 2004; Arvidsson, 2006; Aronczyk & Powers, 2010). The increasing ties between popular music and advertising have also been a focus of interest, particularly in terms of whether such relationships are undermining the value of music as art or culture (Klein, 2008; Klein, 2009; Allan, 2005; Frank, 1998; Carah, 2010). In a similar vein, Meier (2011) has investigated the use of music in branding campaigns to create an entirely new media object in its own right. The nexus of automotive culture and sound has also received attention. Bull (2003) and LaBelle (2010), for example, have looked at the immersive sonic experiences while driving, while Bijsterveld, Cleophas, Krebs, and Mom (2013) have studied the search for auditory privacy in and from cars. The specific issue of the relationship of popular music to sound design in automotive branding, however, has been critically understudied.[2]

This chapter examines the increasing attention given to sound design, and especially sound branding, in automobiles. In particular, I am concerned with how sonic branding plays with, constructs, and reflects the identities of both the car and of the consumer who buys and operates it. The growing complexity of built-in or "intentional" sound sources and of the sonic experience when operating cars also calls into question the relationship between our machines and ourselves. Marketers and sound designers attempt to instill in consumers the "emotional values" they want associated with a product (Lim, 2012, p. 217). As a result, cars (and other commodities) are marketed to us as anthropomorphic, often even sentient entities that give the appearance of sharing our values and enabling our lifestyle choices. To a large extent, consumption has become more than the simple acquisition and use of goods. Particularly in the case of the automotive experience, as outlined below, it has evolved into how we can relate to our cars as anthropomorphized allies in the construction and projection of our own identities.

Automotive sound-branding concepts

Sound plays an important role in product branding in general, and has become more central to customers' experiences, not only with cars but also with a wide variety of appliances and electronic devices. More than a simple jingle or sound logo, audio branding entails the creation of an entire sonic language for a brand. Based on that brand's essence, values, and "personality," and often casting the brand in an anthropomorphic light, this language is expressed across all points of contact between the company/product and the consumer. The wide range of these so-called "touchpoints" includes the product's online and software presence, trade shows, television and other media, the retail environment, and, as will be shown, the aesthetic of the sounds that the product generates.

Selling sound and music in automotive advertising

Anthropologist David Howes (2005) argues that "consumer capitalism has ... increasingly made it its business to engage as many senses as possible in its drive for product differentiation and the distraction/seduction of the consumer" (p. 288). Employing the term "hyperesthesia" to describe the phenomenon, Howes suggests that manufacturers and brand advisers are moving toward a conceptualization of brands as multisensory experiences. Branding therefore increasingly seeks to connect inanimate products to sensory bodily experience that will appeal to consumers. In the case of automotive branding, this might mean emphasizing the powerful sound of the engine, the luxurious feel of the interior, the smooth, responsive handling, and the advanced features of inter-active or "intelligent" technology. The use of music is, of course, an especially compelling form of sensory experience, one that, since at least the time of the ancient Greeks, is believed to have exercised a particularly powerful form of influence on our emotions and actions. Extending this inquiry, advertising and media studies scholar Devon Powers discusses the practical use of music as a central tool in branding, convincingly arguing that its impact on consumerism's phenomenology is based on three longstanding assumptions about the power of musical sound and the psychology of hearing:

> The first assumption is that musical sound is a natural, universal lan-guage that trades on bodily, rather than mental, experience. The second assumption follows closely: the sounds of music are a vector of pure affect, a direct and untroubled way to access, trigger, and control emo-tional states. Third, music is a sonic "science," a code which can be unlocked and exploited (Powers, 2010, p. 288).

As such, musical sound branding has the capability, albeit perhaps culturally conditioned, to actively work on and in our bodies, triggering desired emo-tional states.

Since the establishment of commercial radio in the mid-1920s, many com-panies have employed musical jingles and sound logos in order to distinguish themselves in the marketplace. Automobile manufacturers, however, have recently been particularly determined in their attempts to project an easily recognized and coherent sonic brand. German manufacturer Audi, for exam-ple, currently attempts to project a consistent sonic message across all aspects of the company, including: the consequential sounds of engines, door handles, and other parts; advertising music and voiceovers; and even the ideal tone and timbre of voices perceived as fitting the brand in commercials and automated phone menus. In order to achieve this sonic saturation and identification, the company developed a system in 2010 that it terms its "Corporate Sound Con-cept," which uses a holistic approach to complement the brand's visual identity and is understood to embody "the sound of Audi" (Audi Sound Studio, 2011). According to Audi's corporate strategy, the objective of the Corporate Sound

Concept is to ensure that the Audi brand values of "sportiness, progressiveness and sophistication" can be recognized and experienced at all acoustic touch-points, from the sounds made when operating the actual car to the music used in its marketing, and all the way down to the customer experience when contacting the company by phone (Audi AG, 2011).

In order to produce its distinctive corporate sound, the company devised what it refers to as the Audi Sound Studio. This strategy involved developing a limited catalogue of musical motifs, the so-called "Audi sounds." Employing a series of central sound-based themes, its goal is to create a flexible sound brand with a high recognition value; that is, each sound must be distinct enough that consumers will be able to recognize and associate it with Audi whenever they hear it. Audi then built and continues to build the music for its promotional materials, using sounds that spokespersons refer to as, for example, "Audi strings," "Audi synthesizer," "Audi pizzicato," and the "Audi heartbeat." The company thus created a series of adaptable modular sounds that could be deployed at various touchpoints.

Since 1996, Audi's most prominent sound trademark has been its "Audi heartbeat." According to Alexander Urban, head of brand and customer strategy at Audi AG:

> The heartbeat has become an acoustic icon for the Company. … The sound signature has become just as closely connected with the brand as the claim *Vorsprung durch Technik* [advancement through technology]. We have now refined the acoustic quality to make two aspects stand out—great technical expertise and the brand's emotional appeal (Sound file, 2010).

The "Audi Heartbeat" logo, comprised of two synthesized dynamic bass pulses, seeks to make the car sound alive, as if possessing an actual human heart. "This heartbeat really gets under your skin," Urban claims. "And it stays in your head. We've backed the pulsating heart with synthetic sounds that fit with our 'Vorsprung durch Technik' philosophy. They boost the sound logo's impact and make it memorable" (Sound file, 2010). In addition to being heard at the end of all the company's television and radio advertising, the heartbeat logo sounds like an engine start-up chime in several Audi models, actively reinforcing not only the corporate sound branding within the product but also its synthesized human characteristics as the car figuratively and sonically pulses into life. The effect is perhaps also intended to make the driver feel like an all-powerful god, giving life to an inanimate object and then commanding it. This sonic anthropomorphization underlines the increasing premium placed by car companies on intelligent driving technologies that promote an ever-evolving man–machine hybrid. Indeed, the act of driving itself can be understood to represent a cyborg-like bonding between human and machine. The car essentially becomes an extension of ourselves as we enter, inhabit, and operate it.

As Mimi Sheller (2007) notes, the car is grafted onto human systems of cognition such that "we not only feel the car, but we feel through the car and with the car" (p. 181). Moreover, we listen to the car in order to feel reassured that it is functioning properly. Ideas of automobile "intelligence" have now expanded to include not just data processing and automated responses to driving environments (e.g., keyless entry and start-up, parking assistance, automatized navigation, and accident sensing) but also more "human" elements of intelligence, such as feeling, intuition, and emotion.[3] Presaging its heartbeat sonic branding, the 2004 Audi A8 L was advertised for its "Multi Media Interface," a navigation-infotainment unit, as a "central nervous system" that is not only innovative, but "the most intuitive," "straightforward," and "effortless" system to use (Sheller, 2007, p. 183). As such, the integrated sonic branding that promotes and reflects Audi's corporate identity can be likened to a form of digitized audio DNA code that permeates all aspects of the company and its products, imparting a consistent emotional form of life to its brand. The beating-heart sonic logo is thus found not only in the soundtrack of commercials but also throughout Audi's branding: for instance, it conveys the reassurance of car "health" when it is heard in engine start-up sounds and in the various warning indicators and sonic touchpoints of many models.

French automaker Peugeot has also employed the concept of DNA-like sound branding. But whereas many automotive brands develop audio identities rooted in the sounds of cars and engines, Peugeot has broken away from timeworn sounds and instead built a musical identity to reaffirm the brand's upmarket move and bring depth to its corporate tag line, "Motion & Emotion." Like Audi, Peugeot aims to humanize its products by reaffirming and reinforcing the idea that its cars embody and project some form of humanly recognizable emotion. As described by Sixième Son, the marketing company responsible for designing Peugeot's sound strategy, the sound logo (and variants used across different touchpoints) nonetheless falls back on some familiar clichés, such as the association of classical music instrumentation with timeless elegance, quality, and wealth:

> The musical composition creates a very surprising musical alchemy: at once simple and mysterious, both deep and light. Piano guides the main melody and is accompanied by noble instruments like the cello. The melody's crystalline clarity illustrates the uncompromising standards of the brand. The futuristic sound design and the rhythm section convey the concepts of movement and modernity. The airy female voice, [*sic*] reinforces the emotion and reflects sensuality and driving pleasure (Sixième Son, 2015).

Yet, in addition to the "noble" instrumental accompaniment, the logo employs a "futuristic sound design and rhythm section"—largely consisting of an up-tempo techno 4/4 drum machine beat and various sampled and synthesized squelches and blips—to convey "movement and modernity," which hardly seems ground-breaking in the auto industry. Indeed, Timothy Taylor (2007) persuasively links the initial rise of techno to the use of licensed, previously recorded music in automobile advertising. As outlined by Taylor, the overtly futuristic sounds associated with techno are commonly employed by advertisers to reinforce the perception of similar technological forwardness in automobiles.

Audi and Peugeot are by no means the only automobile manufacturers concerned with building a comprehensive corporate sound image. BMW is also actively involved in creating a unique sonic-brand identity. For some 14 years, the BMW sound logo was a synthesized "double gong" sound heard at the end of every commercial and official video created by the company. However, all BMW products and brand films created after 2013 end with a new sound logo that reflects the brand-specific sounds and, according to the accompanying press release, its "innovative power and dynamism" (BMW Group, 2013). The new logo, also played at the end of radio and television ads, features brand-specific dynamic sound elements meant to represent the company's reimagined identity. The corporate model of "flexible mobility"—a company initiative begun in 2013 that emphasizes a mix of electric, hybrid, and conventional gas engine-powered cars—is sonically symbolized by playing the same sound elements simultaneously backwards and forwards. The BMW press release alongside the announcement of the new logo described the melody and its intention:

> Reverse technology is used to play sound elements forward and backwards in a way that symbolizes flexible mobility. The melody is introduced by a rising, resonant sound and underscored by two distinctive bass tones that form the sound logo's melodic and rhythmic basis. The sounds build toward a shimmering, sophisticated finish. This combination of different elements represents the joy of progress, of dynamism, and Sheer Driving Pleasure (BMW Group, 2013).

While it is perhaps debatable how two sounds simultaneously played forwards and backwards portray "the joy of progress," the distinctive sonic identity of various makes of cars is something on which sound designers are increasingly focused. Not only do the consequential sounds of the power windows, seat belt warning, indicators, and so on define and project the brand and model identity of the car; they also serve to define and project the identity of the buyer and the driver. BMW employs over a dozen sound designers (officially titled "acoustic artists") specifically for the purpose of crafting the perfect sonic experience to match its various products. The company, which also owns the Mini Cooper and Rolls-Royce brands, is careful to separate the sound designs imagined for each of its brands. BMW acoustic artist Emar Vegt describes the process of engineering sounds to match a car's "character":

> Most important the sound must suit the car's character and fit the brand's image. BMW is almost quite classic in its orientation—its sounds have a longer finish, the Mini has more of a crunch to it—a playfulness almost. The next step is Rolls-Royce, which currently has this check control sound. ... A harp. With BMWi ... you can't really associate the sound with an instrument, but that's what we wanted because this is something quite new; it's not immediately recognizable (BMW, 2013).

Although the sounds are digitally synthesized, the more resonant "longer-finish" sounds associated with BMW series or the "harp" sounds associated with Rolls-Royce reinforce a socio-economic stereotype that links classical music with leisure, luxury, and wealth. The more affordable Mini, however, is characterized by shorter, more techno-sounding blips, evincing a playfulness that identifies it with younger, possibly less wealthy consumers.

There are, perhaps, other, more subtle stereotypes of gender and race projected by these sounds. The playful techno dance music sounds of the Mini may be calculated to appeal to female buyers. According to one study from 2010–2011, among all car brands the Mini had the highest percentage of retail sales to women, while the Rolls-Royce, with its soothing and classically inspired harp sounds, was more likely to be valued by older white men (Woodyard, 2012). In essence, these sounds fall into a stereotypical Cartesian binary that sees "simple" dance music associated with the non-rational body, and therefore the feminine, while supposedly more complex and cerebral classical music is coded as masculine. The same study found that in 2010 five brands—Ferrari, Lotus, Lamborghini, Maybach, and Rolls-Royce—had retail sales to women that did not exceed 10 per cent. It is also the case that, despite the long and involved history of interrelationship between African-American culture and the automobile (discussed in Chapter 2), such in-car sounds appear not to include influences from stereotypically African-American-derived stylistic idioms, such as jazz, r & b, or hip hop.

Often, the synthesized electronic operating sounds produced by our cars, and sometimes other appliances, are initially selling points. They may attract consumers with sounds that evoke the possibilities of a technologized future. Arguably, however, the sonic beeps and chimes repeatedly and unalterably emanating from our cars and appliances may, in fact, ultimately alienate us from the machines. The cold, immutable repetitiveness of the sounds reminds us that these machines evince very little ability to adapt or respond to the tastes of individual users. Over time, they become constant reminders of the subhuman rigidity of our technologized culture. Until recently, car-alert sounds were static and hardwired into the product. The familiar "chirp" of remotely locking and unlocking one's car doors through a keyless entry system has become a ubiquitous and sometimes annoying source of sonic performance. The dynamic level of many keyless entry systems can now be altered or even disabled, and there is a wide variety of beeping and chirping tones and timbres often unique to various brands and models. As such, keyless entry tones enact another form of branding identification, albeit one that occurs in a much more public forum.

Some car manufacturers, such as Tesla (2010), are working on ways to allow consumers the ability to customize the music and sounds tags that are played when operating their vehicles. Thus they are effectively facilitating personalized sonic interactions and social performances by and with our machines. Sonic branding in automobiles and other products, then, has the potential to take on a function of personal sonic identification similar to a ringtone and other customizable sound notifications and alarms on our phones (de Vries & van Elferen, 2010; Gopinath, 2013). Indeed, BMW's and Audi's start-up and seat belt chimes and engine sounds are already available to consumers as downloadable ringtones. While current automobile and product sounds are not as customizable, when activated they nonetheless instigate a performative process (though possibly an unwanted one) that takes place between users and their surroundings. Drivers, moreover, carry with them the connotations of the music and designed sounds. By adding this cultural marker to their physical appearance and presence, drivers brand the product as much as it brands them—in effect, becoming corporeal representatives of the machine.

The increasing propensity for car advertising to employ anthropomorphic language and sounds appears to reflect the notion that it is through interaction with human-like machines that we, as individuals, will essentially be brought to life. Such thinking is underscored by recent interpretations of the growing human immersion in technology. Sociologist John Urry (2007), for example, claims that the twenty-first century will be marked by the presence of "inhabited machines" that will be "desired for their style … and [that] demonstrate a physical form often interwoven with the corporeal. It is through inhabiting machines that humans will come to 'life'" (pp. 179–180). Inasmuch as automakers attempt to imbue cars with anthropomorphic qualities, it is ostensibly up to the consumer to accept or reject their car's claim to liveness (Auslander, 2012). Nevertheless, whether consciously accepted as a "live" entity or not, it seems that we are more likely to identify with a car that reminds us of ourselves in some way or other. The sonic branding found in Audi's beating heart or BMW's carefully crafted musical chimes that project various aesthetic proclivities and lifestyles is part of that human desire for self-reflection.

Car manufacturers such as BMW and Audi are clearly putting as much thought into designing the acoustic identities of their products as the visual ones. Such thinking is not simply limited to car branding, but is also a major part of branding other consumer products and appliances that produce sound. GE, for example, has spent considerable time developing a range of distinctive sound chimes for its various lines of kitchen appliances. Like automotive companies creating anthropomorphic identities for their cars, GE attempts to invest its appliances with human feelings and identity. David Bingham, who heads the sound initiative at GE, explains its approach:

> We had a lot of back and forth coming up with different expressions and images that collectively gave us a feeling for [each particular] brand. In brainstorming sessions, designers would ask each other questions like, "If this brand was a band, what band would it be?" (Vanhemert, 2015).

GE here can be seen as not only anthropomorphizing its appliances but even as viewing them as representing and potentially fulfilling the same popular cultural space as an actual band. A similar question to that asked by GE above is often asked, albeit more tacitly, by car companies. As we shall see in the variety of endorsement deals discussed below, car manufacturers often regard their products as being embodied by and aligned with the music and spirit of various musical celebrities.

Automotive celebrity sound branding

Sound branding encompasses tactics intended to convey organizational or product identity (i.e., what an organization is and what it stands for) to enhance consumers' experiences when using a product or service, or to extend an organization's relationship with its audience. Another, perhaps more familiar form of sound branding involves an organization's public association with or sponsorship of a musical enterprise, such as a concert tour or an artist. Ostensibly intended to demonstrate the sponsoring organization's good will as a patron of the arts, practices like these seek to brand the organization by calling attention to its values and aesthetic sensibilities.

Taylor has commented on automobile manufacturers' employment of previously composed techno and electronica dance music styles in television commercials. In particular, he highlights Volkswagen and Mitsubishi ads during the 1990s and early 2000s that featured the music of UK acts such as Stereolab, the Orb, and Wiseguys. Employing Pierre Bourdieu's concept of the "new petite bourgeoisie" (groups and professions, including advertising agencies, that mediate notions of high and low culture), Taylor (2007) opines that the prevalent use of electronic music in car advertising in the 1990s represented the new petite bourgeoisie of "the advertising industry ... bringing their taste for underground music to the mainstream" (p. 253).

Of course, electronica represents only a fraction of the musical styles that have been employed by car companies in their long history of drawing on popular music to sell their products. Indeed, from the very inception of mass-produced automobiles, music has been a central marketing tool for auto manufacturers. Car companies were quick to realize and seize the advertising potential of Tin Pan Alley, and many began to commission and distribute sheet music to the public, hoping to bring in potential customers. Songs such as L. Marda's "The Studebaker Grand March" (1899) or C. R. Foster and B. Gay's "The Little Ford Rambled Right Along" (1914) were commissioned by the eponymous manufacturers as promotional odes to the reliability and safety of their products. More recently, automobile advertising has regularly featured a diversity of genres and styles of popular music licensed from contemporary artists. At the less well-known end of the spectrum, punk and alternative music has been prominent in several influential television car commercials. In 2007, for example, Cadillac featured Iggy Pop and the Teddybears' "Punkrocker" (2006) in its campaign for the XLR. In similar fashion, songs by iconic British post-punk bands, such as The Jam's "Pretty Green" (1980) and The Fall's "Blindness" (2005), were employed in North American commercials for the Mitsubishi Outlander in 2007. With the use of these relatively obscure songs (at least in North America), car companies appeared to be trying to connect their products to a more rebellious notion of petite bourgeoisie: a more aggressive consumer than the stereotypically passive, dance-oriented consumer evoked by the use of techno music.

Although Taylor (2007) concentrates his analysis on techno music, the alternative rock examples cited above demonstrate that automobile advertising regularly uses music by a variety of artists from diverse genres and styles. For example, from 1990 to 2004, Chevrolet trucks ads featured Bob Seger's song "Like a Rock" (1986). Similarly, Ford employed country artist Toby Keith for its "Ford Tough" truck campaign. Ford sponsored Keith's concerts, including his 2009 "Biggest and Baddest" tour, in which the song "Big Ol' Truck" (1995) featured prominently. In a humorous juxtaposition of genres, the 2008 Jeep Cherokee commercial entitled "Grand Ol' Opera" used a full-voiced operatic duet sung by a helpful police officer and a stranded motorist.[4]

One of the more prominent examples of popular music cross-marketing occurred in 2002, when Celine Dion signed a $14-million, three-year deal with Chrysler to be its celebrity spokesperson. Dion was subsequently featured in Chrysler Pacifica ads that used her hit single, "I Drove All Night" (2003). The unveiling of the car was designed to coincide with the premiere of her Las Vegas show at Caesar's Palace, "A New Day … Presented by Chrysler." The intimacy of the relationship is evident in a press release from Dion:

> The sponsorship package for A New Day … includes Chrysler placement on the new Caesar's Palace marquee on the Las Vegas strip. Chrysler also has the option to name each lobby level of the Coliseum. A special area of the Coliseum lobby will feature Chrysler tonality with display room for two vehicles, and a mural wall at the entrance will showcase Chrysler. Additional advertising, print, signage and video displays will support the partnership (PR Newswire, 2003).

"This sponsorship is a natural extension of the Chrysler brands partnership with Celine Dion," said Jim Schroer, executive vice president, global sales and marketing for the Chrysler Group. "A New Day … is the epitome of innovation in entertainment. It fits perfectly with the innovation in automotive design that is inherent in every Chrysler vehicle" (PR Newswire, 2003). The union did not result in increased sales, however, and Chrysler pulled out of the partnership after a little more than a year (see Chapter 3).

For automakers the success of these arrangements is often difficult to track in terms of the effect on sales. In 2019, however, one of the more influential and successful sponsorship arrangements was struck between K-pop boy band sensation BTS and Hyundai. The band signed on as Hyundai's global brand ambassadors, endorsing the manufacturer's 2019 SUV Palisade. The group appeared in multiple commercial spots, and even stepped out of the vehicle during the 2019 Grammy awards. Commercials featuring the band played off the fact that the Palisade's three rows of seating were accommodating enough to comfortably hold all seven members of their "family." Testifying to the influential reach of BTS, in the immediate aftermath of the endorsement demand for the vehicle skyrocketed. Hyundai doubled its annual sales of the vehicle, from a projected 25,000 units to over 52,000, and incurred a production backlog that saw customers facing up to a ten-month wait on their orders (Biz, 2019).

Other examples of the role of popular music in automotive marketing are not difficult to find. In 2005, the up-market manufacturer Jaguar sponsored two days of events tied to the annual Coachella music festival, including a VIP reception that included a pre-show pool party. Potential customers were lured into committing to test-drive Jaguar products with the free offer of an exclusive two-CD set from up-and-coming artists (Halliday, 2005).

Jaguar's association with rock artists began in 2000 when singer-songwriter Sting licensed the company his song "Desert Rose" (2000), recorded with Algerian raï singer Cheb Mami. The two sides then collaborated on developing television commercials that were similar to the video Sting had previously shot for the song. However, the deal between Sting and Jaguar raised some eyebrows among Sting's fans, considering that the singer was an avid environmentalist who was seemingly endorsing a gas-guzzling vehicle. The Jaguar ads, however, helped turn "Desert Rose" and the album *A Brand New Day* (1999) into one of Sting's biggest hits. The ad ran in high rotation across North American and European markets and, responding to listener demand, the song was soon being played on commercial radio. "Desert Rose" stayed in the US music charts for a full six months and had top-ten status all across Europe. By January 2001, the album had sold more than three million copies and earned Sting several Grammys for the year 2000.

Jaguar, for its part, was certainly satisfied with the immense success of its association with Sting's song, and the experience appears to have had an impact on the company's thinking about how to package itself thereafter. Owned by the US auto giant Ford, Jaguar is a venerable UK company known not only for its luxury cars, but also for its somewhat stuffy image. However, following its relationship with Sting, Jaguar continued to use popular music in other ads, including Deep Purple's "Hush" (1968) and Spoon's "I Turn My Camera On" (2005). Songs by The Clash, Queen, Moby, and Propellerheads have also been employed. Granted, not all of these generated the same success as "Desert Rose" but, taken together, pop and progressive music tracks have helped Jaguar generate a new brand image, which in turn has helped the company reach new groups of potential buyers.

Indeed, the list of licensed songs and styles is lengthy. In addition to those already mentioned, some of the more memorable songs include George Thorogood's "Bad to the Bone" (1987), heard in Buick Regal ads between 1984 and 1987; Sheryl Crow's "Everyday is a Winding Road" (1996) in Subaru Impreza advertising (2006–2007); and Eminem's "Lose Yourself" (2002) spot for the Chrysler 2000 that debuted during the 2011 Super Bowl. This list, while nowhere near exhaustive, testifies to the variety of styles employed and the scope of the practice as car manufacturers seek to appeal to and mine new demographics of buyers.

As I have argued, sound design that emanates from an automobile or appliance (e.g., chimes or musical notifications) serves to heighten our relationship with that product, essentially humanizing it and mitigating potentially alienating interactions and/or unsafe or faulty interfaces with a machine (Johansson, 2007). Associating a famous musician with a car brand is a different form of implied sonic branding, but one that largely achieves the same effect as intentionally designed sounds. The musician helps make the machine familiar, putting a human face to it that, in combination with the similarly associative memory of their music (typically reinforced in television advertising soundtracks), serves to humanize the machine (and its corporate manufacturer) in much the same manner as the sonic tags it emits.

In the past decade, popular music licensing agreements with brands have become even more common, and form an increasingly important revenue stream for both bands and record labels. It is also a sign of the growing intimacy between popular music and advertising (Powers, 2010). This relationship has become so close that advertising executive Bill Meadows has claimed that "[p]eople should look at advertising like they would radio" (Barhard & Rutledge, 2009). In part, this aligns with the emphasis advertisers place on creating sensory experiences for consumers; and, indeed, to a large degree, advertising *is* becoming the new radio as artists commonly use licensing agreements to promote their works and brands actively seek out new artists with whom to align themselves. Apple's MacBook Air television ad, for example, used Yael Naim's "New Soul" (2008), resulting in this previously unknown artist selling over a million downloads within six months of the commercial airing (Barhard & Rutledge, 2009). Both brands and musical artists now function in a new media environment, where information and communication are prime sources of capital. As a form of production, brands are no longer simply promotional devices for products, but facilitators of contexts or "platforms" for interaction (Lury, 2004; Aronczyk & Powers, 2010).[5] Music, particularly that employed in service of branding, functions in much the same way.

While automotive manufacturers can increase their market share and heighten their brand identity through music sponsorship deals, increasingly common are individual artists who endorse automotive brands for many of the same reasons. Indeed, as described above, musicians and automobile brands have had a symbiotic relationship for some time now. Taylor (2012) notes the growing convergence of commerce and artistic content, and, citing the example of Sting's relationship with Jaguar, claims that "the erosion of meaningful distinctions between the advertising and music industries has resulted in a convergence not only of content and commerce but also of the marketing of popular musicians" (p. 224). Furthermore, he concludes that:

> there is no longer a meaningful distinction to be made between "popular music" and "advertising music"—virtually all musics today that are heard outside the school or church ... are produced in commercial circumstances ... the sounds of capitalism are everywhere (Taylor, 2012, p. 229).

To a large extent, commercially successful artists are already in essence "brands" in and of themselves. They promote their lifestyle and the products with which they associate themselves to audiences through the songs they write and perform. Many artists, such as those described above, overtly align themselves with various corporate brands in the form of tour sponsorships, product endorsements, and other partnerships. In so doing they ascribe to a notion of celebrity as "consumer role model" (Meier, 2011, p. 401). Furthermore, recent statistics reveal that there has been a marked increase in product placements within popular song lyrics over the past 15 years, a fact that would seem to reinforce Taylor's contention that popular music and advertising music are no longer distinguishable—and perhaps also that the ubiquity of marketing has so saturated our daily existence that artistic expression references it as a means of speaking our vernacular. Automobiles, it should be noted, accounted for the largest portion of those product references in song lyrics, with "Mercedes-Benz, Bentley, Corvette, Cadillac, and Chevrolet ... among the most mentioned brands" (Gloor, 2014, p. 48). The cross-marketing of popular music and artists with automotive advertising is among the most pronounced manifestations of the increasingly blurred relationship between artistic content and commercial branding.

One of the more overt of such cross-marketing initiatives took place in 2006 when Volkswagen employed virtuoso guitarists Slash and John Mayer for its "V-Dub Rocks" television advertising campaign. Featuring either Slash or Mayer riffing on an electric guitar plugged into a car's stereo system and accompanied by the beat of windshield wipers, the commercials promised a free GarageMaster electric guitar to purchasers of its car. Against the tag line "Rock your V-dub from bumper to bumper!" Mayer draws his guitar neck over the top of the car door in an exaggerated version of a distorted bottleneck slide, effectively playing the car itself (Mayer, 2006). The free guitar, in turn, displayed the corresponding vehicle's vehicle identification number (VIN) and the pick guards were coloured to match the vehicle. The guitar was also covered with VW logos on the knobs, neck, and other places, and came with VW-branded picks and a guitar strap made out of seat belts. Even the blue indicator light on the guitar was the same shade as VW's panel lighting (Neff, 2006). As such, Mayer's solo was improvised specifically for the commercial, and, at the time, was a rare example of content uniquely created to converge with a product, and an equally rare example of a product adapting its content to popular music. Testifying to the impact of such advertising, the commercial featuring Mayer's improvised solo has received over two million YouTube views, and there are numerous "how-to-play" videos of Mayer's solo from the commercial and dozens of websites offering guitar tabs (Mayer, 2006).

While automakers such as Volkswagen have actively engaged pop musicians to endorse their products, others have also pursued sponsorship of popular music events and culture. Honda, for example, regularly sponsors music festivals, including the Austin City Limits Music Festival. Mike Accavitti, senior vice president of auto operations for American Honda Motor Co., boasts that:

> at Honda we are just as passionate about music as our owners and being a part of these festivals allows us to connect with them in an authentic way. … Attendees can expect that the Honda Stage will host the best and brightest bands in the country (Honda uses music festival sponsorship, 2013).

Manifest in these comments, Honda uses the cultural capital of the music festival to underline the sincerity of its "passion" and "authentic" connection to its customers. As Leslie Meier argues with regard to the ever-increasing licensing of original pre-existing songs by popular musicians, such a strategy is part of a branding trend to speak to consumer identities in a way that is perceived as authentic:

> Not only are artists recruited to the ranks of sales and marketing through … licensing agreements, they are coached to brand themselves as artists up to the tasking of branding—to sell themselves as up to the task of selling. Their purpose, first and foremost, is to function as instruments of brand differentiation. The use of the music of recording artists in this manner is, I suggest, related to "authenticity"-oriented differentiation strategies (Meier, 2011, p. 408).

And as such automakers appear to frequently co-opt the outsider cultural capital associated with and ideologies of independent and alternative musicians, and look to align and associate themselves with artists perceived as embodying real or "authentic" musical expression. These associations have met with various levels of success, as the following example and others discussed in the remainder of this chapter show.

In 2007, the critically acclaimed alternative rock band Wilco came under criticism for their decision to license six songs from their album *Sky Blue Sky* for use in a series of Volkswagen GTI commercials. Underlining the effort by car manufacturers to appropriate Wilco's reputation for integrity and to brand its products as a human machine, the ads were connected by the vaguely disturbing tagline, "When you get into a Volkswagen, it gets into you." In light of the fact that Wilco's artistic credibility and ideology were forged, in part, by two tribute albums to leftist folk icon Woody Guthrie, the band was heavily criticized by fans and bloggers (Swash, 2007).[6] In response to what appeared to many of their fans as a sell-out, Wilco took to their website to explain that they were finding it increasingly difficult to get their music played on commercial radio:

> As many of you are aware, Volkswagen has recently begun running a series of TV commercials featuring Wilco music.
>
> Why? ... With the commercial radio airplay route getting more difficult for many bands (including Wilco); we see this as another way to get the music out there. As with most of the above (with the debatable exception of radio) the band gets paid for this. And we feel okay about VWs. Several of us even drive them.
>
> If you're keeping track, this is not the first time Wilco has licensed a song to or even been involved in a commercial—most recently a TV spot for Telefonica Mobile in Spain. ... Wilco have [also] licensed hundreds of songs to television shows and films worldwide (Stereogum, 2007).

Pointing out that several band members drove Volkswagens and that their music was already licensed in other commercials, even Wilco, one of the most left-leaning alternative bands of recent times, felt compelled to partner with Volkswagen in order have their music heard and be paid for it. Volkswagen, for its part, briefly trumpeted the partnership on its website before removing all mention. The original VW post, however, celebrated the originality of the agreement and the closeness of the relationship, proclaiming:

> In a new form of music/promotion/communications, the band Wilco's recently released album *Blue Sky Blue* is the soundtrack to Volkswagen's latest TV campaign. This new form of marketing collaboration has the creative forces of Wilco and VW combining to launch both an album and a VW campaign in the same week (May 22nd). The partnership spans multiple commercials and multiple songs. ... The Wilco Volkswagen union will run for the summer and all songs can be streamed on vw.com. It's also the first-ever licensing deal for Wilco (Perez, 2007).

Described as a collaboration of "creative forces," this announcement was removed from the website after only a couple of days in the wake of the controversy and Wilco's response to their fans that refuted the claim that this was the band's "first-ever licensing deal." Regardless of the controversy, this case highlights the rising intimacy and creative alignment between artists, particularly alternative artists, and corporations in mutual commercial promotion. It also underscores the manufacturer's desire to highlight the brand experience for consumers who were able to stream Wilco's songs from the VW website. As for the efficacy of Wilco's avowed desire to find an alternative media platform to radio, *Sky Blue Sky* became the band's highest charting *Billboard 200* album to that time, peaking at number 4.

Over the past several years, such licensing agreements have become even more commonplace—with, as I will argue below, the notable difference that automobile manufacturers are now extending their influence into the creative content of the music they are licensing. In effect, not only are such commercial agreements a primary means of broadcasting and exposing new music; they are also directly influencing the musical/lyrical content itself as bands either seek to align their sound with particular brands or openly compose songs in response to licensing deals.

Automobile maker as hit maker

Perhaps no other automaker has affiliated itself more overtly with popular music than Scion. In 2009, Scion (owned by Toyota) began Scion Audio Visual, an in-house record label and arts marketing division. Despite folding the operation in 2017, Scion AV worked with approximately 1,500 artists and produced over 143 records, mainly in the genres of urban popular music—including metal, hip hop, alternative, and techno. Scion AV also operated a collection of 17 Internet radio channels (Scion AV Streaming Radio) that streamed from the company's website, sponsored an annual heavy metal festival (Scion Rock Fest), and hosted an annual music industry conference. Jeri Yoshizu, manager of marketing strategy for Scion, claimed, "We wanted a consistent voice, and combining lifestyle and audiovisual content … was [a way] to capture the lifestyle branding, and not have mixed messages about product and brand awareness" (Castillo, 2016).

In all senses of the concept, Scion AV was a fully functioning record label, similar to other brand-led initiatives like Red Bull Records and Mountain Dew's Green Label. It released albums, music videos, films, and web series, as well as producing live events, and even hosted pop-up record shops. Although music and video content was posted on its main website and bore Scion branding, the artists owned the masters of and rights to their content. In becoming a car/music hybrid brand, Scion firmly aligned itself with the alternative urban styles and politics of the music it promoted in order to legitimize itself with its target market of younger, entry-level car buyers. Artists who worked with Scion were typically independent, relatively little known, and often echoed Wilco's lament that only by licensing their songs to an automotive company could their music achieve widespread promotion. Independent electronic music artist and producer Steve Aoki, for example, worked with Scion AV for the last decade. According to Aoki, Scion helps "bands that have no recognition at all. They really are in it for all the right reasons" (Castillo, 2016). Challenging the common assumption that independent musicians would disavow corporate influence, Aoki says he embraced Scion because he believes it came from an honest place:

It makes sense to attach ourselves to brands that are pushing culture forward and in more youth-driven demographics, that are doing something that's meaningful instead of short-lived. ... Working with bands consistently over a longer period of time shows Scion knows it's all about the culture (Castillo, 2016).

Thus Scion, while not actively influencing content, actively supported and aligned itself with the creation of independent music, and reaped surplus social and economic value from its alignment with the independent ideals of the artists it supported.

A particularly fruitful commercial association that emphasizes the growing convergence between automotive branding strategies and popular music content, and that also quite literally relies on the musician to humanize the car, is that of Lexus and The Black Eyed Peas' will.i.am. In marketing its redesigned 2014 NX model SUV, Lexus teamed up with will.i.am to produce a television commercial and longer video entitled *Striking Angles*. The luxury brand has traditionally appealed to the over-55 market, and in this collaboration was seeking to challenge the "big three"—Mercedes, BMW, and Audi—by capturing more of a younger demographic.

Striking Angles begins with a shot of will.i.am looking directly into the camera, the film focusing on his blinking eye as the round shape of his iris shifts into that of the Lexus icon, directly highlighting the idea that his body is an extension of the car, and vice versa. The film, shot in super slow motion, transitions to the set of a Madrid nightclub as will.i.am exits. Brandishing a Puls "smartwatch"—yet another product that he endorses and sells on his website—he looks at the Lexus and turns on the music inside with his watch. The audience is then plunged into his mind's eye, entering a digitized fantasy world where practically everything shares the car's shifting planes and sharp-angled design aesthetic. The image of will.i.am is refracted across multiple surfaces, splitting into eye-catching fragments as he dances in ultra slow motion. The commercial concludes with a return to reality as will.i.am flips his shades back on and walks away, smiling to himself.

All the imagery is set to a remix of will.i.am's "Dreamin' About the Future" (2014), a song he originally wrote for a digital art installation called "Pyramidi" as part of London's Barbican Centre's Digital Revolution exhibit. Both the television ad and the longer commercial film reference the digitized face-morphing techniques used in the original art exhibit. However, both also notably omit the overt Afrofuturist references to Egyptian pharaohs and pyramids that marked the art installation, perhaps for fear of limiting or alienating the target demographic. In all versions—art installation, commercial, and commercial film—both will.i.am's heavily autotuned voice and a pulsating drum machine bassline that represents his heartbeat further the cyborg-like merging of man and technology that seems to be the overriding message. In the film, the artist's head, instead of transforming into the headdress of an Egyptian pharaoh as in the Barbican exhibit, merges into the shape of the grill of the car; will.i.am essentially becomes one with the car. In both the television ad and the longer video, the imagery is highly technologized and presents a digitized angular future (complete with holographic clones of will.i.am) and underscores the lyrical message of the quest for technological innovation shared by both the performer and the car company: "We've been dreaming about the future / We've been thinking about technology … we're a part of everything, ain't no separation."[7] Such lyrics, in the context of a car commercial, directly underscore the connection between the product, the company, the artist, and presumably the audiences and customers in underlining a mutual preoccupation with dreaming about the future.

At first glance, this might seem, on the one hand, a conventional case of the car company benefiting from the celebrity, yet, on the other, the celebrity's art and career benefiting from the product endorsement. However, given the growing prevalence of music licensing and the fact that it forms an ever more important revenue stream for musicians and record labels, notions of "selling out" are increasingly seen as anachronistic by artists (such as Wilco, above) and marketers alike (Meier, 2011). Indeed, few critics saw the relationship with Lexus as an artistic sell-out on the part of will.i.am. Instead, many more regarded the visuals of the commercial as an innovative and compelling blending of message, music, and image, and it received a substantial amount of positive press coverage, both online and in print. The September 2014 press release for the campaign describes the closeness and reciprocal nature of the relationship, including the rationale for choosing will.i.am:

THE LEXUS NX AND WILL.I.AM FRAME FUTURE DESIGN IN NEW STRIKING ANGLES TV AD

The Lexus NX and will.i.am are the stars of Striking Angles, a television commercial for the new luxury crossover that has its premiere in Europe tonight and will break in the UK in October. Using rich visuals and a soundtrack featuring an exclusive remix of will.i.am's Dreamin' About the Future, the ad transports viewers into an imagined modern world of angular design.

It depicts the NX travelling through a futuristic cityscape, giving hints of the car's progressive design as it passes beneath stylised road signs and through multi-faceted tunnels. As the journey unfolds, will.i.am appears on angled TV screens in a shop window before emerging in person from a facet-fronted club, stopping in his tracks to admire the passing Lexus.

Speaking about the ad, will.i.am said: "As a musician and an entrepreneur, I want my ideas and my presence to impact on the world around me. The team at Lexus applied the same vision to the ad—showing how the NX impacts the design of the world around it."

Alain Uyttenhoven, Head of Lexus Europe, said: "We wanted to bring our design philosophy for the Lexus NX to the forefront, transporting consumers to a world built entirely on revolutionary and striking design.

It's an attitude that we apply to everything we do at Lexus, from the design of the car to the innovative technology within. Will.i.am perfectly complements the world that we created, fusing our joint passions for progressive design and technology."

As part of the NX Striking Angles campaign, Lexus has created a one-off model, designed by will.i.am. The highly stylised car will be unveiled in Paris on 24 September during Paris Fashion Week (Christian, 2014).

The reciprocity between the car manufacturer and the musician are taken to new heights here. In addition to his "exclusive remix" of "Dreamin' About the Future," will.i.am praises the ability of Lexus to "design the world around it," just as he does as a musician. All the stakeholders deliberately described the project as a "collaboration"—i.e., not simply an endorsement: a relationship characterized by the fact that will.i.am and the Lexus are both "stars" of the ad, with the former even designing a bespoke NX.[8]

The use of relatively mainstream commercial artists such as will.i.am, Sting, Celine Dion, or John Mayer in automotive branding may be unsurprising. Perhaps more unexpected is that the use of traditionally non-commercial indie groups in car advertising, à la Wilco's collaboration with Volkswagen, also seems to be on the rise. In the past several years, there has been a flood of indie acts that have licensed their music in the service of car advertising campaigns. A brief list of the more conspicuous deals include Fun's "We Are Young" (2011) for the Chevy Sonic Super Bowl ad (2012), Phoenix's "1901" for the Cadillac SRX (both 2010), Royal Teeth's "Wild" for the Buick Verano (both 2012), and Saidah Baba Talibah's "Revolution" for the Chevrolet Volt (both 2011). In almost all cases, the television commercial was released within months of the release of the song so as to best capitalize on the latter's inevitably fleeting social impact.[9]

Of course, to a large extent the allure and incentive for independent and alternative artists to license their music is a financial one. A one-year licence for an existing song by a relatively unknown band runs from $10,000 to $25,000, while an original composition can cost $25,000–$30,000. For a year-long national campaign, a marquee-name band could get $150,000 for existing work, and up to $300,000 for an original composition for a multi-year campaign (Hopper, 2013). This can mean significant sales and radio play, as well as fast-tracking an unknown artist into the mainstream. Music brand supervisor Bryan Ray Turcotte believes that this new marketing world is overtly affecting the thought processes of new artists:

I'm seeing baby bands talk about advertising the way that baby bands used to talk about getting signed. ... It's like the in-house music producers are the new A&R guys, and the bands want an ad, just the way they wanted a record deal. That's what they aspire to have (Hopper, 2013).

Although licensing a song to an ad is lucrative for an artist, as brand manager Grant McDonough claims, the benefits of this relationship are potentially even more valuable for the corporate licensee.

> Eight out of ten of the most-followed people on Twitter are musicians. Nine out of ten of the most-viewed things on YouTube are music videos. What's the value of having [a musician tweet] about something to 20 million followers? That's more than a primetime ad buy on NBC you could spend gazillions on. And musicians are finally starting to realize that this is worth more than any song [they] could write. *That's* money (Hopper, 2013).

So far I have only discussed bands that have licensed their pre-existing work to appear in automotive commercials. However, artists are also subject to the allure of writing and releasing music consciously tied to advertising campaigns. Although not concerned with automotive advertising, one of the most overt instances of corporate influence on an artist's music occurred in 2003, when McDonald's enlisted Justin Timberlake for its ubiquitous "I'm Lovin' It" campaign. More than simply use Timberlake to sing its iconic "ba da ba ba ba" jingle in commercials and sponsor his forthcoming tour, the collaboration began several months before the commercial aired, when Timberlake released a fully fledged single and video employing the jingle, also called "I'm Lovin' It." Steve Stoute (2011), the former music marketing executive who introduced McDonald's to Timberlake, described this approach as "reverse engineering," a process that boosts the credibility of a brand's message by "first putting it in a pop culture form that isn't connected in any way to the brand" (p. 220). As Stoute explains, "Commission a song to be performed by an iconic artist; promote it months before [the] McDonald's campaign; and at the same time start promoting the marketing slogan" (p. 221). Such a covert advance approach is not uncommon in movie promotion—indeed, Timberlake released his 2016 hit "Can't Stop the Feeling," featured in the *Trolls* soundtrack, several months before the movie appeared in theatres. For Timberlake, "I'm Lovin' It" was a marketing and financial coup, earning him an estimated $6 million (Elliott, 2003). It also prefigured other agreements he and other major pop stars have recently made with major corporations, including Taylor Swift unveiling her *1989* song "Style" (2014) in a Target commercial or Jay Z releasing his *Magna Carta Holy Grail* (2013) album in partnership with Samsung.[10]

Timberlake, Jay Z, or Swift, mainstream brands in their own right, all created artistic content to align with other major brands. Little-known emerging and independent artists, however, are also increasingly being sought by brands to write music that will intentionally promote their products.[11] Brooklyn-based indie band X Ambassador's hit single "Renegades" (2015), for example, was written and released as a conscious commercial tie-in with the release of Jeep's 2015 Renegade ad campaign. X Ambassadors and

Interscope Records producer Alex da Kid were approached by Fiat Chrysler for a song that would complement its new Jeep Renegade marketing. In an interview with *Adweek*, da Kid noted that the band and the brand considered how to market the message in a way that would be "authentic and organic" to everyone involved (Monllos, 2015). For its part, Fiat Chrysler, parent company of Jeep, created a micro-website that allowed consumers to watch short videos of the band exploring the Jeep Renegade; and, of course, the band was featured in television marketing for the car.

The collaboration enjoyed immediate success. Previous to the release of "Renegades," X Ambassadors had achieved their highest *Billboard* chart position, #87, in 2014 with the song "Jungle." "Renegades," co-written with da Kid, reached #1 on *Billboard*'s Top 40. Fiat Chrysler chief marketing officer Olivier François proclaimed:

> The music is a smash, the hook is super catchy. But what really made me feel that [song] was the campaign was the way they speak of the millennials being the modern renegades. The genius here is that you tie the name of the car, which is "Renegade" to the mindset of the target, which is the millennial target (Monllos, 2015).

In a company press release, François went even further in openly announcing the musical influence:

> Through this unprecedented collaboration with X Ambassadors and Alex da Kid to build a campaign around an original song, *we're staking a new claim to music* and setting the stage for the Jeep brand's North America marketing launch for the all-new 2015 Jeep Renegade. ... Together, we've created a one-of-a-kind platform that features lyrics and track written with the modern renegade in mind—its name invoking the very spirit and mindset of Millennials—and features traits inherent in the Jeep Renegade DNA that will allow the campaign to have global relevance (FCA, 2015, emphasis added).

The claim of "staking a new claim to music" that is part of the "Jeep Renegade DNA" highlights the brand as a new media "platform" and underscores its emotional human connection to millennials. It seems likely that more examples of the overt infiltration and influence of automotive companies in popular music will emerge in the future. Marketers in search of currency with millennial consumers possessing a growing need for digital content and dealing with a music industry still attempting to adapt to new technologies and marketing strategies have helped create a scenario in which alternative or independent music and corporate culture, two once-polar opposites, are increasingly happily attracted.

In addition to its debut as a television commercial, X Ambassadors created their own official music video for the song, released a few days after the Jeep

Renegade television campaign began. Unlike the car ad, which depicts the band arriving at a gig juxtaposed with able-bodied surfers, skateboarders, and hikers—purported renegades all—the music video shows a collection of inspirational clips of people with physical disabilities performing various athletic feats. The song "Renegades," beyond its Jeep tie-in, was inspired in part by X Ambassador keyboardist Casey Harris, blind since birth. Lead vocalist Sam Harris, Casey's brother, described the band's thinking behind the video: "This video is about people who defy the odds; who, when all the cards seem to have been stacked against them, still find ways to accomplish incredible things" (KROQ, 2015). Lyrically, this message is portrayed in somewhat different terms, as film directors Steven Spielberg and Stanley Kubrick are evoked as renegade "underdog" and "outlaw" icons: "All hail the outlaws, Spielbergs and Kubricks."[12] On the surface, what might be construed as a naked commercial co-option of X Ambassadors' artistic agency by the Jeep campaign is, at least in part, mitigated by the socially conscious message of the band's official music video. On one level, we see alternative music and its "renegade" values being converted into yet more commercial capital, while at the same time the band maintains its socially progressive image—as, in turn, does Chrysler by its association with the band (the Jeep Renegade still features prominently in the band's official video). X Ambassadors' indie image and music help humanize the car in Chrysler's media advertising, while the band's video simultaneously highlights the bodies and physical abilities of disabled athletes and thus serves to humanize the band and, by extension, the Jeep Renegade and Chrysler Corporation. Through this collaboration, the Jeep Renegade seeks to become an inclusive extension of both the able and the disabled body.

The politics of automotive musical branding

As we have seen, the cross-marketing of popular music performers and automobiles hopes to humanize the corporation and car brand by inducing the consumer to associate the product with a "human" face and lifestyle and the aesthetic qualities of the music it promotes. Social science research has looked to the concept of values to explain successful celebrity endorsement. Defined by psychologist Milton Rokeach (1968) as "centrally held enduring beliefs which guide actions and judgments," values are central to people's lives and guide behaviours and judgments across many situations (p. 550; also Rokeach, 1973; Kahle & Timmer, 1983). Because values are higher-order constructs that can affect other consumer-related constructs, such as attitudes and behaviours, the congruence between celebrity values (as perceived by consumers) and values represented by products is typically considered an addition to attractiveness (likeability) and expertise (credibility) of the celebrity matched to the product. For instance, celebrities who are associated with success-related values (e.g., a sense of accomplishment) by consumers can be matched with products that represent success-related values. This is most notably highlighted in the will.i.am/Lexus "collaboration." Chris Taylor, head of European marketing for Lexus, explains that will.i.am was perceived as sharing the values that the company wished to be known for:

> From a brand perspective ... we thought long and hard about getting a celebrity who was relevant and credible and from a values perspective had empathy with the brand. Will is a champion of design, creativity, innovation, it's exactly what Lexus stands for (Sparey, 2014).

In their quest to align their cars with consumer tastes, automotive manufacturers associate themselves with celebrities whose values align with the constructed and desired identity and "values" of the car to be marketed. In many respects, this again represents a form of human–product hybridity whereby the celebrity embodies the values of the car/product, thus imbuing the car/product with those same human attributes. To some extent, such marketing is a natural outcome of the totalizing effort of consumer capitalism. We are encouraged to understand the automobile in human terms, as a sympathetic living entity that shares our values and that helps enable the construction of our self-identity through our lifestyle choices.

It seems that, for car companies, the values they wish to embody, and with which they believe consumers will identify with the most, are becoming those that appear to criticize the very corporate/capitalist system of which they are part. As manifest in the Jeep cross-branding with X Ambassadors, corporate marketing departments are co-opting critical and aesthetic approaches of artists who are more commonly associated with inverting power relationships. Marketers are adopting positions and strategies in line with populist political empowerment. Marketers and brands attempt to convince (sometimes inveigle) consumers that they have adopted attributes of an ideal culture by emphasizing values such as inclusivity, empowerment, liberation, and pleasure. At the same time, however, musical culture becomes a valuable resource for the accumulation of capital as it conforms to the logic of commercial branding. Often it is the very resistance to corporate branding—the cynicism, irony, and suspicion of corporate values with which much alternative and indie musical culture is typically associated—that becomes the very source of capital value.[13] With their consistent efforts at developing new and improved ways to simulate authenticity in commodity form, brands now even stand in for political values. Seemingly in an attempt to counter the stereotype of the conservative corporate and environmentally unfriendly automotive industry, brands such as Jeep Renegade align themselves around, and co-opt, progressive, liberal values, stressing innovative and independent ideals. The micro-website for the 2015 Jeep Renegade, for example, includes the following under the title "Doers. Dreamers. Adventurers":

> Renegades never stand still. They see opportunity where others give up and love to share their discoveries. Adventure is defined by the moment

they're in, the company they're with and the potential for making memories. They don't follow the same old routes. They follow their instincts (Jeep, n.d.).

This, in combination with videos showing the members of X Ambassadors (described as "the perfect voice to represent the Renegade spirit") exploring the vehicle, highlights the liberal and creatively independent values of the brand and its target demographic.

As demonstrated by the Jeep Renegade campaign, contemporary marketers also appear to be moving from a "customer satisfaction" model to a "consumer empowerment" one, adopting ethically sensitive, inclusive, and often participatory language. On the Renegade website discussed above, ideas of opportunity, sharing, responsibility, adventure, independence, defiance, and discovery permeate. This can also be seen in BMW Mini's 2016 "Defy Labels" campaign. The website for the campaign features a variety of celebrities, including tennis star Serena Williams and musician T-Pain, and invites the viewer to "watch as these icons speak about the labels they've overcome and even embraced on their paths to success. So what defines you and what you're capable of? Do you defy all labels and carve your own path?" (Defy Labels, n. d.). BMW here attempts to empower potential customers by challenging them to "defy all labels" by associating themselves, ironically, with its brand.

Marketers and branding agencies thus create a new ethical language in partnership with culture makers like musicians. In so doing, corporations reframe their position in culture in ways that are conducive for brand building. Artists such as X Ambassadors, who in the past may have spoken out against the potentially negative social and environmental impact of cars and car manufacturers, now increasingly praise corporate investment in local culture, believing, or at least rationalizing to themselves, that their music and local scenes retain their autonomy (recall Steve Aoki's unreserved support for Scion outlined earlier). In attempting to legitimize their own cultural subjectivity, their discourse also serves to authenticate and reinforce the corporate brand. Separate from their music licensing deals, through their association and identification with various brands, artists, and by extension their audiences, provide a form of unpaid advertising labour—promoting the corporations and products by their very attendance and performances at sponsored events—and implicit cultural capital that make these marketing initiatives appear both authentic and successful (Carah, 2010, p. 106).[14] Indeed, the notion of "selling out" is perhaps a moot point as we are all complicit in capitalism—though one might conceive selling out as an inauthentic/deceptive relationship between artist and product.

The imagined social world that marketers and bands co-construct is nonetheless dependent on the extraction of surplus value (the monetary value) that brands accrue through the association with culture makers. As such, the extraction of surplus value seemingly results in an asymmetrical sharing of power. Brands accrue value off the labour of their cultural collaborators. The myth-making of musicians, imbued in notions of authentic creativity, produces a popular culture that evades or at least mitigates its contradictions. Musicians must ultimately negotiate between the ideology of authenticity—often based on romantic and unattainable notions of artistic freedom from external monetary influence—and the demands of corporations that want to profit from that ideology. Ironically, despite the sentiments of the song and commercial campaign, it seems doubtful that any of us are truly renegades given our inability to escape the ubiquity of industrial capitalism. Our identities are at least in part bounded and shaped by the commercial imperatives of both bands and brands.

Conclusion

Celebrity sound branding has become a common strategy used by automobile companies to reach their target audiences. The licensing of music and the association with the artists who create it enables car brands to sensorially connect with or latch on to human consumers. The music and musician used in a branding campaign associates the car with a recognizably human activity, and immediately connects the machine to a recognizable human face. The music used in the campaign is heard by the listener/consumer, is felt in their body, and conjures an emotional response that, if successful, allows the consumer to identify the car with attributes of their own life, real or imagined.

But celebrity sound branding has taken a further step whereby commercially artistic content is actively tailored in the service of branding. In influencing the creative process of artists like X Ambassadors, in commissioning them to write a commercially released pop song that intentionally promotes their product and brand, Jeep-Chrysler employs the band as product sound designers. Perhaps recalling historical models of aristocratic artistic patronage, it is another form of automotive sound branding, like the sound logos and chimes used in operating the vehicle itself. What Kurpiers (2009) says about sound designers is also true of sonic branders: they "enact and concretize sonically ideas [and] cultural norms about social relations, behaviors, and ideologies [and] organize musical sounds in ways that convey meaning within a multilayered, sometimes thorny labyrinth of constituents, ideologies, and popular culture" (p. 205; also see Powers, 2010, p. 300). When music is specifically commissioned by car companies to align with company goals—such as the notion of being an outsider or renegade—the creative process becomes a performative political act by a corporation, for this type of sound branding is one that has the additional benefit of harvesting surplus capital from the band's independent image and like-minded fan base.

Branding campaigns now serve as alternative media platforms from which to launch both new artists and new music as, almost by default of the declining efficacy of more traditional media such as radio, artists now create their music in alliance with car company ideals. It is a collaborative performance that structures our taste, not only in automobiles but also in popular music itself. In turn, car companies reap benefits from both the commercial cachet of the associated artist and, particularly in the case of alternative or independent acts, the cultural capital due to the perception that their "authenticity" is imparted to the brand and its promotional activities. Car companies employing popular music and musicians thus connect to consumers in what is perceived as an authentic way. In essence, the licensing and commissioning of popular music are performative acts in their own right that create what might be termed a "hyperstition" in which the respective mythical "authenticities" of product, artist, and their relationship are made "real" in the minds of consumers (Priest, 2013). As a result, the proliferation of music licensing and, now, of commissioning and influencing the content of commercially released popular music in support of branding is one more step in David Hesmondhalgh's (2007) belief that we are witnessing an "extension and gentle acceleration of the long-term process of commodification of culture" (p. 301). This may not be an unexpected outcome, however, as the end product of capitalism, if taken to its logical conclusion, is the commodification of everything. An early critic of popular music and the culture industry, Theodor Adorno (2001), argued that popular music promoted the creation of a distracted or obedient listener in service of maintaining an illusion of subjective choice to further social control. Adorno's claim that "the listener is converted, along his line of least resistance, into the acquiescent purchaser" seems even more cogent today under the weight of sound-branding practices that seek to alter our behaviour through increasingly naturalized relationships between brands and popular music (p. 32; see also Powers, 2010, p. 292).

The situation is equally pronounced in terms of the sound design emanating from our cars that seeks to sensorially connect us to it. As computer chips and digital technologies become ever more powerful and less costly to produce, it can only be assumed that sound branding in cars and other appliances will become ever more sophisticated and omnipresent. In many ways, the practice of sound branding appears to overtly reinforce philosopher Marshall McLuhan's famous dictum (introduced in 1964) that the medium is the message (see McLuhan, 1994). In the case of car or appliance sound marks or alert chimes, the sonic "message"—so to speak—is inherently fused with the attempt to brand and sell the product (the medium) that conveys that message.

Be it in automobiles or the increasing use of sonic chimes and notifiers in stoves, washing machines, or almost any other appliance with which we interact, more and more attention is being paid to the sonic relationship between humans and our tools. I use the term "relationship" intentionally as it seems evident that, at least in part, what is occurring is an emphasis on creating increasingly intimate anthropomorphic relationships between ourselves and the inanimate (albeit "smart" or "intelligent") technologies that surround us. The sounds and music emanating from our cars, whether consequential or intentional, serve not only to further promote brand identification but also to promote and advertise our own identities. Whether influenced by advertising or not, it is we as consumers who have chosen, albeit often subject to budgetary restrictions, to identify ourselves with the products and their associated branding.[15] Just like a pop song, sound tags and sonic logos (whether musically inspired or not) are designed to produce an "I like it and would like to associate myself with it" response from consumers. As such, the technology of sound chimes and sonic branding serves not only to represent both company and product but also, simultaneously, representations "of the self to the self." In the words of communications scholar James Katz (2003), they become fashionable "accoutrements to our self-creation and symbolic interpersonal communication" (p. 318).

As discussed in Chapter 1, the history of sound design in cars, as manifest in numerous advertising campaigns devoted to the idea of a quiet ride, was initially about reducing noises that were perceived as a portent of a car's lack of reliability and quality (Bijsterveld et al., 2013, p. 173). While manufacturers have by no means abandoned the idea of equating quietness with quality and luxury, they now, ironically, add sounds to the driving experience—e.g., warning sounds and engine start-up chimes—in order to achieve that same sense of well-being. Moreover, through the concept of holistic sound branding, such as Audi's Corporate Sound Concept, those reassuring sounds become associated with the corporate brand.

Both composed music or specifically designed product sounds and soundtracks remove the perceived threat of both the chaotic and the consequential noise of the machine. In essence, they give the user of the appliance a sense, whether real or illusory, of control and security. Brandon LaBelle (2010) recognizes this sense of auditory bonding when he argues that "music affords a kind of auditory device on to which one can latch in some way or other" (pp. 143–144). Thus, the increasing sonification of our technology helps to humanize it. It provides the user with the assurance of a human presence, a vibratory sonic interface between machine, its creators, and its operators. LaBelle further opines that "auditory latching can be appreciated as existing below the audible field, and within the vibratory sensing … granting us a deep vocabulary of how to feel" (p. 138). Indeed, the sound of our computer booting up, or of the engine of our car starting, often provides us with a distinct feeling of reassurance, that everything is working properly. Furthermore, both the intentional sounds and perhaps the more subconscious consequential sounds (the vibrations of which are more likely to be felt than consciously heard) are important in establishing how we feel about and relate to our machines. Product sound designers thus essentially supply a sonic vibratory language through which we communicate and bond with our cars and appliances. Our cars, then, are designed to both physically and emotionally "move" us.

The car, of course, is the product of a vast array of human labour, from the designers and engineers to the parts manufacturers and assembly line workers. There is a sense that the car does, in fact, take on a life of its own. For Karl Marx (2002, n.p.), machines "are organs of the human brain, created by the human hand; the power of knowledge, objectified." Gerald Raunig (2010), channelling Marx, even claims that machines and technology take on a virtuosic component separate from the human content that creates it. He writes:

> The machine emerges as a virtuoso, *having a soul of their own* (taken from workers), whose virtuosic handling of their implements and whose labour on and in machines merges into an activity … that is determined and regulated by the movement and parts of the very machine itself (p. 113, emphasis added).

In this manner, automobiles can be said to transcend the limitations of their apparent inanimate construction and actively inherit the "souls" of their creators. Thus, automobiles evince a hauntological humanity through the unseen presence of sounds and labour of past producers. Furthermore, in the ability of these durable goods to transcend the present—indeed, as fetishized in vintage car cultures—these past traces of labour ultimately project themselves into a circulation of multiple presents and futures that disrupt and dislocate any sense of absolute temporal flow.

The increasing use of intentional and consequential sound design in automobiles haptically sutures the human to the machine and often serves, perhaps ironically, as reassurance of our own humanity. As discussed earlier in this chapter, this is a prime example of Urry's (2007) contention that "[i]t is through inhabiting machines that humans will come to 'life'" (pp. 179–80). Of course, in the case of the automobile, the reverse is also true. The machine essentially only comes to life when it is inhabited by a human (and when a human is present to perceive it in that manner). Facilitated and enhanced through sound, music, and touch, the car–driver experience thus exemplifies the notion of technogenesis, which, as outlined by N. Katherine Hayles (2012, p. 104), involves the coevolution of, and feedback between, humans and technology in a highly complex media ecology that mimics, on a deep level, a complex simulation of life itself.

The increasing ubiquity of sonic branding in automobiles and elsewhere also testifies to the growing proclivity to commodity fetishism and the penetration and assimilation of corporate culture into our individual daily consciousness. Bombarded by and immersed in a myriad of advertising touchpoints of which many may not even be aware, we are increasingly becoming, or at least encouraged to become, branded individuals. Like it or not, branding, sonic or otherwise, is part of a culture industry that creates fantasies that structure our social reality. Our consumption choices, while overtly subjective, are fundamentally limited by product availability and price point while marketers attempt, in part through music and sound, to influence our perception of the world to align with their corporate goals. Additionally, the notion of consumption has become more than the simple acquisition and use of goods, but expanded to be about how we relate to our goods as almost social entities. In this manner, sonic branding (including music licensing) and its concomitant goal of creating a human relationship with a product fit well with the legal definition of a corporation. Derived from the Latin word *corpus* (or body), the corporation is itself an anthropomorphic entity referring to a company or group of persons authorized to act as a single entity with many of the same legal rights and responsibilities of an actual living person. Thus, the corporation births products that are extensions of itself and that, in turn, through advertising and branding strategies, help construct our own sense of corporality through advertising and branding strategies. The sonic chimes, beeps, warnings, sound logos, songs, and other forms of audio branding all combine to imbue us with aurally haptic connections to the products we are using and, by extension, the corporate body that produces them. As such, sound branding, whether through celebrity musical associations or intentionally designed product sounds, serves both to mitigate the consequential and potentially alienating sounds of the car or appliance while simultaneously creating anthropomorphic brand "identities" for that same machine, its manufacturers, and even its users. Moreover, as manifest in the commercial success of intentionally branded songs, sound branding increasingly shapes and influences recent popular music. Practices such as "reverse engineering" a song such that listeners are initially unaware that it is advertising a product seem ethically dubious at best, and challenge our perception of reality in popular music. They essentially attempt to manipulate the social imagination in order to structure the collective psyche—like "fake news" and "alternative facts," they create virtual realities that, in turn, deliberately distort our construction of reality.

Notes

1 A section of this chapter appears in *The Oxford Handbook of Music and Advertising,* edited by James Deaville, Siu-Lan Tan, and Ronald Rodman (Oxford University Press, forthcoming).
2 The exception to this is a few studies that have looked at related issues, such as the prominence of techno music in automobile television commercials (Taylor, 2007) and the influence of car audio systems on hip hop production practices (J. A. Williams, 2010).
3 With the increasing inevitability of "intelligent" autonomous or self-driving cars coming to market in the near future, it seems likely that use of anthropomorphic identities, sonic and otherwise, by car manufacturers will only be exacerbated.
4 Some of the stranger automotive endorsements by musicians occur overseas. In 1980, for example, Michael Jackson appeared in a Japanese Suzuki "Love" Scooter commercial underscored by his hit "Don't Stop 'Til You Get Enough" (1979). In a spoken English voiceover, he proclaims, "Love is my message!" Perhaps even more odd is French automaker Peugeot's commercial from 1994, which aired in various European markets, using the blind musician Ray Charles shown driving around the Bonneville Salt Flats in Utah in its 306 Cabriolet, underscored by his hit song "Georgia."
5 A brand platform emphasizes sensory consumer experiences and typically consists of several core components, including a brand's vision, mission statement, values, personality, and tone of voice (Weintraub, 2013). Many of these components assign human attributes to the brand in order to encourage consumers to relate to the product.

6 In the late 1990s, Wilco and British leftist singer-songwriter Billy Bragg wrote music that was applied to unpublished lyrics by Woody Guthrie. These songs were recorded and released as the albums *Mermaid Avenue* (1998) and *Mermaid Avenue Vol. II* (2000).

7 Lyrics and music by William Adams. Copyright Warner Chappell Music, Inc.

8 It should be noted that in addition to its collaboration with will.i.am, Lexus also sponsored talent such as Studio XO, Hellicar & Lewis, Lunice, and LuckyMe from the worlds of fashion, design, and music to showcase its artistic views, and was inspired by the NX in a digital art exhibit called NX-Perspectives.

9 One of the stranger ads to employ an independent musician was North American Mitsubishi's campaign for its 2018 Eclipse Cross, called "Freestyle Test Drive." The ad uses a white salesman who invites potential customers at a dealership for a test drive. While on the test drive the salesman shows them the "great sound system," and then busts into a full-blown freestyle rap that rapidly spits innumerable aspects of the car's features in an impressive flow that takes the drivers by surprise (Mitsubishi, 2018). Unbeknownst to the customers, the salesman in the ad is, in fact, independent freestyle phenomenon Harry Mack.

10 The Samsung deal included giving away one million Jay Z albums to purchasers of Samsung's smartphones a full 72 hours before the album was officially on sale and available to other consumers.

11 Canadian indie folk-pop duo Tegan & Sarah, for example, teamed with Oreo cookies for an original song in their "Wonderfilled" campaign of 2014.

12 Lyrics and music by Adam Levin, Alexander Junior Grant, Casey Wakeley Harris, Noah G. Feldshuh, and Samuel Nelson Harris. Copyright Kobalt Music Publishing Ltd.

13 Ryan Moore's *Sells Like Teen Spirit* (2010) deals with this question in the context of the rise and fall of grunge rock.

14 X Ambassadors are not the first artists to adapt their creative process to satisfy a corporate branding partner. In 1968, Buick offered The Doors $75,000 to alter the lyrics to "Light My Fire" from "Come on, baby, light my fire" to "Come on, Buick, light my fire." Singer Jim Morrison quashed the deal and the ad was never made. When such attempts have been made, they typically take the form of a request to modify a song's lyrics to fit with a product after the song has gained popularity, rather than an initial creative decision by songwriters. A rare example of the latter is Chris Brown's "Forever" (2007), which prominently features the slogan of Wrigley's Double Mint gum in its chorus: "Double your pleasure / Double your fun and dance." Almost a year later, Wrigley revealed that the song was actually part of a cleverly orchestrated branding move conceived by a former senior executive at Interscope Records, Steve Stoute. Interscope is also the label responsible for the Jeep/X Ambassadors relationship. Sometimes artists employ brand names unsolicited, as a way to attract brand attention and hopefully earn sponsorships down the line. In Busta Rhymes' hit "Pass the Courvoisier" (2001), for example, management claimed the liquor brand was simply an artistic choice. After the song's release coincided with "a double-digit uptick in U.S. sales" of Courvoisier, the company penned a sponsorship deal with the rapper (Kaufman, 2003).

15 The decision to buy a car or other product is still largely predicated on utilitarian precepts. The product has to work well for us, and we still test-drive cars to ensure that we like the fit and feel. Marketers, however, have realized that taste in music contributes to identity formation, and that by aligning their products with certain music and sounds that link is something that can be capitalized on by creating that extra spur to buy.

5 The sound of cars as musical objects
Tuning, engine sound enhancement, and the quest for quiet

As discussed in Chapter 4, from its inception the automobile has made a sonic impact on society. Throughout its history, the car has projected a variety of both consequential (and often unwanted) sounds generated by its operation and intentional sounds of horns, and later radios and stereo systems. The sonic component of cars has meant that they have lent themselves well to musical metaphors and to considering them in musical terms. The "pitch" of an engine, for example, is one of the prime characteristics that distinguishes one car from another, and forms a key component of brand identification for manufacturers. This chapter traces the sonic and musical components of automotive culture, from the penchant for using musical names in branding cars and metaphors of music that are used to codify and identify engine sounds to the seemingly endless quest for a quiet ride that marks many automotive advertising campaigns.

What's in a name?

One of the most overt connections between car culture and music is the plethora of musical terms, like Sonata or Prelude, that are used in automotive branding in nearly every part of the globe. David Placek, president of the marketing firm Lexicon Branding, believes this has to do with familiarity: "Music is universal. … A lot of the words and phrases used to describe certain phrases in music are fairly well recognized" (Wise, 2013). A stirring or lyrical name can be a powerful selling tool, particularly when it comes to marketing more eco-friendly designs. According to Placek, musical car names "reflect women coming more into the marketplace, younger people driving more and cars getting more economical and more ecological." Conversely, "if it's a big muscle car you don't want something softer and smoother" (Wise, 2013). While such an opinion may be somewhat generic, unscientific, and informed by stereotyping, there is no doubt that musical names form their own subcategory of car branding.

Likely no manufacturer is more wedded to musical names than Kia. The South Korean manufacturer has a legacy of cars with musical names: the premium Cadenza, the multi-purpose Rondo, and the compact Forte. Its rival

Hyundai, however, likely has the most well-known musical brand in its mid-size Sonata. In 2010, Hyundai rolled out its "music to the eyes" ad campaign that directly played off the Sonata brand name.[1]

Japan's Honda also has a long history of musical car names. The Honda Prelude was one in a series of vehicles with music-themed names the company developed in the 1980s. The Prelude was the most popular, undergoing five iterations from 1978 to 2001. Others were the Quintet (1980–1985), Concerto (1988–1994), Ballade (1980–1986), and Jazz (1982–present; it is also sold under the name Fit in North America, Japan, and China). Between 1998 and 2004, Toyota marketed a subcompact car called the Duet in Japan (known as the Sirion internationally). The Nissan Note, a five-seat hatchback, is a rare example of a single-syllable musical name.[2] North American cars featuring musical names include the Ford Tempo (a commercial from its early days encouraged consumers "to pick up the tempo of your life"), the Buick Encore, and the Pontiac Vibe.

The penchant for musical names transcends the major automotive manufacturing regions of South Korea, Japan, and North America. Testifying to the international appeal of musical car names are the Czech-manufactured Škoda Octavia, and the Aria, a crossover SUV from India's Tata Motors. The latter is also a rare example of a car that explicitly references opera in its name, and seemingly attempts to link its product to the typical social elitism associated with European opera.

Indeed, with the possible exception of the Honda Jazz, the vast majority of these musical names are terms associated with classical music. While automobile companies often rely on a variety of popular music styles to sell their products in television commercials, as actual brand name association, classical music is the preferred genre. Beyond being often mellifluous and friendly, musical terms and names tend to transcend associations with national languages and countries, and so are more universally recognizable. Above all, however, it seems clear that there is a desired perception of a transferred cachet from classical music to the automobile. The stereotypical notions of enduring history, quality, exclusivity, and intellectual and upper-class connotations that are commonly attached to classical music are, in turn, transferred to the car brand in question. It is likely no accident that the brands listed above are all relatively inexpensive and, as such, the classical music labels invoke an aspirational image for entry-level middle-class buyers.

Sounding cars: tuning up

Aside from musical car names, the nexus of cars and music occurs most overtly in the parameters of rhythm and sound. While it is important to distinguish between the intentional sounds that designers have added to enhance the experience of car travel and the consequential sounds associated with the operation of the car itself, the internal combustion engine car is, by its very nature, a dynamically expressive piece of machinery. Spark plugs, crankshafts, valves, pistons, carburettors, fuel injectors, and exhaust systems all emit various frequencies and often overlapping rhythmic pulses that, working in unison, create what we would commonly recognize as the sound of an engine—for many a sound as aesthetically pleasing as conventional music. The combination of overlapping and, at times, synchronous rhythmic pulses and sounds might be likened to the complexity of baroque counterpoint—indeed, the mechanistically repetitive *Fortspinnung* sequencing found in much baroque music led to it being derisively labelled by some as "sewing machine music."

Add to the sounds of the engine the vast array of other consequential sounds, including tyres on the road, windshield wipers, and various squeaks and rattles of car seats, pedals, shock absorbers, and loosening parts of the cars assembly, to say nothing of the similar cacophony produced by numerous other cars on the road. All told, it is easy understand the premium that car manufacturers and the public alike place on obtaining a "quiet" ride. As any automotive mechanic knows, despite the increasing proliferation of computerized system checks, the ability to listen to a car when it is operating is crucial for the diagnosis of many problems. Indeed, the historical cross-pollination of cars and music finds one of its most dominant metaphors in the common notion of the "tune-up," in which various systems, indicators, and engine parts are brought back into an optimal harmonious state.[3] In more recent times, the concept of car "tuning" has expanded to mean the modification and personalization of car performance and appearance. Exterior modifications might include changing the aerodynamic characteristics of the vehicle with side skirts, spoilers, or non-factory air vents and rims. However, tuning also extends to the modification of engines, electrical systems, suspensions, and, notably, audio systems.

The traditional notion of an engine tune-up involves more than just a sonic musical metaphor, and reaches into the realm of sound perception in an active sense. Engine sound is often perceived as an integral part of a car's identity. Aside from visual design, it is the distinctive tone of a Ferrari's six-cylinder engine that separates it from a four-cylinder Toyota. Indeed, the tune-up is often more than just a musical metaphor for car health. Car engines are typically discussed in terms of their pitch. The sound of a car engine originates from vibrations causing air-pressure disturbances that hit our eardrums. The frequency, or hertz (Hz), of a sound wave—how many times the wave oscillates in a second—determines how our brain processes and interprets it as a distinct pitch. A higher frequency makes for a higher pitch, and vice versa. A car's engine under load (the torque output of an engine; as the load or stress on an engine increases its speed will decrease) plays a range of frequencies; but its root note—its characteristic pitch, the core musical voice, so to speak, that it is built on—is defined by its so-called dominant frequency. These sound-generating vibrations derive from the combustion in each cylinder and the corresponding pressure waves in the intake and exhaust systems. They are all keyed to the engine's rotational speed; as these revolutions rise and fall, the pitch also perceptibly rises or falls.

Calculating that dominant frequency at any given number of revolutions per minute (rpm) is relatively straightforward. First, one must convert engine rpm to hertz using the following formula: 60 rpm = 1 revolution per second, or 1 Hz. Thus, a V-6 (six-cylinder) engine rotating at 1800 rpm can be said to be running at 30 Hz (1800/60 = 30). Multiplying the 30 Hz value by three (the number of ignition events per crankshaft revolution for a six-cylinder engine) produces a 90-Hz dominant frequency that defines the six-cylinder engine sound at 1800 rpm (Tingwall, 2015). As the engine speed increases, the firing frequency rises proportionally. In a six-cylinder engine, it is also called the "third-engine order" because the frequency is three times that of the engine's rotation. In an eight-cylinder engine, the firing frequency is the fourth-engine order; in a V-10, it is the fifth, and so on.

This is only part of the picture, however, as the engine's overall timbre, namely the distinctive quality that separates the sound of a six-cylinder Toyota from a six-cylinder Ferrari, involves thousands of variables. The firing frequency of the pistons induces multiple additional vibrations throughout the engine's structure and inner workings. Most throaty, aggressive-sounding cars have very high half orders, such as 2.5 and 3.5 times the firing frequency (Tingwall, 2015). These produce the growl often desirable in a sports car, and are normally adjusted through exhaust tuning. The relative loudness or dynamic amplitude of the higher orders defines an engine's distinct timbre. Those are the pitches that build on the root note to create the engine's distinctive chord.

A noise, vibration, and harshness (NVH) engineer determines which ancillary frequencies are allowed to sing and which are muted. An exhaust muffler cancels some unpleasant frequencies that might otherwise resonate in the cabin when the engine operates at a certain load and rpm. Every engine's sound is the product of a network—an orchestra of sorts—of bushings, pipe diameters, and hundreds of sheet metal pieces of varying thicknesses, as well as design factors such as exhaust layout, insulation, and body shell.

Electronic engine sound enhancement

When Milli Vanilli admitted that the vocals for which the group won a Grammy in 1990 were not their own, the award was returned, contracts were voided, and their musical careers were effectively over. What is less known, though hardly a secret to those immersed in the latest automotive technologies, is that many cars are effectively faking the sound of their engines. Electronic sound enhancement uses the cabin speakers or an electromagnetic shaker attached to the firewall to generate its own internal-combustion soundtrack. Artificial enhancement may be taboo among car engine purists, but it is increasingly popular among automakers because it is cheap, effective, and adds minimal weight.

Car manufacturers such as Cadillac, Lexus, Ford, BMW, Volkswagen, and many others have been turning to various incarnations of the process to alter the perceived sound of their engines. Unlike Milli Vanilli and other infamous incidents of musical performance enhancement, most car companies have been transparent about their use of artificial noise; and, as I have written about elsewhere (McLeod, 2011), we are likely to be far more forgiving of artificial performance enhancement when it is applied to machinery. Some observers, however, think otherwise. Karl Brauer, a senior analyst with Kelley Blue Book, for example, says automakers should stop the lies and come clean with drivers:

> "If you're going to do that stuff, do that stuff. Own it. Tell customers: If you want a V-8 rumble, you've gotta buy a V-8 that costs more, gets worse gas mileage and hurts the Earth," Brauer said. "You're fabricating the car's sexiness. You're fabricating performance elements of the car that don't actually exist. That just feels deceptive to me" (Harwell, 2015).

Although there are varying ways by which the sound of engines can be electronically enhanced, BMW's M-series can serve as a case in point.[4] M-series engineers discovered that the F10 chassis, like that of many other new cars these days, is so effective at insulating the cabin from road and engine noise that the M5, likely BMW's most iconic M-series model, lost one of the sonic characteristics that made previous iterations so viscerally thrilling and compelling to its buyers. In order to give the driver a better aural feel for the engine, an exterior recording of the M5's motor plays through the car's stereo. The precise sample is determined by engine load and rpm. Some of the real engine sounds are still audible to the driver, so the recording is essentially more of an enhanced backing track to the original lead vocal of the engine. BMW claims that the setup helps the driver shift by ear and reduces the chances of bumping the rev limiter (a device typically used to prevent damage to an engine by restricting its maximum rotational speed).

Among purists, such technological trickery has resulted in something of an identity crisis that calls into question the authenticity of the driving experience. The "aural experience" of a car, some would argue, is an aesthetic intangible that is just as valuable as the technology revving under the hood. Musical metaphors, much like the idea of tuning, are therefore commonly used in automotive discourse. Commenting on Ford's recent decision to use "Active Noise Control" on its iconic Mustang brand, one enthusiast remarked, "For a car guy, it's literally music to hear that thing rumble" (Harwell, 2015). For many in the automotive world, the sound of a car is a complex symphony of hundreds of moving parts that function like an actual orchestra and produce something similarly aurally pleasing.

In 2015, German car manufacturer Porsche AG produced a book curated by their director of historical archives, Dieter Landenberger (2015), and dedicated to the distinctive engine sounds of their cars. Entitled *Porsche Sounds*, the book features archival photographs of classic Porsche models, and comes paired with a CD of corresponding engine sounds. Landenberger sees the engine sound as creating an "emotional" bond with the consumer:

The sound of a Porsche sportscar is as iconic as its design or performance. Many car aficionados can make out a Porsche from a far distance, just by its engine sound. The idea behind the book was to combine the unique history of the Porsche brand with the emotional aspect of sound (Jamshed, 2015).

Responding to the controversial use of artificial noise enhancement, Landenberger posits:

> The typical soundtrack of a Porsche is a unique mix between the thrilling melody of the boxer engine, the crescendo of the valve trains, and the tempered trumpeting of the exhaust system. And it's the real thing, [because] artificially generating sounds and adding them to the drive spectrum through speakers is absolutely out of the question (Jamshed, 2015).

Here, Landenberger employs musical terms to describe engine sound, from the "crescendo" of the valve trains to the "trumpeting" of the exhaust. Like the use of classical terminology described in terms of car brands, his language draws on the cachet of classical music to imply a similar notion of class, refinement, and history to Porsche products.

Despite its detractors, artificial engine sound enhancement has played a central role in establishing the identity of several leading brands. The influence of music and musical acoustics, for example, was underlined in press releases announcing the 2014 Cadillac CTS models. Under the title "Cadillac Applies Art and Science to CTS Engine Sounds," Cadillac engineers applied "the principles of psychoacoustics" to "create powerful and pleasant exhaust notes" for its new models. The complete press release for the system reads as follows:

> Knowing that engine sound communicates throttle response to the driver, CTS engineers uniquely tuned each selectable driving mode—Tour, Sport and Track—to provide the driver with a specific sound impression of what's happening under the hood.
>
> Tour mode purrs with refinement. Sport mode growls with power. Track mode, only available on the CTS Vsport equipped with Cadillac's first Twin-Turbo engine, roars even more aggressively.
>
> The team drew upon its knowledge of what tones sound the most pleasing to human ears based on the study of psychoacoustics, surveyed the sounds made by competitor models and relied on their own ears when selecting final tones.
>
> The integrated electronic sound enhancement system gathers and measures information from the engine and uses Bose digital signal processing to deliver desirable tones through the Bose audio system inside the normally quiet passenger cabin.

"The sound enhancement system acts like a choir conductor, calling forth certain engine sounds to sing the loudest depending on the driving mode," said Dave Leone, CTS executive chief engineer, Performance Luxury Vehicles. "We used our ears to tell us what sounded the best and programmed the system to listen for those tones. It is Cadillac's Art and Science design philosophy applied to engine sound" (Cadillac, 2013).

Cadillac, a relatively exclusive brand name, here associates its sound enhancement features with the prestige associated with classical music and a "choir conductor." Consumers are given a choice of sound enhancement modes that will each give them a different sonic "impression of what's happening under the hood."

A variety of other manufacturers have adopted similarly musically inspired approaches to their marketing of engine sound enhancement. In the case of Porsche's 911 model for 2012, "emotion" was cited by engineers as a key factor in developing the car's acoustic signature with their "Sound Symposer" technology. "Sound was a major design and engineering focus," said Wolf-gang Hatz, Porsche's main board member for research and development (New Porsche 911, 2011). Unlike other manufacturers such as BMW, Porsche eschewed electronically synthesized noise, so the engineers developed the Sound Symposer system that is standard in all versions of the car. The system works by using an acoustic channel to pick up intake vibrations between the throttle valve and air filter; then a membrane incorporated in the channel reinforces the vibrations and transmits them as an engine sound into the cabin. It is driver activated or deactivated via a "Sport" button that controls a valve ahead of the membrane. The result is a direct acoustic link between the cabin occupants and the engine, providing optimal transmission of the engine load-dependent sounds. In addition to this optimizing of engine sounds, the sound of gearshifts can also be enhanced. The Sound Symposer incorporates a tuneable Helmholtz resonator to achieve a harmonious sound pattern, damping out unpleasant noise occurring at around 5000 rpm. Complementing the emotion generated by the Sound Symposer, when the driver completely lifts off the accelerator at high revs (around 7400 rpm) the system generates a transient, essentially artificial, backfire.

Aside from its technical features, Porsche's emotion-based Sound Symposer title is clearly a conflation of the words "symphony" and "composer." Somewhat apropos, Porsche creates an artificial word that describes a feature that creates an artificial sound. Like Cadillac, Porsche also thereby manages to connect itself to the creative status typically associated with classical music.

Lexus has employed a similar approach. When it launched its LFA super car model in 2009, the company wanted drivers to experience the full range of the car's V-10. To achieve this, Lexus contracted Yamaha—not the Yamaha Motor Company that built F1 engines in the 1980s and 1990s, but rather the musical instrument division—and its Center for Advanced Sound Technologies to tune the LFA's "symphony hall" (cabin) for the "audience" (driver), with the goal of creating an interactive loop linking a "musical instrument, space, and performer" to an "engine, body, and driver" (Yamaha, 2009). It treated the engine as a sound generator (instrument) and developed components to direct the V-10's wail to the driver. In a press release, Yamaha described its acoustic design concept and reasoning:

> The objective of this acoustic design was to utilize sound as a medium that can achieve a direct link between the driver and the vehicle. To accomplish this goal, Yamaha and Yamaha Motor decided to base the design on the following two goals.
>
> 1 Create an engine sound that reacts instantly to even delicate alterations by the driver in the vehicle's operation.
> 2 Effectively convey all of the high-grade engine sound to the driver.
>
> This approach was based on Yamaha's expertise in creating relationships between performers and musical instruments to give the performers the full enjoyment of playing an instrument.
>
> When playing a musical instrument, performers hear the delicate changes in volume, tone, and nuances that they produce themselves. Hearing these subtle changes allows performers to make instant revisions as they play the instrument. For these performers, access to high-quality audio feedback is vital to achieving the best possible performance. In this case, sensing the direct feedback of the musical instrument is what provides the performers with the enjoyment of playing an instrument (Yamaha, 2009).

Lexus thus directly identifies the car's engine with an instrument, and equates the driver with a "performer" who adjusts their driving "performance" based on "delicate changes in volume [and] tone" of the engine sound.

It is not just automobile manufacturers who are adopting musical metaphors when discussing the enhanced sound of cars. Many automotive journalists also make musical comparisons. Consider the following opinion on engine sound enhancement that directly compares the process to Milli Vanilli (a common target for writers) and the prevalent practice of Auto-Tuning:

> Most mainstream music uses some form of autotune or pitch correction, so why can't our cars? Tough as it may be to accept, "fake" engine noises are probably here to stay. Don't expect a V12 Ferrari to pull a Milli Vanilli any time soon, but continuing improvements to sound deadening and the bitter articulations of high-efficiency turbo powerplants will likely encourage automakers to use this technology to keep cars scoring high (Hard, 2014).

Of course, in recent years the relative cacophony of sounds produced by the internal combustion engine has been drastically altered and often muted by the advent of hybrid and electric cars, which have been both lauded and decried for their relative lack of noise. This change has prompted debate in many quarters. The switch to quieter hybrid engines in Formula One racing, for example, touched off an enormous controversy among fans and drivers alike. In 2014, Formula One decided to make new hybrid-style engines mandatory for all teams. The new 1.6-litre V-6 turbo engines (which replaced 2.4 litre V-8 engines) had extensive energy recovery systems, and cars had to complete races using no more than 100 kilograms (about 130 litres) of fuel. The changes were ostensibly made to make Formula One more environmentally aware and, con-comitantly, to attract more commercial partners for the 2014 season. However, after the initial race using the new power plants (the Australian Grand Prix held in March of that year), Bernie Ecclestone, the then chief executive of the Formula One Group that manages Formula One and controls the commercial rights to the sport, claimed he was "horrified" by the sound of the new cars, and prophesized that it would drive promoters and spectators away from the sport (Bernie Ecclestone horrified, 2014). Similarly, four-time world champion driver Sebastien Vettel complained about the new engines. When asked for his view on the sound of the new engines, he claimed:

> It is s***. … I was on the pitwall during the race, and it is better [quieter] than in a bar! I think for the fans it is not good. I think F1 has to be spectacular—and the sound is one of the most important things. … I remember when, although I don't remember much because I was six years old, but we went to see the cars live in free practice in Germany, and the one thing I remember was the sound.
> [I remember] how loud the cars were, and to feel the cars through the ground as it was vibrating. It is a shame we don't have that anymore (Johnson, 2014).

Others have defended the sound of the new engines, and claimed that it con-nects the sport to the new realities of consumer and car manufacturer demands for more environmentally friendly engines that produce less noise pollution. For example, former McLaren Racing team boss Eric Boullier supported Formula One's new engines in the wake of complaints over their uninspiring sound. He pointed out that the engines mirror the direction of the road-car industry and have been embraced by manufacturers. According to Boullier, "This new power-unit we have developed is a completely industry-relevant engine formula and this is why we could attract some new engine manufacturers and keep some of them on board actually" (Benson, 2014). Indeed, the past few years have seen several companies threatening to pull out of Formula One if the sport does not more accurately reflect real-world demands. Renault, one of the three companies producing the engines, claimed that it would quit Formula One if the sport did not introduce a new formula engine that reflected the greater efficiency now popular in road-car power plants. Honda, which quit Formula One in 2008, returned with McLaren in 2015 because of the switch to industry-relevant engines. Williams racing deputy team principal Claire Williams has claimed, "Personally I like the sound of the engines. ... I think people will pretty quickly get used to what F1 engines sound like." Similarly, Mercedes executive director (business) Toto Wolff has pointed out, "This is modern technology, this is where road cars are going" (ibid). At the time of writing, in 2019, hybrid engines are still in use and with noticeably fewer complaints, as fans and practitioners seem to have reconciled themselves to the new engine sounds. Whether Formula One continues to use these engines, time will tell—though it is a distinct possibility that it may yet turn to the type of engine sound enhancement technology found in road cars, as discussed above.

Safety and engine sound

Orchestrated engine noise has become a necessity for electric cars, which run so quietly that they can provide a dangerous surprise for inattentive pedestrians, the blind, or the visually or aurally impaired. In 2016, the US National Highway Traffic Safety Administration finalized rules requiring all hybrid and electric cars to play synthesized engine sounds to alert bystanders, a change that experts estimate could prevent thousands of pedestrian and cyclist injuries (NHTSA, 2016). With traditional engines, some advocates have even celebrated artificial noise as an added luxury. Without it, drivers would hear an unsettling silence or only the kinds of ambient road noises they would most likely rather ignore, such as bumps in the pavement or the whine of the wind.

Multiple studies have shown that crashes involving pedestrians and cyclists occur more frequently with electric and hybrid electric vehicles than with vehicles powered by traditional internal combustion engines, particularly when engaging in low-speed manoeuvres such as parking or reversing. A study by the NHTSA (2009), for example, found that a hybrid electric vehicle (HEV) was two times more likely to be involved in a pedestrian crash than was a conventional internal combustion vehicle when slowing or stopping, backing up, or entering or leaving a parking space. The study also found that the incidence rate of pedestrian crashes in scenarios when vehicles make a turn was significantly higher for HEVs. The NHTSA study additionally concluded that the incidence rate of bicyclist crashes involving HEVs for the same kind of manoeuvres was significantly higher compared to conventional vehicles.

In order to combat such safety issues associated with HEVs, several companies have begun to design sound emission systems that artificially create an engine sound. The Nissan Leaf, for instance, uses a soft whirring tone, the company's "Vehicle Sound for Pedestrians," that is emitted through speakers located in the driver's side wheel well. The sound changes pitch as the car accelerates when the vehicle is moving forward. The noise, designed with the help of acoustic psychologists and Hollywood sound designers, is a sine wave that sweeps from 2.5 kHz to 600 Hz (McClellan, 2011). The range was selected to be audible across all age groups. GM's (now discontinued) Chevy Volt, on the other hand, emits a subtle chirp, generated by the car's horn, to perform the same function. The GM system used on the Volt is called the "Pedestrian-Friendly Alert System," and was developed to alert but not startle pedestrians. Hyundai's warning system is called "Virtual Engine Sound System" (VESS), and it generates a synthetic sound that is supposed to represent an idling internal combustion engine. Finally, the Toyota system, called "Vehicle Proximity Notification System" (VPNS), produces an electric motor sound that rises and falls in pitch relative to the vehicle's speed.

After-market manufacturers are also interested in developing sound systems for electric vehicles and hybrids. Enhanced Vehicle Acoustics (EVA), founded by two Stanford students, developed an after-market technology called "Vehicular Operations Sound Emitting Systems" (VOSES) (McClellan, 2011). The device makes HEVs sound more like conventional engine cars when the vehicle goes into the silent electric mode, though still at a significantly reduced sound level compared to most internal combustion vehicles. At speeds higher than 20 miles per hour (32 km/h) or when the combustion engine engages, the sound system shuts off. The system employs miniature speakers placed in the wheel wells that emit specific sounds based on the direction the car is moving to minimize noise pollution yet maximize acoustic information for pedestrians. If the car is moving forward, the sounds are only projected in that direction; if the car is turning left or right, the sound changes on the left or right accordingly. The company argues that common warning sounds such as chirps, beeps, and alarms are more distracting than useful, and that the best sounds for alerting pedestrians are those traditionally car-like.

The luxury of silence

In something of a contradiction to the attempts to artificially enhance the sound of engines and the desire to artificially add or shape the sounds heard while driving, the automotive manufacturing industry also places huge emphasis on developing technologies and methods to subdue the effects of consequential engine and road sounds when riding in their products. Writing in 1892, Arthur Schopenhauer (2008) said, "Noise is the most impertinent of all forms of interruption. It is not only an interruption, but also a disruption of thought. Of course, where there is nothing to interrupt, noise will not be so particularly painful" (p. 47). It was not the noise pollution of cars and engines that bothered Schopenhauer, but rather another transportation-related noise: "The most inexcusable and disgraceful of all noises is the cracking of whips— a truly infernal thing when it is done in the narrow resounding streets of a town." For Schopenhauer, such noise was also associated with the "very unmannerly and ill-bred" (ibid). Our apparent revulsion to noise, and its stereotypical association with seemingly uneducated or marginalized lower social class, seems little changed today.

According to a Zagat (2013) survey, noise ranks as the number one complaint of restaurant-goers in the US. In the midst of honking car horns, screeching subway trains, and the general din of the street, noise is also the most frequent complaint (registering over 260,000 calls) submitted to New York City's 311 hotline (Dobnik, 2014). As Schopenhauer's irritation demonstrates, such complaints are nothing new. The ancient Greek colony Sybaris, for instance, mandated that certain noisy tradesmen (e.g., potters, tinsmiths) had to live outside the city walls; and Julius Caesar issued an edict banning wheeled vehicles during the daytime. Thomas Carlyle attempted to insulate himself from the noises of the Victorian street—as well as the "crowings, shriekings, and half-maddening noises of a stock of fowls which my poor neighbour has set up for his profit and amusement"—by attempting to build a soundproof attic to serve as his study (Froude, 1884, p. 116). Today, however, quiet and silence are often marketed as indulgences or as a high-tech features of a product. From noise-cancelling headphones to the popularity of silent retreats, there has never been quite so great a social and economic premium placed on silence. Not only do we value it in a general sense, we are also willing to pay for it. Silence has, in effect, become the ultimate luxury.

Recent examples of technology that attempts to cash in on this quest for quiet are not hard to find. An iPhone app called Stereopublic, for example, crowdsources the search for placid urban spaces by encouraging "ear-witnesses" to map these locales. Another example of the worlds of sound engineering, business, and popular music colliding is provided by John Paluska, manager of the rock band Phish, and his restaurant in Berkeley, California. Paluska employed Meyer Sound, a world-renowned audio engineering company located in Berkeley, to test a relatively new technology that digitally controls reverberation levels in designed spaces (Finz, 2012). By using a combination of sound-absorption materials, microphones, speakers, and a digital processing program, Paluska can make his restaurant as loud or as quiet (in terms of the level of sound absorption) as he wishes. Previously, the technology had only been used in live musical performance spaces. According to John Meyer, president and founder of Meyer Sound, "We've (only) used it in live performance venues including Zellerbach Hall at UC Berkeley, Cirque du Soleil productions, experimental music rooms, Bob Weir's (of the Grateful Dead) recording studio, even churches" (Finz, 2012). The cost of such a project, according to the contractors, can range from $10,000 to $100,000. In a way, this technology allows those who desire and can afford it to have an ambient sound volume control knob in their living space.

Such attempts to control and refine noise levels are increasingly found in other, more public arenas, and often achieved by means other than high-technology noise cancellation. The "quiet car" car concept in commuter train transportation, for example, is becoming increasingly prevalent. A number of rail lines around North America, including Amtrak US and Go Transit in Toronto, now offer silent seating areas for those wishing to avoid the disruption of phones and loud conversations. Moreover, people seem willing to pay extra for this small luxury. According to the *Boston Herald*, with the impending likelihood of in-flight cell phone use becoming a reality, 53 per cent of airline passengers would offer to pay a premium to sit in a silent zone (Burke, 2014).

Household products are also being marketed with an increasing emphasis on noise reduction. The 2015 Bosch dishwasher line advertised itself as "the quietest, dishwasher line in the U.S." (Bosch, 2015). Meanwhile, Electrolux markets a model called the "UltraSilencer" vacuum. In 2011, Electrolux conducted an extensive brainwave study (polysomnography) in order "to explore how vacuum cleaner sound affects sleep quality." While the reason is unclear why a vacuum might be used in the presence of someone sleeping, the study nevertheless concluded that "18 out of 21 times, the test subjects remained asleep as the vacuum cleaner was turned on" (Electrolux, 2011).

Among the most well-known brands devoted to the luxury of quiet culture, Bose has been offering high-end noise-cancelling headphones to consumers since 2000. While Bose is famous for its stereo systems and headphones, it is actively trying to apply aspects of its patented noise-cancelling technology to the automotive industry. In 2004, Bose unveiled the prototype of a radically new automobile "semi-automatic" suspension system based on more than 20 years of research. The system employs electromagnetic motors to retract or extend specially designed shock absorbers that will isolate the vehicle in response to uneven bumps or potholes in the road. When a wheel drops into a pothole, the motors extend the struts to isolate the vehicle body from the bump. On the "far" side of the pothole, the motor works as a generator and sends power back through the amplifier so that the strut retracts and allows the wheel to absorb the rising impact. The result is a smoother ride over all types of roads. The technology uses similar principles to noise-cancelling technology for speakers and earphones. The unevenness of the road is sensed and processed much like a sound wave. A cancelling wave is then generated and applied to the wheels through linear motors. Although the system is close to being perfected, no auto manufacturers have yet committed to the technology, possibly because the system is still costly, even after many years of development (Shuldiner, 2007).[5]

As evident in the Bose initiative, sound-mitigated travel is a particularly valued feature of car use and features heavily in various advertising campaigns. In a US print advertisement, the Kia K900 boasts of being "so quiet, it's left our competition speechless." The full ad reads as follows: "K900: Certified to deliver a quieter cabin and a smoother, better overall ride than the Audi A8 4.0T, BMW 750i. … Because sometimes the most luxurious sound is nothing at all. Challenge the luxury you know" (Kähler, 2014). The ad for the mid-priced Kia clearly challenges the company's higher-priced competitors' claims to the luxury of silence.

In 2011, Chevrolet posted a video on YouTube as part of its Department 180 online promotional video series, entitled "Dept. 180 Chevrolet Cruze Quiet Science." Set to the backdrop of a live Detroit hard rock/heavy metal band to emphasize the quiet technologies of its new Cruze model, the promotional clip features an acoustic engineer standing in the middle of the live band while a second engineer and narrator drive around them in the car listing the various sound-damping technologies employed in the car, including a "premium dash mat that filters out high frequency noise of the engine … a liquid sound dampening material applied by robots … and sound insulating material made from 70% recycled denim" (Dept. 180, 2011). After listing these features, the engineer rolls up the window and significantly reduces the volume of the band playing outside the car. Although the spot is intended to be a light-hearted take on the noise-reducing aspects of the brand, it is also somewhat ironic that such technologies are used to diminish the apparent "noise" of the band while in other advertising they actively promote the quality of the sound system that would presumably bring the sound of the band, or other music choices, to even greater heights. Car companies must strike a fine balance between the need to subdue the uncontrollable exterior car noises and sounds of the road with sound-damping technologies while simultaneously using other sound-enhancing technologies—be they sound systems or engine sound enhancement—to create more nuanced sensorial driving experiences.

In 2010, Honda's luxury brand Acura introduced two-page print advertisements for its TSX models. Under a campaign titled "Interesting Sound," the ads proclaimed, "Our speakers can create an interesting sound. 'Silence'." The ad goes on to explain, "Microphones inside the cabin constantly monitor unwanted engine noise. When noise is detected, opposing frequencies are broadcast through the speakers to eliminate it, literally fighting sound with sound." What is particularly notable about the two-page ad is that, in a move reminiscent of John Cage's *4'33"*, the facing page consists of four completely empty staves of music.

Likely the most famous maker of luxury cars, Rolls-Royce, has placed a particular premium on delivering a quiet ride. Its top brands, the Phantom and the Ghost, are even (perhaps oddly given the association with death) named for their quiet, stealth-like qualities. The advertising for the 2011 Ghost, an updated version of the classic Silver Ghost that first appeared in 1906, states:

> In the 1950s Rolls-Royce produced a car that was so well engineered that the loudest thing you could hear at sixty mile per hour was the ticking of the clock. … The sound inside a Rolls-Royce Ghost isn't just about sound levels it's about sound quality. A buzzing mosquito may not be loud but

it is annoying. The interior of a Rolls-Royce has been designed so that conversation should always be effortless (New Rolls Royce Ghost, 2011).

The driver in the video then takes the car up to a speed of 140 miles per hour to illustrate that he does not have to raise his voice.

The quest for quiet has, perhaps, had its most profound and radical manifestations in the world of luxury cars. However, this quest has even invaded the relatively mundane middle-class world of pick-up trucks, a category of vehicle and of buyers not typically connected with a concern for a quiet driving experience. In introducing its redesigned 2014 Silverado pick-up truck, Chevrolet devoted a 30-second commercial to its "quiet cab" that, reinforcing the immersive exclusivity of the urban driving experience, "helps keep the outside out!" (Quiet Cab, 2014). The enhancements to the cabin's soundproofing included upgrades like enhanced baffling inside the doors and thicker, better-sealed windows. Such sound-reduction features, whether in pick-up trucks or luxury vehicles, help to literally and figuratively insulate the driver and passengers from the outside world, creating a heightened feeling of privacy and control.

As evidenced in the Rolls-Royce commercial and elsewhere, the increased emphasis on a quiet ride and the technology used to achieve it is creating something of a paradox within advanced car design: the more automakers succeed in muting sounds coming from outside, the more drivers are hearing the annoying little chirps, rattles, and drones on the inside. After making huge strides in diminishing the worst offenders—engine and road noise—automakers are now going to new lengths to quiet their vehicles' interiors, fine-tuning acoustics on everything from the whoosh of the climate-control vents to the *ka-thump* of the door locks. In their book *Sound and Safe*, Bijsterveld et al. (2013) discuss the history of the obsession with "seeking auditory privacy on public roads" and "the phenomenon of acoustic cocooning, or the driver's ability to relax by controlling the car's interior acoustic environment, in traffic situations" (p. 2). Among other claims this study makes about the search for silence in the driving experience, including the rise of acoustic sound barriers on roads in the 1970s, the authors state that drivers pay decreasing attention to the sound of their cars to diagnose engine problems. While drivers may rely on computer-driven system warning lights and the like to recognize many issues with their car, in the modern car's increasingly acoustically cocooned environment, it is perhaps ironic that the imposition of the actual sound of a problem, even a small rattle associated with a loose fitting, becomes all the more heightened.

Limiting and eliminating car sounds

It takes a surprisingly large team of people to design optimal sonic experiences for drivers. Throughout most of the period between initial drawings and full production, often spanning several years, a special team of engineers will work exclusively on a single car. There is typically a working group that worries only about what noises the engines make. One person might handle the sound of the air conditioning, another all the chassis work, and so on. While car manufacturers and engineers put a great deal of effort into isolating and sealing the cabin, they put equal effort into designing the sounds we do hear. This involves isolating the car with sound-insulating materials and designing customer-actuated sounds activated by pushing buttons or clicking seat belts.

Kara Gordon is a noise and vibration performance engineer with GM. She works to ensure that customers like what they hear from their cars. She is part of the team that designed and tested the soundscape of the 1999 Chevy Impala. Underscoring the cyborg-like, human-machine experience of driving, automotive sound designers such as Gordon often use a specialized recording device called an Aachen HEAD. This "listening" device is directly modelled on, and looks like, a human head, with microphones in place of ears. After driving a prototype car in various conditions, engineers can put on headphones and experience what the Aachen HEAD "heard." They then employ equalization filters to locate and isolate noises to determine their source, with the ultimate aim of mitigating or eliminating them. It is not just loudness that engineers and sound designers are concerned with, but also the sound's quality and whether it is perceived as annoying. For car owners, an unexpected noise is often the first sign that it is time to visit a mechanic. And, since aspects of aural perception are especially important in the process of buying a new car, manufacturers take great pains to ensure that their brands have the perceived quality that we associate with a lack of noise. Designers and engineers are particularly concerned about the noises that originate from moments when the car makes a sound because of something instigated by the operator, like clicking buttons, moving levers, or opening and closing doors. According to Gordon, "The Impala has a wonderful [dashboard] display that moves out of the way. ... We spent a good deal of time tuning that noise to sound just right" (Maley, 2013).

Of course, as discussed in Chapter 4, what might be considered "just right" changes from model to model, and is related to the brand identity of the car and the consumer most likely to purchase it. A luxury touring car would be more likely to have a highly insulated cabin that protects passengers from road and engine noise, whereas a sports car might have less cabin insulation so that the driver can hear and feel the roar and rumble of the engine. A family sedan might be more concerned with making sure passengers can communicate with each other and clearly hear the entertainment system.

Many of the sounds associated with user-activated events are now intentional, designed and synthesized artificially. The iconic clicking of a turn signal was once an artefact of the mechanical process that turned the light on and off. But that mechanism has long since been replaced by an electronic circuit that operates silently. Audible feedback, however, is valuable for both safety and aesthetic reasons, so cars now play an MP3 file of a turn signal over the speakers. According to Gordon, "It could sound like anything. ... We asked [a customer survey group], 'What if we wanted it to sound like birds?' They said no" (Maley, 2013). What was once a consequential sound of automotive use is now something intentionally created and designed into the product—a friendly and reassuring synthetic ghost, one might say, of the sonic history of the car. It is essentially a sonic skeuomorph, an anachronistic design feature that is no longer functional in and of itself. Moreover, it is suggestive of how we have been trained to think like the machine, rather than the machine adapting to us.[6]

In contrast to the artificial enhancement of user-actuated sounds and engine sounds, some automakers add sophisticated noise-cancellation systems to offset sounds that, due to noisier cabins and engines, were once inaudible. John Pepas, vice president of engineering at Mahle Behr (an auto-parts manufacturer of heating, air conditioning, and ventilation system components), claims, "Ten years ago most interior noises couldn't even be heard because of the engine and road noise." However, recent progress in damping those sounds, he says, has forced manufacturers to lower noise levels "even on little parts like the tiny motor that runs the vent door that opens and closes in a heater" (Bennett, 2014). Mahle Behr spent more than $1 million to develop its sound-testing facility, which includes two acoustic rooms built on shock absorbers to stop noise from bleeding in through the ground. In one room, the skeleton of a car cockpit is connected to a massive air chamber, while a tripod-mounted microphone records and measures every whoosh. Niranjan Humbad, the company's acoustic validation manager and a noise-tracking veteran, listens to the sounds and reviews visual representations of them on a computer monitor to target problems. Humbad and his team have compiled a database of more than 1000 noises caused by the motor and blowers inside a car's heating, ventilation, and air conditioning (HVAC) unit, ranging from low throaty rumbles to a high screeching whistle or chirp tone. The database is paired with computer software to help identify sounds that need muffling.

In the future, automakers may even allow customers to turn on a white noise option. To most consumers, the *thump* of a closing door or lock conveys the quality of the vehicle—the quieter, the better. To be sure, sound or lack thereof is an active agent in shaping consumers' perceptions of a product's quality. Door-lock maker Kiekert AG, which provides latch systems to carmakers such as Mercedes-Benz and Bentley, built an acoustic lab at its 90-person production facility in Wixom, Michigan. The company has recorded thousands of different door-locking sounds from its own products and those of its competitors. Mike Hietbrink, vice general manager of the company's US operations, explains that "[a] high-frequency sound you get from metal hitting metal is usually perceived as bad because the 'tingy' sound is annoying to the human ear [whereas] a lower sound like a closing bank vault is considered more acceptable" (Bennett, 2014).

The search for silence is perhaps simply an extension of a desire to shed the increasing non-aural "noise" of modern life—the information overload yielded by advertising, emails, texts, and other social media that clutter our consciousness. This is not to discount, however, the actual irritation and, indeed, potential health issues associated with exposure to excessive amounts of audible noise. The Centers for Disease Control and Prevention (CDC, 2014) estimate that in the US 4 million people work amid "damaging" noise every day; 10 million people US have noise-related hearing loss; and 22 million workers are exposed to potentially damaging noise each year. The deleterious effects of noise, however, are not just limited to our ears. A 2003 study found that long-term exposure to aircraft noise could impair reading comprehension and long-term memory in children. In 2011, the World Health Organization released a report that estimated, based on "disability-adjusted life-years … at least one million healthy life years are lost every year from traffic-related noise in the western part of Europe" (WHO, 2011, p. v). In looking at the nexus of sound and music in automotive culture, it is imperative to keep in mind the potentially negative mental and physical effects of the increasing environmental din produced through automotive culture's quest to create ever-more audible and finely tuned engine sounds and powerful and immersive sound systems. The potentially harmful effects of sound and noise (including music) while driving yet again calls into question the ways in which our bodies and, indeed, our human identities are forced to adapt and interact with, if not fuse with, the seemingly non-corporeal machine.

Auto and audiomobility: merging man and machine

The quest for quiet in our driving experiences in many ways reflects a desire to be at one with our cars, undistracted by external noises or sounds. As Mimi Sheller (2007) notes, "Cars are technologies that re-shape corporeal existence, material environments and social temporalities in diverse and complex ways, with impacts on all people, spaces and times, not only those that are explicitly 'automobilized'" (p. 175). As I have previously discussed, we are often emotionally attached to our cars. In many ways, as Paul Gilroy (2010) has remarked, "cars are integral to the privatization, individualization and emotionalization of consumer society as a whole" and "have redefined movement and extended sensory experience" (p. 89). Drawing on Jack Katz's (1999) studies of the practices of "tacit automobilized embodiment," Nigel Thrift (2004) suggests that we might

> understand driving (and passengering) as both profoundly embodied and sensuous experiences, though of a particular kind, which "requires and occasions a metaphysical merger, an intertwining of the identities of the driver and car that generates a distinctive ontology in the form of a person-thing, a humanized car or, alternatively, an automobilized person" … in which the identity of person and car kinaesthetically

intertwine Thus driving ... involves the capacity to "embody and be embodied by the car" (pp. 46–47).

The remainder of this chapter looks at the increasing emphasis that car-makers place on merging the corporeal, flesh-and-blood, driving body with technology. In many ways a manifestation of actor-network theory in action, they often attempt to bestow "agency" to the automobile, and would have us understand cars as empathetic, emotional actors with which we both merge and interact.[7]

The automotive industry characteristically focuses on the subjectivity—body and agency—of the car driver, though in ways that subtly, or often not so subtly, undermine human agency. In their advertising campaigns, manufacturers often highlight the cyborg-like, human–machine hybrid that driving implies. In 2012, Jaguar kicked off a global marketing campaign to relaunch itself as a brand that makes drivers feel "alive." The campaign, by agency Spark44 (part-owned by Jaguar Land Rover), introduced the luxury marque's "alive" brand positioning, which targets "contemporary and open-minded, sophisticated and daring" consumers. The campaign's television ad, called "Machines," explains how the historical development of technology has improved human life, but employs a voiceover that warns of machines that want to "replace" people. It then claims that "there is one machine which makes us greater ... which is alive as we are," before cutting to a shot of a Jaguar. The ad ends with the brand's new catchphrase, "How alive are you?" (Brownsell, 2012). It is unclear how the concept of a car that is "as alive as we are" altered sales; but it underscores the overall public perception, if not reality, that cars are becoming smarter, more intuitive, and indeed more human-like in their capabilities. Perhaps the deeper and more unsettling question is less whether machines are becoming more "human" than whether actual humans are in control. There is something uncomfortable about promotions that claim a machine is human-like but that we control it.

Daimler-Benz's "smart" brand is, perhaps, the most well-known manifestation of this trend. The smart car, however, is only "smart" because of its eco-friendly electric and/or hybrid engine and compact design. Other car manufacturers tout the ability of their products to provide, through various enhanced information and entertainment systems, "intelligent environments" (Sheller, 2007, p. 181). Indeed, manufacturers attempt to appeal to the senses in offering new driving environments that link driver to machine in increasingly sophisticated ways. Most new cars now offer options such as Wi-Fi connectivity, satellite-linked navigation (typically with real-time traffic monitoring), Bluetooth wireless phone technology, and various forms of enhanced surround-sound stereo systems and video screens. As Sheller (2007) describes,

> with a design team devoted to the "Human–Machine Interface", Infiniti claims to have utilized the "advanced technology of touch, known as

haptics" to develop a unique dashboard configuration, and "the science of psychoacoustics" to develop the Bose TrueSpace "immersive surround-sound experience" (p. 187).

Some manufacturers are apparently even moving to eliminate human decision-making altogether. Tesla (2018), for example, proudly advertises that:

> All Tesla vehicles produced in our factory, including Model 3, have the hardware needed for full self-driving capability at a safety level substantially greater than that of a human driver.

Tesla's self-driving system is called "Autopilot," and the company further claims that:

> Enhanced Autopilot adds these new capabilities to the Tesla Autopilot driving experience. Your Tesla will match speed to traffic conditions, keep within a lane, automatically change lanes without requiring driver input, transition from one freeway to another, exit the freeway when your destination is near, self-park when near a parking spot and be summoned to and from your garage.
>
> Tesla's Enhanced Autopilot software has begun rolling out and features will continue to be introduced as validation is completed, subject to regulatory approval. Every driver is responsible for remaining alert and active when using Autopilot, and must be prepared to take action at any time (Tesla, 2018).

Tesla looks at the processing power needed for Autopilot as part of a "neural net" that goes "far beyond the human senses":

> To make sense of all of this data, a new onboard computer with over 40 times the computing power of the previous generation runs the new Tesla-developed neural net for vision, sonar and radar processing software. Together, this system provides a view of the world that a driver alone cannot access, seeing in every direction simultaneously, and on wavelengths that go far beyond the human senses (Tesla, 2018).

Many vehicles offer dashboard configurations and entertainment and driving systems that are, conversely, ergonomically designed for the human body, offering the driver "at your fingertips" controls for seat adjustment, lumbar support, climate control, and heating and massage features (e.g., Volkswagen Phaeton, 2005). Tesla's online promotional material for its Model S also touts its interior as "[b]uilt around the driver":

> The cabin combines meticulous noise engineering with Tesla's uniquely quiet powertrain to obtain the sound dynamics of a recording studio. The gem of the interior is the 17-inch touchscreen, which is angled toward the

driver and includes both day and night modes for better visibility without distraction. It puts rich content at your fingertips and provides mobile connectivity so you can easily find your destination, favorite song or a new restaurant (Tesla, 2018).

As Sheller (2007) points out, "Features such as these not only 'free' drivers from direct manipulation of the machinery, but embed them more deeply in its sociality, producing what might be described as a 'cybercar'" (p. 182).

Furthermore, car manufacturers are increasingly attempting to "humanize" their products by promoting their increasingly sentient qualities. Ideas of automobile "intelligence" have now expanded to include not just data processing and automated response to the driving environment, but also more "human" elements of intelligence such as feeling, intuition, and emotion. The 2004 Audi A8 L advertised its "Multi-Media Interface" as a "central nervous system." Saab also asserted that the "driver's environment" in its cars offers "exceptional control over a vehicle that seems to communicate with you, for intuitive driving" (Sheller, 2007, p. 183). Adding to this cyborg-like hybridization of human and machine is the increasing presence of, and interaction with, the synthetic "voice" of the car in the form of various onboard navigation and safety systems, such as GM's OnStar.[8] As drivers, we can now listen to and follow navigation commands as well as issue our own spoken requests via Bluetooth and other hands-free devices. As these voices become more intuitive, we are often confronted with the sense of an uncanny co-presence in our driving experiences as we attempt to navigate correctly according to the spoken instructions so as to not disappoint our immaterial co-pilots. As Sheller (2007) has suggested, "The implication is that the car is like a living organism, with which the driver can connect intuitively and emotively" (p. 183).

The emotional connection to our cars is a factor that manufacturers are increasingly focused on, and music is among the most prominent means by which this can be achieved. As outlined by Sheller (2007), in 2002 a Toyota/Sony Pod concept car promised that it would:

> measure your pulse and perspiration levels to gauge your stress levels. If you are becoming aggressive it will calm you with cool air and soothing music. It will even warn other drivers about your mental state by changing the colour of the strip-lights on the bonnet! (p. 184).

The car was able to "emote" by raising or lowering its body, wagging its antenna, and illuminating its hood with different colours (e.g., red for angry, yellow for happy).

A research group at MIT's Media Lab calling itself AutoEmotive has even grander plans to reduce the stress of drivers by adding emotion-sensing technologies inside the cockpit of the car. Its website declares:

Regardless the emotional state of drivers, current cars feel impassive and disconnected. We believe that by adding emotion-sensing technologies inside the car, we can dramatically improve the driving experience while increasing the safety of drivers.

Although we experience hundreds of emotions on a daily basis, one of the most relevant (especially when driving) is stress. While certain amounts of stress is [*sic*] beneficial to be alert and attentive, too much stress or too little can negatively affects driving performance.

We are looking forward to a future when AutoEmotive would not only be used at the individual level to enhance the driving experience but also to empower greater social awareness by capturing the emotional state of a large city, providing the means to live healthier lives and create more liveable cities.[9]

The team hopes to develop an empathetic car that senses a driver's emotions and moods via a small camera that reads expressions on the driver's face. In theory, a car that responds to your emotions could be instantly personalized. It could be customized, for example, with various soothing sounds, lighting, smells, or seat positions in order to fit different moods, routines, or commonly occurring tasks (the stress around one's daily commute, say, might be different from that associated with picking the kids up at school).

Yet another team of engineering students at the University of Waterloo in Canada has developed technology to detect road rage and defuse driver anger by playing soothing music. The technology relies on data from three sensors that measure the driver's heart rate, the pressure of the driver's grip on the steering wheel, and the driver's facial expression. According to project manager Dipshikha Goyal, "If the [heart rate and grip] values are above the normal threshold, we trigger the camera and check if the person is actually angry" (Winter, 2014). Each new driver must first train or teach the software by demonstrating a normal face and an angry face. When road rage is detected, the car automatically selects a favourite soothing song from the driver's smartphone playlist by using a mood music app. Those who would rather not have Rage Against the Machine start up every time someone cuts them up could also program alternative calming methods. According to Goyal, "A person can choose whether he'd prefer to have music come on, or to have the AC turn on, or have the windows roll down. ... Some cars nowadays even have massage systems" (ibid). The Waterloo team is attempting to patent its technology, and is approaching carmakers about installing the road rage detectors. Several car companies, including Volkswagen and Ford, have already introduced driver attention and drowsiness systems, which use sensors and cameras to monitor factors like a driver's steering habits, ability to remain within a lane, and time at the wheel.

The overall push towards intelligent cars underscores the increasing and quasi-spiritual metaphysical bond between humans and our machinery. Sailing boats and horse-drawn carriages aside, we have been increasingly dependent on machines for our mobility at least since the inception of the bicycle in the nineteenth century. Cars that can sense and respond to our emotions with music or soothing sounds will doubtless make us more reliant on them, and emotionally bring us closer to them as they begin to exhibit more human-like characteristics. As discussed in Chapter 4 in regard to sound-branding practices, one might recall Urry's (2007) contention that "[i]t is through inhabiting machines that humans will come to 'life'" (pp. 179–80) and Katherine Hayles' (2012) idea of "technogensis," the coevolution of, and feedback between, humans and technology in a drive to simulate life itself. Several technology companies have recently expressed interest in the creation of driverless vehicles. In a well-publicized initiative, Amazon, for instance, is developing flying drones to deliver packages by remote control. In 2010, Google announced that it would be developing driverless cars. Its first 25 prototypes began operating on roads in California in the summer of 2015. The ultimate goal, according to Google co-founder Sergey Brin,

> is computer-controlled cars that can eliminate human error, which is a factor in an estimated 90 per cent of the 1.2 million road deaths that occur worldwide each year. Self-driving cars could also improve traffic congestion and transport the elderly and disabled (Associated Press, 2015).

Brin also stated that "[w]e want to partner to bring self-driving to all the vehicles in the world" and that "our goal is to create something safer than human drivers" (ibid.). Google, however, is not alone in its attempt to develop self-driving cars. Mercedes-Benz, Infiniti, and other carmakers already have advanced driver assistance systems such as lane keeping and adaptive cruise control that can pilot a car on the highway with minimal input from its driver.

This hybrid cyborg human–car assemblage has many parallels in the musical world. At the same time that we are increasingly giving over control of driving and decision-making to our cars, popular music has witnessed an increasing tendency to either de-emphasize or technologically enhance the body in performance and musical production.[10] As in the hybrid human–car assemblages that have facilitated easier human mobility, musicians have long relied on prosthetic enhancement to improve performance. Microphones and amplifiers artificially project the human voice. Earphones and headsets allow musicians, as well as consumers, to hear sounds that would otherwise be inaudible. A variety of studio devices, such as the ubiquitous Auto-Tune, artificially enhance the vocal tracks of many singers. Digitally created holographic performers, such as the famous Tupac Shakur hologram from Coachella in 2012 or Japan's fictional animated pop star Hatsune Miku, now populate stages around the world. Like the promise of self-driving car technologies, such completely controlled holographic performers abrogate the human errors of flesh-and-blood musicians. Digital computer technologies and simple software programs now aid us in the creation and animation of any sound that can be imagined. Similarly, our consumption of popular music is almost always mediated by technology. In animating any recorded sound, we are only listening to a virtual performance of a body. Whether our music listening is mediated through radios, stereo systems, MP3 players, headphones, or, indeed, through car sound systems, the line separating human and machine seems to be increasingly blurred. In many ways, the production and consumption of music, like our interaction with cars, has long instantiated a state of man–machine hybridity.

Conclusion

This chapter has looked at how the automotive industry has conceived of itself in musical terms, from the use of a plethora of musically inspired automobile names to musical metaphors used in tuning the pitch of an engine. It has also looked at aspects of the sonic aspect of car engines and the industry's attempts to both artificially enhance engine sounds and mitigate its associated noise. Such attempts typically use many of the same techniques and studio wizardry employed by sound engineers in music recording studios. Although not typically thought of as connected, the two industries share a bond in their attempts to produce carefully designed and engineered sonic experiences for consumers—experiences on to which manufacturers hope their customers will emotionally latch.

Paralleling these attempts, the quest for silence, or at least the mitigation of uncontrolled noise, is another ongoing obsession of the automotive industry. Today, there is double-edged element to our obsession with silence: technology has both increased our perceived need for silence and created (or at least improved) the means of attaining it. We are assaulted by incessant technological "noise" (cars, planes, radios, televisions, stereos, cell phones), and yet we are simultaneously reliant on technology to control it. We plug into our iPods and noise-cancelling headphones and climb into our noise-controlled cars in order to tune out the technological din that surrounds us. The noise-cancelling systems in automobiles are ironically a similar product of years of research and refinement that create the increasingly pristine sound reproduction of contemporary car entertainment systems. Automotive manufacturers place a premium on quietness, as evidenced by both their marketing materials and the extensive resources they allocate to refining intentional sounds and alleviating unwanted consequential sounds in their products.

Finally, automotive marketers continue to attempt to imbue cars with sentient emotional "agency" that would impel us to understand cars as empathetic, emotional actors with which to merge as a human–machine cyborg hybrid, attempts that often rely on musical or sonic means of car–driver (or car–passenger) interaction. Such a merging of human and machine, however, is just as omnipresent in the production and consumption of current music. Thus, in both the automotive and the popular music industry, we look to ever-advancing technologies to recognize ourselves as technogenetic creatures.

An underlying issue in this book is the ability of industry, particularly the automotive manufacturing industry, to influence the sound and style of popular music. We might think of this relationship as manifesting a similar two-part categorization of "consequential" and "intentional" sonic outcomes of sounds produced by manufactured products. On the one hand, popular music is "consequentially" influenced by the sounds of automobiles and the processes used in their manufacture that have seeped into the popular imagination. As outlined earlier, the repetitive nature of the assembly line, the rollicking syncopations of engines, and the inherent signification of horn honking have all stimulated the creation of various songs and sounds, from Berry Gordy's Motown sound to the proto-rock n' roll tempos of "Rocket 88." Such instances reflect the ubiquitous nature of industrial, automotive sounds in society and how they inspire analogous sounds in the medium of popular music. This sonic transference can be seen, at least to some degree, as helping normalize and humanize what would otherwise be considered disturbing, non-natural, and mechanically chaotic noise. Through such consequential transference, the typically undesirable sonic by-product of automotive culture becomes regularized, controlled, and transformed into something aesthetically desired.

Yet, on the other hand, the intentional sounds produced by the car have also been subject to transformation and refinement throughout its history. This refinement, and the associated increasing desire and ability to listen to music in our cars, has had many consequences for the popular music industry. As will be discussed in the following chapter, characteristics such as recording studio mixes created specifically for car speakers or the advent of various communities whose identity is tied to car stereo modification are inherently tied to the intentionally designed sounds of the car.

Notes

1 The commercials featured voiceovers by actor Jeff Bridges, who compared the Sonata to classical music sonatas from composers such as Mozart, and how the paint process can help the body stand the test of time. The tag line read: "Because beautiful works of art are meant to last."

2 Ironically, as one reviewer observed, "Despite the musical inference of its name, the Note's engine was disappointingly cacophonous" (Booth, 2006).

3 The common verbal replication of car problems made by customers to mechanics was made famous in the popular Peabody Award-winning NPR radio show *Car Talk* that was hosted from 1977 to 2012 by brothers Tom and Ray Magliozzi, also known as Click and Clack, the Tappet Brothers.

4 BMW M-series cars (the "M" stands for motorsports) feature modified high-performance engines and other non-standard additions gleaned from the company's racing program.

5 In 2010, Bose introduced a system called Bose Ride for reducing road-induced vibration in drivers' seats. The system is aimed at long-distance truckers to alleviate problems with back pain and fatigue.
6 In something of a take on Jean Baudrillard's concept of the simulacrum, cars often manifest other visual and tactile skeuomorphs, such as artificial wood grain panelling and simulated leather upholstery.
7 Actor-network theory (ANT), as developed by Bruno Latour and others, seeks to understand how complex material–semiotic networks come together to act as a whole. Among other issues, it deals with how various actors can engage with, transform, influence, and become part of a larger complex system of relations (such as driver merging with car).
8 As discussed in Chapter 3, the vast majority of these systems have been voiced by women. For example, Dianne Williamson performs GM's OnStar, Patrizia Lipp Audi's "autocheck," and Susan Bennet voices Siri for Apple's CarPlay. Somewhat reinforcing maternal female stereotypes, relatively non-threatening voices of women seem to be the default choice used by these companies to ensure that we will be comfortable with their technology.
9 http://autoemotive.media.mit.edu/ (accessed January 29, 2019).
10 The politics of technology in relationship to music have been discussed at length elsewhere (e.g., Gilbert & Pearson, 1999; Katz, 2010), with most authors decrying the increasing disembodiment of popular music and the tendency to submerge the body beneath the machine while creating relatively lifeless musical experiences.

6 Sound systems, sonic performance, and the car as instrument of identity

As has been outlined in earlier chapters, automotive culture and popular music are clearly linked through: the lyrical celebration of cars in popular songs; the influence of engine and road sounds on popular music's sound; their combined roles in the construction of diverse identities; and the use of popular music (and popular music personalities) in automakers' television and print advertising campaigns. This chapter concerns itself with the car as a vehicle for both the consumption and production of music and expressive sound. The car represents one of the most popular venues for listening to music, and one of the most prominent means of its reproduction in history. Long before the iPod, car radios established the concept of mobile music consumption. Whether through the medium of car radios, cassette tapes, CD players, MP3 player ports, or the latest in infotainment and cell phone interface systems, cars have facilitated our listening habits and reflected the latest developments in listening and playback technology. This chapter begins with an overview of the evolution of car sound systems—from early car radios to today's in-dash information and entertainment systems—and their influence on music. The ubiquity of radios in cars by the 1960s, for example, influenced radio programming through the advent of morning and afternoon "drive-time" shows. Following this, the discussion moves to how the car has been used or conceptualized as an expressive musical instrument in and of itself, whether in television commercials, through car horns and sirens, or in car modification scenes. Finally, the chapter discusses theoretical issues surrounding sound systems and the practice of listening to music in our cars.

The evolution of automotive sound systems

The symbiotic relationship between the car and popular music consumption was evident from an early stage in automotive development. As popular music began to incorporate the car into its thematic iconography in Tin Pan Alley and blues songs, so too the car manufacturing industry began to incorporate the capability for music reproduction as optional and, later, standard equipment. The history of car sound systems is marked by constant innovation and refinement made by manufacturers around the world, and is likely worthy of its own book-length study. Perhaps the earliest instance of a radio in a vehicle occurred in 1901, when Guglielmo Marconi fitted a radio to a Thornycroft steam-powered carriage in England. The radio, however, was only capable of receiving data, not sound, and it would not work while the carriage was in motion. In order to get the radio to function, a tall, roof-mounted, cylindrical aerial was lowered to a horizontal position before the vehicle moved. The first truly successful car audio systems were associated with monophonic AM radio, which remained the norm for many years. The first of such car radios were battery-operated domestic sets that were usually placed on the back seat, used to provide entertainment only once car and driver came to a halt. Eventually, more robust radios were constructed and placed in weatherproof steel boxes that could be mounted under the car or on the running board. As radios became smaller and car interiors more enclosed and weatherproof, they were installed inside the car, often on the floor or bulkhead with cables reaching up to the steering column or dashboard.

In 1922, George Frost of the Lane High School radio club in Chicago installed a modified battery-operated portable radio in a Model T Ford, with a high impedance cone loudspeaker fitted in the car's passenger door (Ham, 2011, p. 53). This was likely the first instance of a radio that could be heard above the engine and road noise while the car was in operation. Early loudspeakers were either ordinary horn or cone speakers, though sets were sometimes equipped with headphones. That same year, American newspaper advertisements for Chevrolet sedans stated that for an extra $200 (nearly $3000 today) it was possible to purchase a car fitted with a Westinghouse "two-step amplifying radio receiving set." The ad's title made an allusion to classical opera, suggesting that that would be the main draw for the product: "go anywhere within 100 miles of a broadcasting station and take the concert with you" (Grand opera in Chevrolet cars, 1922, p. 31).

The first commercially successful car radio debuted in 1930, the dashboard-mounted Motorola model 5T71 produced by the Galvin Corporation—Paul and Joseph Galvin in association with William Lear, later of Learjet fame. The Motorola, a blended word from the term "motorized Victrola," was initially fitted to a Studebaker (Brodsky, 2015). These devices were initially expensive, estimated to cost around $130 (approximately $1800 today), yet wildly popular. Motorola went on to sell millions of car radios, and, later, two-way radios for police and fire departments, home stereo systems, and televisions before moving into transistors, solid-state electronics, and semiconductors. Meanwhile in Germany, Blaupunkt fitted its first radio to a Studebaker in 1932, and in the United Kingdom Crosley first offered a factory-fitted wireless in its models in 1933. After 1938, cars in the UK fitted with a radio further required a special radio licence (Jones, 2013).

One particularly interesting partnership that underlines the extent of the symbiotic relationship between music and the auto industries is provided by the Radiomobile 100. In England, a company called Smith and Sons

(Radiomobile) Limited was formed in 1945, a joint venture between EMI's Gramophone Company (EMI's full name is Electric and Musical Industries Ltd) and Smiths Motor Accessories Ltd. The aim of the company was to "market car radios manufactured and developed by Gramophone Ltd" (Gramophone, 2007). The newly formed company produced its first car radio, the Radiomobile 100, in 1946. It was priced at £40 and carried the famous "His Master's Voice" Gramophone label, the trademarked moniker associated with Nipper the terrier that had been in use since the early twentieth century. Thus, a manufacturer predominantly associated with musical equipment collaborated with an automotive parts company to produce one of the earliest successful car radios in the UK.

By 1932, over 100 different car radio models were available in the US, and at least one report states that, by 1933, about 100,000 cars in the US were fitted with a radio (Erb, 2007). In the US, the Crosley Corporation, which by 1924 had become the largest radio manufacturer in the world, began mass production of car radios for the likes of Chevrolet and GM. Crosley was later bought by GM and, operating under the Delco Radio brand, introduced the first instrument panel radio in 1935. As manufacturing costs of car radios began to radically fall because of mass production, and in combination with innovations such as automatic volume and frequency controls, their popularity increased exponentially. In the US, between 1930 and the start of 1936 the number of cars equipped with radios grew from 34,000 to 3 million. By the end of the decade roughly 20 per cent of all cars were equipped with built-in radios (Brodsky, 2015).

Following the rapidly increasing sales and adoption of car radios, the 1950s saw a number of failed experiments to incorporate other musical media into the car over which the operator would have more choice and control, including record players and reel-to-reel tape players. Motorola, for example, produced the first 7-inch rotating disc player for cars in 1956. The feature was called a "Highway Hi-Fi" and was installed by Chrysler as an optional accessory on 1956–1958 model years of select Plymouth, Dodge, DeSoto, and other Chrysler cars. The system was described in the official Chrysler press release of September 12, 1955.

> Highway Hi-Fi, a record player that provides music and speech as you go, has been developed exclusively for the 1956 Chrysler Corporation cars. ... For driver and passengers who prefer the lively scores of Broadway musicals, Highway Hi-Fi provides the lilting and memorable tunes from the hit show, "Pajama Game."
>
> And if the children are restless on a long ride, Davey Crockett and Gene Autry are ready at hand to help keep them quiet.
>
> Highway Hi-Fi plays through the speaker of the car radio and uses the radio's amplifier system. The turntable for playing records, built for Chrysler by CBS-Columbia, is located in a shock-proof case mounted just below the center of the instrument panel. A tone arm, including

sapphire stylus and ceramic pick up, plus storage space for six long-play records make up the unit.

Using a new principle of design worked out by CBS Laboratories, the player and position of the stylus on a record are not affected by the angle of a car, its highway speed, or even severe cornering. Tests demonstrate it is extremely difficult to jar the arm off the record or even make the stylus jump a groove.

The special records also developed by CBS Laboratories, are seven inches in size, transcribed on both sides, and pressed especially for Chrysler by Columbia Records. They give up to 45 minutes of music and up to one full hour of speech per side. A collection of six disks will be presented to customers with each player.

Making up the collection are Tchaikovsky's Sixth Symphony, Borodin's Polovtsian Dances, Ippolitov-Ivanov's Procession of the Sardar, the complete score of the Broadway musical show Pajama Game, Walt Disney's Davey Crockett, Gene Autry and Champion, Romantic Moods by Percy Faith and his orchestra, quiet jazz by Paul Weston and his orchestra, Music of Cole Porter and Victor Herbert by Andre Kostelanetz and his orchestra, and dramatic readings from Bernard Shaw's Don Juan in Hell by a cast of top Hollywood and Broadway artists (Chrysler Historical Services, 1955).

As indicated in this colourful press release, a button controlled whether one listened to the radio or the record player, and a proprietary stylus was used with an unusually high pressure of 2 grams to prevent skipping or skating despite normal car vibrations. The featured recordings ranged from classical and jazz to dramatic readings and selections aimed at "restless" children to "help keep them quiet." This diverse range was meant to emphasize the potential cross-section of customer tastes, as well as to emphasize the individual control one might exercise beyond the limitations of what was being broadcast over commercial radio.

Despite car ads promising "a complete modern record library on wheels," Columbia Records' proprietary 16⅔ rpm format meant that consumers were at the mercy of a rather limited and eclectic catalogue. Chrysler drivers must have puzzled over titles like "Ken Griffin at the Wurlitzer Organ," Irving Berlin tunes, and a dramatic re-enactment of the signing of the Magna Carta. Part of the problem, admitted the system's inventor, Peter Goldmark (who also invented the 33 rpm LP for CBS Laboratories and the first colour TV system), was that CBS chief William Paley apparently "didn't think pop music was a market at all" (Collins, 2011). Chrysler executives apparently agreed with Paley, imagining the car-buying public to be tired of noisy rock n' roll. As one Chrysler VP argued,

If you want to listen to classical music and relax and you can't get anything on the radio but rock and roll, it can be irritating. … Did you ever try to get classical music on your radio at three in the afternoon? (Collins, 2011).

Regardless of the Chrysler press release's optimistic tone and advertising trumpeting the system's innovations, the Highway Hi-Fi was doomed to failure. The tone arm, despite its extra weight, still skipped, and the records available exclusively at Chrysler dealerships were in relatively limited supply. Columbia Records produced only 42 album releases in the 16⅔ rpm format. Furthermore, the records had to be changed manually—an extremely difficult and dangerous manoeuvre while driving.

The Highway Hi-Fi was not the last attempt to incorporate a turntable into mass-produced cars. In 1960, RCA Victor introduced the "Auto Victrola," also known as the "RCA 45," which could be fitted into many models of cars. Notably, it could play a stack of up to 14 standard 45 rpm records, thus allowing drivers to bring along records from their own collections. Chrysler, seemingly not daunted by the failure of the Highway Hi-Fi, adopted the Auto Victrola for several models. The sales brochure for the 1960 Plymouth Fury contained the following description of the system:

> Music to while away the miles? You can choose between Plymouth's Push-Button DeLuxe radio at a truly low price, or a new Hi-Fi radio with push-buttons that pull in stations that are states away with a sound that compares well with a living room console.
>
> *And* [emphasis in original] you can enjoy, if you will, your own favorite phonograph records from home. This is another feature you will not be able to get in any other low-price car this year. To make it possible in Plymouth, RCA perfected an unusual automatic record player that fits handsomely within reach, right under Plymouth's instrument panel.
>
> This RCA Victor "45" record player handles your standard 45 rpm records smoothly and safely. It plays up to 14 of them consecutively—about two hours of uninterrupted music of your own choosing. As the records play, the automatic changer stacks and stores them for you. The storage space actually holds many more than 14 records, so you can change the repertoire after each stack if you enjoy your records as much as we suspect you might (Plymouth, 1960, p. 23).

The system presaged much later in-car CD changers and, in contrast to the Highway Hi-Fi, emphasized control and choice in musical selections by playing regular 45 rpm records that one could buy anywhere. RCA further made the unit available on the aftermarket, theoretically widening the consumer base to any brand of car.

From the autumn 1959 to summer 1960 television season, Plymouth sponsored Steve Allen's weekly variety show on NBC. This resulted in marketing opportunities such as the 45 rpm single recorded by Allen, "Come Along for a Ride in the Solid New Plymouth" (1960). Both sides were identical, and consisted of Allen pitching the features of the 1960 Plymouth Fury while accompanying himself on piano. It was clearly created to be played while a prospective customer took the car for a test drive. A partial transcription of the recording reads:

Howdy, this is Steve Allen. No—wait a minute, don't go looking in the glove compartment. I'm not there. I'm not really in the car at all. Not personally, that is. But you have to admit, that RCA Auto Victrola's a fooler.

You know, I enjoy sitting at my piano. I guess, uh, any musician does. But you! Man, you're really in solid—sitting behind the wheel of a new, solid '60 Plymouth. ... Solid, man. Really solid! (Collins, 2011).

Despite such celebrity endorsements, increased ease of listening, and much greater variety and access to recordings, the RCA 45, like the Highway Hi-Fi, only survived through the 1961 model year. The success of these record-playing car audio systems could be characterized as limited at best. It was not until 1965, when Ford introduced the 8-track tape player in select 1966 models (including the Mustang's "Stereo-sonic" 8-track), that drivers were successfully able to program their own music.

The 8-track tape recording system was popular from 1965 to the late 1970s. While today it has become an icon of obsolescence, it was initially commercially successful. An 8-track tape consisted of an endless loop of standard ¼-inch magnetic tape, housed in a plastic cartridge. On the tape were eight parallel soundtracks, corresponding to four stereo programs. For many, it is a technology associated primarily with in-car listening, yet it was first developed not by the auto industry but by a leading aircraft manu-facturer, the Learjet Corporation.

William Lear, famous for his successful business plane company, announced in 1965 that he had developed a cartridge with eight tracks that promised to lower the price of recorded tapes without sacrificing music qual-ity. In 1963, Lear became a distributor for Muntz Electronics, which had developed an early 4-track cartridge cassette system called Fidelipac, mainly in order to install units aboard his planes. Dissatisfied with the Muntz tech-nology, he contacted two of the leading suppliers of original equipment tape heads, the Nortronics Company and Michigan Magnetics. Lear specified that he needed a head with much thinner "pole-pieces" and a new spacing that would allow two tracks (or one stereo program) to be picked off a quarter-inch tape that held a total of eight tracks. Although a departure from the Muntz player, the technology of the closely stacked multitrack head was, by the early 1960s, well established in fields like data recording. Lear developed a new version of the Fidelipac cartridge with somewhat fewer parts and an integral pressure roller, and in 1964 his aircraft company constructed 100 "Stereo-8" players for distribution to executives at the auto companies and RCA (Heitmann, 2010).

The early Learjet Stereo-8 player was designed with convenience in mind, as well as safety. The minimal knobs and controls were intended to make it quick and easy to play tapes while driving, essentially without the driver taking his or her eyes off the road. Lear also secured the backing of both Ford and the recording industry. After getting RCA Victor to commit to the mass production of its catalogue on Learjet Stereo-8 cartridges, Ford agreed to offer the players as optional equipment on its 1966 models. Over 65,000 8-track players were installed that year alone. Ford's electronics supplier, the Motorola Corporation, initially manufactured the player—the same firm that Lear and the Galvins had employed in the 1930s to pioneer the "motorized Victrola" car radio. In 1965 Ford became the first automobile manufacturer to introduce dealer-installed 8-track players as an option on many of its models, and thus 8-track was the first tape format to achieve a true, national mass market. While the promoters' projections for reel-to-reel tape players had fallen short during the 1950s and 1960s, car sales of 4- and 8-track tape machines grew spectacularly from the early 1960s through the 1970s.

Meanwhile, in 1952 German electronics manufacturer Blaupunkt was the first company to offer automotive FM receivers. Then in 1964, following unsuccessful experiments to incorporate 45 rpm disc players and reel-to-reel tape machines, Dutch-based Philips launched the "Compact Cassette" tape player that competed with the 8-track cartridge system throughout the 1960s and 1970s. Tape players in cars using reel-to-reel tape technology could also be found in the 1950s, but their large size and finicky components limited their popularity. This changed when Philips launched its cassette configuration. To overcome the sonic deficiencies of this thinner tape format, engineer Ray Dolby adapted his hiss-reduction technology (versions of which had previously appeared in high-end and reel-to-reel recorders) for cassettes in 1968. The introduction of better-quality home cassette decks by Ampex and others in the late 1960s and early 1970s elevated the reputation of the format and helped make it acceptable to hi-fi and car stereo enthusiasts alike.

Cassette tapes had also become the technology of choice for those interested in making copies of records for use in battery-operated portables or in-car tape players. Pre-recorded cassette sales overtook 8-track in the mid-1970s, and then overtook LPs in the early 1980s. For a time in the 1980s, the cassette was the most popular home music format for both home recording and pre-recorded listening applications. Dolby steadily improved his technology for cassette tape, and the venerable gamma-ferric oxide tape formulation, used since the 1940s for reel-to-reel tape, was superseded by mixtures that contained iron oxide and/or chromium dioxide or metal particles. The 90-minute tape became the best-selling blank tape, reflecting the fact that two full LP albums could usually be recorded on a single 90-minute cassette.

In 1975, the Japanese company Pioneer introduced the first in-car compact cassette player, and in 1984 the first car CD player (Pioneer was also responsible for the first car GPS navigation system in 1990). The arrival of CD technology in the early 1980s led to the decline of both 8-track and compact cassette tapes. The early 1970s also brought the true advent of what is now referred to as the aftermarket. Custom stereo makers like Crutchfield began to cater to owners who wanted to improve their vehicles' audio capabilities beyond what any car manufacturer or dealer offered. Car audio manufacturers such as Alpine, Blaupunkt, Kenwood, and Pioneer began to do brisk business selling aftermarket cassette players and higher-quality speakers. The early 1980s also saw the advent of the first pull-out box-style stereo receivers, a response to the plague of break-ins and thefts that afflicted many car owners in the US at the time.

The late 1970s and early 1980s saw FM radio stations explode in popularity (including those focusing on sports and talk radio). This prompted the construction of car receivers that could pick up FM signals while in motion, giving drivers a much more expansive listening choice. The quality of the signal, combined with the variety of formats and programming, meant that FM stations became far preferred by drivers over AM stations (Brodsky, 2015).

Beginning in the early 1980s, and coincident with the arrival of compact disc (CD) technology, car stereos began to rival home stereos in their sophistication and sound quality. The first car audio competitions began around this time. Multiple speaker configurations took hold in earnest. It became common to find upgraded or custom systems with two or three separate (or "component") drivers per side, with tweeters and mid-range speakers in the front plus mid-range rear deck speakers to "fill" out the sound, and one or more subwoofers either in their own separate enclosures or mounted in the rear trunk. The 1990s saw the arrival of higher-end systems, often incorporating a centre channel to improve sonic imaging.

Multiple-disc CD changers appeared in the late 1980s. These allowed the operator to store as many as ten CDs at a time and effortlessly switch between them while driving. By the mid-1990s, it was common to find many cars with a CD changer mounted in the trunk or underneath the front passenger seat. CD technology was a tremendous advance over tape technology in sound quality, durability, and even safety. Indeed, it was a step forward in almost all respects save one—customizability. For most of the 1980s and 1990s, CDs were fixed albums, like vinyl records. Although CD burners were introduced in the early 1990s, affordable consumer products did not take hold until around the turn of the millennium.

MP3 technology represented yet another leap forward, one that largely solved the issue of customization. Virtually at the moment the iPod and competing MP3 playback models took off in popularity, sales and usage of CDs began to decline, and what remained of the compact cassette market disappeared almost overnight. MP3 players allowed for the storage of thousands of songs, made it easy to create custom playlists, and let operators easily search by song title, artist, or album. But when it came to automobiles, there was still tension in the market. Even as people began to buy iPods and other players by the millions, it was not always simple to connect them to car stereos—and, in some cases, it can still be complicated today. For example, by the mid-2000s, cars began to come with auxiliary inputs that connected to any MP3 player's headphone jack. But true iPod integration remained elusive for much longer. Some early BMW and MINI Cooper systems notwithstanding, it has only been relatively recently that cars have come standardized with USB jacks (already outdated in many cases) that can read iPod and iPhone playlists, albums, artists, and songs, or even work with mobile phone apps.

Currently, manufacturers offer a dazzling array of ways to play music and of electronic entertainment possibilities for our cars. The days of the limited programming associated with the Highway Hi-Fi are long over. There are now multiple ways to connect a portable music player or smartphone to one's car and choose specifically what songs to hear. Most new cars come with a Bluetooth system that allows for wireless phone connectivity. It lets operators not only dial by voice and talk hands-free, but also stream music stored on the phone or received through a data connection. With the ability to stream Internet audio, which is often free, the need for purchasing a satellite-radio receiver and subscription like SiriusXM may soon be obsolete. Alternatively, a person can link their smartphone to a modern infotainment system such as Apple CarPlay or Android Auto and stream Internet radio stations or online digital music services such as Spotify or SoundCloud, perform web searches, and check local fuel prices, weather forecasts, or road conditions from the driver's seat. Drivers can have the car read text messages to them; and, with an integrated navigation system, one could even look up local restaurants, make an online reservation, and get turn-by-turn directions how to get there. Many of these functions can often be controlled by voice (using the Siri voice assistant in Apple's CarPlay system, for example), which lets drivers keep their eyes on the road and hands on the wheel. A recent trend is for auto-makers to develop their own entertainment systems that let the driver access various content from their smartphone. Toyota's 2018 musically titled Entune connectivity system, for example, essentially duplicates the function of Car-Play or Android Auto.

In-car electronics are among the fastest-growing area of auto technology, as automakers scramble to outdo one another. Demand for the latest in-car media technology has exploded, and savvy dealers train their sales staff to be electronics experts who can effortlessly guide customers through sometimes complex systems. Electronic features such as CarPlay or Android Auto are popular options, even overtaking demand for a GPS. The controls for many of these advanced systems can be nebulous and distracting. To reduce driver distraction, some functions are usually deactivated while the vehicle is moving. And while there can still be features that take the driver's eyes off the road, using an in-car system is generally easier than trying to operate the small buttons of a portable device while driving—an operation that is obviously dangerous and increasingly illegal. However, the best designs offer an unprecedented level of versatility and convenience that is changing how we live with our cars.

The market for connectivity has even extended into a burgeoning after-market business. There are currently numerous aftermarket options to bring an older model car up to speed, so to speak. According to Jeffrey Fay, direc-tor of mobile electronics at Crutchfield, an online electronics retailer, "Today, with a five-year-old car you can add as many or more modern conveniences than you can find in many of the brand-new cars" (Connect with your car, 2013). Common aftermarket upgrades include iPod or iPhone integration and Bluetooth capability. With growing concern about distracted driving and increasing bans on using handheld phones, a Bluetooth add-on to allow hands-free calling is a common upgrade. Both are achievable with relatively low-priced plug-and-play systems using the existing car radio or by changing an existing radio for an aftermarket system with Bluetooth capability and the ability to control a music player.

This brief survey serves to point out the emphasis placed on improving audio playback quality, the safety of sound system operation and ease of delivery, and, finally, though perhaps most importantly, the increasing desire to facilitate the driver's choice and availability of music that can be heard. As such, the development of car sound systems was and still is largely driven by the desire to cater to individual tastes and sonic identities.

Sound systems and influence on music

Advances in automotive sound systems (including advances in sound quality, ease of delivery, and increasing means of choosing the music available to be heard) represent another distinct way in which car manufacturers have (often unintentionally) influenced the sound of popular music. As discussed, the evolution of various sound systems and media players has greatly enhanced and facilitated the ease and experience of listening to music in our cars. The ubiquity of music consumption in cars has, in turn, led audio engineers to turn to car speakers in studios for mix downs. Many engineers use their cars as a reference, and some studios (such as Sony in New York) have car speakers built into their range of mixing reference speakers.[1] Thus, the literal sound of the music we listen to is often conditioned by automobiles and their sound systems, regardless of whether we are actually listening to that music in a car.

A particularly overt example of this phenomenon can be found in hip hop artist Dr. Dre's creation of "G-funk," a genre that emerged from California in the early 1990s and which features slow hypnotic grooves, melodic synthesizer passages, and high-pitched portamentos that contrast with deep bass frequencies. In its slow tempo and booming bass-oriented feel, the music was a perfect soundtrack for slow cruising with the top down. Indeed, as Justin Williams (2014) argues, G-funk "was created and mixed *specifically* for listening in car stereo systems" (p. 110, emphasis in original). Williams outlines Dre's production style specifically in relation to his work on Snoop Doggy Dogg's debut single "Who Am I? (What's My Name?)" from 1993:

> The contrast between the high and low synthesizer frequencies in "Who Am I" and other examples in that style are particularly effective in aftermarket car sound systems where the highly directional car tweeter can exclusively support the high end frequencies, and the power of the

> subwoofer(s) produce the corporeal sensations from the bassline. ... Synthesized sound, dynamic range compression, and prominent bass frequencies are but three elements that seem most compatible with the automotive sounds-scape (Williams, 2014, pp. 132–33).

Distinct from the consequential sounds of cars that have influenced the sound and content of popular music, the consequential implications of the car's sound system itself influence the overall sound of the mix, as engineers intentionally emphasize certain frequencies in order to shape the sound of the recording to best align it with the conditions in which it is to be ideally heard. Such influences of automotive design may be subtle, and most consumers may not be aware of them, but they speak to the powerful, if perhaps unintended, impact the automobile has had on shaping the sound and experience of popular music today. Whether it is the noise of the car itself that affects the recorded sound and written content of the music or the refinement of the automotive sound system that facilitates the ubiquity of listening to popular music in cars (and by extension affects the music mix-down process for an optimal sonic experience of that music), such influences should be understood as a consequential or unintentional imprinting of automotive culture on to popular music.

Intentional influences of the automotive industry on popular music are more difficult to trace. However, there is at least one other powerful way in which the automotive industry has actively and willingly influenced popular music: namely in its ability to influence our taste for which types and styles of cars we might purchase and, by extension, which music we might buy/consume. As discussed in Chapter 4, in studying the alignment of products with various artists (or even genres of music), we can profitably understand the complexities of how the automotive industry is affecting our taste in music—and hence what kinds of music are being commercially and successfully produced.

Drive-time radio

Another important outcome of the evolution of automotive sound systems is the effect that automotive listening has had on actual media content. The "drive-time" radio format, in particular, would not have existed without previous advances in automotive sound design. Beginning in the early 1960s, a growing number of mostly AM radio stations began to focus exclusively on news- and talk-format programming. Although all-news formats were expensive (far more so than formats playing recorded music), such stations did extremely well in large markets. Stations typically mixed updated newscasts with various "call-in" talk shows. At the same time, a growing number of stations dropped news and public affairs programming and devoted themselves exclusively to "all-music" or "all-talk" formats. Drive-time radio became important around the same time as the rise in suburban living meant that morning and evening commutes in most urban areas grew longer.

The drive-time format continues to be a mainstay, attracting the medium's largest audiences and most popular and well-known on-air DJs and hosts. Such programs continue to thrive despite decades of competition from broadcast and cable television and the Internet. New York-based "shock jock" Howard Stern's morning program was widely re-broadcast across the country beginning in 1986, and in 1996 talk-show host Don Imus' popular *Imus in the Morning*, also originating in New York City, began to be simulcast on the 24-hour cable television news channel MSNBC. For popular music-oriented stations, morning drive time is typically dominated by the hyperactive, zany routines of "morning zoo" radio programming, while the afternoon portion is often given over to music (often in commercial-free blocks, especially in markets with long commute times) and light entertainment features.

Furthermore, the rise of satellite radio (e.g., SiriusXM) was due in large part to its associations with the automotive industry, which regularly offers it as an option. In 1999, GM invested in XM and entered into a 12-year distribution agreement between XM and GM's subsidiary, OnStar Corporation. The agreement called for exclusive installation of XM Satellite Radio in GM vehicles from November 2001 until November 2013. Following this agreement, other car manufacturers started installing satellite radio receivers. Electronics companies also began launching several models of portable after-market satellite radio receivers soon thereafter. A "corporate overview" of SiriusXM Satellite Radio listed on its website proudly states:

> SiriusXM has arrangements with every major automaker for installation of satellite radio in their vehicles. SiriusXM products for cars, the home or office are available through shop.siriusxm.com and at retail locations nationwide.
>
> SiriusXM is also a leading provider of telematics and connected vehicles services, providing safety, security and convenience services to a host of major automotive manufacturers.
>
> SiriusXM also provides premium traffic, weather, data and information services for subscribers in cars, trucks, RVs, boats and aircraft through SiriusXM Traffic[TM], SiriusXM Travel Link, NavTraffic®, Nav Weather[TM], SiriusXM Aviation, Sirius Marine[TM], Sirius Marine Weather, XMWX Aviation, and XMWX Marine[TM].[2]

Recently, however, the expanding number of digital music services and podcasts, coupled with the increasing availability of in-vehicle Wi-Fi, may make satellite radio service irrelevant. SiriusXM has a distinct market advantage because it is already built into many new vehicles, and is thus familiar and easy to use for many customers. However, this advantage may disappear as cars manufacturers offer systems that easily integrate with smartphones. Thus, complete vehicle connectivity looks to be inevitable. A report by Mearian (2014) projected that by 2020 most cars in Europe and North America would be connected to the Internet: "about 150 million vehicles will be connected via Wi-Fi, and 60% to 75% of them will be capable of consuming, creating and sharing Web-based data." Underscoring the emphasis placed on car-connectivity that mobile phone and computer manufacturers are envisioning, industry analyst Thilo Koslowski opined:

> To facilitate that kind of shift, connected-vehicle leaders in automotive organizations need to partner with existing ecosystems like Android Auto or Apple CarPlay that can simplify access to and integration of general mobile applications into the vehicle (Mearian, 2014).

As advertised by Apple on its website, CarPlay "is a smarter, safer way to use your iPhone in the car." The system takes iPhone functions and places them in the car's built-in screen:

> CarPlay features Siri voice control and is specially designed for driving scenarios. It also works with your car's controls—knobs, buttons, or touchscreen. And the apps you want to use in the car have been reimagined, so you can use them while your eyes and hands stay where they belong.[3]

As of March 2018, there were over 300 models of car that support the system (Charlton, 2018). Aftermarket manufacturers like Alpine, Clarion, JBL, JVC, Kenwood, Pioneer, and Sony also sell car stereo systems with CarPlay, as well as systems for Android phones, such as Android Auto. The operating interface for these systems ranges from physical knobs and touchscreens to automated voice commands (à la Siri) and eye movements in heads-up displays.

In the almost obsessive desire to refine and improve our in-car music and entertainment experience, it is evident that manufacturers are attempting to provide customers with as much choice and ease of use as possible. It is also evident that entertainment and sound systems are becoming ever more automated and integrated into the overarching goal of self-driving cars. A car that will respond to the driver's/passenger's eye movements and voice commands increasingly merges, as it were, into their very thoughts—a car that seems to be becoming more and more an extension of the human body itself.

The car as instrument of identity

Although audio sound systems have evolved considerably over the past century or so, such that they greatly enhance and facilitate our experience of engaging with music while driving, it is often the very sonic features of the car itself that become transformed into expressive musical objects. The following section looks at the car as it can be understood, and has been used, as a musical instrument in and of itself.

Cars transformed into musical instruments

As discussed in Chapter 1, various car songs have incorporated the sound of the car itself into their musical soundscape. From the syncopated motoristic rhythms of "Rocket 88" to the ambient use of engine and highway sounds in Kraftwerk's "Autobahn," the sounds of cars themselves have infiltrated and influenced the sound of popular music. Madness' "Driving in My Car" (1982), for instance, features a sampled rhythmic pulse of a car engine and horn, as well as the percussive clinking of a disassembled exhaust pipe. The song, featuring the line "I've been driving in my car, it's not quite a Jaguar," is a satirical ode to the joys of driving in the band's "Maddiemobile," a 1959 Morris Minor, which appears in the video.[4] The off-beat sounds, accompanied by a slightly out-of-tune piano and mechanically delivered, dead-pan vocals, are meant to convey a whimsical sense of UK working-class identity. While there are a large number of such pop songs featuring actual sounds of cars, the realm of marketing and advertising of cars has also witnessed significant manifestations of the car as musical object.

Almost from its origins as a mass-marketed industry, popular music has formed an integral part of automotive advertising. As discussed in Chapter 4, television soundtracks and product endorsements by musical celebrities form the largest component of this advertising. Some companies, however, have taken the musical relationship one step further. Several television advertisements, for example, have imaginatively used parts of the vehicle itself to create their musical soundtrack. In 2009, Ford introduced its new Focus model in Europe with "The Beautifully Arranged, Ode to a New Ford" advertisement.[5] The ad features a tuxedo-clad orchestra of 31 instruments assembled out of Focus parts. Instruments include: a clutch guitar ornamented with a backdrop from the inside of a door; a fiddle made from a rear suspension mount and a shock absorber; a Ford Fender bass made from fenders and a pillar/roof support; a sliding trombone-like instrument made from shock absorber parts; a transmission case cello-dulcimer; a window frame harp; and an opera window violin. In what sounds like a conventional, if somewhat pop-hook-laden orchestral arrangement, the group performs "Ode to a New Ford" accompanied by the text "The new Ford Focus. Beautifully arranged." The commercial, with its formally attired musicians and clear nod to orchestral tradition, links the Focus to the perceived precision and values of classical music in much the same manner as the common use of classical music for car names described in Chapter 5.

In recent years, it has become something of a recurrent trope in car advertising to build a soundtrack from samples drawn from the sounds of a car's operation. These soundtracks, often devised by techno musicians and DJs, tend to be more techno or industrial pop in style, as opposed to the classical music resonances of the Ford Focus campaign described above. Among the earliest of these cars-as-sound-source ads was Nissan's 2002 Altima "Samplers" commercial, which features two DIY music engineers sampling various sounds from the car—the engine starting, doors opening and shutting, automatic door locks—that eventually become the sole sources for an original techno-sounding composition.[6] The tag line for the ad was "Shift Expression." In 2008, pioneers of ambient techno The Orb were responsible for creating a soundtrack for Volkswagen Golf's "Everyday" campaign. The track is similar to the "Samplers" ad, and is composed of altered samples of sounds of the car itself, such as closing doors and pitch-shifted engine sounds interspersed with sampled and rhythmically modified snippets of "everyday" in-car conversations.[7]

In similar fashion, in 2011 Chevrolet posted a video on YouTube highlighting the "solid fit and finish" of its Chevrolet Cruze model. The video takes place in an anechoic chamber and consists of a series of sounds—slamming doors, hoods, and trunks, and wipers and horns—that build into an industrial percussive soundtrack.[8] In 2013, to celebrate its tenth anniversary, Scion released ten exclusive tracks celebrating its products for download on its music site. The first track, "Celebration Anthem," was accompanied by a commercial announcing the new Scion 10 series of cars, with the tag line "Join us in celebrating 10 years of making our own tracks," and directing viewers to "get the tracks at scion.com."[9] "Celebration Anthem" was composed by experimental electronic musician Jeesh, and comprised sounds drawn from all five of Scion's models at the time, as well as from samples of happy club goers stating the names of all five models. To cite but one more example, in 2015 Lexus released the ad "Make Some Noise" as a Super Bowl spot for its new NX turbo hybrid. The ad featured (again) percussive samples of car doors, the stick shift, and various electronic indicators under a voice-over proclaiming, "Be seen, be heard! Make some noise!"[10]

If nothing else, these examples again underscore the close connection between cars and music in popular culture. The commercials are ostensibly intended to promote and advertise to consumers the identity of the car models in question. Typically linked through a common technological emphasis, these commercials also help to humanize the machine, breaking down the advanced technology into an approachable and recognizably human leisure/entertainment activity. In all these advertisements, the stark, and what are usually considered to be unmusical, sounds of the mechanics of wiper blades and door latches—underscored by the scientific sterility of the anechoic testing chamber in the case of the Chevy Cruze ad—transform the otherwise non-human machine into a recognizably human expressive product. The cars are literally turned into musical instruments, underlining the combined sonic components of the car as an expressive device, and thereby tying into advertisers' desire to have consumers generate emotional experiences with their inanimate products. Like the "smart" technologies and like the association with musical soundtracks and musical celebrities that are promoted in conventional automotive advertisement, commercials that emphasize cars morphing into instruments attempt to connect the machine to our humanity, and highlight the ability that both cars and music have to emotionally move and transform us. Understood in this light, both cars and music are synchronously expressive vehicles of transformation.[11]

The car horn

Predating even the radio, one of the most overt connections between automobiles, music, and the projection of human presence, if not of identity, is the car horn. Both car and audio manufacturers have continually sought to refine the automotive sound system and make the consumption of music and other forms of entertainment a more individualistic experience. The same might be said of the horn, which is perhaps the most overt musical component of the car itself.

The sounds of car horns have become a ubiquitous part of the soundscape of our everyday urban life. The horn is also a sonic icon of popular culture, as manifest in everything from the animated Road Runner's characteristic "beep beep" to the General Lee's horn that played "Dixie" on the television show *The Dukes of Hazzard*. Horns and automobiles are virtually synonymous, and date back to the earliest days of the horseless carriage. In the early 1800s, steam carriages were becoming popular in Britain. For the safety of pedestrians and animals, the Red Flag Act or Locomotives on Highways Act (1865) stated that "self-propelled vehicles on public roads must be preceded by a man on foot waving a red flag and blowing a horn" (Matteucci, 1970, p. 392). Of course, it did not take long to realize that a horn in a moving automobile, operated by the driver, was much more efficient.

In the late 1800s, motorists were able to choose from a range of signalling devices that included bulb horns, whistles, and bells. In America, most chose bells. Despite the noise made by these devices, they were considered a quieter alternative to the clatter of horses' hooves and the bouncing of metal carriage wheels on cobblestones. Testifying to the early suspicion of automobiles, the Farmers' Anti-Automobile Society of Pennsylvania demanded adequate warning, but added: "If a horse is unwilling to pass an automobile, the driver should [sound the horn and] take the machine apart and conceal the parts in the bushes" (Karolevitz, 1968, p. 192).

According to motoring periodicals of the day, the proliferation of vehicles using bells contributed to the likelihood of accidents because those vehicles could be easily mistaken for anything from "cable or trolley cars, to bicycle [hot rods], even to bakers' wagons, at greater or lesser distances" (Garfield, 1983, p. 217). To counter this problem, some writers advocated the bulb horn as an alternative warning signal. By the turn of the century, the bulb horn, which was already popular in France, became the standard in North America. Its sound was considered more novel and penetrating than a bell. However, much as today, complaints about the constant din of horn honking abounded. Charles Johnson (1913) of *Motor Magazine* opined,

> The dull, monotonous, and utterly innocuous droning of the bulb horn has become such a continuous noise in many sections and cities that people pay no more attention to it than one does to the buzz of machinery in the building where he may be located (p. 66).

By 1910, some were calling for a more effective warning device, one that could be heard at least an eighth of a mile ahead. Manufacturers responded with a variety of whistles, chimes, sirens, and horns, some of which ran off exhaust gases. The Sireno, named after the Greek mythological creatures that lured mariners to their destruction with the irresistible charm of their song, was advertised as a "one-mile signal." Another device, called the Godin, was publicized with the slogan, "You press as you steer and your pathway is clear" (Garfield, 1983, p. 217). Likely the most famous horn in the early age of the automobile was the Gabriel. A multi-toned horn, it was publicized by the manufacturer as being musically pleasing in character: "Everybody likes its organ-like tone and cheerfully moves aside as it sends forth its warning" (p. 218).

The main rival to the Gabriel was the harsher and more abrupt tone of a device called the klaxon. This horn got its name from the Greek word *klaxo* (to shriek). Comprised of an electric-powered vibrating metal diaphragm, the klaxon had one notable advantage over other horns—rather than having to be sounded continuously, one touch on the klaxon sufficed. The power and dynamic level of the klaxon was such that it was advertised as "the only horn which would instantly move cows and bullocks" (Garfield, 1983, p. 218). Unlike the musically pleasing sound of the Gabriel, the klaxon injected a less mellifluous and less natural, and thus attention-getting, sound onto landscape.[12]

More recently, car horns have been engineered as a combination of two pitches: a low one that carries a greater distance; and a high one that supersedes the din of busy city streets and the sound interference of the highway. Until the mid-1960s, many North American cars were tuned to the notes E flat and C, a consonant combination that manufacturers felt was not too disturbing. Current electronic automobile horns are often arranged to produce two frequencies between 500 and 420 hertz and moved up the scale to F# and A# (Garfield, 1983, p. 218). Of course, horns and sirens used on emergency vehicles have a distinctive and immediately recognizable sonic voice, meant to get the immediate public's attention and announce presence. Albeit serving a far more practical purpose than playing music through a sound system or revving a powerful engine at a stoplight, horns and sirens project yet another car-enabled sonic marker of identity.

Despite their practical and safety purposes, automotive sirens and horns are nonetheless often condemned for their contribution to urban noise pollution. At various times and places in the history of the automobile, people have attempted to curb this noise problem by making it illegal to honk too much, too loud, or in particular locations at certain times of the day. By 1912, a number of cities in America—among them Chicago, St. Louis, Los Angeles, Cincinnati, Seattle, and Dallas—had enacted laws requiring motorized vehicles to have audible warning devices, but forbidding their excessive use. Some cities also made it illegal to use loud electric horns within city limits. While endorsing the new horseless carriage, *Scientific American* asserted, "Specialists have many times expressed an opinion that the nervous disorders which exist in the city are aggravated, if not caused, in many cases by the city's great traffic" (The horseless carriage, 1899).

The use of car horns is also marked by significant gender differences. Women are not only less inclined to honk their horns than men, but are also more likely to be honked at. In a study by Deaux (1971), participants were asked to drive cars to a particular intersection, wait for the light to turn green, and then sit at the intersection for 15 seconds or until the car behind them began to honk. The results indicated that the sex of the driver was the most important influence on horn use: only 52 per cent of male drivers were honked, at compared to 71 per cent of female drivers.

Despite the fact that Deaux's study was written nearly 50 years ago, today car horns are still a leading source of noise pollution in urban centres. India's honking problem is so severe (some 18 million honks per hour in Mumbai alone) that the response to it—by both activists and government officials— mirrors the response to an actual epidemic, with national distribution of pamphlets and bumper stickers requesting people to avoid honking when not required (Stancati, 2013; Zee Media Bureau, 2018). Officials in Peru, mean-while, began treating honking as a serious crime in 2009, threatening to con-fiscate the cars of people who honk unnecessarily (La Rue, 2009). In 2013, Shanghai expanded the reach and areas covered by its 2007 car horn law. Originally aimed at reducing noise pollution downtown, officials also wanted to curb the use of car horns "by airports, subway stations, and the intersec-tions of major roads" (Xiaoru, 2013).

The situation is little different in North America. In recent years, various states and municipalities have attempted to restrict unnecessary horn use by instituting fines. Yet those laws have not solved the problem. In 2013, New York City all but gave up attempting to control its citizens' passion for honking, and decided to remove all its "Don't Honk" signs. There is still a $350 fine on the books for illegal use of a car horn, but, according to the *New York Times*, the law is rarely enforced (Flegenheimer, 2013).

Despite its reputation as a public irritant, the car horn as a musical device has a long and continuing history in popular music. As previously mentioned, one of the earliest automotive songs to come out of Tin Pan Alley incorpo-rated the sound of a honking car horn. Hamilton J. Hawley's "The Auto Race," as performed by the Edison Concert Band and recorded in 1905, for example, features an early recording of car backfiring as it starts up, followed by several hoots from a hand-pumped car horn that are imitated in the winds. Later, Clarence Gaskill wrote a song tellingly entitled "I'm Wild About Horns on Automobiles That Go Ta Ta Ta Ta" (1928), and in 1950 Arkie Shibley and his Mountain Dew Boys recorded George Wilson's "Hot Rod Race" with a striking horn-honking lead guitar accent.

Perhaps the most famous instance of the incorporation of car horns in popular music is in The Beatles' onomatopoeic chorus, "Beep beep'm, beep beep, yeah," on "Drive My Car" (1965).[13] The onomatopoeic quality of car horns has been incorporated into many popular music recordings, including the aforementioned "Rocket 88" and Madness' "Driving in My Car" (1982). Other songs, from Kraftwerk's "Autobahn" (1974) to Common's 1999 rap hit "Car Horn" (featuring a sampled horn that provides the main beat to the song), also foreground the sound of the horn. While it is perhaps a stretch to call the sounding of car horns "music" in the traditional sense, horns are certainly a recognizable part of the ambient urban soundscape that represent an immediate sonic connection to motorized mobility and, as such, have been commonly incorporated into the poetics of popular music and culture. Moreover, since the function of the car horn is to signal or announce one's presence, it can be understood as an early form of mobile sonic projection of identity and a related colonization of space and place.

Recently, car horns have been used as the main instruments in recreating various songs. Musician Wendy Chambers constructed a "Car Horn Organ" that she has played at concerts throughout North America, including on *The Tonight Show with Jay Leno*. Searching on YouTube also uncovers a number of instances of people creating music on car horns (e.g., synchronized beeping by a group of drivers) or on virtual car horns, as in the popular video game series *Grand Theft Auto*.

The technology of car horns has also improved to the extent that after-market "musical car horns" are now capable of playing various extended tunes, from the ever-popular "Dixie" to the latest pop hits. The following advertisement for one supplier of musical horns underscores the variety of songs that can now be programmed into a car horn:

> Musical Air Horns play the easily recognizable tunes straight out of Hollywood! They are available with four, five and six trumpets.
>
> You can choose from funky tunes like "The Tequila", "The Calvary Charge", "Call to the Post", "Wedding March" and "Eyes of Texas". These Musical Air Horns come with four trumpets playing these popular tunes that you love.
>
> The popular Dixie Horn plays the first 12 notes of "Dixie" at the touch of a single button. It comes with five trumpets that play the powerful Dixie notes at 118 decibels.
>
> You can choose from "The La Bamba", "Oh Susannah", "Never On Sunday", or "Macarena" Air Horns that come with five trumpets. If you are a fan of La Cucaracha, the five-trumpeted Air Horn plays the most easily recognized notes of the La Cucaracha song and help you get instant attention on the road!
>
> If you crave extra loud, trumpeted sound, you can choose the "The Godfather" or the Dr. Zhivago theme Horn that comes with six trumpets that play the soulful themes in a super-loud 118-decibel blast.
>
> Musical Air Horns are made of impact-resistant, resilient plastic materials and fit easily into any engine compartment. They do not require bulky air tanks to install (J.C. Whitney Autoparts, n.d.).

This ad underscores the ability to project "in a super-loud 118-decibel blast" a variety of musical identities, ranging from the Southern redneck stereotype associated with "Dixie" to Hispanic and Latino ("La Bamba," "Macarena," and "La Cucaracha") to Italian and Greek ("The Godfather" and "Never on a Sunday").

Some companies are marketing programmable and recordable musical car horns and public address systems. COGApa's Automotive PA System, for example, is promoted as:

> The first fully integrated, musical, recordable automobile horn with built in public address system. ... Use Coga's built-in songs and sounds or record your own. Record your school fight song, your favorite pop music, your dog barking—you name it! The possibilities are endless![14]

With the ability to program one's own sounds and songs and, like MP3 playlists for in-car sound systems, programmable car horns represent completely customizable projections of sonic identity. Ostensibly intended as a warning device, the car horn can now actively project a personalized musical or sonic identity that, much like a personalized ringtone, publicly announces one's presence. To "honk (or toot) one's horn" is a commonly used expression of self-pride and self-identity, and represents yet another form of car–music sonic latching of identity on to daily lived experience. The horn is, however, merely one public sonic component of the car that projects identity and presence. Another closely related manifestation of this is found in the siren.

Sirens

As sonic objects, musical horns also manifest a transhistorical representation of military power and control over people, whether as sounded on the battlefield to control troop movements or used to alert and warn a civilian population of threat. The evolutionary offshoot of the horn is the mechanical siren. Sirens are thought to have been invented in the 1790s by physicist John Robison (an associate of James Watt, inventor of the steam car); and although it now has multiple uses, it was initially intended to serve as a musical instrument, specifically as a way of powering pipes in an organ (Popa, 2012).[15] Sirens were first added to motorized police vehicles in the 1920s and, along with their use on ambulances and other emergency vehicles, have become synonymous with the sound of state control and associated regulation and disciplining of bodies. Whereas a car horn is a statement of presence, a siren is a statement of authority.

The association of sirens with danger, control, and authority has made them ripe for inclusion in anti-establishment pop songs such as The Clash's "White Riot" (1977), Black Sabbath's "War Pigs" (1970), or The Ramones' "Psycho Therapy" (1983). Moreover, they are especially prominent in hip hop. In many predominantly black neighbourhoods, and as reinforced in numerous movies and television police dramas, the short rhythmic *chirp chirp* or *whoop whoop* sound of a police siren has become synonymous with the "driving while black" phenomenon, general police surveillance, and interventions with both pedestrians and drivers. The characteristic sound has consequently been sampled and incorporated into many hip hop works, such as Nelly and P. Diddy's "Shake Ya Tailfeather" (2003), Chamillionaire's "Hip Hop Police" (2007), or Kendrick Lamar's "XXX" (2017). For black men and women (and, indeed, for most people regardless of their race), hearing the siren, whether in the form of an actual police car or sampled in a hip hop track, evokes a particularly immediate bodily and emotional response, one that incorporates both visceral muscular tension and nervousness, even fear. Socially conditioned to evoke the sound of authority, the siren thus effects an immediate disciplining and control of our bodies.

Rather than using samples of actual sirens, some hip hop works use vocal imitations, such as in Wyclef Jean's "Thug Angels" (2000). One of the most overt and telling examples of police siren vocalization is KRS-One's "Sound of Da Police" (1993), which begins with the rapper intoning, "Woop-woop! That's the sound of da police! That's the sound of da beast!"[16] He goes on to compare the police to "overseers"—the plantation managers formerly responsible for the daily policing of slaves and their work.

The incorporation of police sirens in rap calls attention to the sonic environment and the police state reality that many black people still experience on an everyday basis. The siren is used in these works primarily to protest and reclaim (at least as imagined in a fictive song) power from the police and, by extension, the state. In addition to the culture of resistive car and stereo modifications, it is yet another manifestation of the incorporation and importance of the automobile in the construction of African-American identity. Much as earlier jazz and swing incorporated the sounds and rhythms of machines and factory work to sonically recover their potentially de-humanized daily existence (Dinerstein, 2003), the onomatopoeic vocal *woop* imitation of police sirens in "Sound of Da Police" breathes human life back into the mechanical sound of state control.

"Booming" and car sound system modification cultures

Aside from being a venue from which to consume music in evermore varied ways, as manifest in such ongoing refinements to both horns and sound systems, the car is increasingly being modified and used as an expressive music reproduction device in and of itself. Music is an integral part of a larger culture of car modification loosely known as "tuning." YouTube is rife with tens of thousands of videos showing off the automotive handiwork of various individuals (the vast majority of whom are young men), all accompanied by aggressive musical soundtracks, mostly techno, independent alternative, or heavy metal. Online series such as *Fine Tuned* and documentaries like *We Are Driven* (2013) underline the sense of personalization and individual expression that tuning a car provides for practitioners. As one informant in *We Are Driven* claims, "If somebody says to me, 'Do you know Mike?' I'll say, 'No, what does he drive?' ... Because you know [the car] is an extension of that guy."[17]

The fetishization of the car sound system in particular is a rite of passage in some subcultures of tuning, notably in the lowrider or Houston SLAB cultures (as discussed in Chapter 2). The desire to sonically brand and customize one's automobile works as both a projection of self-identity and, often, an overtly socially resistive act. Such cultures of customization both resist and co-opt the active homogenizing mass marketing of corporate automotive culture—typically dominated by middle-aged white men—and even, by extension, of the American military industrial complex as a whole. Indeed, two central innovations that facilitated the massive increase of car audio systems in the 1950s, transistors and alternators, directly resulted from technological advances during World War II (Morris, 2014, p. 329). Furthermore, returning soldiers exposed to the advanced audio and listening technologies found in sonar and other devices brought that knowledge home, and they began to alter and tinker with their home stereo systems to achieve more pristine reproductions of perceived sonic reality (Keightley, 1996, p. 151). In essence, much as with car modification in hot rod culture, these returning soldiers can be said to have begun the ongoing passion among enthusiasts to experiment with and customize automotive sound systems.

Underscoring the expressive aspect of automotive sound, car sound system competitions have become evermore commonplace. Car audio competitions started in the early 1980s in a quest to find the loudest and/or most outrageous installations. Little consideration was given to sound quality early on; but in the early 1990s, several organizations, notably the International Auto Sound Challenge Association (IASCA), began holding car audio competitions that focused on sound quality. The two styles—sound production, or pressure, level (SPL) and sound quality level (SQL)—have become almost mutually exclusive. SPL or loudness competitions are also known as "dB drag racing," and are often associated with transgressive values of "deviance and defiance," whereas SQL events represent less transgressive attempts to focus on the refinement of the sound system and overall listening experience (Morris, 2014, p. 340). Sound and vibration levels during SPL competitions can become so acute that the cars sometimes begin to self-destruct. The sound systems produce a visceral effect on both occupants and surrounding listeners that often borders on the painful, and, if taken to an extreme, can even be lethal. Media studies scholar David Morris (2014) describes the unnerving experience of being in a dB drag racer:

> [As the driver] slowly raised the volume, the bass began to press down into my lungs and make the bones in my face vibrate. I found myself reflexively fighting for escape, scrabbling frantically for the door handle as the sound went from entertainment to existential threat (p. 327).

"Booming," as the practice of building and playing extremely loud car stereos is commonly known, is popularly practised around the world. As Morris outlines, booming first gained public notoriety within African-American hip hop culture in the 1980s, but has subsequently transcended simple demographic categories of race, class, or geography. Like SLAB and lowrider cultures of modification, the appeal of driving a sonically disruptive and obtrusively noisy car accentuates social positions of marginality. Booming provides participants with a means to creatively impose themselves on both their machines and their surroundings, thus enacting the ability to confront, if not outright threaten, received social order. As Morris (2014) writes, "Booming has been framed as an epidemic by law enforcement and governments, which have undertaken a decades-long battle to shut down boomers, an effort rich with subtle and overt expressions of racial antipathy—and also so far unsuccessful" (p. 328). Booming and the preoccupation with loud stereos have long been considered a public annoyance. An editorial from the *Orlando Sentinel* in 1988 concluded that the "preoccupation with building the world's greatest ear-splitting stereo system for your cars is just the latest evidence that young American males are public nuisance No. 1 in this country" (Lowery, 1988). The critique called attention to the overt stereotypical association of the practice with youth and masculinity, but also positioned practitioners as marginal outsiders who behave improperly or who challenge normative or dominant conceptions of sonic behaviour.

Hip hop has been the dominant locus of much of the practice of booming for the genre's propensity to emphasize and project bass heavy beats, a key aspect of booming. "Jeep beats" is a colloquial expression in hip hop for a bass-heavy beat that is particularly effective for projection from a car. The defiant 1991 debut album by DJ Terminator X (previously a member of Public Enemy), *Terminator X & The Valley of The Jeep Beets*, for example, brings together notions of threatening bass sound emanating from a car and racial empowerment. The album is intensely political, and concerned primarily with issues of black empowerment. It features songs with titles such as "Vendetta" and "Buck Whylin'," which begins with Sister Souljah's impassioned call to arms: "We are at War." Other artists associated with "Jeep beats" include Sir Mix-a-Lot and 2 Live Crew. In much of this repertoire, artists specifically articulate conventional masculinity, as can be heard in the use of deep bass, and an aggressive colonization of space and territory through sound. For instance, L'Trimm's "Cars That Go Boom" (1988), a Miami bass electro-funk influenced song, features the lyrics "So turn down the treble, and flaunt your bass so your car can be heard almost any place ... / yo, if your speaker's weak, then please turn it off 'cause we like the cars that sound so tough."[18]

As with many sound-projection cultures, exceptionally loud bass frequencies are a particular feature of booming. Bass frequencies take the most power to broadcast—literally, in terms of the amperage and watts needed, and figuratively, in terms of financial ability to buy the necessary equipment—and they also project the furthest distance, and thus sonically colonize a greater territory than shortwave treble frequencies. Bass territorialization therefore represents a sonic projection of power that inverts typical codes of musical value that often fetishize higher frequencies (i.e., of a lead vocalist or lead guitar). In lowrider, SLAB, and booming culture, there is literally a bottom-up flow of power that confronts and potentially threatens the more normative convention of top-down political and socio-economic power arrangements. Moreover, despite these overtly loud pronouncements of presence and defiance, the greater width of bass frequencies makes the origin of the sounds difficult to accurately locate. If the listener is not within sight or near distance of the booming car, they are left with an indistinct muddy pulse that can be heard for many blocks. Thus, the booming car, not unlike the sonic boom from a high-flying military jet, is often heard but not actively seen, and thereby functions as something of a sonic warning—an indistinct yet clearly audible threat as car and driver travel through the urban landscape.[19]

Booming culture and its antithesis, the quasi-ubiquitous quest for quiet that marks so much of mainstream automotive technological innovation and marketing (as discussed in Chapter 5), can be understood along racial perspectives. As we have seen, silence has become particularly associated with luxury and exclusivity, as manifest in the premium placed on a quiet ride by prestigious brands such as Rolls-Royce. A less understood aspect of this quest for quiet results from the Great Migration of African Americans from the rural South to urban centres of the North. At the end of World War II, the influx of African Americans to city cores, combined with advances in mass transit and highway infrastructure that allowed for easier commuting, triggered what is commonly known as "white flight" into newly established outlying bedroom communities and suburbs. The result was a form of sonic segregation wherein people of colour and the working poor were largely relegated to the crowded, noisy confines of the cities while economically advantaged white people were able to access the relative peace and quiet and privacy of suburban life. The longer highway commute times synchronically resulted in a desire for quiet automotive experiences—more private and acoustically insulated car cabins and more pristine car stereo sound that could drown out the "noise" of the lower-class urban existence they sought to escape.[20] Marginalized black and Latino members of car booming cultures effectively invert, or "flip the script," on such predominantly white notions of privacy. Just as the emphasis on bass frequencies inverts a musical power relationship, so too does the booming car turn the private, interior act of driving and car audio listening into public, outside noise. As David Morris (2014) observes:

> This inside-outness is also, often, a racial subversion. Not all boomers are black, but all boomers project blackness. Obscured in the body of the car, a white driver blasting hip-hop becomes, like early white rock DJs, a racial ventriloquist, an audio minstrel (p. 346).

Thus, while booming facilitates a public projection of individual identity, its popularity and co-option by white adherents has facilitated a blurring of racial identity.

In addition to hip hop "Jeep beats" and Houston SLAB styles, a variety of distinct booming car modification subcultures exist throughout the US. "Donks," also known as hi-risers or skyscrapers, for example, are characteristic of the South Coast hip hop scene, particularly prevalent in Florida and especially Miami, and consist of older sedans sporting massively oversized wheels in addition to their powerful stereo systems. But likely the most well-known car modification culture in the US is the lowrider.

Lowriders

More than the literal lowering of a car, the term "lowrider" refers to a specific set of aesthetic and mechanical preferences within the broad range of practices of car modification and recreational cruising that emerged in mid-twentieth-century America (Chappell, 2012). It connotes a close relationship to the history of Mexican-American communities, where the style spread among family and friends through vernacular social networks. Lowriding also developed as a distinctive social activity, comprising public cruising, car club organizations, magazines devoted to the culture, and competitive show events. Lowriders are distinguishable from other custom cars by the prevalence of specific consumer products such as Chevrolet Impala vehicles and Dayton Wire Wheels; functional modifications such as the use of industrial hydraulic lifts innovated by California customizer Ron Aguirre; and visual iconographies, both figurative and ornamental, that reference other media, such as public murals, film and television, and religious art. Other modifications include lowering the car, upholstering its interior with fake leopard skin, intermixing parts from various models, and adding side-rails and chrome bumpers or stripping it down to a stark, lead-grey underpaint. These modifications, predominant in white working-class hot rod culture and other car modification cultures, function as appropriative acts of resistance against the automotive industry's homogenous mass production aimed at the white middle class. In the hands of Chicano lowriders, the car becomes a creative site for "self-determined labor whose value was gained on the street, where cruising formed social activity and competitiveness lent to the formation of self-determined rituals and codes" (LaBelle, 2008, p. 195).

The term lowrider came into use as a marker not only of aesthetic style but also of a particular social identity in the 1960s' context of rising Chicana/o consciousness. The public display of lowrider style came to represent ethno-racial and local pride, with aesthetic competence in lowrider style exemplifying local knowledge gleaned from the shared experiences of urban Mexican America. Thus, while Anglos, African Americans, and others have long participated in lowrider style, it remains generally recognized as a Mexican-American invention and modern tradition. As stated by one lowriding enthusiast,

In white culture, they like their cars jacked up in the back and fast; we have to be different so we have them low. The US is a car culture, and whether you're white or Chicano, your car is an expression of yourself (Thayer, 2012).

Lowrider scholar Brenda Jo Bright (1995) interprets lowrider modifications as "performances of self-imagined identity enacted against an inverted background of cultural stereotypes and racially marked experiences" (p. 96).

Lowering cars to their lowest possible point also, of course, puts practitioners into confrontation with the law. Lowriders flout legal car height restrictions, but also literally place their bodies in a low position, whereby they would be less likely to be identified by police. Physically lowering the car is also matched by an emphasis on acoustically low frequencies. As Brandon LaBelle (2008) explains, the introduction of mega-bass sound systems into the arsenal of lowrider modifications, influenced in part by hip hop car modification culture, "turns the car into a message machine, in which customization expresses social and cultural dissent through appropriative tactics" (p. 200).

The soundtrack to lowriding today is typically comprised of old r & b and doo-wop, which lowriders generally refer to as "oldies." Just as the cars are a hybridized mix of old and new, of stock and modified, lowrider music mixes Mexican mariachi influences and African-American r & b that reflect the influx of black workers to Southern California in the 1930s and 1940s. In the postwar period, the primary taste for *musica tejana* (Texas-style music) led to the inclusion of *conjuntos* (small musical groups) and *orquestas* (dance bands) (Tatum, 2011, p. 113). What Chicanos refer to as oldies represents a loose category spanning the period from the 1930s to the recent past. The songs are often slow-tempo ballads with narrative Spanish lyrics called *corridos*, which often relate the social and racial oppression of Mexican Americans and thus became a form of cultural resistance to Anglo musical culture. In the postwar era, swing and eventually rock influences began to blend with traditional *corridos*, culminating around LA in what became known as "the Eastside Sound." This style borrowed and merged sounds from r & b, rock n' roll, funk, Latin salsa, and traditional Mexican styles. The most well-known Chicano artist associated with the Eastside Sound is likely Ritchie Valens, who achieved success among white and African-American audiences with songs such as "Come On, Let's Go" (1958) and his version of the Mexican folk song "La Bamba" (1958). Other significant Chicano acts influential in lowrider Eastside style include Cannibal & the Headhunters, Thee Midniters, and later, in the 1980s, the somewhat new wave-inflected sound of Los Lobos. In the early days, lowriders simply listened to their favourite music on their car radios. With the more recent popularity of rap, lowriders began to outfit their cars with customized sound systems, adding yet another layer of hybridized resistance. While African-American rappers are often popular, Chicano rappers such as Frost and Lil Rob also enjoy much success.

The most famous work associated with lowriding, however, is War's classic song "Low Rider (On the Boulevard)" from 1975. Reaching #1 on the *Billboard* r & b chart and #7 on the pop singles chart, the song has subsequently become an anthem that immediately evokes the relaxed casual cool of Chicano lowrider culture. The song features cowbell and timbale percussion, and a muscular pumping bass line overlaid by an iconic catchy harmonica melody played by Lee Oskar. The song ends with a saxophone riff emulating the sound of a police siren and alluding to the fact that lowriders were often pulled over for having their suspension too low to the ground. The song also features the laid-back baritone lead vocals of saxophonist Charles Miller. Many mistakenly interpret the relaxed vocals, relatively slow tempo, and lyrics—such as "take a little trip" and "the low rider is a little higher"—as references to drugs.[21] However, in keeping with the identity implications of lowriding, the lyrics are actually about raising one's sense of pride. According to War's drummer, Harold Brown (n.d.): "We were trying to convey that the Lowrider gets a little higher by riding in his automobile, being proud of how he takes care of his ride. It's like riding around in your trophy." Thus War again flipped the script by lyrically playing off the irony that riding low in a modified car actually lifted and empowered the rider to a higher sense of pride. Here, the lowrider culture of car modification, much as in African-American car culture, is reinforced as a manifestation of a human–machine assemblage in service of promoting a distinct socio-cultural identity that resists the mainstream and the related quest for literal and figurative social mobility.

"Tuning" the world

Car modification and tuning scenes, often associated with African-American hip hop and Hispanic lowrider cultures in North America, are also commonly found in other parts of the world. England, for example, has its South London Look that concentrates on lowering and tricking out 1950s'–1970s' era low-end British Ford models (such as Cortinas and Escorts); and Germany similarly has a German Look modification culture of VW Carmen Ghias with lowered suspensions and mag wheels to improve handling and cornering. Sweden's *Reggare* (essentially translated as "greasers") cruising subculture features restored American cars from the 1950s and '60s accompanied by suitable period American rock n' roll and rockabilly. *Reggare* is likely Sweden's largest pop subculture, and is largely comprised of disaffected young working-class males who adopted large American cars as a symbol of their sense of foreignness from and resistance to mainstream Swedish cultural norms. The large cars and connotations of much of the accompanying musical culture have also led many middle-class parents to regard them as a sexual threat to young women (O'Dell, 2001).

Japan has also been a particular hotbed of car modification cultures. Japanese VIP tuning culture (aka *Bippo*) refers to the modification of Japanese luxury cars, often making them lower in stance and wider looking, with aggressive negative camber wheels, suspension, and body kits.[22] Typical examples include high-end sedans from Nissan or Toyota with paint colours generally limited to black, white, silver, or grey. Some practitioners modify their mufflers and engines in order to make them much louder, in what is known as "Yankee Style." The trend has its roots in the Yakuza, Japanese organized crime syndicates, who wanted to drive luxury vehicles but also to blend in and avoid detection by the police and rival gangs. Another sub-culture of Japanese car tuning is the *Bosozoku* (roughly translated as "violent speed tribe") youth gang form of car modification, which originates in motorcycle gang modification. It is characterized by futuristic Japanese manga- and anime-inspired designs, bright gaudy paint jobs, aerodynamic roof fins, and extreme protruding spoilers with fancifully angled, sky-high exhaust pipes. The music associated with the style is either hyper aggressive hardcore punk or hip hop, and, as with their counterpart North American scenes, is often heavily invested in projecting an aggressive, confrontational form of youthful masculinity. One online playlist of *Bosozoku* music titled "Fried and Fucked Up," for example, subtitles it as "a rough mix for a lot of rough boys."[23]

Finally, the Japanese *dekotora* ("decoration truck") phenomenon must also be mentioned.[24] *Dekotora* trucks are extravagantly modified and ornately decorated versions of larger working trucks that can include anything from garbage trucks and dump trucks to big-rig transport trucks. Often influenced by the art and design characteristic of the *Gundam* mecha anime series, they are characterized by fantastic futuristic chrome add-ons and elaborate LED lighting schemes that make them look like moving pinball or pachinko machines. The trucks originate in working-class trucking culture, but cost millions of yen (hundreds of thousands of dollars) to create and maintain. Yet, enthusiasts see them as a creative means of self-expression.

Although it is hardly an obvious connection, the *dekotora* craze has its roots in popular music. Throughout the late 1960s, '70s, and '80s, American-inspired bluegrass, folk, and country experienced a notable boom in Japan, with aspiring Japanese banjo-pickers and fiddlers across the nation modelling themselves on the country sounds coming out of the US. Country artists such as Ralph Stanley began touring Japan, engendering an unexpected cultural cross-pollination. Buck Owen's live album *In Japan!* (1967), for example, features the song "Tokyo Polka." The interest in all things American saw a concomitant Japanese interest in trucker culture and its related outlaw persona. In an answer to films like *Smokey and the Bandit* (which co-starred country musician Jerry Reed and featured Reed's trucking songs in the soundtrack) in 1975, the first of ten *Torakku Yaro* ("Truck Rascals") movies was released. Each *Torakku Yaro* instalment followed a duo of *dekotora*-driving heroes on a different, lovelorn wild goose chase. And while the slapstick plots and affable characters were light-hearted, it was the glittery *dekotora* trucks that inspired an ongoing expressive culture.

The *dekotora* phenomenon and, to some extent, much of car modification culture in general speaks to notions of transformation and the resistant struggle of being two things simultaneously. Recall W. E. B. DuBois' (1897) notion of the double consciousness of African Americans: "One ever feels his two-ness—an American, a Negro; two souls, two thoughts, two unreconciled strivings; two warring ideals in one dark body" (p. 194). The shape-shifting aspects of *dekotora* are also reminiscent of another Japanese truck phenomenon, the Transformers—the famous animated vehicle–robot hybrids. The personality associated with the impact of a *dekotora* truck, as well as the personification of Transformers, hint at the innate duality, if not multiplicity, of our mechanized yet human shape-shifting experience of identity.

Car modification also changes the static car–driver relationship scripted by the manufacturer. The physically embodied and sonic assemblages become individualized. As Mimi Sheller (2007) writes, car modification culture

> [e]vade[s] the rhetorics, embodiments and practices of the mass industry, hence producing alternative materializations of the car and driver, and different kinds of mobilities and attunements between the person and the environment. "Lowriders" in places like East Los Angeles, El Paso and Northern New Mexico, for example, have long customized their cars with elaborate painted murals, powerful stereo systems, chrome-plated chain-link steering wheels, and hydraulic suspensions that enable the car to scrape the ground, bounce up and down, or ride on three wheels (p. 185).

For Hispanic lowriders, individualized car modifications result in a unique hybridized physical experience when riding, one resulting from an expressive assemblage of personal, cultural, and technological identities. Indeed, in all varieties of car-modification cultures, cars are hybrid creations that reflect the multifaceted, non-conformist identity of the owner. Cruising in modified cars with tricked-out stereo systems performs and embodies alternative hybridities of various ethnic, racial, class, and locational identities.

There are nonetheless important communal identities in these modification cultures that are played out through similarities of car-modification techniques and for which music performs a central role. Participants in various identities of music-related car cultures are not merely interpreting and enacting their belonging, or "competence" within a community, but are feeling, in a sensorial way, what it is to belong with others when they coordinate their musical choices and modification techniques. Music's sensual quality—the way it makes us *feel* with others in specific times and places—communicates to those who simultaneously experience it that they share a fundamental bond with others in the group.

Booming, dB drag racing, SLAB, lowrider, and other cultures of automotive and sound system modification all represent the resistive outcomes of multiple acts of marginalization. In part, they are projections of sonic power, aural representations of territorialization, and reclamations of socio-

cultural power. They can be regarded as noisy and even threatening statements that protest against the privileged exclusivity of privacy and quietness
associated with upper- and middle-class white values. They are also, however, creative articulations of individual and community identity and sonic
and visual expressions of place and location expressed by both the particular styles of modification and the music and sounds being incorporated
into the expression.

Approaches to sound systems and listening to music in cars

In car sound system modification culture and elsewhere, the interconnection
of cars and popular music reproduction represents a powerful indicator of
individual and group identities. Modification cultures highlight the personalized bond many people have with their vehicles. In some cases, we are emotionally tied to our car almost as much as we are tied to family members and
pets, often giving it a name and investing it with a personality—or, to quote
the Queen song, the feeling that "I'm in love with my car." We literally enter
and inhabit our car, we are protected by it, we become one with it. It becomes
a mobile extension of ourselves, a momentary bonding of human and
machine that is augmented by a simultaneous musical experience that takes
us out of our immediate bodily experience. In many ways, the subdued sounds
of the engine and road notwithstanding, the automobile represents an ideal
listening experience: it is isolated and immersive, with sound systems perfectly
designed and tuned for the space at hand. Moreover, the changing visual
landscape as we drive is often enhanced by the presence of a personalized
soundtrack. To be sure, there is a certain irony in that we are expressing
ourselves and experiencing one of our most profound sensations of liberation
through mass-produced assembly-line products, both music and cars. In both
cases, and with the notable exception of marginalized cultures of car customization previously discussed, we have been co-opted by our military industrial complex society that relies on machines to greater and greater degrees to
ensure both our security and our liberation.

   In some respects, the car is literally a vehicle of change, be it terms of location or emotion. In the *System of Objects*, Jean Baudrillard (1996) discusses the
euphoric intimacy of driving:

> Effortless mobility entails a kind of pleasure that is unrealistic, a kind of
> suspension of existence, a kind of absence of responsibility. The effect of
> speed's integration of space-time is to reduce the world to a two-dimen-
> sionality, to an image, stripping away its relief and its historicity and in a
> way ushering one into a state of sublime immobility and contemplation
> (p. 66).

In this manner, the experience of effortless musical animation of modern
sound playback mimics the displacement of humanizing attributes and the

minimization of human participation that Baudrillard recognizes in driving. The combined experiences of listening to music and speed only act to further enhance a state of distractive, effortless euphoria.

The automobile functions as a nexus of mobile sound technologies: the personal stereo, the car radio and stereo system, the mobile phone. The use of stereos in cars directly presaged the mobile soundspace that has gradually become ubiquitous since the invention of the Walkman, and even more so since the iPod. An increasing number of consumers demand the engrossing blend of noise, proximity, and privacy while on the move. The use of personal sound technologies, including the automobile, informs us about how we attempt to "inhabit" the spaces in which we live. The use of these technologies binds the disparate threads of urban movement together for many consumers, both occupying and structuring the time and spaces between various activities. The use of sound and music while on the move—whether in automobiles, through personal stereos, or on mobile phones—thus appears to represent wider social transformations of everyday life.

Though, as we have seen, cassette recorders enabled listeners to assemble their own listening experiences in various locations, the advent of car radios represented the first instance in which musical space was not necessarily a static experience. Iain Chambers (1994), writing about the Walkman, describes how a nomadic listening identity is constructed as subjects recreate the landscapes that surround them, effectively "constructing a dialogue with it, leaving a trace in the network" to create what he calls a "diasporic identity" (p. 50). The mobile listening experience associated with the Walkman and MP3 players, however, was already presaged experientially in automobiles. Even the limited ability to switch radio stations allowed drivers the opportunity to actively shape their journey to suit their mood or changing surroundings. The freedom enabled by automobile travel was mirrored in the freedom to choose a soundtrack that would enhance the journey. Unlike the relatively pristine interiority afforded by headphones on most mobile audio devices, the aleatoric nature of the automobile listening experience, including the presence of radio static, road noise, and other ambient sound sources, results in a continual dialogue with the external sonic world. Listening to music while driving inevitably involves a liminal play between a cinematic experience of our imaginary sound scene and the sonic exigencies of the real physical world.

We often inhabit our cars as a type of secondary home (for those without access to affordable housing it can too often become a primary residence). Today almost all cars come with sophisticated sound systems that enable the driver to easily switch between radio, CD, or MP3, helping to transform notions of automobility from an experience of "dwelling on the road" to one of "dwelling in the car" (Urry, 2000; 2004). For many drivers, a listening experience is integral to and indeed defines car habitation. Drivers often describe the unsettling nature of spending time in their cars without music.[25] Driving with only the sounds of the road and engine, and without the mediation of music or conversational voices of passengers, qualitatively alters the experience. According to Michael Bull (2004a), "Many drivers habitually switch on their radio as they enter their automobile ... mediated sound thus becomes a component part of what it is to drive" (p. 246). In this sense, the use of music in cars is similar to the use of personal stereos, creating an intimate and unbroken flow of music or sound from one place and space to another. Bull (2006) describes the cinematic experiences of people listening to personal listening devices to argue that "the aesthetic re-creation or reappropriation of the urban through the act of looking is mediated through the subject's desires, stimulated both by desire and music" (p. 155) Therefore, as we listen to music while driving, the external physical world at times becomes endowed with heightened new meaning or, alternatively, is not even consciously regarded at all.

Bull (2001) identifies a number of recurrent themes in drivers' descriptions of their music-accompanied driving experiences. For example, he reports that the use of media in vehicles masks random environmental sounds, creating an "accompanied" form of aural privacy in which music provides an experience of "connection" with others. This "private space" makes possible a range of other experiences that facilitate expressions of personal identity. Drivers report that they listen to whatever they like, as loudly as they like, and can even sing along because, despite the fact they are in a glass bubble of sorts, they feel less observed than at home. They report finding potential frustrations of driving transformed by listening to music. Furthermore, Bull notes the reappropriation of "empty" or "stolen" time that listening to music while travelling allows.

A personal listening device, while often castigated for ostensibly manifesting a refusal of sociability (Sterne, 2003), nonetheless "reaffirms participation in a shared environment" (Chambers, 1994, p. 50). It is less clear that this is the case for music consumption in automobiles, for in a car our sense of security and safety is such that we operate more as in a self-contained world detached from other cars and their inhabitants. Surrounded by the exoskeleton of a machine, we are often unconscious, and seemingly often uncaring, of the presence of other human bodies in our midst and of their concomitant sonic worlds. Consequently, we tend to interact with other drivers not as human beings but as unfeeling machines, unaware of the grid and din of the multitude of soundscapes that are simultaneously travelling around us.

In an essay on Formula One racing, Baudrillard (2002) discusses the merging of driver and car, observing that, "The driver, for his part, is alone. In his cockpit he no longer is anyone. He merges with his double, with the car, and so no longer has an identity of his own" (p. 167). Add in the distraction of a musical soundtrack, and the driver is immersed in an interior world that separates them from the potentially mundane reality of who they are. Drivers, even at normal highway speeds, often achieve a state of calm—"the equivalent of the eye of the storm, the stasis of speed, the trance-like state: you are no longer in the same world" (p. 168). The background becomes televisual;

the physical perception of other cars fades as the car itself becomes an extension of the driver's body, in keeping with recent automobility conceptions of the hybrid entity of the "autoself" as discussed in the Introduction (Randell, 2017). There is little reference here to a real landscape or experience. As Baudrillard (2002) claims, "you pass into virtual imagery. You approach real time, the instantaneity of motion—but also, of course, catastrophe" (p. 168).

As indicated by Baudrillard's analysis and evident in many songs centred on cars, the "crash" is often, consciously or subconsciously, at the centre of car culture. Well-known car songs such as "Teen Angel" (1959), "Tell Laura I Love Her" (1960), "Leader of the Pack" (1964), and "Dead Man's Curve" (1964) likely peaked in the early 1960s on account of the advent of the teenage tragedy genre in songs and literature. Bands such as the Crash Test Dummies and songs such as Pearl Jam's rendition of "Last Kiss" (1998), Usher's "Crash" (2016), or Marilyn Manson's "Just a Car Crash Away" (2007) testify to something of an ongoing fascination with the theme. Going beyond the mere subject matter in car crash songs, many studies have focused on the detrimental relationship of listening to music while driving, particularly the potential impairment to concentration that listening to music may incur. A study by Ayres and Hughes (1986), for example, finds that visual acuity is significantly impaired by the presence of louder music. Together with Beh and Hirst's (1999) study that found driver response times reduced by loud music, this research suggests that listening to music at a high volume can be detrimental to driving performance.

The effects of musical tempo on driving have also been subject to testing. In rare studies that focused on the effects of tempo, 28 students were played music with tempos that ranged from 60 to 120 beats per minute while they navigated a virtual car through the streets of Chicago (Brodsky, 2002; see also Dibben & Williamson, 2007). The conclusions indicated that drivers were two times more likely to make bad judgments, or even have an accident, when they listened to fast music compared to slow or medium tempos. Furthermore, both the speed of their driving and estimates of their speed rose as the tempo of the music increased. Brodsky concludes that the tempo of music results in distraction effects, whereas intensity can result in arousal effects, and posits that the temporal character of music may influence the experience of time, and therefore of speed. In 2015, Brodsky further asserted that "music is a distraction because the sounds themselves prevent drivers from making the best use of attention needed to drive a car" (p. 185). For Brodsky, "*music intensity evoked arousal* (i.e. overly rambunctious driving), *music tempo generated distraction* (i.e. hampered longitudinal and lateral control), and *music-genre induced aggression* (i.e. a habitual driving style beset with risk-taking and unfriendliness)" (ibid., emphasis in original).

These studies indicate that extremes of volume and tempo can significantly affect driving performance, and potentially compromise road safety. The situation is further problematized because musical complexity may also be implicated in this question (Furnham & Allass, 1999). Theoretically, the greater the complexity of the music we listen to, the greater the effect on our attention resources, level of arousal, and emotional state. In addition, as Dibben and Williamson have recognized, any effects of music are going to be mediated by features such as the driver's musical preferences and familiarity with the music (Wiesenthal et al., 2000), their personality and level of sensation-seeking (Barnett, 2004), gender (Turner et al., 1996), and the variable amount of concentration needed to safely drive at any specific moment. In an extensive study of English drivers, when questioned about their listening experiences, 62 per cent believed that music calmed and relaxed them while driving, while just under 25 per cent claimed that music increased or helped their concentration. The same study concluded that there was also a significant difference between the genre of music playing and driver performance. Dance/house music, for example, was singled out as particularly distracting for drivers aged 18–29 (Dibben & Williamson, 2007). The loud, dynamic, repetitive, potentially hypnotic beats apparently contributed to a potential lack of focus and awareness on the road.

Conclusion

This chapter has provided an outline of the history of the car sound system and its influence on the evolution of music production and consumption. The automobile and its sonic accoutrements—such as radios and sounds systems, but also horns and sirens—have been employed to sound and announce presence and identity since their inception. The car often acts as a sonic, if not overtly musical, instrument of identity in and of itself. Moreover, the act of listening to music in our car through its sound system represents one of the most potent representations of identity in the music–car intersection. As discussed, the modification of the sound system itself is characteristically an intimately personal expression, just as is the broadcast performance of one's chosen music to the outside world. At the same time, listening to music in cars reduces, distracts from, and tames the often unwanted or threatening sounds of the machine and external road noise. It can stimulate a virtual experience, providing cinematic and highly personalized soundtracks to our travel that enhance and contribute to the often euphoric experience of effortless travel. However, the musically enhanced generation of such distracted euphoria would seem, at least to some degree, to also increase the chances of real-life driving accidents. Despite this potential for causing distracted driving, automotive sound systems have evolved to facilitate listening experiences that both reflect and project our sonic identities, and have changed how we live with and emote through our automobiles. Indeed, listening to music in our cars arguably represents one of the most ubiquitous and influential sonic performances of identity in contemporary culture.

Notes

1 For a more detailed explanation and description of music producers mixing down with and using car speakers as references in the studio, see Williams (2014, pp. 118–120).
2 https://www.siriusxm.com/corporate (accessed March 29, 2015).
3 https://www.apple.com/ios/carplay (accessed March 29, 2015).
4 Lyrics and music by Cathal Joseph Smyth, Christopher John Foreman, Daniel Mark Woodgate, Graham McPherson, Lee Jay Thompson, Mark William Bedford, and Michael Barson. Copyright Sony/ATV Music Publishing LLC.
5 https://www.youtube.com/watch?v=w4y272NI7J8 (accessed June 7, 2017).
6 http://adland.tv/commercials/nissan-altima-samplers-2002-030-usa (accessed June 6, 2017).
7 Previously, The Orb were responsible for the hit song "Little Fluffy Clouds" (1990), which was used as the soundtrack for Volkswagen's 1998 "What Color Do You Dream In?" ad campaign for its new model Beetle.
8 https://www.youtube.com/watch?v=Oze4fmuOVxo&feature=player (accessed November 7, 2015). See also Chapter 5.
9 http://adland.tv/commercials/scion-10-series-celebration-anthem-jeesh-2013-30-usa (accessed June 7, 2017).
10 http://adland.tv/commercials/lexus-nx-make-some-noise-2015-60-usa (accessed June 7, 2017).
11 The act of turning a car into an instrument has earlier, non-commercial roots, as in the Car Music Project initiated by musician and composer Bill Milbrodt in 1995. The Car Music Project is both a band and a compositional endeavour that turns car parts into musical instruments. Repurposing parts from his own worn-out car, Milbrodt created playable musical instruments that replicate the four instrument families of a traditional orchestra: wind, brass, percussion, and strings. He hired professional auto mechanics to disassemble his car, and commissioned sculptor Ray Faunce III to craft the instruments, which were given car-related names such as Convertibles and Tube Flutes (winds), Strutbone and Exhaustaphone (brass), Percarsion (percussion), and Tank Bass and Air Guitar (strings). The Car Music Project is also a band formally begun by Milbrodt in early 2005. Although currently on hiatus, the members include Eric Haltmeier ("winds"), James Spotto ("brass"), William Trigg ("Percarsion"), and Wilbo Wright and Milbrodt ("strings"). The ensemble has made a number of recordings and performed several live concerts, including at Lincoln Center Out of Doors on August 5, 2007. Milbrodt describes his motivation for repurposing his old car into what he refers to as "hybrid" instruments: "I always loved the idea of making a soundscape or music from 'stuff' like brake drums, sirens, and radios in the way that John Cage and Edgar Varese did. I often imagined doing similar things with bottles, cans, vials of pills, sandbags, kitchen utensils, tools, buildings, and all sorts of other things. … The result of [this] was the idea of creating instruments that I referred to as 'hybrids', a combination of car parts and musical instrument parts." http://www.carmusicproject.com (accessed May 12, 2015). Although motivated by artistic experimentalism, it is Milbrodt's connection to his car that seems to have spurred his repurposing or transformation of it into a more overtly expressive instrument.
12 Until recently klaxons were commonly used on Navy vessels where there was less need for niceties concerning noise, and clear urgency in their use.
13 Lyrics and music by John Lennon and Paul McCartney. Copyright Sony/ATV Music Publishing LLC.
14 http://www.cogapa.com/index.htm (accessed March 28, 2015).
15 Alexander Rehding (2014; Rehding, 2016) has discussed the rise and incorporation of sirens in experimental art music, and credits the invention of the modern siren to French scientist Charles Cagniard de la Tour in 1819.

16 Lyrics and music by Lawrence Krsone Parker, Rodney Lemay, Eric Victor Burdon, Bryan James Chandler, and Alan Lom. Copyright Universal Music Publishing Group.

17 https://www.youtube.com/watch?v=kqek1F2ZUDo (accessed July 10, 2018).

18 Lyrics and music by Rachel de Rougemont and Elana Cager. Copyright Essential Media Group LLC.

19 This form of sonic dislocation from location, of course, stands in distinction to the police siren "chirps" that, as described previously, intentionally announce presence.

20 The quest for aural privacy (or "acoustic cocooning") from unwanted external sound continues, of course, in the pervasiveness of mobile headphone culture, first manifested in the late 1970s with the Sony Walkman and then later in iPod and other MP3 players (Bijsterveld et al., 2013). Although the quest for aural privacy and unadulterated listening experiences is certainly prevalent in the automotive audio sector, it is perhaps even more prevalent in the use of headphones, as evident in the explosion in popularity of noise-cancelling headphones.

21 Lyrics and music by Sylvester Allen, Harold Ray I. Brown, Morris Dewayne Dickerson, Le Roy L. Jordan, Charles Miller, Lee Oskar, Howard E. Scott, and Jerry Goldstein. Copyright Universal Music Publishing Group, Henstone Music.

22 One particularly unique subset of Japanese tuning culture is *Onikyan*, which is primarily marked by the use of extreme negative camber wheels that make the vehicle difficult, if not dangerous, to drive and control.

23 https://8tracks.com/yankizuwari/fried-and-fucked-up (accessed June 16, 2017).

24 Though it is largely outside the parameters of this study, truck decoration is found in Afghanistan, Pakistan, India, and throughout South Asia. Haitian "Tap Taps" and the Philippine "Jeepneys," for instance, are private buses and omnipresent symbols of the art and culture of their respective nations, and of the personal creative expressions of their owners. Often featuring elaborate floral patterns and various forms of calligraphy (sometimes with religious verses requesting safety on the roads), they are frequently known by the term "Jingle Trucks" in reference to the sound made by chains and other accoutrements hanging from the vehicles.

25 Since the 1970s, when radios and tape players became standard features in most American cars, people have been able to listen to recorded music while driving. More recently, with the inclusion of compact disc and MP3 players in vehicles, the opportunity for self-selected music listening while driving has grown. A study of American drivers shows that audio (most often the radio) was playing in vehicles 72 per cent of the time, with only 4 of the 70 participants not listening to any audio (Stutts et al., 2003; see also Dibben & Williamson, 2007, p. 572).

7   Spare parts
Cars and soundtracks, spiritual connections, location, and theoretical musings

Soundtracks: cars, television, and movies

An important but little considered aspect of the symbiotic relationship between popular music and automotive culture is found in the music and soundtracks used for the many car-themed television shows and movies that arose in the postwar period. When World War II ended, there were no privately owned television sets. However, over 7,500,000 sets were sold in 1950 alone, with a comparable number of cars (6,665,000) rolling off the assembly lines (Marling, 2002, p. 354). Alongside the rise of affordable suburban housing, televisions and cars represented the frontiers of consumerism, and helped shape new forms of popular culture and entertainment. Nowhere was this more in evidence than in television programming. Beginning in the 1960s, a series of iconic cars graced the television screens of North America, including *Batman*'s Batmobile, the *Munster*'s Koach, the *Beverly Hillbillies'* truck, *Starsky and Hutch*'s 1974 red Grand Torino, the *A-Team*'s customized 1983 GMC van, the *Dukes of Hazzard*'s 1969 Dodge Charger ("The General Lee"), and, perhaps most famously, *Knight Rider*'s talking 1982 Firebird, "KITT." Among the most musically related of these television automobiles were the *Monkees'* Monkeemobile, a customized Pontiac GTO that featured as the band's car on their eponymous show and followed them on tour in actual concerts; and the *Partridge Family* bus, a 1957 Chevrolet Series 6800 Superior School Bus with a Mondrian-inspired patchwork paintjob. Falling out of the hippie Volkswagen van fascination of the 1960s, the prominence given to vehicles in these latter examples manifests a common identification with the road and touring musicians in the late 1960s and 1970s.

Paralleling automakers' desires to design and market cars in our human image, one of the most notable features of automobiles on television and in film is the propensity for anthropomorphizing them. Such cases exemplify the duality of automotive culture, emphasizing on the one hand the extent to which human and machine might bond and work together for an improved quality of life, or, on the other hand, the extent to which cars—and machinery and technology in general—might dominate and threaten or diminish our humanity. Likely the most infamous example of the former case was *My*

Mother the Car, a 1965 NBC comedy starring Jerry Van Dyke as the hapless owner of a fictionalized 1928 Porter that contains the ghost of his late mother who regularly communicates with him. The theme song that opened and closed each of the 30 episodes outlines the show's premise—"my mother dear decided she'd come back as a car"—and asserts the friendly and benign nature of the mother–car–son relationship: "she helps me through everything I do."[1] "Mother" talks to Van Dyke's character (and only Van Dyke's character) through the car's radio, the dial light flashing in synchronization with "Mother's" voice.

A similar case of automotive anthropomorphization occurred with Disney's *The Love Bug* (1968), the first of a series of five movies (plus a television series in 1982 and a television movie in 1997). The films featured Herbie, a lovable little Volkswagen Beetle with a personality all its own. In *The Love Bug*, Herbie is abused by one racing driver (David Tomlinson), but is rescued by another, benevolent, one (Dean Jones). Out of gratitude, Herbie enables the previously luckless good guy to win one race after another. A central character in the story is the happy-go-lucky and artistically inclined mechanic, Tennessee Steinmetz (Buddy Hackett), who, having spent time with Buddhist monks in Tibet, extols the virtues of spiritual enlightenment. In keeping with his Buddhist principles, Tennessee believes that even inanimate objects may be sentient beings and befriends the car, naming it Herbie. Music does not play an enormous role in the film, but Tennessee's Buddhist experiences echo and sympathize with that of the Beatles and of 1960s' pop and hippie culture in general. "The Love Bug (Theme Song)," also known as "Herbie's Theme," is an instrumental work written by George Bruns that recurs throughout most of the Herbie films. The calypso-flavoured music, with 1960s' psychedelic rock-styled electric guitar fills, is notable for its flutter-tongue flute melody that seems to represent the airy and light-hearted, though unspoken, voice of Herbie.

Unlike *My Mother the Car*, *The Love Bug* was enormously successful, ranking as the third-highest grossing movie of 1968, with domestic US box office receipts in excess of $51 million. Both *My Mother the Car* and *The Love Bug* are testimony to our propensity to humanize our automobiles. The quasi-spiritual connection (evinced by the ghostly haunting and faux Buddhist philosophy embodied in Mother and Herbie, respectively) that sometimes links us to our cars stems from the fact that we are often incredibly dependent on them in times of need. Most drivers have little understanding of the complexity of a car's mechanics, and so cede their safety and themselves to a higher intelligence—albeit one purely mechanical—when they get behind the wheel. We can often be grateful to our vehicles when they do not break down and when they successfully transport us to a new place. Moreover, cars protect us from the elements and perils of other drivers and obstacles on our respective journeys. *My Mother the Car* and *The Love Bug* tap into the feelings of spiritual connection and empowerment that we may feel when we get behind the wheel.

Both Herbie and Mother are examples of friendly or benign anthropomorphic automobiles, a concept taken to new heights of popularity in 2006 with Pixar's Academy Award-nominated animated film *Cars*. The film (and its subsequent franchise releases) is set in a world populated entirely by anthropomorphic cars and other vehicles, and features the voices of well-known car enthusiasts Owen Wilson and Paul Newman. It is notable that many of these anthropomorphized cars are intended for younger viewers. They are typically presented as friendly animated machines that project unthreatening personalities. Optimus Prime, the leader of the Autobots from the *Transformers* media franchise, is a case in point. Optimus Prime, who transforms from a robot into a Kenworth truck, is dedicated to building a peaceful and mutually beneficial co-existence with humans, and repeatedly utters his signature phrase "All are one." As such, he represents a charismatic machine with ideals to which humankind might aspire, but also calls for a cyborgian sense of oneness with our technologies. To some extent, automotive characters such as Optimus Prime or Herbie inculcate automotive culture into children, allowing them to see cars as benevolent and well-meaning technology. It is thus no accident that several car manufacturers regularly advertise on children's television channels and during children's programming (Brodsky, 2015).

The NBC television series *Knight Rider* (1982–1986), starring David Hasselhoff as Michael Knight, was yet another popular example of the tendency to humanize automobiles.[2] The show features a car named KITT (an abbreviation for Knight Industries Two Thousand), a heavily modified Pontiac Firebird Trans Am with numerous crime-fighting features. KITT is controlled by a super computer with artificial intelligence, and features a nearly indestructible body, various electronic cloaking and listening systems, and several offensive weapons systems, including a flame thrower, tear gas, and laser. Like Mother, KITT can talk to its driver. Voiced by actor William Daniels, it has mastered multiple languages and accents and, thanks to its artificial intelligence capability, interacts with humans, displaying a sensitive, kind, and dryly humorous personality. Unlike the affable examples of Herbie and Mother, however, KITT is a machine designed for offence, albeit in a positive crime-fighting role.

The fear of dystopic machines taking on a destructive life of their own is a trope that seems far more common than the good-natured anthropomorphic vehicles discussed above. Multiple horror stories and films have portrayed the car as possessing a sentient capacity for evil. *Killdozer* (1974), *The Car* (1977), *The Hearse* (1980), *Maximum Overdrive* (1986), *The Wraith* (1986), and *Road Kill* (2010) all feature a plot line of driverless, murderous automobiles that have a mind of their own. In part, these negative depictions serve as a warning against North America's overreliance on and growing obsession with automobiles. One of the earliest such horror stories aired in 1960 as an episode from *The Twilight Zone* entitled "A Thing About Machines." The plot revolves around Bartlett Finchley, an ill-tempered gourmet magazine critic who reviles humanity and is as inept with machines as he is with people. Finchley constantly abuses his appliances and comes to believe that they are conspiring against him. Eventually, every appliance and machine in his house turns on him. His typewriter taps out "GET OUT OF HERE FINCHLEY"; a woman on television and a voice on his unplugged phone impart the same message; and his electric razor takes on a cobra-like pose, rising menacingly into the air. Finchley eventually becomes so frightened by these machines running amok that he flees his house, only to be chased by his driverless car, a 1939 Lagonda coupe. The car follows him to his pool and pushes him in. Finchley sinks to the bottom and drowns.

Another episode of *The Twilight Zone*, "You Drive" (1964), features a similar tale of the fear of automotive control over our lives. This episode finds the car of a hit-and-run driver forcing the latter to confess to his crime. The car, a 1956 Ford Fairlane, is able to act and think independently, and self-drives the perpetrator back to the scene of the accident before chasing him down the road as if to run him over. Eventually the car stops and the door opens, and the driver goes to a police station to confess.

With its movie trailer and poster ominously proclaiming, "She was born in Detroit," John Carpenter's *Christine* (1983) ranks as the most famous of the angry-car movies. The story, set in 1978, follows a sentient and violent automobile nicknamed Christine and her relationship with her teenage owner. The film is based on Stephen King's novel of the same name, and both versions employ the familiar car–woman conflation. In this case, it is an empowered and vengeful female-gendered car, a red-and-white 1958 Plymouth Fury, that plots revenge against those who have damaged or abused her in some way. Two soundtracks were released in association with the film, one consisting of an album of electronic music composed exclusively by director John Carpenter and music director Alan Haworth, and the other comprised of pop songs (mostly from the 1950s) featured in the movie. Of the newly composed music, the most notable work was the instrumental "Christine Attacks (Plymouth Fury)," the only piece to appear on both albums. "Christine Attacks," like all the incidental music composed for the movie, is an electronic composition and bears something of a resemblance to the music of Kraftwerk. It consists of a synthesized car engine whose revs and backfire are turned into an obsessive electronic drum beat that slowly builds in intensity. The synthesized engine sounds recur frequently in the track. The stark electronic music cleverly captures the notion of a car transformed into an obsessive and vengeful killer.

As has been discussed throughout this book, the automotive industry often seeks to have customers regard their products as perceptive, human-like entities. They incorporate human-like qualities such as various "intelligent" driver-assist systems, with the eventual goal of realizing driverless cars. Such advanced technology seems to promote a utopian future in which humans are able to safely surrender control of their bodies to the machine. The anthropomorphic cars in Hollywood and television as described above, however, often paint a darker picture—one that envisions a dismal, dystopic future in which the intelligent machines have turned against us, symbolically warning us of the threat of our reliance on technology and of corporatism and consumerism.

Regardless of the appeal of the threatening anthropomorphic car movie, it is not insignificant that the automobile and movie industries evolved during the same era. Filmmaker Cecil B. DeMille attributed the common "love of motion and speed, the restless urge towards improvement and expansion, and the kinetic energy of a young, vigorous nation" embodied in the two industries as reasons for their mutual success in America (Ling, 2012, p. 67). Both industries were symbols and material manifestations of accelerated mechanized utility. Indeed, the proliferation of car-themed movies specializing in kinetic overdrive—such as *The Fast and the Furious* franchise (2001–), *Gone in 60 Seconds* (2000), the *Death Race* series (1975–), or even *Speed Racer* (2008)—would seem to confirm DeMille's assessment. The common connection between these racing-obsessed movies is often sensory, and a sonic one at that. These films are characterized by the noise of roaring engines, the grinding of gear changes, the screaming of tyres, and the rumble of the road disappearing under the bumper. The accompanying musical soundtracks generally reflect the aggression and speed of the narrative, and are also often extremely commercially successful. The soundtrack for the original *Fast and Furious*, for example, reached number seven on the *Billboard* Top 200 (and number one on the soundtracks chart), and features amped-up hip hop and hard rock pieces by artists such as Ja Rule and Limp Bizkit. The soundtracks of the *Fast and Furious* series all captured a general zeitgeist of hip hop culture at the time of their release.

To be sure, cars are often at the forefront of many Hollywood offerings, from road movies and crime dramas to overt hot rod and drag racing films, and relate to a wide spectrum of characters and aspects of everyday life. In the 1950s, for example, American International Pictures released a number of low-budget films, including the original *Fast and Furious* (1955), *Hot Rod Girl* (1956), *Dragstrip Girl* (1957), *Dragstrip Riot* (1958), and *Hot Rod Gang* (1958), that overtly linked hot rods, rock n' roll, and delinquency. Outside of these formulaic movies that were primarily aimed at American male teenagers, and although it has received little scholarly attention, popular music inevitably plays a profound role in depicting a variety of car-related activities, such as chase scenes, travel, and racing montages. Frequently reinforcing stereotypical notions of masculine aggression (often exacerbated by various supposed racial or ethnic traits of characters), the musical backdrops to chase and racing scenes, in particular, provide important narratives of identity within these films. Marvin Hamlisch's disco-inflected "Bond 77" theme (inspired by the Bee Gees' 1976 *Saturday Night Fever* hit "You Should Be Dancing") is the soundtrack to an epic James Bond car chase in *The Spy Who Loved Me* (1977). Bond drives a stereotypically macho high-performance, white Lotus Esprit, and the music employs a powerful brass bass melody with accompanying disco guitar riffs that evoke the glitter-ball ambience of a nightclub. It underlines Bond's hedonism and suave sophistication as he outruns motorcycles, cars, and even a helicopter, all while smooth-talking his female passenger. Skilfully evading his pursuers in his white super car while seducing his own prey and accompanied by music evoking a white disco group makes this scene the epitome of the mythology of heterosexual, white masculine control.

One of the most iconic intersections of pop music and cars in film is the famous "head banging" scene that takes place in an AMC Pacer while listening to Queen's "Bohemian Rhapsody" in the movie *Wayne's World* (1992). Although the movie is set in 1992, the oddball 1970s' car and Queen's anthemic tongue-in-cheek music from the same period wonderfully capture five misfit male friends and a sense of white suburban youth cruising culture. Going beyond individual car–music scenes, some movies such as *American Graffiti* (1973) or *The Blues Brothers* (1980), the latter complete with its "Bluesmobile," are fully based on the intersection of automobile culture and popular music. The soundtrack to George Lucas' *American Graffiti*, a homage to 1950s' youth culture and cruising in cars, is drawn directly from the car radio. The entire soundtrack is comprised of a selection of 1950s' rock n' roll hits played by the enigmatic disk jockey Wolfman Jack. Every car radio in town is tuned to the same radio station, and each listener feels they have their own personal relationship with the hip DJ. Many times, the characters seem to feel even closer to the slightly mysterious and disembodied voice of Wolfman Jack than to the person sitting next to them in the car. In this manner, the diegetic sounds of the car radio and rock n' roll stations supplant the traditional symphonic score, bridging the distance between characters and audience with familiar music heard in a familiar automotive context.

Although it is somewhat outside the realm of the current study, the use of popular music in car-related video games also forms an important locus within the nexus of automotive culture, popular music, and identity formation. In many games, music is used to both identify players (in the case of user-controlled soundtracks) and construct stereotypical characters and situations within the games. In the *Grand Theft Auto* series (1997–), for instance, the choice of various radio stations is a key element in establishing historical and character context. One of the most overt musical car-racing games was *Rock n' Roll Racing* (1993), a battle-racing video game developed by Silicon & Synapse for the Sega Mega Drive/Genesis and the Super Nintendo Entertainment System. The background music consists of instrumental versions of several heavy metal and rock songs, reflecting the game's title. It is important also to note the difference between games such as *Grand Theft Auto* or the popular *Grand Turismo* series (1997–), which rely on licensed, pre-existing soundtracks and curate and integrate Top 40 songs to fit into the gameplay, and those that employ originally composed soundtracks specifically designed for the game at hand. Of the latter, Sega's *Out Run* (1986) was one of the best-selling and most influential video games of its time. A 3D driving game based on a player controlling a Ferrari Testarossa Spider, it is also famous for its user-selectable soundtrack, composed by Hiroshi Kawaguchi. Depending on their mood, players could choose between instrumental tracks inspired by Latin jazz fusion and titled, for example, "Passing Breeze," "Splash Wave," and "Magical Sound Shower." Moreover, many of the sounds were later adapted into various vaporwave mixes,[3] and "Magical Sound Shower" was even given words for vocaloid Hatsune Miku to sing in her own subsequent video games.

Real talking cars

As demonstrated by GM's OnStar and Apple CarPlay's Siri capabilities, interactive voice communication systems are now relatively common. To some extent, such interactive systems represent the ultimate in human–machine merging. As we engage in active conversations with voice assistants on our phones and other devices, in the case of cars the trend might seem, at least by some, to be the potential realization of the dystopic threat of technology and killer-car scenario discernible in movies such as *Christine*. Interactive talking and/or intelligent cars, however, have long been the stuff of Hollywood and science fiction fantasy. As mentioned above, the one of the main characters of the 1980s' television series *Knight Rider* was KITT, a heavily modified, technologically advanced Pontiac Firebird Trans Am with features that included the ability to talk thanks to a computer with artificial intelligence. At about the same time, and presaging electronic voice interfaces such as the OnStar safety system (the earliest analogue version of which launched in 1995), the 1981–1984 Datsun/Nissan Maxima, 200SX, and Z-cars were fitted with Nissan's patented Voice Warning system (Martin, 2015). The latter featured a breathy female voice that would warn the driver about open doors, low fuel level, and other areas of concern. The system was essentially a small record player placed inside the car that would operate when the Voice Warning switch was activated. The technology was based on a small spinning phonograph record driven by a motorized rubber-belt drive located inside the Voice Warning box. The spinning record had six parallel grooves, each with a different short message such as "left [or right] door is open," "key is in the ignition," "parking brake is on," "lights are on," or "fuel level is low." When the correct inputs were sent to the box, a needle dropped on to the start of the appropriate groove and, following a warning chime, the particular voice message would play. The system was essentially a small 6-track record player. As in keeping with many electronic voice messaging systems, and an apparent need to associate technology as non-threatening as possible, Apple's Siri voice assistant (among others) is female, speaks in a seemingly calming tone, and uses vaguely American-accented English.

From 1983 to 1987, all WR engine Audi ur-Quattros were equipped with an autocheck unit that included an electronic voice synthesizer. This unit was developed so that some 20 sensors could be monitored without cluttering the dashboard with a plethora of warning lights. It also allowed warnings (e.g., "Attention! Brake system defective") to be prioritized over cautions (e.g., "Please check washer level"). Like the Nissan system, the Audi autocheck was voiced by a woman, Patrizia Lipp, though the voice reproduction quality was quite poor, producing rather raspy and robotically abrupt commands (Isham Research, n.d.).

Between the anthropomorphic cars portrayed in movies and television and the sounds actively emanating from cars through real-life, interactive voice commands and information systems, our industrialized society has clearly been encouraged to understand our machines as humanized entities. Daniel Miller (2001) points out that "[t]he car's humanity lies not just in what people are able to achieve through it ... but in the degree to which it has become an integral part of the cultural environment within which we see ourselves as human" (p. 2). As such, automobiles can be understood as embodying a form of human spirit, an amalgam, perhaps, of their designer/ creators, including actual design engineers, marketers, factory workers, and even owners. In many ways, as further discussed below, cars have come to fulfil a quasi-spiritual role in society, a role that popular music helps to both facilitate and promulgate.

Cars, music, and spirituality

More than simply inanimate machines, cars represent major cultural creations replete with their own spiritual mythologies. Likewise, the infrastructure surrounding them—the roads and highways on and through which they operate—have often evolved similar mythologies and metaphysical identities commonly celebrated in song. As evinced in the earlier discussion of the ghostly haunting and pseudo-Buddhist philosophy that imbued *My Mother the Car* and *The Love Bug*, car owners can develop a quasi-spiritual relationship with their cars. This would seem to be linked at least in part to the fact that we are often incredibly reliant on cars to get us where we want or need to go in a variety of potentially threatening or urgent conditions. First dates, rushing a loved one to the hospital, taking a newborn home, the daily commute to work, family vacations, and funeral processions—in all these major markers of human experience the car is often an integral and relied-upon mechanical participant. Moreover, this mechanized companion also physically and emotionally takes us to new and different places and returns us to the safety and stability of home.

Although perhaps thought of as more ephemeral and immaterial, music similarly takes us on metaphoric emotional journeys to different mental states and places. It likewise is often intimately entwined in defining life moments—marriages, funerals, and ceremonies of all kinds—and standout memories not infrequently have their own associated soundtracks. Furthermore, Western tonal music often functions by taking the listener from the stability of home—manifest variously in a home or tonic key, tonal centre or harmony, or rhythmic pulse—then moving through less familiar tonal, harmonic, or rhythmic places in order to build tension that typically gets released by the return to the familiar stability of the original, key, harmony, or rhythmic pulse. In these ways, both cars and music replicate the trajectory of our lives, to some extent the breath of life itself, as they facilitate and embody our life journeys through moments of tension and release, moving emotionally and physically from moment to moment, from stability to instability.

The car can even take on the characteristics of a living entity, having a metaphoric life that facilitates and intimately entwines with our own. Recall from Chapter 4 that for philosopher Gerald Raunig (2010), "The machine emerges as a virtuoso, *having a soul of their own* (taken from workers), whose virtuosic handling of their implements and whose labour on and in machines merges into ... the very machine itself" (p. 113, emphasis added). In this manner, a car, alongside other machines, can be understood to literally possess the spirit of its creator. However, because it functions essentially as a mechanical prosthesis of the human body, we often ascribe qualities and attributes to it that imply it is not just a mechanical tool but a mechanical creature, one with which we can establish an intimate partnership that involves a reciprocity and transference of energy. We wash our car, change the oil, listen and monitor for subtle changes in its engine sounds and health, and feed it fuel when it is hungry. In exchange for this caretaking, the car transports us to different places and events, and can serve as an extension of ourselves and an agent of new ways of being with people. Not unlike a family pet, we often give our car a name, and may feel sadness when a valued car eventually "dies." Many fear that if our objects leave, our identities will go with them. It seems that it is often only the advertisers that understand how we are defined by our relations to things and the company we keep. This, at least in part, accounts for car advertising that commonly focuses on the anthropomorphic, intelligent features of the products.

Certain civilizations openly ascribe spiritual valence to their vehicles. Among the Pitantjatjara people of South Australia, the car is regarded as a body that is either alive or dead. According to Diana Young (2001), "the engine and the battery of a vehicle are regarded as having a life force. When engines are swapped between car bodies the carcass without an engine is ... 'useless'" (p. 50). Abandoned car dumps are often even found near sacred and burial sites, and are thought to carry forward the spirits of deceased owners (ibid., p. 52). In Nigeria, different aliases are attached to various car models. These aliases are suggestive of either the social status or gender of the owner or of a particular aesthetic or mechanical feature of the automobile in question. The Volkswagen Beetle, for example, is known as the "Ijapa" (tortoise); the BMW is "Be My Wife"; the Toyota Corolla is "First Lady"; and the Toyota Camry is either "Senior Brother" or "Godfather," depending on the year of production. The 2009 Honda Accord, meanwhile, is known as "The Evil Spirit" (Obadare, 2013). While Western society seldom attaches such degrees of life to its vehicles, instances of people wanting to be buried in their cars or having car-themed coffins and funerals are not unheard of.[4] And, as manifest in the number of crosses and rosaries hanging from rear-view mirrors and religious-themed bumper stickers, the automobile can even be transformed into a space of worship, one that both advertises religious inclinations and becomes a place of religious contemplation.

The transference of life or corporeal qualities to automobiles is facilitated by the music we listen to within them. As previously discussed, listening to music while driving a car is an immersive experience, and helps humanize and bond us with what might be considered intimidating or threatening machinery. The sounds of human performers appear to emanate directly from the car. Despite the absolute location of speakers, the nature of listening to music in a car—with the presence of road and engine noise—makes it difficult to pinpoint exactly from where the sound is emanating. This characteristic is even more pronounced in cars with high-end sound systems that strive to provide as pristine a listening experience as possible. The result is that musical sounds are often perceived as originating from an unfixed, ephemeral place, from the general material of the car itself—as if it is speaking directly to us in the manner of a disembodied and intimate, headphone-like, experience.

Of course, popular music has not failed to recognize the metaphysical, spiritual aspect of car culture. Mark Dinning's prototypical teen tragedy song "Teen Angel" (1960) describes the attempt to communicate to a lover "somewhere up above" who died in a car–train accident.[5] Janis Joplin's "Mercedes Benz" (1970) opens with the now iconic prayer to consumerism: "Oh Lord, won't you buy me a Mercedes Benz." Carrie Underwood's debut country hit "Jesus, Take the Wheel" (2005) tells the story of a woman, with her baby in the back seat, who surrenders control of her car when she hits a patch of black ice. The near-accident serves as a wake-up call to make changes in her life and return to her faith. The song's protagonist proclaims "I'm letting go ... Save me from this road I'm on / Jesus, take the wheel."[6] These songs represent the car's status as an icon of both wealth, as in "Mercedes Benz," and its association with (near-) death experiences, as in "Teen Angel" or "Jesus Take the Wheel."

Several other artists have also had hits that evoke the spiritual side of automobiles. Alternative band Dishwalla's "Counting Blue Cars" (1995), for example, finds the singer in a conversation with a young boy who has some deep questions: "Tell me all your thoughts on God."[7] In a much different approach, industrial metal band Ministry, in their song "Jesus Built My Hotrod" (1991), openly makes the connection between cars and religion, proclaiming: "Jesus built my car / It's a love affair / Mainly Jesus and my hot rod."[8] In these and other examples, metaphysical and ephemeral/incorporeal music serves as a sonic vibratory fusion to the materiality of the car, a synthesis that has often served as an almost religious obsession in North American life. Both driving a car and listening to popular music offer a means of spiritual empowerment and uplift that are enhanced in combination with one another. It is often said that life is a journey, and both popular music and cars offer transitory experiences that mimic and facilitate that trip.

Beyond the intimate bonding and relationships drivers may establish with their cars, highways and roads also sometimes take on spiritual characteristics. The building of Germany's autobahn freeway system, for example, became entwined in the spiritual ideology and politics of the German National Socialists in the 1930s. In 1938, Fritz Todt, who directed the construction of the *Autobahnen* before becoming Reich Minister for Armaments and Ammunition and directing Hitler's war economy, explained how the intention was that the *Autobahnen* would be "absolutely adapted to the German landscape," encapsulating an "artistic feeling and a love of Nature" and reflecting the "deeper and spiritual movement of the National Socialist revolution" (Merriman, 2007, p. 37). Subsequent architectural design and landscaping policies—e.g., mandating that only regional plants were used—ensured an aesthetic and spiritual connection to the German character.[9]

Such nationalistic policies regarding the representation of place, as Peter Merriman (2007) has pointed out, were later adapted to the construction of England's motorways. Some 36 years later, in 1974, Kraftwerk released their ode to the highway in the form of the album *Autobahn* and 22-minute *Gesamtkunstwerk*-like single of the same name. In its enigmatic length, soporific repetitive beat evoking the monotony of long-distance freeway driving, diffuse automotive soundscape, and disembodied, electronically altered, robotic-sounding vocals largely consisting of iterations of "We are drivin' on the Autobahn," the song evokes its own ethereal and liminal state of being and identity.[10] Although perhaps inescapably embedded in German-ness and the potentially disturbing parallels between the nation's industrialized Nazi past and its contemporary industrial economic success, it nonetheless points to something of an instability in or question mark over German spiritual identity. The car and its associated highway infrastructure, in combination with disembodied electronic music, appear as symbols of both a past and potential future characterized by a lack of humanity. At the same time, the future and the promise of its technology—the road forward, as it were—might still be a path to Germanic enlightenment and salvation. Melanie Schiller (2014) discusses something like this metaphysical process in terms of the song's various configurations of nationalized space:

> By fragmenting spatiality into different components, "Autobahn" points to the simultaneous multiplicity of spaces in national narratives. Here, spatiality can be conceived as an inherent element of storytelling (in this case the sonic component of the narrative), it can be interpreted as an indicator of ideological shifts (the reinterpretation of the autobahn as a symbol for German supremacy towards becoming a sign of the Federal Republic's modernity), and it can be argued to illustrate the fundamental unclosedness of any national narrative (the automobile moving along the figurative autobahn, symbolizing the unfolding and constant reconfiguration of Germanness as a process of becoming rather than of being) (p. 627).

"Autobahn," in its detached electronic erasure of the human body, encapsulates a form of techno-spiritualism. It represents a (perhaps stereotyped) German ideal of salvation through technology, and a process of becoming potentially both more and less human.

If for some the car is an object of almost religious self-identification, a material object of beauty and reverence that promises the perfection and transformation of man, its close relationship to music only reinforces and further actualizes this spiritual potential. Recall from the Introduction Roland Barthes (1991) describing the 1957 Citroën DS as:

> the best messenger of a world above that of nature: one can easily see in an object at once a perfection and an absence of origin, a closure and a brilliance, a transformation of life into matter (matter is much more magical than life) (p. 88).

If one were to replace the word "matter" with "sound," Barthes' words would readily apply to music as much as to cars. For Barthes, the car represents a magical, spiritual transformation of life itself. The impermanent ebb and flow of music represents a similar transformation of life, underlining its transitory nature. It may be this spiritual connection, at least in part, that has inspired so many popular songs about the car, so many hymns to its capacity for liberation and transformation.

Soundtracks: roads and location

The German autobahn system is but one example of how the road has the capacity to signal and create identities. As discussed in Chapter 6, car modification cultures are often tied to various locations. Houston's SLAB, Southern California's lowrider, the South London Look, Swedish *Reggare*, and Japanese *Bippo* and *dekotora* scenes, for example, all evince musical counterparts that are representative of their particular country, locality, or place. However, the simple act of driving, as with diaspora and mobility in general, facilitates the physical movement from place to place that imbues one, almost by necessity, with different locational identities. Car-listening practices are key in activating a symbolic creativity that humanizes the experience of car travel and invests it with meaning (Willis, 1996, p. 2). Indeed, we typically use music to define the situation and sometimes the location of driving. The soundtracks we create for a stressful city commute, for example, are likely to be markedly different from those listened to when transporting young children to school. Our racial, ethnic, and locational identities all play a role in the music we choose to play and with which we identify while driving, and, in turn, symbiotically reinforce those same identities. Thus, we use music to construct a sense of ourselves—or even varied senses of ourselves—as we utilize the car for differing purposes and in travelling to different locations.

In addition to the often liquid or liminal identities created while driving, specific roads have been linked to popular music in such a manner that they become identified with particular musical styles or events.[11] As the location of everything from musical and fashion trends to graffiti and advertising art, the street is often both the real and mythical location of cultural production. The iconic "Route 66," one of the oldest American highways, established in 1926, was immortalized in Bobby Troup's 1946 r & b song "(Get Your Kicks on) Route 66." The song was first recorded by Nat King Cole but subsequently covered by numerous artists, from Perry Como to The Rolling Stones, and featured in the Pixar film *Cars* (2006). It is a descriptive travelogue of actual places along the highway as the lyrics recount how it "winds from Chicago to LA" and goes through various towns including St. Louis and Joplin, Missouri; Oklahoma City; Amarillo; Gallup, New Mexico; Flagstaff, Arizona; and "don't forget" Winona.[12] After the establishment of the Dwight D. Eisenhower National System of Interstate and Defense Highways in 1956, American highways became crucial vectors of economic development and industrial growth, and the idea of the nation connected by a web of federally run roadways an exhilarating notion. Thus, "get your kicks" underlines the romance that the highway system acquired in the popular American imagination.

Travel has been a popular theme in blues lyrics, and roads and highways have symbolized the potential to quickly leave one's troubles behind, or seek out new opportunities elsewhere. Reflecting something of the same romantic ideology, Bob Dylan titled his influential album *Highway 61 Revisited* (1965) because the title road spanned a trail of places associated with famous blues musicians. Now popularly known as the "Blues Highway," it travels from the Canadian border through Duluth, Minnesota, where Dylan was born, down to New Orleans, passing along the way the nearby birthplaces and homes of influential musicians such as Muddy Waters, Son House, Elvis Presley, and Charley Patton. The highway, thereby, physically and emotionally connected Dylan to his blues heroes.[13]

Likely the most famous instance of the confluence of popular music and a particular street is New York's renowned Tin Pan Alley. Although the term gradually came to be applied to the American popular music publishing industry in general, it originally referred to an actual location in New York— West 28th Street between Fifth and Sixth Avenue. This was where a number of music publishers and songwriters set up business in the late 1800s, their influence growing well into the twentieth century. The origins of the term "Tin Pan Alley" are vague. Some accounts claim it derived from the cacophonous sound of the many pianos emanating down to the street, while others point to a modification to pianos intended to create a more percussive sound. Either way, the connection of the sounds and the music industry to the street has made it an indelible part of the American imagination.

Other streets and roads around America have similar associations with popular music. Beale Street in Memphis, for example, is the heart of that city's storied blues scene and is lined with blues clubs and bars. Historically a bustling centre of African-American-owned businesses and nightclubs, it is the topic of W. C. Handy's 1916 popular song "Beale Street Blues," which influenced the street's re-naming from Beale Avenue. Other blues legends— Louis Armstrong, Muddy Waters, Albert King, Memphis Minnie, and B. B. King—frequented the clubs and helped develop the danceable and heavily syncopated "Memphis Blues" style.

Nashville's famed "Music Row" (sometimes used as a nickname for the commercial music industry in general) refers to the area centred on 16th and 17th Avenues, where many music businesses are located. Predominantly relating to country music, contemporary gospel, and Christian styles, the two streets (situated in a residential neighbourhood) house a large number of recording studios, record labels, music publishing and licensing companies, and other related businesses that serve the commercial music industry.

Los Angeles' Sunset Boulevard, in particular the 1.5-mile section of the road running through West Hollywood and known as the Sunset Strip, is yet another street whose identity is intimately fused with the popular music industry. Originally existing outside the jurisdiction of the City of Los Angeles, where gambling was illegal, the Sunset Strip developed a reputation for wild nightlife during the 1920s with the arrival of several casinos and notorious nightclubs and bars such as Ciro's and Mocambo. In the 1960s, it became the centre of LA's countercultural scene, with clubs such as the Troubadour, Whisky a Go Go, the Roxy Theatre, Pandora's Box, London Fog, and later, in 1993, Johnny Depp's infamous Viper Room. The street's music venues held concerts by bands and performers such as The Doors, The Byrds, Linda Ronstadt, Joni Mitchell, The Eagles, Frank Zappa, Buffalo Springfield, and Led Zeppelin. In the late 1970s, the Sunset Strip became the host for punk and new wave music and, in the 1980s, glam and heavy metal music, with bands such as Van Halen, Mötley Crüe, Poison, and Guns N' Roses performing in its clubs. Cruising Sunset Boulevard, and the Sunset Strip in particular, has been a rite of passage for visitors and many musically inclined residents of the city. These examples—Route 66, the Blues Highway, Tin Pan Alley, Beale Street, Music Row, and the Sunset Strip—are part of the musical map of America, and each is connected to distinct musical identities and, by extension, distinct urban identities.

Apart from these music industry connections to various thoroughfares, it is often overlooked that roads and streets also have individual complex sonic complexities or soundscapes that, though often considered only as chaotic noise, can nonetheless evince what might be considered a musical or at least music-like ebb and flow. The sound of traffic and emergency vehicle sirens passing, of pedestrian footsteps and conversations, or of nearby street or building construction all contribute to the unique ambient sonic experience of the urban street. Moreover, traffic lights, stop signs, speed limits that regulate car movement and sounds, and the general grid of sidewalks and streets impart subtle rhythms to these sonorities through their loose but repetitive patterns of tension and release. It is a flow of sound that can be considered ambient music and a unique sonic fingerprint for each street. In his posthumous book *Rhythmanalysis*, Henri Lefebvre (2004) discusses the subtle yet complex pulse of the rue Rambuteau in Paris as heard and viewed from the window of his apartment:

> At the green light, steps and words stop. A second of silence and then it's the rush, the starting up of tens of cars, the rhythms of the old bangers speeding up as quickly as possible ... buses cutting across other vehicles. The harmony between what one sees and what one hears (from the window) is remarkable. ... On this side [of the street] people walking back and forth, numerous and in silence. ... After the red light, all of a sudden it's the bellowing charge of wild cats, big or small ... the noise grows in intensity and strength, at its peak, becomes unbearable. ... Then stop. Let's do it again, with more pedestrians. Two-minute intervals. ... Sometimes, the old cars stall in the middle of the road and the pedestrians move around them like waves around a rock, though not without condemning the drivers of the badly placed vehicles with withering looks. Hard rhythms: alternations of silence and outburst, time both broken and accentuated, striking he who takes to listening from his window, which astonishes him more than the disparate movements of the crowds (pp. 28–29).

Lefebvre paints a poetic picture of the momentary sonic life of one street as impacted by car culture.[14] He captures the abstract sounds and rhythms of the street, akin to how an impressionistic painter might paint a busy street scene.[15] It is a representation of the music of the city, the music of a single street. But it is only one street in one city and as heard from one location on that street, Lefebvre's apartment window. There is a tendency to believe that the "noise" of urban traffic homogenizes cities, creating urban soundscapes that erase locational and personal identities. However, as intimated by Lefebvre, every street has its own complex sonic identity, its own subtly unique soundscape. The traffic and street sounds in, say, New York are different from those experienced in London; and the distinctive sound marks, as opposed to visual landmarks, of individual streets are no less notable if one takes the time to listen for them. Moreover, this sonic identity can change and evolve depending on the time of day (e.g., as the flow of traffic increases or decreases with rush hour) and one's shifting location along the street (as one's position will necessarily create subtly different resonances and exposures to different sounds). Although we may not always be consciously aware of these sonic identities acting around us, the rhythms of our daily exposure to them in turn impact our own identities.

Traditional ideas of place and space as being limited by physical boundaries have been transcended in favour of trying to understand how movement and flows of people and transport networks of products and information have contributed to identity formation (Morley & Robins, 1995). No less influential, though receiving less attention, are the micro influences of the sonic spaces in which we live our daily lives. Ambient street and traffic sounds reflect the particularity of the location or place, but also must necessarily act on individuals who are continually exposed to it—sonically shaping and influencing their daily existence. Thus we become, in part, sonically constructed individuals, the product of our sound environment. Several recent studies have sought to understand the impact of traffic and street sounds in the construction of identity. MIT researchers, for example, have been asking people all over the world to send in two-minute soundbites, what they refer to as "audio portraits," of their streets and neighbourhoods in order to glean information about locational social and economic dynamics (Poon, 2015). In combination with related concerns surrounding noise pollution and building on recent ecomusicological studies on popular music geographies and environments (Pedelty, 2012), the car–sound–music relationship contributes to and reflects the overall transitory complexity and rhythmic soundscape of the street and constructs spaces of identity constituted in assemblages of bodies, cars, and landscapes, and their sounds and movements.

Apart from the ambient car-related street "music" that reflects various locations and helps aurally construct the people who are continually exposed to these sounds, as discussed in Chapter 1 and above, numerous popular songs evoke the experience of travel on various roads and highways. Many of these refer to actual, real-world roads and places, such as the aforementioned "(Get Your Kicks) on Route 66," "Beale Street Blues," or Robert Johnson's "Crossroads"—the latter purportedly located at the junction of Highways 61 and 49 near Clarksdale, Mississippi. Many songs, however, have also been based on mythical roads that appeal to a sense of a journey to an imaginary, often utopian place. This was especially prevalent in the 1970s in the wake of the socio-cultural upheavals of the 1960s and the ongoing war in Vietnam. Songs such as the Beatles' "The Long and Winding Road" (1970), John Denver's "Take Me Home, Country Roads" (1972), America's "Ventura Highway" (1972), Don McLean's "American Pie" (1972), Gordon Lightfoot's "Carefree Highway" (1974), Gerry Rafferty's "Baker Street" (1978), Joni Mitchell's "Refuge of the Roads" (1979), Van Morrison's "Bright Side of the Road (1979), and Willie Nelson's "On the Road Again" (1980) were all odes to travelling on roads that led to imagined better times and places. Such songs resonated with how ingrained the car was in everyday life, and reflected the ongoing love affair with the automobile in the 1970s. Yet, they also depicted the car as a powerful marker of the potential for change and the creation of an imagined identity. Of course, some road songs—such as AC/DC's "Highway to Hell" (1979), Talking Heads' "Road to Nowhere" (1985), Chris Rea's "The Road to Hell" (1989), and Foo Fighters' "Long Road to Ruin" (2007)—portended more dystopic destinations and outcomes. These songs largely followed in the wake of the hoped-for utopianism expressed in songs from the 1970s and reflect something of the disenchantment with, if not rejection of, the idealistic values of the 1960s and '70s.

Similar to songs celebrating various real or mythical highways, the connection of cars and rock music is often a particularly strong identifier of more general locations. Detroit, "the Motor City," for example, boasts one of the proudest popular music heritages of any city in the world, much of it directly related to the automobile industry. The manufactured Motown sound, the working-class hard rock of "The Motor City Madman" Ted Nugent, Bob Seeger's assembly line ode "Making Thunderbirds" (1982), the urban hip hop of Eminem, and the proto-punk garage rockers such as Iggy Pop's the Stooges and The MC5 (an acronym for the Motor City Five) have all been overtly affected by Detroit's car manufacturing to one extent or another. Iggy Pop, in particular, claimed that the Stooges' sound was inspired by the "pounding clangor" of Detroit's auto factories (Reynolds, 1999, p. 13).

Detroit is also the birthplace of techno, a genre highly influenced by the auto industry. Dan Sicko (1999) described the emergence of the Detroit techno scene and showed how it centred on Detroit's Gratiot Avenue, a street that became commonly known as "Techno Boulevard." In the 1980s, the street housed pioneering techno record labels and studios such as Juan Atkins' Metroplex, Kevin Saunderson's KMS, and Derrick May's Transmat, a trio collectively known as the Belleville Three. According to another critic, techno was invented by the sons of the auto industry: "a generation of black middle class youth in Michigan who grew up accustomed to affluence, thanks in part to the racially mixed United Auto Workers union" (Reynolds, 1999, p. 15). Indeed, the onomatopoeic sounds of automobiles and their manufacturing process, as well as European synth-pop songs such as Kraftwerk's "Autobahn" and Gary Numan's "Cars" heavily informed the genre's creation. The darkly mechanistic style of the early African-American techno pioneers Cybotron (Juan Atkins and Rick Davis) spoke to Detroit's economic collapse in the late 1970s. The influence of the mechanical automobile aesthetic is evident in titles such as "Cosmic Cars" (1982) and "Night Drive (Thru Babylon)" (1985). "Cosmic Cars," as discussed in Chapter 2, employs a mechanically repetitive beat redolent of the insistent rhythmic flow of an assembly line, punctuated by analogue synthesizer squelches and TR 808 claps, and overlaid with robotic vocals. Perhaps the most overtly recognizable human-like sound (though it, too, is mechanical) in the work is synthesized horn honking. As evinced by the concepts of advanced technological travel in such works, the car and its attendant technology were viewed as a metaphoric spaceship—in some sense an Afrofuturistic form of escape from economic and racial oppression. The musical associations with the auto industry in Detroit have not, however, been without controversy. Ford's decision to use Juan Atkins' "No UFO's" in a television advertisement for the 2001 Ford Focus, along with a host of subsequent techno songs used in car ads, led many in the scene to lament its co-option by the mainstream.

Outside of Detroit, no other location and period has inspired more car-related songs than the hot rod scene of Southern California in the early 1960s. Legendary guitarist Dick Dale, for example, had hot rod hits with

"Hot Rod Racer" (1963), "Grudge Run" (1963), "Nitro Fuel" (1964), and "Mr. Eliminator" (1964). Jan and Dean also had a number of hot rod hits, such as "Drag City" (1963), "Dead Man's Curve" (1964), "My Mighty GTO" (1964), and "The Little Old Lady from Pasadena" (1964). Perhaps the kings of the hot rod song, however, were the Beach Boys. Their album *Little Deuce Coupe* (1963) contained, in addition to the title track, a series of car songs, including "Car Crazy Cutie," "Cherry, Cherry Coupe," "409," "Shut Down," "Our Car Club," and "Custom Machine." Often tied to actual locations in California, the hot rod song was to a large degree predicated on maintaining the mythos of the duelling culture of the gunslinger, a figure embodying quasi-superhuman speed and skill, taking on all-comers, and maintaining a fiercely independent spirit, thereby symbolizing the history and location of the "Wild West."

The driving experience is, of course, located at least as much, if not more, in the realm of the visual as the sonic. In the face of increasingly extensive freeway systems, some theorists believe that the act of driving creates a diminished experience of place and location. In his book *America*, Jean Baudrillard (1988) meditates on the visual spectacle of driving along the Los Angeles freeways and desert highways. Driving through the desert is understood to create an "invisibility, transparency or transversality in things," as well as what Baudrillard, citing Paul Virilio, terms an "aesthetics of disappearance" (pp. 7, 5). In this manner, Baudrillard contradicts the poetics of the particularity of place. Nonetheless, he still incorporates and evokes these "transversal" effects and experiences into his geography of Los Angeles and the American desert. Virilio addresses similar themes in his writings. However, unlike Baudrillard's framing of the experience in the spaces of Los Angeles and the desert, he abstracts the practices and experiences of driving from site-specific landscapes, and instead traces an even more dystopian, futuristic, abstract, and dislocated geography that effaces the multi-sensory nature of driving. In *Polar Inertia*, perhaps anticipating the driver assistance and virtual reality technologies, Virilio (2000) writes of a future where "the audiovisual feats of the electronic dashboard will prevail over the optical qualities of the field beyond the windscreen" and "the temporal depth of the electronic image prevails over the spatial depth of the motorway network" (p. 15). Virilio believes that physical movement, if played out to its maximum potential, would cease to be important, as "dynamic automotive vehicle[s]" such as cars would be replaced by "the static audiovisual vehicle," marking "the definitive triumph of sedentariness" (p. 18). Actual physical location and place would thus cease to matter entirely. In many ways, the Internet and smartphone technologies have already begun to minimize the need for embodied travel. It should be noted, however, that Virilio's future predictions of virtual travel appear to contradict contemporary sociological studies that point to the continuing importance of corporeal travel and physical co-presence alongside the increasing use and importance of virtual communication technologies (Urry, 2002; Urry, 2003).

Cars, art, and modernity

Beyond the association of automobile and music with which this book is primarily concerned, it is worth making a brief detour to note how other arts have also often focused on the automobile. The contradictory images of cars as agents of destruction and death, yet simultaneously of liberation and utopian modernity, have paved the way for their celebration in a variety of art objects—such as the collective Ant Farm's line of ten half-buried Cadillacs (the so-called "Cadillac Ranch") on Route 66 in Amarillo, Texas, or even sculptor Henry Moore's beloved Jaguar Mark II, which he described as "sculpture in motion" (Wollen, 2002b, p. 35). To some extent, artistic fascination with automobile art was already present in the world of hot rodders and car customizers who regularly altered the aesthetic appearance of stock cars. Famous hot rod customizer George Barris, for instance, was among the first to add decorative racing stripes and lettering to floor model cars. For many artists and thinkers, such as the Italian Futurists, the car symbolizes speed, noise, and power—attributes integral to the aesthetics of modernity. Thus Filippo Marinetti believed that the modern-day car was more beautiful than the ancient Greek *Winged Victory of Samothrace*, a second-century BC sculpture prominently displayed at the Louvre and described as "the greatest masterpiece of Hellenistic sculpture" (Janson, 1995, pp. 157–158). Much like those who relish the "music" of a roaring car engine, for the Futurists and many other subsequent enthusiasts the automobile was not only functional but also a work of sonic and visual art.

Imitating the common car–woman conflation characteristic of early Tin Pan Alley songs (see Chapter 1), photographers began to make use of the car in erotic imagery as early as the 1920s. Guillermo Giucci (2012), for example, explains that:

> In photos combining the women and the car, the naked figure and the importance of the sexual position were retained. … The coupling of the "women and car" was highly photogenic. One and the other, female and machine, were fused into one as objects of masculine desire (p. 171).

Both were essentially treated as objects of sexual desire and works of art, and staging this conflation contributed to the overall notion of the car as a cathected, humanized machine that has been discussed throughout this book.

Much as with their various endorsement deals with popular musicians, a number of car manufacturers have aligned themselves at different times and places with the art world for marketing and publicity purposes. In one of the most remarkable and celebrated car-themed artworks, in 1932 Ford commissioned Mexican artist Diego Rivera to paint for the Detroit Institute of the Arts a giant 27-panel, 4-wall mural of the Detroit River Rouge factory featuring its assembly line. At about the same time, between the 1930s and 1954, the modernist Italian artist Mario Sironi was creating a number of advertising posters for FIAT. French carmaker Renault soon followed in its patronage of the arts, and even went so far as to create a department of "Recherches, Art et Industrie" in 1967. The department was notable for commissioning numerous sculptures, logo designs, paintings, and even building designs from artists such as Arman, Victor Vasarely, and Nicolas Schöffer, and amassed a large collection of kinetically inspired artworks between 1967 and 1985. Renault justified its support of the arts "by pointing to the role played by the creative imagination in an increasingly technological world—the search for new creative solutions and so on" (Wollen, 2002b, p. 32).

A prominent sculptor who collaborated with Renault was the French-American artist Arman, who produced a series of sculptures titled *Accumulations Renault* in the late 1960s. These works are minimalist inspired, created from individual car parts supplied by Renault, and often feature repetitive components that arguably take on a quasi-musical rhythm. Despite his successful partnership with Renault, Arman also produced works quite critical of car culture. *Long Term Parking* (1982) consists of 60 automobiles embedded in concrete. *White Orchid, exploded MG car* (1963), a burning car piece dating from before his collaboration with Renault, indicates a conscious element of conflict between the commercial interests of car manufacturers and the artistic beliefs and principles of the artists they patronized. Other artists involved with Renault included Robert Rauschenberg, Jean Tinguely, and Henri Micheaux. While Renault may not have condoned every work of automotive art produced by the artists it associated with, it clearly embraced its connection to the exclusivity associated with the highbrow art world.

Following the example of Renault, throughout the 1970s and 1980s BMW engaged the leading figures in modern art to decorate some of its cars. In 1975, for instance, it commissioned Alexander Calder to decorate the body of its BMW 3.0 CSL, which was entered in that year's Le Mans 24 Hour race. The following year it similarly commissioned Frank Stella, a race car enthusiast, to emblazon his trademark geometrical patterns on a car in the same race. In subsequent years, Roy Lichtenstein, Andy Warhol, Ed Rauschenberg, and David Hockney were likewise enlisted to design various "art cars" (Wollen, 2002b, p. 37).

While these artists happily aligned themselves, at least temporarily, with the prestige and popularity of the motor racing world (whether to advertise their art to a wealthy racing elite, to cash in on a commission, or simply for the fun of it), numerous other artists have crafted more negative, often dystopic, visions of the automobile. In 1964, Judy Chicago created the wall-mounted sculpture *Car Hood* from a steel car hood taken from a Corvair and painted in traditional automotive paint. In her memoir, *Through the Flower: My Struggle as a Woman Artist*, she describes the gendered symbolism of *Car Hood*: "the vaginal form, penetrated by a phallic arrow, was mounted on the 'masculine' hood of a car, a very clear symbol of my state of mind at the time" (Chicago, 1975, p. 36). In this work, Chicago consciously co-opts and deconstructs the stereotypical masculine conflation of female-as-car. The car-related works of Krzysztof Wodiczko, including his 1991 *Poliscar* (a human-powered vehicle designed as a modern-day survival centre to transport homeless people), or Sarah Lucas' *Car Park* and *Concrete Void* (both from 1997 and featuring vandalized and/or destroyed cars) evince an ironic critique of the disposability of postmodern car culture. Finally, worthy of mention is French sculptor César (Baldaccini), who shocked the Paris art world in the late 1950s and 1960s with his *Compressions*, discarded automobiles and car parts that he had crushed using a large hydraulic pressing machine. In this manner, César employed one form of mass-produced machine to mechanically transform another. In so doing, he created an eloquent critique of our affluent throwaway society whose scrapping practices he turned into a creative artistic act, an anti-utopian metamorphosis and the manifestation of his disenchantment with the automotive fetish.

As functioning vehicles, the "art cars" commissioned by BMW (such as those by Calder and Stella, discussed above) have a clear sonic presence. Indeed, many might simply regard them as intentional forms of kinetic-sonic sculpture. Other apparently silent works, even pessimistic or anti-car works by César or Lucas, nevertheless also evoke a sonic presence. César's *Compressions*, his "Car Horn Relief" (1962) or "Dauphine" (1959), for instance, instantaneously recall the implied dissonant metallic sounds of a car being crushed, or perhaps even of the horrific sounds of a devastating car crash. In their mechanically smashed and crumpled transformations, such works represent the sound of late twentieth-century industry, and perhaps its eventual grinding and cacophonous collapse. It is also notable that, as in the case of "Dauphine" (named for the Renault Dauphine that was compressed), César typically retained both the car name and enough recognizable material of the original to maintain the car's brand identity.

Much as with Renault's and BMW's sponsorship of art cars, car manufacturers have often placed a high value on integrating themselves into the artistic cultural life of their respective countries and communities. Wolfsburg, Germany's fifth largest city, is home to Volkswagen's world headquarters and the world's largest automobile production plant. It is, in short, a company town. Adjacent to its factory, Volkswagen's theme park, Autostadt (German for "automobile city"), is the country's most visited tourist attraction. It displays a variety of pavilions in an open-air, futuristic, World's Fair-like atmosphere, and is sponsored by manufacturers in the Volkswagen group (Bentley, Ducati, Lamborghini, SEAT, and Škoda, among others). Many of the displays, such as that of Lamborghini, are heavily centred on the sound of the car's engine, and feature an impressive sound and light show that is presumably intended to sonically and visually overwhelm the visitors' senses, to create an emotional connection with the car and its manufacturer. Beyond the displays, Autostadt presents a selection of revolving musical entertainments at various locations on the grounds, staging everything from classical ensembles to pop, rock, and heavy metal artists. Aside from regular day-to-day musical programming, various public and private concerts are held on the site, including a six-week summer festival. In addition to underwriting Autostadt and its cultural attractions, Volkswagen also sponsors a world-renowned modern art gallery, the Kunstmuseum Wolfsburg, that regularly exhibits automobile-themed works and displays.

Volkswagen's highly automated plant in Dresden, Die Gläserne Manufaktur, is yet another successful tourist attraction that regularly schedules public concerts. Purchasers of high-end Bentleys and Phaetons (assembled at the plant) were, until the plant's retooling in 2016, serenaded with classical music and presented with opera tickets when they took delivery of their cars. In keeping with its perhaps ironically elitist cultural associations with classical music, given its genesis as the accessible "people's car," Volkswagen is also a major sponsor of the Dresden opera.

The cultural outreach of car manufacturers is particularly acute in Germany. In addition to Volkswagen's various initiatives, the BMW Group (formed by BMW, Rolls-Royce, and MINI) is headquartered in Munich as part of BMW Welt and the associated BMW Museum. BMW Welt is a somewhat smaller version of Volkswagen's Autostadt, though it still attracts over three million visitors a year. As at the Gläserne Manufaktur, customers picking up special custom-ordered cars are given a dramatic, staged experience in a futuristic glass-walled hall. The company also sponsors the prestigious annual BMW Welt Jazz Award, along with numerous jazz and classical concerts throughout the world.

Such automotive public outreach is not limited to Germany. Among several Ferrari museums in the company's home country of Italy, the Museo Ferrari in Maranello is centred on an interactive exhibition highlighting the evolving looks and sounds of its racing car engines through the decades. Visitors can stroll by a chronologic display of Ferrari Formula One cars and push a button to activate the recorded sound of each year's car as it revs up and goes through the gears. The mediated sounds are reproduced at an extremely loud decibel level, roughly equivalent to that of the actual car in

Figure 7.1 Autostadt Summer Music Festival Stage

operation, and are felt as much as heard by whoever triggers them. It is a bodily impactful experience that testifies not only to the sheer sonic thrill felt by many racing fans, but also to the value placed by Ferrari, its racing fans, and its customers on sonic and visual aesthetics.

In addition to underlining the car culture that is ingrained in the identity of these particular cities and countries, car companies in each of these cases have set up interactive opportunities for the public to participate in sonic and musical experiences. They often appropriate the cultural and social prestige of jazz and classical music as stereotypical representations of exclusivity and taste in order to elevate, by association, their more exclusive and luxury models. In so doing, they encourage potential customers to see automobiles as another cultural product of the region, on a par with the arts and music. Moreover, through these venues, car manufacturers such as Volkswagen and BMW overtly integrate themselves into the cultural fabric and identity of their communities and of the people who live there. Such efforts, by consequence, help to suture, or at the very least mitigate, the common perception of a divide between the arts (including musical arts) and industry.

Conclusion

Testifying to the overall complexity and density of their relationship, this chapter has discussed a variety of cultural intersections between cars and popular music. While issues of more focused racial and gender identity are never far from the surface, these intersections speak more to our identity as human beings and how we regard ourselves and our locations in general. Movie and television soundtracks often reinforce utopian or dystopian ideals of anthropomorphic cars, the former of which automakers seek to imbue in their products, as evident in the variety of "talking car" voice systems. Such features project various levels of machine intelligence. This, beyond our dependence on automobiles, can lead drivers to regard their cars as being instilled with some sense of a human "spirit," and, in turn, serves as a prime instigator for the development of quasi-spiritual relationships with cars and the creation of songs about cars that evoke spirituality. Likewise, the roads on which we drive our cars, and even the locations where they are manufactured, have often developed metaphysical, often mythical, identities that are commonly celebrated in song and through popular musical culture. Finally, in order to cement their place in the identity of various regions and countries, auto manufacturers have often aligned themselves with the arts. Beyond songs about cars, the sonic and musical influence of cars, or the role of music in advertising them, this chapter has outlined and reinforced some less obvious aspects of just how deeply culturally embedded the car–popular music relationship has become and how the two industries have combined, and even been re-combined, to meaningfully contribute to various constructions of human identity.

Notes

1 Lyrics and music by Paul Hampton. Copyright Red Cape Songs, E Red Cape Songs, EMI U Catalogue Inc.
2 *The Knight Rider* franchise spawned several unremarkable movies, and returned to NBC in 2008 as a series that updated the original technology (with a new Ford Shelby Mustang replacing the original Firebird). However, it was cancelled after one season.
3 Vaporwave is a popular online genre whose practitioners creatively repurpose the pre-existing sounds of advertising jingles, easy-listening commercial pop, and designed sounds of various products and video games to critique consumerism and capitalism. The subculture surrounding vaporwave tends to be characterized by an ironic nostalgic and often surrealist engagement with popular entertainment, technology, and advertising of previous decades.
4 For example, in May 1977, socialite Sandra Ilene West was buried upright at the wheel of her powder-blue 1964 Ferrari 330, as instructed in her will.
5 Lyrics and music by Dion Di Mucci, Frederick Patrick, and Murray Singer. Copyright Sony/ATV Music Publishing LLC.
6 Lyrics and music by Brett James, Gordon Sampson, and Hillary Lindsey. Copyright Sony/ATV Music Publishing LLC.
7 Lyrics and music by George Pendergast, George Edward Pendergast, Gregory James Kolanek, John Robert Richards, Rodney Browning, and Scott Preston Alexander. Copyright Sony/ATV Music Publishing LLC.
8 Lyrics and music by Allen Jourgensen, Paul Barker, William Fredrick Rieflin, Gibson Haynes, and Michael Bruce Balch. Copyright Warner Chappell Music, Inc.
9 Such nationalistic policies regarding the representation of place, as Merriman has pointed out, were later adapted to the construction of England's motorways.
10 Lyrics and music by Emil Schult, Florian Schneider-Esleben, and Ralf Hütter. Copyright Sony/ATV Music Publishing LLC.
11 For a more in-depth look at the nexus of popular music and the American road see Slethaug (2017).
12 Lyrics and music by Bobby Troup. Copyright Music Asset Management.
13 As the major route northward out of Mississippi, US-61 has been of particular inspiration to blues artists. The highway has also been the subject of several blues recordings, including Roosevelt Sykes' "Highway 61 Blues" (1932), Jack Kelly and Will Batts' "Highway No. 61 Blues" (1933), and the Sparks Brothers' recording of "61 Highway" (1933).
14 Brandon LaBelle (2010) similarly sees the sidewalk and the sonic experience of the pedestrian as mediating space by acoustically "interlocking private lives and public organization" (p. 124). Through a mixture of vibrational energies produced by both the sound of the engine and interior stereo systems, the car is a form of mobile sonic expressiveness that both mediates and impacts the experience of private and public spaces.
15 Indeed, presaging Lefebvre by some 80 years, in 1922 the Canadian painter Lawren Harris wrote the poem "Morning and Evening," which was based on the sounds of a street in Toronto: "Bathed in the morning Sun I walk up the street … The rattle and clanging of the street cars, the roar of the heavily laden trucks, the piercing bleat of arrogant motor horns—all discordant noises of the street. / Bespeak to them the romantic import of human affairs" (Harris, 2007, pp. 7–8).

Conclusion: shut down

Music is designed to "move" us, emotionally and physically. It induces physical kinaesthetic responses—most often expressed in dance but also in toe tapping or head bobbing—that, through sympathetic vibration, invigorate and stimulate recognition of our corporeal existence. Mechanized transportation, particularly as experienced in automobiles, produces a similar hyper-stimulated state. Cars, like our response to music, often "move" us emotionally, as objects of design and aesthetic contemplation, and physically, as a means of practical bodily transport. Seen in this light, that music is so intimately connected to the history of transportation, and of cars in particular, may perhaps be unsurprising. Each experience would seem to reinforce and heighten the other, with the combination perhaps even greater than the sum of its parts. Both the car and the pop song are also, of course, outcomes of industrial mass production, commodities that play on our emotions and that are fused into our construction of self and community. Nonetheless, the relationships between these two worlds seem, at least on the surface, diametrically opposed. Although both are industrial products, the car—with its emphasis on industrial engineering, mass production, and functional user experience—would seem to have little to do with the artistic, aesthetic realm of popular music. For their part, popular music and musicians have often decried any association with the potentially corrupting commercialism of corporate culture. Yet, as I hope this book has illustrated, the two industries are indeed intimately connected and have mutually influenced each other in a variety of ways that have, in turn, acted as influential agents in human identity construction.

Personal human and branded automobile identities are equally constructed. As individuals, we are assemblages of various and evolving racial, gender, sexual, religious, class, and locational identities and personas. Cars are similarly (though perhaps more intentionally) constructed and designed to appeal to our sense of self. Identity formation, partly shaped by car and other industrial manufacturers, thus evinces a form of transhuman evolution, what N. Katherine Hayles (2012) might call a commercially induced "technogenesis," as we are increasingly encouraged to merge with and see ourselves in our products (if not, in fact, regarding ourselves as one) and other non-human actors with which we engage. It is a merger that the automobile manufacturers (and corporations more generally) increasingly seek to achieve, and which we, as consumers, increasingly buy into. Car manufacturers and the popular music industry create products in our image that, in turn, impact not only our perception of reality or sense of self identity but actually change our realities, and thus who we are. Such a proposition evokes philosopher Bernard Stiegler's notions of human co-shaping by and through technology. The central idea guiding his work is that human beings are marked by an "originary absence of origin" (*défaut d'origine*), a fundamental lack of qualities that makes them originally and inherently in need of technical prostheses. This means that we are fundamentally constituted and conditioned by technics. For Stiegler, much as with Hayles, humanity is co-extensive with technics (Lemmens, 2011).

Despite ever-increasing environmental concerns and a push for mass transit around the world, there is no shortage of motorized vehicles on the road. According to one study conducted by Sousanis (2011), approximately one billion cars were built in the last century, and already roughly another billion are on the road today. Not surprisingly, China leads the way in vehicle growth, with the number of cars on Chinese roads increasing by 27.5 per cent since the last century, amounting to half the entire global growth and roughly 33 per cent of the world's current yearly car production. That gives China the world's second largest car population, with 78 million vehicles. But the United States still constitutes by far the largest vehicle population in the world, with 239.8 million cars. The same study also claims that the world vehicle population passed the 1 billion mark in 2010, only 24 years after reaching 500 million in 1986. Prior to that, the vehicle population doubled roughly every ten years from 1950 to 1970, when it first reached the 250 million threshold (see also Voelcker, 2014). Global production numbers continue to increase at a rate of roughly three million cars a year.

As outlined in the conclusion to Chapter 1, the automotive industry is currently undergoing a period of radical change. Hybrid cars, fully electric cars, hydrogen fuel cells, and various forms of autonomous driverless systems dominate the industry's and the public's imagination. New electric car companies such as Tesla and Lucid Motors seem poised to make major inroads on the sales of traditional North American manufacturers, who are likewise scrambling to improve and upgrade their own vehicles. The peer-to-peer ride-sharing company Uber has even announced plans to bring vertical take-off and landing (VTOL) cars—essentially, flying cars—to Los Angeles by 2020 (Stewart, 2017).

Whether it is autonomous or driverless cars, electric cars, flying cars, or some other variant, the future of cars will be determined by new and as yet unrealized technology. The fusion of humans with some type of mechanized mobility device seems likely assured for the next stage of our existence as a species. Automobility—i.e., the "automatic" moving of people—thus fuses in many ways with the notion of "automaton." As John Urry (2007) states,

> [The] double resonance of "auto" demonstrates that the "car-driver" is a hybrid assemblage of human competences and will, and machines. ... "Auto" mobility thus involves the powerful combination of autonomous humans together with machines possessing the capacity for autonomous movement along the paths, lanes, streets and routeways of each society (p. 118).

Such an observation will for many raise the spectre of a dystopic post-human society of human–machine hybrids. However, as evinced in the work of Stiegler and Hayles outlined above, in many ways humans have always been the hybrid products of technological and social evolution.

Of course, humans are not simply constructed by the whims of corporate techno-culture, automotive or any other. Car modification and tuning culture across the globe has enabled the personalization of otherwise mass-produced cars to reflect purposeful individual and/or group identities. Automotive sound and entertainment systems have likewise evolved to the point where we can customize the driving soundtrack to directly reflect our individual tastes and moods behind the wheel.

As I have discussed at several points throughout this work, popular music—whether of the kind used in car advertising or that to which we listen while in a car—has the effect of humanizing the machine, making it more approachable, more familiar, and often subdues the potentially alienating or unwanted sounds produced by the machine itself. However, something of a reverse reading can also be true. Instead of making the machine feel more human and potentially less threatening to users, music in car advertising and played through sound systems also helps to haptically suture us to the car, making drivers and passengers become more machine-like. Through heard and felt vibrations, we are sonically and emotionally fused with the culture of industrial mass production, both of the music and of the automotive industries.

The history of music making is rife with similar incarnations of hybrid human–machine experiences, from microphones that artificially project the human voice to the use of any instrument. Playing an acoustic guitar is, in many ways, as much of a hybrid, human–machine fusion as driving a car. Indeed, car drivers fuse with their machines such that, in certain manoeuvres and situations (e.g., while parallel parking or changing lanes), they simply "feel" the car as an extension of themselves. This is similar to Marshal McLuhan's (1994) concept of "extensions," whereby the "wheel is an extension of the feet in rotation" (p. 60). As such, the automobile is simply a refined extension of the feet and legs. It allows humans to travel places as if on foot, only faster and with less effort. This extension further enables one to travel in relative comfort in extreme weather conditions. Similarly, musical instruments are simply extensions of the voice, allowing us to sonically communicate and connect in newly creative and expressive ways beyond our vocal range and without straining or injuring ourselves.[1]

Both the experience and practice of music and automobility involve the manipulation of technology, and not for purposes as different as one might imagine. While the driver's experience is one rooted in the practicalities of mobility, enabling easier physical movement from one place to another, music, too, has the capacity to figuratively move us. Both hybrid activities involve distortions of time and space, altering our perception of time passing and, combined with developments in communication and computer and Internet technologies, embodying notions of what both Baudrillard (1988) and Urry (2007) refer to as "instantaneous" time. Both music and automobile, then, serve as counterbalancing agents to the restrictive and oppressive codified objectification of time as found in working hours, train and plane schedules, and other expressions of rigid clock time. The flexibility afforded by cars and music can be linked to the increasing significance of these personalized and subjective temporalities; and so it is not surprising that both have contributed to the contestation and construction of identities, either discretely or in combination with each other.

Cars and recorded music should be regarded as expressive products that result from the intersectional labour of numerous, if not innumerable, people. In the case of automobiles, designers, factory workers, and marketers all contribute to the identity of each model. In the case of popular music, composers, singers, session musicians, producers, and engineers together help create the sonic fingerprint of each song. In both cases, a trace of each individual person, and hence a trace of their identity, is left in each product. As individuals, our identities are constructed from the confluence of a multitude of internal (genetic) and external (socio-cultural) influences. Indeed, individual agency can be regarded as the product of an intricate nexus of both past and present labour and technologies.

The concept of "intersectionality" was initially broached by legal scholar Kimberlé Crenshaw (1989). Since then, intersectionality has become a term most often applied in critical theory, particularly feminist theory, to describe the ways in which oppressive systems—e.g., racism, sexism, homophobia, transphobia, ableism, xenophobia—are interconnected and cannot be examined separately from one another. To a large degree, this book has been about a different form of intersectionality—namely, the intersection of humans, music, and automobiles; and their modes of interaction not as a system of oppression but rather as one of identity construction. Since their invention in the late 1800s, cars have figuratively driven our identities and, in turn, been driven by them. The added influence of music—whether to enhance the driving experience, as an effective aid in marketing the product, or in the resulting pop songs that celebrate or evoke cars—has helped create a cultural feedback loop whereby cars and popular music are intimately connected actors that co-evolve and help shape and sell each other. Rather than representing oppression (though some might argue there is a repression of humans in both industries), cars and popular music have typically been viewed as liberating forces, with music sonically manifesting an emotional and mentally expressive freedom that heightens the physical freedom and mobility that the car promises.

I began this book by quoting Filippo Marinetti's 1909 "Founding and Manifesto of Futurism" and his characterization of the future as a beautiful "roaring car" that would construct a hymn to the driver. To a large degree, Marinetti's vision has proven accurate as car culture and its attendant sonic and musical components have exerted an undeniable influence on society and culture around the globe over the past century. With ongoing environmental questions and the advent of hybrid, electric, self-driving, and even flying car technologies, the future of the automotive industry would appear to be in flux. However, one of the most telling statements about the currency of the nexus of automobiles and popular music occurred on February 6, 2018, when Elon Musk shot one of his cherry-red Tesla Roadsters into space aboard a test flight for his SpaceX Falcon Heavy Rocket. As was widely reported at the time, the car was driven by a space suit-wearing mannequin that was listening to David Bowie's "Starman" (1972) playing on an infinite loop on the car's radio. The imagery was compelling—an electric car on the ultimate road trip, on a trajectory that would take it out beyond Mars, past the asteroid belt, and into a permanent elliptical orbit around the sun while Bowie's song played for eternity. In a press conference held after the launch, Musk said he expected the car to be "out there in space for millions or billions of years" (Freeman, 2018). The life-sized car also a carried a small, toy Hot Wheels Roadster. Maintaining something of the religious fascination that surrounds the automobile, Musk speculated: "Maybe [it will be] discovered by an alien race, thinking, 'What were these guys doing? Did they worship this car? Why do they have a little car in the car?'" (Malik, 2018).[2]

This act was and is a testimony to the enduring power of the intersection of car and popular music.[3] It was a spectacular attempt to pull off the ultimate act of liberation promised by both popular music and automotive culture—an infinite, interstellar freedom of the mind and body (albeit in the form of a non-human mannequin) that we could all potentially be a part of if, as Musk would prefer, we buy a Tesla.[4] It also points to the futuristic, often idealized aspects of both the automotive and popular music industries in their common concern with and reliance on advancing technologies that make similarly haptic connections to the human body, and, much like Marinetti and the Futurists, project the hope for an accelerating, forward-moving, utopian future.

Notes

1 Most individuals will readily understand and accept the concept of extension, but many show more resistance when it comes to what McLuhan calls "amputations," his counterpart to extensions. We conceivably do not wish to be made to think about the time we spend alone in our cars, isolated or "amputated" from other humans, the fact that the resulting amputation from relying increasingly less on physical bodily movement has made us generally less healthy, or that our ubiquitous headphone culture similarly isolates us in public spaces.

2 In early 2020 Elon Musk furthered his connection to music by releasing an electronic dance music (EDM) track on SoundCloud and Spotify, titled "Don't Doubt Ur Vibe," which made SoundCloud's top ten most played tracks for the first week of February that year.

3 Another telling aspect of the continued currency of the intersection of cars and popular music in constructing our identities is the song "Daddy's Car" (2016). In 2016, Sony Computer Science Laboratories (CSL) set out to create popular music solely by means of artificial intelligence. The AI system employed, called Flow Machines, works by first analysing a database of 13,000 lead sheets, and then following a particular musical style to generate similar compositions. The first song to be created using this database approach was, perhaps tellingly, a car song. The melody and harmonies to "Daddy's Car" are somewhat reminiscent of the Beatles, the style that the software was programmed to emulate (Goldhill, 2016). The final result does bear a human imprint, however, as French composer Benoît Carré arranged the song and wrote the lyrics.

4 Later in 2018, and beset with a falling stock price and scrutiny about its strategic direction, Ford tapped actor Bryan Cranston to star in its campaign called "Built Ford Proud." The campaign consisted of a series of ads featuring Cranston moving through various roles, including a lecturer at a Ted Talks-like forum, a US president, and an android. One ad features futuristic transportation scenes interwoven with old footage of a Ford factory. In an apparent rejoinder to tech-visionaries such as Musk, Cranston declares, "Talk doesn't get things done, building does," before ending with "Let the other guys keep dreaming about the future. We'll be the ones building it." The soundtrack comprises an orchestral cover of the Rolling Stones "Paint It Black" (1966) and recalls Model T lore and a quote attributed to Henry Ford: "You can have any color as long as it's black." Another of the ads mocks Silicon Valley's attempts to create flying cars by showing a racing Mustang muscle car going airborne over a hill. Cranston dryly intones: "Contrary to what you're about to see, the Ford Motor Company does not condone, nor build, flying cars."

Works cited

Adams, H. (2013, July 4). Indiana woman "voice of OnStar." *Louisville Courier-Journal*. Retrieved May 14, 2015, from http://archive.azcentral.com/business/news/free/20130704indiana-woman-voice-onstar.html

Adorno, T. (1941). On popular music. In A. Easthope & K. McGowen (Eds.), *A critical and cultural theory reader* (pp. 211–223). Toronto: University of Toronto Press.

Adorno, T. (2001). On the fetish character in music and the regression of listening. In J. M. Bernstein (Ed.), *The culture industry* (pp. 29–60). New York: Routledge.

Adorno, T. (2005). More haste less speed. In *Minima moralia: Reflections on a damaged life* (p. 162). New York: Verso. (Original work published 1951)

Allan, D. (2005). An essay on popular music in advertising: The bankruptcy of culture or the marriage of art and commerce? *Advertising and Society Review*, 6(1). Retrieved April 19, 2016, from http://muse.jhu.edu/journals/asr/v006/6.1allan.html

Anderson, P. (2001). Gary Numan: Gary Numan drives music more than cars. *Kaos 2000 Magazine*. Retrieved August 7, 2016, from http://www.kaos2000.net/interviews/garynuman/

Aronczyk, M., & Powers, D. (2010). *Blowing up the brand*. New York: Peter Lang.

Arvidsson, A. (2006). *Brands: Meaning and value in media culture*. New York: Routledge.

Associated Press. (2015, May 15). Google's newest self-driving cars hit public roads this summer. *CBC News*. Retrieved March 20, 2019, from https://www.cbc.ca/news/technology/google-s-newest-self-driving-cars-hit-public-roads-this-summer-1.3069370

Audi AG. (2011). Corporate strategy. Retrieved May 21, 2016, from http://www.audi.com/corporate/en/company/corporate-strategy.html

Audi Sound Studio [Video]. (2011). Retrieved June 8, 2015, from https://www.youtube.com/watch?v=HNQam68x2l8

Auslander, P. (2012). Digital liveness: A historico-philosophical perspective. *Journal of Performance and Art*, 34(3), 3–11.

Ayres, T. J., & Hughes, P. (1986). Visual acuity with noise and music at 107dbA. *Journal of Auditory Research*, 26(1), 65–74.

Barhard, R., & Rutledge, J. (2009, June 5). Music + ads: Advertising is the new radio. *Adweek.com*. Retrieved November 11, 2016, from http://www.adweek.com/aw/content_display/news/agency/e3if23ea57e4d01ad14116494ef49f3985d

Barnett, V. J. (2004). *The performance and experience of extraverts and introverts playing a computer racing simulation: Mediating effects of increasing complexity in musical distraction* (Unpublished undergraduate thesis). University of York, UK.

Barris, G., & Featherstone, D. (1996). *Barris TV and movie cars*. Osceola, WI: MBI Publishing.

Barthes, R. (1991). The new Citroën. In *Mythologies* (A. Lavers, Trans.) (pp. 88–90). New York: Noon Day Press.

Baudrillard, J. (1988). *America*. London: Verso.

Baudrillard, J. (1996). *The system of objects*. (J. Benedict, Trans.). London: Verso.

Baudrillard, J. (2002). The racing driver and his double. In *Screened Out* (C. Turner, Trans.) (pp. 166–170). London: Verso.

Bayley, S. (1986). *Sex, drink and fast cars: The creation and consumption of images*. London: Faber & Faber.

Beauty at the helm: Mrs. Harold Harmsworth. (1902, July 2). *Car Illustrated*, p. 191.

Beh, H. C. & Hirst, R. (1999). Performance on driving-related tasks during music. *Ergonomics 42*(8), 1087–1098.

Behling, L. J. (1997). "The women at the wheel": Marketing ideal womanhood, 1915–1934. *Journal of American Culture 20*(3), 13–30.

Bell, J. (2017, December 30). Toyota wants to change the world with Mirai, its new hydrogen car. *Wired*. http://www.wired.co.uk/article/toyota-mirai-hydrogen-car-rep licate-prius-success

Bellis, M. (2016). The Duryea brothers: automobile history. *About Money*. Retrieved August 30, 2016, from http://inventors.about.com/od/dstartinventors/a/DuryeaBroth ers.htm

Bennett, J. (2014, January 8). The quest for a quieter ride: Stepped-up efforts to nix the chirps, rattles and drones. *Wall Street Journal*. Retrieved February 28, 2015, from http://www.wsj.com/articles/SB10001424052702303433304579304791217545938

Benson, A. (2014, March 19). Formula 1: Are the new V6 turbo hybrid engines "too quiet"? *BBC Sport*. Retrieved February 7, 2015, from http://www.bbc.com/sport/0/ formula1/26656258

Berger, M. L. (1979). *The devil wagon in God's country: The automobile and social change in rural America, 1893–1929*. Hamden, CT: Archon.

Berger, M. L. (2001). *The automobile in American history and culture: A reference guide*. Westport, CT: Greenwood.

Bernie Ecclestone horrified at sound of new V6 engines in Formula One. (2014, March 17). *Autoweek*. Retrieved February 5, 2015, from http://autoweek.com/article/formula-one/ bernie-ecclestone-horrified-sound-new-v6-engines-formula-one

Betts, G. (2014). *Motown encyclopedia*. n.p.: AC Books.

Big Hootenanny. (1964, January 15). *The Dispatch*, p. 8.

Bijsterveld, K., Cleophas, E., Krebs, S., & Mom, G. (2013). *Sound and safe: A history of listening behind the wheel*. New York: Oxford University Press.

Biz, C. (2019, February 20). BTS's endorsement was so powerful that Hyundai is literally struggling to keep up with demand. *Koreaboo*. Retrieved March 15, 2019, from https://www.koreaboo.com/news/bts-hyundai-palisades-demand-struggle/

Blanke, D. (2007). *Hell on wheels: The promise and peril of America's car culture*. Lawrence: University Press of Kansas.

BMW Group. (2013, March 18). New sound logo for BMW brand [Press release]. Retrieved September 17, 2015, from https://www.press.bmwgroup.com/canada/p ressDetail.html?title=new-sound-logo-for-bmw-brand&outputChannelId=21&id=T01 38168EN&left_menu_item=node__809

BMW. (2013). *BMW sound designers. BMW quality* [Video]. Retrieved March 24, 2013, from http://www.youtube.com/watch?v=tqZcSPXPhcc

Boggs, J. (1963/2009). *The American Revolution: Pages from a Negro worker's notebook*. New York: Monthly Review Press. Retrieved January 6, 2015, from http://www.historyisaweapon.com/defcon1/amreboggs.html#DIV8

Bono. (2010, January 2). Ten for the next ten. *New York Times*. Retrieved June 28, 2016, from http://www.nytimes.com/2010/01/03/opinion/03bono.html?scp=5&sq=Bono&st=cse

Booth, M. (2006, July 8). Nissan note. *Independent*. Retrieved September 12, 2017, from http://www.independent.co.uk/life-style/motoring/road-tests/nissan-note-406920.html

Bosch. (2015). [Brochure]. Retrieved August 27, 2016, from http://www.bosch-home.ca/Files/Bosch2/Ca/ca_en/2015/Brochures/2015_Dish.pdf

Bowman, D. (2015). *Experiencing Rush: A listener's companion*. London: Rowman & Littlefield.

Bracewell, M. (2002). Fade to grey: Motorways and monotony. In P. Wollen & J. Kerr (Eds.), *Autopia: Cars and culture* (pp. 288–292). London: Reaktion.

Bright, B. J. (1995). *Looking high and low: Art and cultural identity*. Phoenix: University of Arizona Press.

Brodsky, W. (2002). The effects of music tempo on simulated driving performance and vehicular control. *Transportation Research Part F, 4*, 219–241.

Brodsky, W. (2015). *Driving with music: Cognitive-behaviourial implications*. Burlington, VT: Ashgate.

Brown, H. (n.d.). Low rider. *Songfacts*. Retrieved November 16, 2018, from http://www.songfacts.com/detail.php?id=2694

Brownsell, A. (2012, March 2). Jaguar unveils global "alive" strategy. *Campaign*. Retrieved May 7, 2016, from https://www.campaignlive.co.uk/article/jaguar-unveils-global-alive-strategy/1120162

Bull, M. (2001). Soundscapes of the car: A critical study of automobile habitation. In D. Miller (Ed.), *Car cultures* (pp. 185–202). Oxford: Berg.

Bull, M. (2003). Soundscapes of the car: A critical study of automobile habitation. In M. Bull & L. Back (Eds.), *The auditory culture reader* (pp. 357–374). Oxford: Berg.

Bull, M. (2004a). Automobility and the power of sound. *Theory Culture Society, 21*, 243–259.

Bull, M. (2004b). Sound connections: An aural epistemology of proximity and distance in urban culture. *Environment and Planning D: Society and Space, 22*(1), 103–116.

Bull, M. (2006). Filmic cities: The aesthetic experience of the personal-stereo user. In A. Bennet, B. Shank, & J. Toynbee (Eds.), *The popular music studies reader* (pp. 148–155). London: Routledge.

Burdick, A. (2001, July). Now hear this: Listening back on a century of sound. *Harper's Magazine*, 70–77.

Bureau of Transportation Statistics. (2013). Chapter 1. Extent of US transportation system: Vehicles. In *Transportation statistics annual report 2013*. Retrieved September 24, 2016, from http://www.rita.dot.gov/bts/sites/rita.dot.gov.bts/files/publications/transportation_statistics_annual_report/2013/chapter1.html

Burke, B. (2014, January 2). Would you pay for a little silence on your flight? *Boston Herald*. Retrieved February 28, 2015, from http://www.bostonherald.com/entertainment/travel/the_travel_guy/2014/01/would_you_pay_for_a_little_silence_on_your_flight

Cadillac. (2013). Cadillac applies art and science to CTS engine sounds [Press release]. Retrieved July 20, 2017, from http://media.cadillac.com/media/us/en/cadillac/news.detail.html/content/Pages/news/us/en/2013/Sep/0911-cadillac.html

Caesar, I. (1937). *Children's songs*. Retrieved January 25, 2015, from http://www. irvingcaesar.com/childrensSongs.aspx

Caldwell, D. (2005, September 2). Where gay collectors come out of the garage. *New York Times*. Retrieved July 23, 2018, from http://www.nytimes.com/2005/09/02/autom obiles/where-gay-collectors-come-out-of-the-garage.html

Car Music Project. (n.d.). [Website]. Retrieved May 12, 2015, from http://www.carm usicproject.com

Carah, N. (2010). *Pop brands: Branding popular music and young people*. New York: Peter Lang.

Castillo, M. (2016, May 28). Toyota's Scion music label puts artists first. *Adweek*. Retrieved August 14, 2016, from http://www.adweek.com/news/advertising-bra nding/toyotas-scion-music-label-puts-artists-first-164660

CDC. (2014). Noise and hearing loss prevention. Retrieved February 26, 2015, from http://www.cdc.gov/niosh/topics/noise/stats.html

Chambers, I. (1994). *Migrancy, culture, identity*. London: Routledge.

Chambers, J. (2016). Presenting the black middle class: John H. Johnson and Ebony Magazine 1945–1974. In D. Bell & J. Hollows (Eds.), *Historicizing lifestyle: Mediating taste, consumption and identity from the 1900s to the 1970s* (pp. 54–69). London: Routledge.

Chappell, B. (2012). *Lowrider space: Aesthetics and politics of Mexican American custom cars*. Austin: University of Texas Press.

Charlton, A. (2018). Apple CarPlay: Everything you need to know. *Techradar*. Retrieved June 5, 2018, from https://www.techradar.com/news/apple-carplayhttps:// www.techradar.com/news/apple-carplay

Chevrolet Canada. (2018). *The Chevrolet Cruze. Hear Carol Ellyn's Canadian dream* [Video]. Retrieved September 3, 2018, from https://www.youtube.com/watch?v= bO24rbVFuLQ

Chicago, J. (1975). *Through the flower: My struggle as a woman artist*. New York: Doubleday.

Christian, A. (2014, August 6). Lexus partners with will.i.am for NX Striking Angles campaign. *4Wheels News*. Retrieved September 16, 2016, from http://www.4wheelsnews. com/auto/lexus-partners-with-will-i-am-for-nx-striking-angles-campaign-w-video-32429. html

Chrysler Historical Services. (1955, September 12). Hi-fi record player available for 1956 Chrysler Corporation cars [Press release]. Retrieved May 7, 2016, from http:// www.imperialclub.com/Repair/Accessories/HiWay/Chrysler.htm

Collins, P. (2011, July/August). The fickle needle of fate: Who the hell puts a turntable in a car's dashboard? *The Believer*. Retrieved March 6, 2015, from http://www. believermag.com/issues/201107/?read=article_collins

Connect with your car: How to plug in your music, apps, and lifestyle. (2013, April). *Consumer Reports*. Retrieved March 14, 2015, from http://www.consumerreports. org/cro/magazine/2013/04/connect-with-your-car/index.htm

Crenshaw, K. (1989). Demarginalizing the intersection of race and sex: A black feminist critique of antidiscrimination doctrine, feminist theory and antiracist politics. *University of Chicago Legal Forum*, *1*(1), 139–167.

Cubitt, S. (2000). Maybellene: Meaning and the listening subject. In R. Middleton (Ed.), *Reading pop: Approaches to textual analysis in popular music* (pp. 141–160). Oxford: Oxford University Press.

de Vries, I., & van Elferen, I. (2010). The musical Madeleine: Communication, performance, and identity in musical ringtones. *Popular Music and Society, 33*(1), 61–74.

Deaux K. (1971). Honking at the intersection: A replication and extension. *Journal of Social Psychology, 84*, 159–160.

Deaville, J., Tan, S.-L., & Rodman, R. (Eds.). (forthcoming). *The Oxford handbook of music and advertising*. Oxford: Oxford University Press.

Defy Labels. (n.d.). *Miniusa*. Retrieved May 21, 2016, from http://www.miniusa.com/content/miniusa/en/why-mini/programs-and-events/defy-labels.html

Deleuze, G., & Guattari, F. (1987). *A thousand plateaus: Capitalism and schizophrenia*. (B. Massumi, Trans.). London: Athlone.

Dept. 180 Chevrolet Cruze quiet science [Video]. (2011, September 10). Retrieved November 9, 2015, from https://www.youtube.com/watch?v=y_2cj22-tyI&feature=iv&src_vid=Oze4fmuOVxo&annotation_id=annotation_172329

Dery, M. (1993). Black to the future: Interviews with Samuel R. Delany, Greg Tate, and Tricia Rose. *South Atlantic Quarterly, 92*(4), 735–778.

Dettelbach, C. G. (1976). *In the driver's seat: The automobile in American literature and popular culture*. Westport, CT: Greenwood.

Dettmar, K. J. H. (2006). *Is rock dead?* New York: Routledge.

Dhaenens, F., & De Ridder, S. (2015). Resistant masculinities in alternative R&B? Understanding Frank Ocean and The Weeknd's representations of gender. *European Journal of Cultural Studies, 18*(3), 283–299.

Dibben, N., & Williamson, V. (2007). An exploratory survey of in-vehicle music listening. *Psychology of Music, 35*(4), 571–589.

Dinerstein, J. (2003). *Swinging the machine: Modernity, technology and African American culture between the world wars*. Boston: University of Massachusetts Press.

DMEautomotive. (2014, January 13). Baby, want to name my car? Younger and female owners most likely to name their vehicles. *PR Newswire*. Retrieved June 18, 2018, from https://www.prnewswire.com/news-releases/baby-want-to-name-my-car-younger-and-female-car-owners-most-likely-to-name-their-vehicles-nicknames-starting-with-b-most-popular-239905721.html

Dobnik, V. (2014, January 18). Noise is no. 1 quality-of-life complaint in NYC. *AP: The Big Story*. Retrieved February 25, 2015, from http://bigstory.ap.org/article/noise-no-1-quality-life-complaint-nyc

Du Bois, W. E. B. (1897). Strivings of the Negro people. *Atlantic Monthly, 80*, 194–198.

du Lac, J. F. (2008, September 7). Rollin on empty. *Washington Post*. Retrieved September 3, 2016, from http://www.washingtonpost.com/wpdyn/content/article/2008/09/05/AR2008090501060.html

Dunn, J., Jr. (1998). *Driving forces: The automobile, its enemies and the politics of mobility*. Washington, DC: Brookings Institution Press.

Early, G. (2004). *One nation under a groove: Motown and American culture*. Ann Arbor: University of Michigan Press.

Electrolux. (2011). Electrolux vacuum cleaner polysomnography study. *Electrolux*. Retrieved November 5, 2015, from http://www.electrolux.nl/Global/Promotions/UltraSilencer/vacuum_cleaner_polysomnography.pdf

Elliott, S. (2003, September 3). The media business: Advertising; McDonald's campaign aims to regain the youth market. *New York Times*. Retrieved November 7, 2018, from https://www.nytimes.com/2003/09/03/business/media-business-advertising-mcdonald-s-campaign-aims-regain-youth-market.html

Erb, E. (2007). First car radios-history and development of early car radios. *Radio-museum*. Retrieved January 15, 2019, from https://www.radiomuseum.org/forum/first_car_radios_history_and_development_of_early_car_radios.html

Eshun, K. (1998). *More brilliant than the sun: Adventures in sonic fiction*. London: Quartet.

FCA. (n.d.). Chrysler brand launches advertising campaign for the new 2013 Chrysler 300 Motown edition. *Fiat Chrysler Automobiles*. Retrieved May 20, 2017, from http://media.fcanorthamerica.com/newsrelease.do?&id=13626&mid=2

Fennessey, S. (2011, March 23). Love vs. money: The Weeknd, Frank Ocean, and R&B's future shock. *The Village Voice*. Retrieved April 14, 2018, from http://blogs.villagevoice.com/music/2011/03/the_weeknd_frank_ocean.php

Fiat Chrysler. (2015, April 17). Unprecedented marketing campaign [Press release]. Retrieved May 2, 2016, from http://www.prnewswire.com/news-releases/jeep-brand-launches-unprecedented-marketing-campaign-for-all-new-2015-jeep-renegade-through-exclusive-music-platform-with-kidinakornerinterscope-records-and-x-ambassadors-300067734.html

Finz, S. (2012, May 13). High-tech system lets restaurant set noise level. *SFGate*. Retrieved February 26, 2015, from http://www.sfgate.com/business/article/High-tech-system-lets-restaurant-set-noise-level-3554029.php#photo-2928837

Fischer, D. (2006, October 8). The trouble she's seen. *Ottawa Citizen*. Retrieved July 26, 2018, from http://jonimitchell.com/library/view.cfm?id=1459

Flegenheimer, M. (2013, January 28). Stop the honking? New York suggests it's a lost cause. *New York Times*. Retrieved March 27, 2015, from http://www.nytimes.com/2013/01/29/nyregion/new-york-removes-no-honking-signs.html?_r=0

Flink, J. J. (1970). *America adopts the automobile, 1895–1910*. Cambridge, MA: MIT Press.

Flink, J. J. (1975). *The car culture*. Cambridge, MA: MIT Press.

Flink, J. J. (1990). *The automobile age*. Cambridge, MA: MIT Press.

Foster, M. (2003). *Nation on wheels: The automobile culture in America since 1945*. Belmont, CA: Wadsworth/Thompson Learning.

Frank, T. (1998). *The conquest of cool: Business culture, counterculture, and the rise of hip consumerism*. Chicago: University of Chicago Press.

Freeman, D. (2018, February 7). Here's what will happen to the Tesla that SpaceX shot into space. *NBC News*. Retrieved March 5, 2019, from https://www.nbcnews.com/mach/science/here-s-what-will-happen-tesla-spacex-shot-space-ncna845566

Frost & Sullivan. (2015). Women in cars: Overtaking men on the fast lane. *Research and Markets*. Retrieved October 16, 2016, from http://www.researchandmarkets.com/reports/3143701/women-in-cars-overtaking-men-on-the-fast-lane

Froude, J. A. (1884). *Thomas Carlyle: A history of his life in London, 1834–1881*. New York: Scribners.

Furnham, A., & Allass, K. (1999). The influence of musical distraction of varying complexity on the cognitive performance of extraverts and introverts. *European Journal of Personality*, *13*, 27–38.

Garber-Paul, E. (2014, August 8). Jesse J: Why "Bang Bang" is a song young women need to hear. *Rolling Stone*. Retrieved November 19, 2018, from https://www.rollingstone.com/music/music-news/jessie-j-why-bang-bang-is-a-song-young-women-need-to-hear-83185/

Garfield, E. (1983, July 11). The tyranny of the horn: The automobile that is. *Current Comments*, 5–11. In *Essays of an information scientist* (Vol. 6, pp. 216–222). Philadelphia: ISI Press.

Gartman, D. (2004). Three ages of the automobile: The cultural logics of the car. *Theory, Culture & Society, 21*(4–5), 169–195.

Gates, H. L., Jr. (1988). *The signifying monkey: A theory of African-American literary criticism.* New York: Oxford University Press.

Georgakas, D., & Surkin, M. (1998). *Detroit: I do mind dying.* Cambridge, MA: South End.

Gilbert, J., & Pearson, E. (1999). *Discographies: Dance music, culture and the politics of sound.* London: Routledge.

Gilroy, P. (2001). Driving while black. In D. Miller (Ed.), *Car cultures* (pp. 81–104). New York: Berg.

Gilroy, P. (2010). *Darker than blue: On the moral economies of black Atlantic culture.* Cambridge, MA: Harvard University Press.

Giucci, G. (2012). *The cultural life of the automobile: Roads to modernity* (A. Mayagotia & D. Nagao, Trans.). Austin: University of Texas Press.

Gloor, S. (2014). Songs as branding platforms? A historical analysis of people, places, and products in pop music lyrics. *Journal of the Music & Entertainment Industry Educators Association (MEIEA), 14*(1), 39–60.

Goldhill, O. (2016, September 24). The first pop song ever written by artificial intelligence is pretty good, actually. *Quartz.* Retrieved November 13, 2018, from https://qz.com/790523/daddys-car-the-first-song-ever-written-by-artificial-intelligence-is-a ctually-pretty-good/

Gopinath, S. (2013). *The ringtone dialectic: Economy and cultural form.* Boston: MIT Press.

Gordy, B., Jr. (1994). *To be loved: The music, the magic, the memories of Motown.* New York: Warner.

Gramophone Co. (2007). *Grace's guide to British industrial history.* Retrieved March 5, 2015, from http://www.gracesguide.co.uk/Gramophone_Co

Grand opera in Chevrolet cars. (1922, May 14). *The Charlotte News,* p. 31.

Griggs, B. (2011). Why computer voices are mostly female. *CNN.* Retrieved May 29, 2017, from https://www.cnn.com/2011/10/21/tech/innovation/female-computer-voices/index.html

Grushkin, P. (2006). *Rock'n down the highway: The cars that made rock and roll.* St. Paul, MN: Voyageur.

Halberstam, J. (1998). *Female masculinity.* Durham, NC: Duke University Press.

Hall, M. (2001, April). The slow life and fast death of DJ Screw. *Texas Monthly.* Retrieved June 27, 2018, from https://www.texasmonthly.com/articles/the-slow-life-a nd-fast-death-of-dj-screw/

Halliday, J. (2005, May 30). Jaguar seeks influencers with music, events. *Automotive News.* Retrieved September 14, 2016, from http://www.autonews.com/article/20050530/SUB/505300704/jaguar-seeks-influencers-with-music-events

Ham, E. L. (2011). *Broadcasting baseball: A history of the national pastime on radio and television.* Jefferson, NC: McFarlane.

Hard, A. (2014, October 22). Road rave: Like a catchy pop-song hook, synthetic engine noises are playing on repeat. *Digital Trends.* Retrieved February 9, 2015, from http://www.digitaltrends.com/cars/road-rave-fake-engine-noise-debate

Harris, L. (2007). Morning and evening. In G. Betts (Ed.), *Lawren Harris in the ward: His urban poetry and paintings* (pp. 7–8). Holstein, ON: Exile Editions.

Harwell, D. (2015, January 21). America's best-selling cars and trucks are built on lies: The rise of fake engine noise. *Washington Post.* Retrieved February 5, 2015, from http://www.washingtonpost.com/business/economy/americas-best-selling-cars-and-trucks-are-built-on-lies-the-rise-of-fake-engine-noise/2015/01/21/6db09a10-a0ba-11e4-b146-577832eafcb4_story.html

Hayles, N. K. (2012). *How we think: Digital media and contemporary technogenesis.* Chicago: University of Chicago Press.

Hebdige, D. (1988). *Hiding in the light: On images and things.* New York: Routledge.

Heitmann, J. (2009). *The automobile and American life.* Jefferson, NC: McFarland.

Heitmann, J. (2010). A brief history of 8 track tapes and the automobile [Blog post]. *The Automobile and American Life.* Retrieved September 30, 2017, from https://autom obileandamericanlife.blogspot.ca/2010/07/brief-history-of-8-track-tapes-and.html

Hesmondhalgh, D. (2007). *The cultural industries.* Los Angeles: Sage.

Hillstrom, K., & Hillstrom, L. C. (Eds.). (2006). *The industrial revolution in America: Automobiles, mining and petroleum, textiles.* Santa Barbara, CA: ABC-CLIO.

Honda uses music festival sponsorship to connect with fans via social media. (2013, May 13). *Auto Remarketing.* Retrieved September 7, 2015, from http://www.autorema rketing.com/retail/honda-uses-music-festival-sponsorship-connect-fans-social-media

Hopper, J. (2013). How selling out saved indie rock. *Buzzfeed News.* Retrieved November 16, 2016, from https://www.buzzfeed.com/jessicahopper/how-selling-out-saved-in die-rock?utm_term=.ks0gK5aBva#.ebJ6Glvypv

Howes, D. (2005). Hyperesthesia, or, the sensual logic of late capitalism. In D. Howes (Ed.), *Empire of the senses: The sensual culture reader* (pp. 281–303). New York: Berg.

Husband, C., Alam, Y., Huettermann, J., & Fomina, J. (2014). *Lived diversities: Space, place and identities in the multi-ethnic city.* Bristol: Polity.

Inglis, D. (2004). Auto couture: Thinking the car in post-war France. *Theory, Culture & Society, 21*(4–5), 197–219.

Is there anyone finah? (1957, December 16). *Time.* Retrieved August 20, 2018, from http://content.time.com/time/magazine/article/0,9171,893808,00.html

Isham Research. (n.d.). What is ECU training? Retrieved October 25, 2017, from http://www.isham-research.co.uk/quattro/wr_voice.html

J.C. Whitney Autoparts. (n.d). Musical horns. Retrieved March 27, 2015, from http://www.jcwhitney.com/musical-horns/c2599j1s17.jcwx

Jamshed, Z. (2015, November 25). For Porsche, the sounds of revving engines are a crucial design element. *CNN.* Retrieved May 31, 2017, from http://www.cnn.com/2015/11/25/autos/porsche-sounds-book/index.html

Janson, H. W. (1995). *History of art* (5th ed, revised and expanded by A. F. Janson). London: Thames & Hudson.

Johannsen, G. (2007). Human–machine interaction. In *Encyclopedia of life support systems (EOLSS): Control systems, robotics, and automation* (Vol. 31). Paris: EOLSS.

Johnson, C. (1913). The motor car warning signal. *Motor, 20*(2), 66.

Johnson, D. (2014, March 27). Sebastian Vettel says sound of Formula One's new engines is "s***". *Telegraph.* Retrieved February 6, 2015, from http://www.telegraph.co.uk/sp ort/motorsport/formulaone/sebastian-vettel/10726491/Sebastian-Vettel-says-sound-of-Formula-Ones-new-engines-is-s.html

Johnson, J. S. (1949, September). Why Negroes buy Cadillacs. *Ebony*, p. 34.

Jones, M. (2013). *The history of the UK radio licence.* Retrieved November 16, 2018, from http://www.radiolicence.org.uk/emailcontact.html

Jones, M. E. (2000). *Libido dominandi: Sexual liberation and political control.* South Bend, IN: St Augustine Press.

Kahle, L. R., & Goff Timmer, S. (1983). A theory and a method for studying values. In L. R. Kahle (Ed.), *Social values and social change: Adaptation to life in America* (pp. 43–69). New York: Praeger.

Kähler, M. (2014, July 17). Elevating quiet luxury: Kia claims to be quieter than Audi, BMW and Lexus. *Elevating sound.* Retrieved December 18, 2017, from http://eleva tingsound.com/elevating-quiet-luxury-kia-claims-to-be-quieter-than-audi-bmw-and-lexus/

Karolevitz, R. F. (1968). *This was pioneer motoring.* Seattle, WA: Superior.

Katz, J. (1999). *How emotions work.* Chicago: University of Chicago Press.

Katz, J. (2003). Bodies, machines and communication contexts: What is to become of us? In J. Katz (Ed.), *Machines that become us: The social context of personal communication technology* (pp. 320–331). New Brunswick, NJ: Transaction.

Katz, M. (2010). *Capturing sound: How technology has changed music.* Los Angeles: University of California Press.

Kaufman, G. (2003, June 6). Push the Courvoisier: Are rappers paid for product placement? *MTV News.* Retrieved May 12, 2016, from http://www.mtv.com/news/1472393/push-the-courvoisier-are-rappers-paid-for-product-placement

Keightley, K. (1996). "Turn it down!" she shrieked: Gender, domestic space, and high fidelity, 1948–1959. *Popular Music, 15*(2), 149–177.

Kelley, R. D. G. (2004). Looking for the "real" nigga: Social scientists construct the ghetto. In M. Forman & M. A. Neal (Eds.), *That's the joint! The hip-hop studies reader* (pp. 119–136). New York: Routledge.

Kent, J. L. (2015). Still feeling the car: The role of comfort in sustaining private car use. *Mobilities, 10*(5), 726–747.

Kirkova, D. (2014, May 30). Are YOU swayed by a famous face? Women buy twice as many celebrity-endorsed products as men. *Mailonline.* Retrieved June 15, 2018, from http://www.dailymail.co.uk/femail/article-2641476/Susceptible-women-buy-twice-celebrity-endorsed-products-men.html

Klara, R. (2013, June 16). Gay advertising's long march out of the closet. *AdWeek.* Retrieved July 28, 2018, from http://www.adweek.com/brand-marketing/gay-adverti sing-s-long-march-out-closet-150235

Klein, B. (2008). In perfect harmony: Popular music and cola advertising. *Popular Music and Society, 31*(1), 1–20.

Klein, B. (2009). *As heard on TV: Popular music and advertising.* Farnham, UK: Ashgate.

Kozack, G. (2016, September 20). Car culture today: Frank Ocean's blond. *Autoweek.* Retrieved August 15, 2018, from http://autoweek.com/article/car-life/frank-ocean-cut ting-edge-modern-car-culture

Krims, A. (2007). *Music and urban geography.* New York: Routledge.

KROQ. (2015, June 12). Watch X Ambassadors' inspirational "Renegades" video. *The world famous KROQ.* Retrieved May 15, 2016, from http://kroq.cbslocal.com/2015/06/12/watch-x-ambassadors-inspirational-renegades-video

Kurpiers, J. (2009). *Reality by design: Advertising image, music and sound design in the production of culture* (Doctoral dissertation), Duke University, Durham, NC, USA.

Kushma, D. (2008, September 14). America's 100-year love affair with the car often put to music. *Automotive News.* Retrieved August 18, 2016, from http://www.auto news.com/article/20080914/ANA09/809150337/americas-100-year-love-affair-with-the-car-often-put-to-music

Kwong, M. (2016, January 26). At Detroit's auto show, industry offers more of what women want. *CBC Business News*. Retrieved September 16, 2016, from http://www. cbc.ca/news/business/detroit-auto-show-women-cars-1.3414529

La Rue, A. (2009, April 17). Police to start giving out fines to quiet the blare of motorist horns. *Peruvian Times*. Retrieved March 27, 2015, from http://www.peruviantimes. com/17/police-to-start-giving-out-fines-to-quiet-the-blare-of-motorist-horns/2623

LaBelle, B. (2008). Pump up the bass: Rhythm, cars, and auditory scaffolding. *The Senses and Society, 3*(2), 187–203.

LaBelle, B. (2010). *Acoustic territories: Sound culture and everyday life.* New York: Continuum.

Landenberger, D. (2015). *Porsche sounds.* Hamburg, Germany: Edel Classics.

Langeveld, L., van Egmond, R., Jansen, R., & Özcan, E. (2013). Product sound design: Intentional and consequential sounds. In D. Coelho (Ed.), *Advances in industrial design engineering* (pp. 47–73). Rijeka, Croatia: InTech. Retrieved January 9, 2016, from http://www.intechopen.com/books/advances-in-industrial-design-engi neering/product-sound-design-intentional-and-consequential-sounds

Laver, M. (2015). *Jazz sells: Music, marketing, and meaning.* New York: Routledge.

Lefebvre, H. (1991). *The production of space.* Oxford: Blackwell.

Lefebvre, H. (2004). *Rhythmanalysis: Space, time and everyday life* (S. Elden and G. Moore, Trans.). London: Continuum.

Lemmens, P. (2011). "This system does not produce pleasure anymore": An interview with Bernard Stiegler. *Krisis: Journal for Contemporary Philosophy, 1*, 33–41.

Levitt, D. (1909). *The woman and the car: A chatty little handbook for all women who motor or who want to motor.* London: John Lane.

Lewis, D. (1976). *The public image of Henry Ford: An American folk hero and his company.* Detroit: Wayne State University Press.

Lewis, D. (1983). Sex and the automobile: From rumble seats to rockin' vans. In D. Lewis & L. Goldstein (Eds.), *The automobile and American culture* (pp. 123–133). Ann Arbor: University of Michigan Press.

Lezotte, C. (2012). The evolution of the "chick car" or: what came first, the chick or the car? *Journal of Popular Culture, 45*(3), 516–531.

Lezotte, C. (2013). Born to take the highway: Women, the automobile, and rock 'n' roll. *Journal of American Culture, 36*(3), 161–176.

Lhamon, W. T., Jr. (1990). *Deliberate speed: The origins of a cultural style in the American 1950s.* Washington, DC: Smithsonian Institution Press.

Liberatore, S. (2017, 24 February). Why AI assistants are usually women: Researchers find both sexes find them warmer and more understanding. *Daily Mail*. Retrieved July 7, 2018, from http://www.dailymail.co.uk/sciencetech/article-4258122/Experts-reveal-voice-assistants-female-voices.html

Lim, W. M. (2012). Understanding consumer values and socialization: A case of luxury products. *Management & Marketing Challenges for the Knowledge Society, 7* (2), 209–220.

Ling, R. (2012). *Taken for grantedness: The embedding of mobile communication into society.* Boston: MIT Press.

Lipsitz, G. (2006). *The possessive investment in whiteness: How white people profit from identity politics.* Philadelphia: Temple University Press.

Lowery, S. (1988, 26 September). Fed up with those boom-boom-booming car stereos. *Orlando Sentinel*.

Lury, C. (2004). *Brands: The logos of the global economy.* New York: Routledge.

Lutz, C., & Fernandez, A. L. (2010). *Carjacked: The culture of the automobile and its effects on our lives.* New York: Palgrave Macmillan.

Maley, T. (2013, July 30). How GM makes a car sound like what a car is supposed to sound like. *Medium.* Retrieved May 31, 2017, from https://medium.com/thought ful-design/how-gm-makes-a-car-sound-like-what-a-car-is-supp osed-to-sound-like-c23c5fb86266

Malik, T. (2018, February 7). Elon Musk's Tesla Roadster is headed to the asteroid belt. *Space.com.* Retrieved February 18, 2019, from https://www.space.com/ 39619-spacex-falcon-heavy-roadster-to-asteroid-belt.html

Marcuse, H. (1964). *One-dimensional man.* New York: Routledge & Kegan Paul.

Marinetti, F. T. (1909/2009). The founding and manifesto of futurism. In L. Rainey, C. Poggi, & L. Wittman (Eds.), *Futurism: An anthology* (pp. 49–53). New Haven: Yale University Press.

Marling, K. A. (1996). *As seen on TV: The visual culture of everyday life in the 1950s.* Cambridge, MA: Harvard University Press.

Marling, K. A. (2002). America's love affair with the automobile in the television age. In P. Wollen & J. Kerr (Eds.), *Autopia: Cars and culture* (pp. 354–362). London: Reaktion.

Martin, M. (2015, August). When cars talked using tiny phonographic records: Nissan's voice warning system. *Autoweek.* Retrieved November 15, 2018, from https://autoweek. com/article/wait-theres-more/when-cars-talked-using-tiny-phonograph-records-nissans-voice-warning-system

Marx, K. (2002). Grundrisse der Kritik der politischen Ökonomie. In *Economic works of Karl Marx 1857–61* (Notebook VII). Retrieved February 23, 2015, from https:// www.marxists.org/archive/marx/works/1857/grundrisse/ch14.htm

Matteucci, M. (1970). *History of the motor car.* New York: Crown.

Mayer, J. (2006, October 13). *John Mayer Volkswagen commercial* [Video]. Retrieved November 8, 2015, from https://www.youtube.com/watch?v=6jLSUSqH55Q

Mayyasi, A. (2016, June 22). How Subarus came to be seen as cars for lesbians. *The Atlantic.* Retrieved August 6, 2018, from https://www.theatlantic.com/business/a rchive/2016/06/how-subarus-came-to-be-seen-as-cars-for-lesbians/488042/

MC Big Data. (2015, June 9). Riding dirty: The science of cars and rap lyrics. *Cuepoint.* Retrieved August 12, 2016, from https://medium.com/cuepoint/riding-dir ty-the-science-of-cars-and-rap-lyrics-21b8404a9c4d#.v74rxhw4p

McClellan, R. (2011, December). Guaranteeing pedestrian protection: Sound warning systems for EVs and hybrids. *Automotive Industries.* Retrieved January 2, 2017, from http://www.ai-online.com/Adv/Previous/show_issue.php?id=4477#sthash.dlDcHu5U. dpbs

McCracken, G. (2005). When cars could fly: Raymond Loewy, John Kenneth Galbraith, and the 1954 Buick. In G. McCracken (Ed.), *Culture and consumption II: Markets, meaning, and brand management* (pp. 53–90). Indianapolis: Indiana University Press.

McLeod, K. (2003). Space oddities: Aliens, futurism and meaning in popular music. *Popular Music, 22*(3), 337–355.

McLeod, K. (2011). *We are the champions: The politics of sports and popular music.* Farnham, UK: Ashgate.

McLuhan, M. (1994). *Understanding media: The extensions of man.* Boston: MIT Press.

Mearian, L. (2014, December 1). 150M passenger cars will be connected to the Internet by 2020. *ComputerWorld.* Retrieved March 29, 2015, from http://www.comp uterworld.com/article/2853775/150m-passenger-cars-will-connected-to-the-internet-by-2020.html

Mehta, S. (2014, April 14). A primer on Houston's SLAB culture. *The Truth About Cars.* Retrieved May 5, 2018, from http://www.thetruthaboutcars.com/2014/04/a-primer-on-houston-slab-culture/

Meier, L. M. (2011). Promotional ubiquitous musics: Recording artists, brands, and "rendering authenticity". *Popular Music and Society, 34*(4), 399–415.

Merriman, P. (2007). *Driving spaces: A cultural-historical geography of England's M1 motorway.* Oxford: Blackwell.

Miller, D. (2001). Driven societies. In D. Miller (Ed.), *Car cultures* (pp. 1–7). New York: Berg.

Mitsubishi Motors North America. (2018). *2018 Mitsubishi Eclipse Cross: Freestyle test drive* [Video]. Retrieved June 6, 2016, from https://www.youtube.com/watch?v= jmIvhCoWcwM

Monllos, K. (2015, April 17). How Jeep found the perfect song to launch its Renegade campaign. *Adweek.* Retrieved February 6, 2016, from http://www.adweek.com/news/a dvertising-branding/how-jeep-found-perfect-song-launch-its-renegade-campaign-164125

Moore, R. (2010). *Sells like teen spirit: Music youth culture and social crises.* New York: New York University Press.

Morley, D., & Robins, K. (1995). *Spaces of identity: Global media, electronic landscapes and cultural boundaries.* London: Routledge.

Morris, D. (2014). Cars with the boom: Identity and territory in American postwar automobile sound. *Technology and Culture, 55*(2), 326–353.

Morse, D. (1971). *Motown and the arrival of black music.* New York: Macmillan.

Myers, M., & Dean, S. (2007). Cadillac flambé: Race and brand identity. *Proceedings of the 23rd Conference on Historical Analysis and Research in Marketing (CHARM),* 157–161.

Neff, J. (2006, October 3). VW gives customers the axe. *Autoblog.* Retrieved November 6, 2015, from http://www.autoblog.com/2006/10/03/vw-gives-custom ers-the-axe-electric-guitar-comes-with-every-veh

New Porsche 911 features "Sound Symposer" technology. (2011, November 9). *SAE International.* Retrieved February 9, 2015, from http://articles.sae.org/10374

New Rolls Royce ghost silent at 140 mph car commercial [Video]. (2011, January 7). Retrieved February 26, 2015, from https://www.youtube.com/watch?v=YZ2jCrsWT5A

NHTSA. (2009, September). *Incidence of pedestrian and bicyclist crashes by hybrid electric passenger vehicles.* (Technical Report DOT HS 811 204).

NHTSA. (2016, November 14). NHTSA sets "quiet car" safety standard to protect pedestrians. Retrieved July 7, 2017, from https://www.nhtsa.gov/press-releases/nhtsa-sets-quiet-car-safety-standard-protect-pedestrians

Nielson, E. (2010). "Can't C me": Surveillance and rap music. *Journal of Black Studies, 40*(6), 1254–1274.

NissanCanada. (2018). *Introducing 2018 Nissan KICKS—Move to your own beat* [Video]. Retrieved August 28, 2018, from https://www.youtube.com/watch?v=-vizSKFYuyU

O'Dell, T. (2001). *Reggare* and the panic of mobility: Modernity and everyday life in Sweden. In D. Miller (Ed.), *Car cultures* (pp. 105–132). New York: Berg.

Obadare, E. (2013). Vehicular religiosities: Importuning God behind (and concerning) the automobile. *Reverberations: New Directions in the Study of Prayer.* Retrieved

January 18, 2019, from http://forums.ssrc.org/ndsp/2013/04/30/vehicular-religiositie s-importuning-god-behind-and-concerning-the-automobile/#more-3028

Ocean, F. (2012). Frank Ocean's open letter on Tumblr. *Genius.* Retrieved August 17, 2018, from https://genius.com/Frank-ocean-frank-oceans-open-letter-on-tumblr-annotated

Packer, J. (2008). *Mobility without mayhem: Safety, cars, and citizenship.* Durham, NC: Duke University Press.

Parkin, K. (2017). *Women at the wheel: A century of buying, driving, and fixing cars.* Philadelphia: University of Pennsylvania Press.

Passon, J. W. (2011). *The Corvette in literature and culture: Symbolic dimensions of America's sports car.* Jefferson, NC: McFarland.

Paterson, M. (2007). *Automobile politics: Ecology and cultural political economy.* New York: Cambridge University Press.

Pedelty, M. (2012). *Ecomusicology: Rock, folk, and the environment.* Philadelphia: Temple University Press.

Perez, R. (2007, June 4). The thanks they get? Wilco and the Volkswagen campaign flap. *The Playlist.* Retrieved November 11, 2016, from http://theplaylist.net/tha nks-they-get-wilco-and-volkswagen-20070605/

Plymouth. (1960). *The solid Plymouth 1960* [Brochure]. Retrieved June 8, 2016, from http://www.1960plymouth.com

Poon, L. (2015, September 17). What a city's "soundscape" reveals about its character. *CityLab.* Retrieved February 24, 2019, from https://www.citylab.com/life/2015/09/ what-a-citys-soundscape-reveals-about-its-character/405733/

Popa, B. (2012, February 4). History of police lights and sirens: The terrifying duo that scares away criminals. *Autoevolution.* Retrieved April 30, 2018, from https:// www.autoevolution.com/news/history-of-police-lights-and-sir ens-the-terrifying-duo-that-scares-away-criminals-42394-page3.html

Postrel, V. (2008, July 1). Inconspicuous consumption: A new theory of the leisure class. *The Atlantic.* Retrieved January 14, 2015, from http://www.theatlantic.com/ma gazine/archive/2008/07/inconspicuous-consumption/306845

Potter, D. L. (1987). *Dromomania: Reading Paul Virilio.* Paper presented at the Comparative Literature, Cornell University Culture Industry Conference, Cornell University, New York.

Powers, D. (2010). Strange powers: The branded sensorium and the intrigue of musical sound. In M. Aronczyk & D. Powers (Eds.), *Blowing up the brand* (pp. 284–306). New York: Peter Lang.

PR Newswire (2003, January 15). Chrysler brand signs on as presenting sponsor of "A New Day…." Celine Dion's new show opening March 25 at Caesars Palace in Las Vegas. Retrieved September 16, 2016, from http://www.prnewswire.com/news-releases/ chrysler-brand-signs-on-as-presenting-sponsor-of-a-new-day-celine-dions-new-show-opening-march-25-at-caesars-palace-in-las-vegas-73860287.html

Priest, E. (2013). *Boring formless nonsense: Experimental music and the aesthetics of failure.* New York: Bloomsbury.

Quiet Cab: 2014 Chevrolet Silverado TV Commercial [Video]. (2014). Retrieved September 2, 2018, from https://www.youtube.com/watch?v=JStlohIr6OM

Rae, J. B. (1959). *American automobile manufacturers: The first forty years.* Philadelphia: Chilton.

Rae, J. B. (1965). *The American automobile: A brief history.* Chicago: University of Chicago Press.

Rae, J. B. (1971). *The road and the car in American life.* Cambridge, MA: MIT Press.

Ramey, J. (2015, December 18). VW Phaeton production to end. *Autoweek*. Retrieved September 28, 2016, from http://autoweek.com/article/vw-diesel-scandal/vw-susp end-phaeton-anticipation-diesel-crisis-pressures

Randell, R. (2017). The microsociology of automobility: The production of the auto- mobile self. *Mobilities, 12*(5), 663–676.

Raunig, G. (2010). *A thousand machines: A concise philosophy of the machine as social movement* (A. Derieg, Trans.). Los Angeles: Semiotext(e).

Rehding, A. (2014). Of sirens old and new. In S. Gopinath & J. Stanyek (Eds.), *The Oxford handbook of mobile music studies* (Vol. 2, pp. 77–106). Oxford: Oxford University Press.

Rehding, A. (2016). Instruments of music theory. *Music Theory Online, 22*(4). Retrieved January 29, 2019, from http://mtosmt.org/issues/mto.16.22.4/mto.16.22.4.rehding.html

Jeep. (n.d.). *Renegade-Life* [Video]. Retrieved May 7, 2016, from http://www.jeep.com/ en/renegade-life

Reynolds, S. (1999). *Generation ecstasy: into the world of techno and rave culture*. New York: Routledge.

Rituals of Mine's video for "Ride or Die" is a love letter to Oakland. (2016, September 29). Retrieved July 28, 2018, from https://noisey.vice.com/en_us/article/vdbvgx/ritua ls-of-mines-video-for-ride-or-die-is-a-love-letter-to-oakland

Rojek, C. (2011). *Pop music, pop culture*. Cambridge: Polity.

Rokeach, M. (1968). The role of values in public opinion research. *Public Opinion Quarterly, 32*(4), 547–559.

Rokeach, M. (1973). *The nature of human values*. New York: Free Press.

Rose, Tricia. (1994). *Black noise*. Hanover, NH: Wesleyan University Press.

Rosenberg, J. (2018, June 4). Why the Model T is called the Tin Lizzie. *ThoughtCo*. Retrieved November 6, 2018, from https://www.thoughtco.com/nick name-tin-lizzie-3976121

Sarig, R. (2007). *Third coast: OutKast, Timbaland, & how hip-hop became a southern thing*. Cambridge: Da Capo Press.

Savage, J. (1993, September). Liner notes to the album *Interface: The roots of techno* by Cybotron [CD CDSEWD 069]. Southbound.

Schiller, M. (2014). "Fun fun fun on the Autobahn": Kraftwerk challenging German- ness. *Popular Music, 37*(5), 618–637.

Schopenhauer, A. (2008). On noise. In *Studies in pessimism on human nature, and religion: A dialogue, etc.* (T. Bailey Saunders, Trans.) (p. 47). New York: Cosimo.

Sheller, M. (2004). Automotive emotions: Feeling the car. *Theory, Culture & Society, 21*(4–5), 221–242.

Sheller, M. (2007). Bodies, cybercars and the mundane incorporation of automated mobilities. *Social & Cultural Geography*, 8(2), 175–197.

Sheller, M., & Urry, J. (2006). The new mobilities paradigm. *Environment and Plan- ning, 38*, 207–226.

Shuldiner, H. (2007, November 30). Bose says suspension drawing interest from OEMs. *WardsAuto*. Retrieved March 4, 2015, from http://wardsauto.com/news-amp-analysis/ bose-says-suspension-drawing-interest-oems

Sicko, D. (1999). *Techno rebels: The renegades of electronic funk*. New York: Billboard Books.

Simmons, L. (1983). Not from the back seat. In D. Lewis & L. Goldstein (Eds.), *The automobile and American culture* (pp. 153–158). Ann Arbor: University of Michigan Press.

SiriusXM Satellite Radio. (n.d.). Corporate overview. Retrieved March 29, 2015, from https://www.siriusxm.com/corporate

Sixième Son [Website]. (2015). Retrieved September 5, 2015, from http://www.sixiem eson.com/en/audio-identity-sncf.html

Slethaug, G. (2017). *Music and the Road: Essays on the interplay of music and the popular culture of the American road.* New York: Bloomsbury.

Smith, N. (2013, October 17). 10 swang-and-bang anthems for Sunday's SLAB Parade. *Houston Press.* Retrieved June 17, 2018, from http://www.houstonpress.com/music/10-swang-and-bang-anthems-for-sundays-slab-parade-6495494

Smith, S. E. (1999). *Dancing in the street: Motown and the cultural politics of Detroit.* Boston: Harvard University Press.

Soderberg, B. (2012, December 6). Trend of the year: Alt R&B. *Spin.* Retrieved April 12, 2018, from http://www.spin.com/articles/trend-of-the-year-alt-rb-2012-frank-ocean-week nd-miguel

Solid Plymouth. (1960). *Come along for a ride in the solid new Plymouth* [Audio recording PLY 101]. Hanover-Signature Record Corp.

Sound file: The new Audi heartbeat. (2010, July 9). *Fourtitude.* Retrieved January 9, 2016, from http://www.fourtitude.com/news/publish/Audi_News/article_6102.shtml

Sousanis, J. (2011, August 15). World vehicle population tops 1 billion units. *Wards Auto.* Retrieved December 1, 2018, from http://wardsauto.com/ar/world_vehicle_p opulation_110815

Sparey, S. (2014, October 25). Lexus and will.i.am unveil "experimental" marketing drive to target younger consumers. *Marketing This Week.* Retrieved April 15, 2016, from http://www.marketingmagazine.co.uk/article/1314197/lexus-william-unveil-exp erimental-marketing-drive-target-younger-consumers

Stancati, M. (2013, May 6). Quiet? Seriously? India's quixotic campaign to stop honking. *Wall Street Journal.* Retrieved March 27, 2015, http://www.wsj.com/news/articles/SB10001424127887323528404578454972522305946

Stanley, T. L. (2011, October 11). Jennifer Lopez still trying to convince you she drives a Fiat. *Adweek.* Retrieved June 25, 2018, from http://www.adweek.com/creativity/jennifer-lopez-still-trying-convince-you-she-drives-fiat-135716

Stein, J. (2003, November 24). Inside Chrysler's Celine Dion advertising disaster. *Ad Age.* Retrieved June 7, 2018, from http://adage.com/article/news/inside-chrysler-s-ce line-dion-advertising-disaster/38897/

Stereogum. (2007, June 5). Wilco weighs in on the Volkswagon's vitriol. *Stereogum.* Retrieved November 7, 2018, from https://www.stereogum.com/5536/wilco_weighs_ in_on_the_volkswagon_vitriol/news/

Sterne, J. (2003). *The audible past: Cultural origins of sound reproduction* (Durham, NC: Duke University Press).

Stewart, J. (2017, November 9). Uber's plan to launch flying cars in LA by 2020 could really take off. *Wired.* Retrieved December 1, 2018, from https://www.wired.com/story/uber-flying-cars-los-angeles/

Stoute, S. (2011). *The tanning of America: How hip hop created a culture that rewrote the rules of the new economy.* New York: Gotham.

Stutts, J., et al. (2003). *Distractions in everyday driving.* (Report prepared for AAA Foundation for Traffic Safety). Washington, DC. Retrieved August 7, 2017, from http://www.aaafoundation.org/pdf/DistractionsInEverydayDriving.pdf

Swash, R. (2007, June 6). Wilco unapologetic about VW ads. *The Guardian.* Retrieved March 2, 2018, from https://www.theguardian.com/music/2007/jun/06/wilco

Tatum, C. M. (2011). *Lowriders in Chicano culture: From low to slow to show.* Santa Barbara, CA: Greenwood/ABC-CLIO.

Taylor, T. (2007). The changing shape of the culture industry; or how did electronica music get into television commercials? *Television and New Media, 8*(3), 235–258.

Taylor, T. (2012). *The sounds of capitalism: Advertising, music, and the conquest of culture.* Chicago: University of Chicago Press.

Taylor, T. (2016). *Music and capitalism: A history of the present.* Chicago: University of Chicago Press.

Tesla. (2018), Model S [Brochure]. Retrieved April 15, 2018, from https://www.tesla.com/en_IE/models/faq

Tesla Forum (2010, October 19). Give us roadster's engine sound for download! Retrieved November 9, 2015, from https://forums.tesla.com/en_CA/forum/forums/give-us-roadsters-engine-sound-download

Thayer, A. (2012, May). Classic lowriders: Low, slow, and soulful. *The Utne Reader,* pp. 76–79. Retrieved June 12, 2017, from https://www.utne.com/arts/classic-low riders-zm0z12mjzros

The history of the electric car. (2014). *Energy.gov.* Retrieved September 28, 2016, from http://energy.gov/articles/history-electric-car

The horseless carriage and public health. (1899). *Scientific American, 80*(7), 98–99.

The Mustang: A new breed out of Detroit. (1964, April 20). *Newsweek,* pp. 97–101.

Thrift, N. (2004). Driving in the city. *Theory, Culture, and Society, 21*(4–5), 41–59.

Tingwall, E. (2015, January). The physics of engine notes, or: Why a Toyota V-6 and a Porsche Flat-6 sound so different. *Car and Driver.* Retrieved March 2016, from https://www.caranddriver.com/features/this-is-why-various-engine-types-sound-so-different-feature

Tori Amos on being a rape survivor. (2016, February). *HealthyPlace.* Retrieved April 2017, from https://www.healthyplace.com/abuse/articles/tori-amos-on-being-a-rape-survivor

Toyota. (2011, May 3). *Hatsune Miku: Dream harmonic—Compact dream* [Video]. Retrieved February 5, 2015, from https://www.youtube.com/watch?v=Uq0jNcS4BeY

Turner, M. L., Fernandez, J. E., & Nelson, K. (1996). The effects of music amplitude on the reaction to unexpected visual events. *Journal of General Psychology, 123* (1),51–62.

Urry, J. (2000). *Sociology beyond societies: Mobilities for the twenty-first century.* London: Routledge.

Urry, J. (2002). Mobility and proximity. *Sociology, 36,* 255–274.

Urry, J. (2003). Social networks, travel and talk. *British Journal of Sociology, 54,* 155–175.

Urry, J. (2004). The "system" of automobility. *Theory, Culture & Society, 21*(4/5), 25–39.

Urry, J. (2007). *Mobilities.* London: Polity Press.

Vanhemert, K. (2015, August 28). GE's new emphasis in appliances: Sound design. Retrieved April 17, 2016, from http://www.fastcodesign.com/1671333/ges-new-empha sis-in-appliances-sound-design

Virilio, P. (1986). *The politics of speed.* Los Angeles: Semiotext(e).

Virilio, P. (2000). *Polar inertia.* London: Sage.

Virilio, P., & Lotringer, S. (2008). *Pure war.* Los Angeles: Semiotext(e).

Voelcker, J. (2014). 1.2 billion vehicles on world's roads now, 2 billion by 2035: Report. *Green Car Report.* Retrieved September 20, 2018, from http://www.greencarreports.com/news/1093560_1-2-billion-vehicles-on-worlds-roads-now-2-billion-by-2035-report

Volkswagen Phaeton. (2005). [Brochure]. Retrieved March 19, 2019, from http://hel ston.volkswagon.co.uk

Volti, R. (2004). *Cars and culture: The life story of a technology*. Westport, CT: Greenwood.

Waitt, G., Harada, T., & Duffy, M. (2017). "Let's have some music": Sound, gender and car mobility. *Mobilities, 12*(3), 324–342.

Wajcman, J. (1991). *Feminism confronts technology*. Cambridge: Polity.

Walsh, M. (2008). Gendering mobility: Women, work, and automobility in the United States. *History, 93*(3), 377–395.

Watkins, J. (2012). *The 100 greatest advertisements 1852–1958: Who wrote them and what they did*. New York: Dover.

We are driven [Video]. (2013). Retrieved July 10, 2018, from https://www.youtube.com/watch?v=kqek1F2ZUDo

Weingarten, T. (2016, January 28). How these female designers are challenging stereotypes. *CNN*. Retrieved August 16, 2018, from http://www.cnn.com/style/article/female-car-designers/index.html

Weintraub, L. (2013, October 30). The 14 components of a brand platform. *Parkerwhite Brand Interactive*. Retrieved December 2, 2016, from https://www.parkerwhite.com/insights/14-components-of-a-brand-platform/

Werner, C. (2006). *A change is gonna come: Music, race and the soul of America*. Ann Arbor: University of Michigan Press.

Wernick, A. (1991). *Promotional culture: Advertising, ideology and symbolic expression*. London: Sage.

Westbrook, Justin T. (2017, January 28). The unconventional influence of cars felt in Frank Ocean's music. *Jalopnik*. Retrieved August 7, 2018, from https://jalopnik.com/the-unconventional-influence-of-cars-felt-in-frank-ocea-1791730789

Wheelsforwomen. (2013, May 16), How influential are female brand ambassadors? *Wheelsforwomen*. Retrieved June 19, 2018, from http://www.wheelsforwomen.ie/index.php/how-influential-are-female-brand-ambassadors

Whiteley, S. (2000). *Women in popular music: Sexuality, identity and subjectivity*. London: Routledge, 2000.

Widmer, E. L. (1990). The automobile, rock and roll, and democracy. In J. Jennings (Ed.), *Roadside America: The automobile in design and culture* (pp. 82–91). Ames: Iowa State University Press.

Widmer, E. L. (2002). Crossroads: The automobile, rock and roll and democracy. In P. Wollen & J. Kerr (Eds.), *Autopia: Cars and culture* (pp. 65–74). London: Reaktion.

Wiesenthal, D. L., Hennessy, D., & Totten, B. (2000). The influence of music on driver stress. *Journal of Applied Social Psychology*, 30, 1709–1719.

Williams, D. (2010, December 17). Shakira gets SEAT backing for European tour. *Telegraph*. Retrieved July 3, 2018, from http://www.telegraph.co.uk/motoring/news/6834382/Shakira-gets-SEAT-backing-for-European-tour.html

Williams, J. A. (2010). You never been on a ride like this befo': Los Angeles, automotive listening, and Dr. Dre's "G-Funk". *Popular Music History, 4*(2), 160–176.

Williams, J. A. (2013). *Rhymin' and stealin': Musical borrowing in hip-hop*. Ann Arbor: University of Michigan Press.

Williams, J. A. (2014). Cars with the boom: Music, automobility and hip-hop "sub" cultures. In J. Stanyek & S. Gopinath (Eds.), *The Oxford handbook of mobile music* (Vol. 2, pp. 109–145). New York: Oxford University Press.

Willis, E. (2011). *Out of the vinyl deeps: Ellen Willis on rock music* (N. W. Aronowitz, Ed.). Minneapolis: University of Minnesota Press.

Willis, P. (1996). *Common culture: Symbolic work at play in the everyday cultures of the young.* Milton Keynes, UK: Open University Press.

Wilson, M. (2000). *Dreamgirl and supreme faith: My life as a Supreme.* New York: Rowman & Littlefield.

Winter, C. (2014, March 26). Teaching cars to read our emotions. *Bloomberg.* Retrieved March 1, 2015, from https://www.bloomberg.com/news/articles/ 2014-03-26/teaching-cars-to-read-our-emotions

Wise, B. (2013). Why do car makers like musical names? [Blog post] *WQXR Blog.* Retrieved July 28, 2017, from http://www.wqxr.org/story/317455-why-car-makers-li ke-musical-names

Wollen, P. (2002a). Introduction: Cars and culture. In P. Wollen & J. Keer (Eds.), *Autopia: Cars and culture* (pp. 10–20). London: Reaktion.

Wollen, P. (2002b). Automobiles in art. In P. Wollen & J. Keer (Eds.), *Autopia: Cars and culture* (pp. 25–49). London: Reaktion.

Women and their cars. (1949, October 15). *Vogue,* pp. 93–94, 96–97.

Women autoists skillful drivers, not content with electrics, now using high-powered gasoline cars. (1907, September 29). *New York Times,* sec. 4.3.

Woodford, A. M. (2001). *This is Detroit, 1701–2001.* Detroit: Wayne State University Press.

Woodyard, C. (2012, April 24). Top ten car brands for women are long on style. *USA Today.* Retrieved July 30, 2016, from http://content.usatoday.com/communities/driveon/post/ 2012/04/top-10-car-brands-for-women-are-small-and-stylish/1#.VjTdJKSzBFU

WHO. (2011). *Burden of disease from environmental noise: Quantification of healthy life years lost in Europe.* Geneva: World Health Organization. Retrieved March 1, 2015, from http://www.who.int/quantifying_ehimpacts/publications/e94888.pdf?ua=1

Wosk, J. (2001). *Woman and the machine: Representations from the spinning wheel to the electronic age.* Baltimore: Johns Hopkins University Press.

Wright, J. (1978). Croonin' about cruisin'. In J. Nachbar, D. Weiser, & J. Wright (Eds.), *The popular culture reader* (pp. 107–117). Bowling Green, OH: Bowling Green University Popular Press.

Xiaoru, C. (2013, October 15). Car horn ban ill-conceived. *Global Times.* Retrieved March 27, 2015, from http://www.globaltimes.cn/content/817920.shtml#.UufwXGQo7-Y

Yamaha. (2009). Yamaha creates acoustic design for engine of the Lexus LFA super sports car [Press release]. Retrieved February 9, 2015, from http://www.yamaha. com/news_release/2009/20091021.html

Young, D. (2001). The life and death of cars: Private vehicles on the Pitantjatjara lands of South Australia. In D. Miller (Ed.), *Car Cultures* (pp. 35–59). Oxford: Berg.

Your car as a musical instrument. (2008). *Noise Addicts.* Retrieved November 6, 2009, from http://www.noiseaddicts.com/2008/09/car-musical-instrument-melody-roads-japan

Zagat. (2013, December 4). *Dining trends survey: Tipping, pet peeves and more.* Retrieved February 25, 2015, from https://www.zagat.com/b/dining-trends-survey-tipp ing-pet-peeves-and-more#2

Zee Media Bureau. (2018, April 4). An auto that launched a thousand horns: Campaign to stop honking makes a bang. Retrieved March 21, 2019, from https://zee news.india.com/mumbai/an-auto-that-launched-a-thousand-horns-campaign-to-end-honking-makes-a-bang-2096289.html

Index

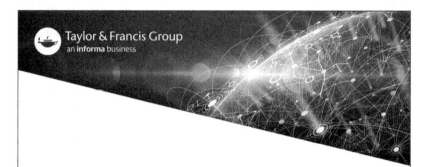

Printed in the United States
by Baker & Taylor Publisher Services